HOLLYWOOD RED

HOLLYWOOD RED

The
Autobiography
of
Lester Cole

Ramparts Press
Palo Alto, California 94303

Library of Congress Cataloging in Publication Data

Cole, Lester.
    Hollywood Red.

    Includes index.
    1. Cole, Lester. 2. Screen writers — United States
— Biography. 3. Blacklisting of entertainers — California
— Hollywood. 4. Blacklisting of authors — California
— Hollywood. I. Title.
PN1998.A3C784   812'.52   81-51701
ISBN 0-87867-085-8   AACR2

Published by Ramparts Press, Palo Alto, California 94303.

First Printing

ISBN 0-87867-085-8
Library of Congress Catalog Card Number 81-51701.

Printed in the United States of America

Contents

Foreword

In October 1947, the House Un-American Activities Committee (HUAC) cited ten Hollywood writers and directors for contempt of Congress. The leading organs of the daily press were outspoken and unhesitating in their criticism of the Committee's purposes and methods. Those of us who had been cited were heartened by the popular support.

About a week later, a cold-war Congress voted overwhelmingly to uphold the contempt citations. A short time after that, the Motion Picture Producers Association met in New York City and produced what became known as the Waldorf Astoria Decision. This document was a "white paper" formally instituting the blacklist in Hollywood. Somehow the mood had changed very rapidly. The recently indignant defenders of the First Amendment made no editorial comment on these latter developments. The news was merely "objectively" reported.

The first book to tell what actually happened at the HUAC hearings was titled *Hollywood on Trial* (Boni and Gaer, New York, 1948). It told who supported us, and who opposed us; it spelled out the consequences for both sides. The author was Gordon Kahn, a film writer and journalist who was one of the nineteen men originally subpoenaed by HUAC (although he was never actually brought to the stand). Kahn's book closed the subject, as far as we ten were concerned, for eight years. Then in 1956, a two-volume *Report on Blacklisting* appeared. Volume I covered the movies, volume II radio and television. The author was John Cogley, executive editor of *Commonweal*, and the book was sponsored by the Fund for the Republic. The back-cover blurb says that Cogley was commissioned to prepare a factual report on the situation. He did — selectively and with discretion. To my knowledge, none of us was consulted about the facts as we knew them.

Over the next twenty-five years, about a dozen more books appeared. At first the authors, if they examined us at all, looked upon us as creatures somewhere between villains and fools — or more generously just as freaks and misfits. Later on, for reasons which will be discussed in the text, we became subjects for more serious young scholars. But they, too, had prejudices and preferences; their political biases also showed, sometimes subtly, sometimes obviously. While some of the writing has been accurate and well crafted, all of these works have been written from the outside. As a result, the political dimensions of the Hollywood Ten have never been personally penetrated. The books have been neither personal nor political.

This story will be personal and political. In the writer's opinion, there can be no separation. Those "on the outside," the historians and investigative reporters whose works comprise most of the literature on the Hollywood Ten, could not have known (although some pretend to) the feelings and thoughts of those who were cited for contempt, fought the convictions all the way to the Supreme Court, and went to prison after a three-year struggle. Outsiders could not convey to the reader the conflicts we experienced — with others, with our families, and within ourselves — as we held fast to principle and firmly held convictions, only partly aware at the time of the pain, humiliation, heartache and punishment that lay ahead.

What were those convictions that I so deeply cherished? For me, it was never a question of friendships with individuals. The quirks and unpredictabilities were too great. Friends and comrades betrayed, just as others did. On the world scene, I witnessed the cruelties of Stalin, his quest for power over those who dared to disagree. But what gave birth to this paranoid, irrational action? To me, the context was crucial: for decades, the Soviet Union was surrounded by military forces which had vowed to destroy the first socialist revolution. Even today, the hostility is as fierce as ever. A recent Reuters dispatch quoted a "high U.S. official" who said "Soviet leaders would have to choose between peacefully changing their Communist system in the direction followed by the West or going to war. There is no other alternative. . ." (*San Francisco Chronicle*, March 19, 1981) No wonder there was paranoia in the Kremlin!

This hostility to socialism is completely unacceptable to hundred of millions, perhaps billions, of people who wish to go their own way rather than accept the dictates of the Western industrial powers. I agree with Friedrich Engels' classic characterization of Western industrial society: it is not just *in*human but *pre*human. Engels said that man is in a stage of his prehistory until there is world socialism, and I share that view. I don't think humanity's history will really begin until racism is wiped out; the exploitation of man by man is abolished; and material, political and social impediments are removed *everywhere.* Only then will the history of man begin.

I believe that. It is what I have fought for all my adult life, and I hope I will never stop fighting for it. The present political mood only intensifies my concern, with Ronald Reagan and Alexander Haig rattling their swords in Washington. They really believe the American people — and the people around the world — are under their thumbs. What the "high U.S.

official" told Reuters in 1981 is the continuation of a doctrine which has flourished for sixty years (except for the brief interlude of World War II).

Hollywood Red tells the story of how I have tried to live by my beliefs. For those writing from the outside looking in, it may be difficult to appreciate the joys and gratification of the victories, the friendships and loyalties that come from the struggle. These have been heightened by the other experiences — the failures, betrayals, the anguish, the disappointments in organizational relationships, in other people, and in one's self. I have tried to tell the story candidly, indicating the defeats as well as the victories.

I felt that I could not complete this memoir without certain documents that formed part of the "official record" of my life and times. I waited two years, and then all but gave up hope that the documents I required would ever appear. I managed to write a first draft without them.

Then on February 11, 1980 the material I had formally requested and paid for finally arrived, pre-paid, first-class mail. Eagerly, I carried the ten-pound cardboard box up the two flights of stairs to my flat and tore it open.

Floating loose on top of the five roughly bound volumes were two letters, polite to the edge of cordiality. One was from David G. Flanders, Chief of the Freedom of Information Privacy Branch, U.S. Department of Justice, FBI; the other was from Clarence B. Kelley, Director.

Mr. Kelley's was a form letter instructing me in the reading of the codes. Mr. Flanders informed me that I would find enclosed 856 pages, stapled into documents as the originals were received and appeared in the files. Further, he wrote that I had been the subject of a "Security Matter" investigation which began in 1940 and continued until October 27, 1972. Also, I was the subject of a "Fraud Against the Government" investigation for three months beginning in September 1949. And, finally, I was again the subject of a "Special Security Matter" investigation in June 1972 while still the subject of the original investigation that had started in 1940.

Of a record containing more than a thousand pages, a hundred odd were blacked out. For these I was not charged ten cents each. But for those on which all but an indecipherable line or two were left intact, with the balance obliterated by black ink — including, on every page, the names of the agents and informers — there was no discount for deletions. It was still ten cents per page or fraction thereof.

After examining what was left, and those sections of it which were understandable, I felt some brief additions from this harrowing tale might be helpful. Whenever I do quote from this source, I will footnote it as such. Much of it will serve to authenticate some of the assertions zealously collected by informers from such sources as Walter Winchell, the commercial press and the film industry trade papers, *Daily Variety* and the *Hollywood Reporter*. For this assistance to one not addicted to clipping such choice items, I can only express thanks to those diligent, special FBI agents and their paid and volunteer informers.

Much time, effort and cost were, of course, wasted. More than a hundred times it was reported that a dark green Buick (or tan Chrysler) bearing such and such a license plate, "which later was discovered to be registered to Lester Cole, was seen to stop in front of the house of Albert Maltz, or Ring Lardner, or John Howard Lawson." As often as not the informer's name was inked out, or such a vital report was followed by this: "(Source unreliable)."

They were on my trail and tail from Hollywood to New York, and when I went abroad vigilance was transferred to the CIA. My mail to and from this country, sent and received, was monitored in the post offices. Some anonymous agent noted all the names on the envelopes of my correspondents. Whether the contents were also read, I do not know. Perhaps the answer could be among the hundred-odd deleted or inked-out pages.

Eager to accept any and all information, there were some matters for which, for political reasons, I was given credit, even authorship, when it was deserved by others. A classic example of this occurred in 1947. A year before James Cain, well-known popular author of such novels as *The Postman Always Rings Twice* and *Double Indemnity*, was weary of the rip-off by the producers. They paid a writer but once for his material, but could use it again and again. Cain came to the Screen Writers Guild with a plan to put an end to this malpractice. His proposal was modeled after the very successful organization of the songwriters, who had formed a licensing company called ASCAP. Under ASCAP rules no song, whether on a record or played live on radio, could be used without paying the authors, composer and lyricist, a fee for each performance. It put an end to free use of their material and changed the miserable economic status of the membership overnight. James Cain was a politically conservative man, and there was no way to attack his plan by red-baiting him. But when I, as vice-president of the Guild, joined in its advocacy, the red-baiters had a target. Suddenly I was publicized as the author of Cain's proposal, which he had entitled "The American Authors' Authority" (the AAA). Cain, easily seduced, apparently believed the canards of those who sought to discredit his plan, and in 1948 angrily denounced me, Ring Lardner and Gordon Kahn as stealing his plan and of being loyal first to the Communist Party and only then to the Screen Writers Guild.

The following FBI report was obviously written not by an agent, but by one of their industry informers, most likely a writer-member of the Hollywood Alliance for the Preservation of American Ideals — about which more later.

FROM FILES OF FBI to ARMY INTELLIGENCE
[Released as no longer confidential on June 20, 1979, upon request through Freedom of Information Act.]

HQ MDW PERIOD FROM 1700, 27 Sept. to 4 Oct. 1946

(Following a section on which is ink-written "Not Relevant")

THE COMMUNIST PLAN TO CONTROL AMERICAN THOUGHT

THE AMERICAN AUTHORS AUTHORITY (AAA) was fathered and hatched up by the (COMMUNIST) SCREEN WRITERS' GUILD and hastily adopted by the RADIO WRITERS GUILD. The purpose of the AAA is to constitute a trusteeship over the brains of all writers. It would not merely control but would own the copyrights on everything from a two line filler or sonnet or magazine article to a book or play. These literary products, it would "lease" or "license" to publishers and producers who accept the AAA's conditions and recognize its domination. In this way all creative writing to reach the public would have to funnel through one narrow and carefully guarded gap. This screen for thought control of America indicates evidence of long, careful preparation as formulated in the eighteen pages of the "SCREEN WRITER." The AAA "Red Front Plan" was adopted at a single meeting without benefit of prolonged discussion which follows all Marxist projected plans in parliamentary procedure. As to personalities, the President of the SCREEN WRITERS GUILD is one EMMETT LAVERY, supported by the Communist Party in his recent unsucessful attempt to get the Democratic Party nomination to Congress. LAVERY is an old time joiner of all the old familiar CP Front organizations. DALTON TRUMBO, editor of the SCREEN WRITER, and one of the propagandists for the AUTHORITY aforementioned, is best known for having written "Johnny Get Your Gun," serialized in the COMMUNIST DAILY WORKER during the time the Communists were working with the Nazis, 1939-1940. It was circulated to make Americans refuse to go to war. LESTER COLE, First Vice President of the Guild, is a notorious follower of the Communist Party line. JOHN HOWARD LAWSON and RING LARDNER, JR., are followers of the Party line undertakings. PETER LYON, a fellow traveler, is also on the committee. It is interesting to note that the DAILY WORKER and other Communist organs endorse the plan of the AAA. It is further reported that the AAA contemplates using this authoritarian plan as a future wedge into the American political structure.

In order to counteract the AAA, fifty prominent writers on 18 [?-unclear] September formed the American Writers Association. The Association lending every effort to expose the nefarious plot of the AAA. Local chapters of the organization are in the process of being formed in Washington, D.C., Chicago, Ill. and Hollywood, Cal.

(A..2) (1074)

All references to "Communist" plotting are not only untrue but preposterous. However, we were in a Cold War hysteria, and the campaign of the "fifty prominent writers" — all anonymous, naturally, was sufficient then, along with producer pressure, to defeat James Cain's much-needed proposal, depriving writers of the benefits ASCAP members have enjoyed for more than fifty years.

At this writing (March 1981) the Writers Guild members are preparing to go on strike to achieve but one part of such an arrangement, and without the help of those "nefarious" red plotters.

There are also some ironically amusing, inadvertent errors in the vast FBI file. One informer reported in 1945, that I attacked the Cagney Brothers, Jimmy and his producer-brother, Bill, for having deleted a portion of my screenplay of the film, *Blood on the Sun.* I had, this unnamed source wrote, accused the producers ". . . of substituting veracity for public reception and . . . writers should be protected from such mistreatment." Obviously, I had written the reverse: that hoped-for "public reception" should not be substituted for "veracity." (More on this later.) But as busy as the FBI was with hundreds in Hollywood being watched and monitored, such innocent slips must be forgiven.

I paid my ten cents a page for even less. One sheet was completely inked out with the exception of this one line:

"ACTION: None. This is for your information."

Over and over different informers sent in similar "information." I was listed in twenty-odd organizations, from the League of American Writers (as vice-president and "lieutenant to Donald Ogden Stewart"), to a member of the Hollywood Anti-Nazi League, the League Against War and Fascism, the Committee to Aid Republican Spain — and on and on. It is true, I was active in them all. Now I wonder where did I ever find time? Somehow I did.

An informer reported that he joined the Communist Party (his name blacked out, of course) and that after becoming

OPTIONAL FORM NO. 10

UNITED STATES GOVERNMENT

Memorandum

~~CONFIDENTIAL~~

TO : Mr. A. H. Belmont

DATE: February 3, 1961

FROM : Mr. J. F Bland

SUBJECT: LESTER COLE
INTERNAL SECURITY - C

ALL IN...
HEREIN IS...
EXCEPT WHERE SHOWN
OTHERWISE...

Tolson
Mohr
Parsons
Belmont
Callahan
Conrad
DeLoach
Malone
McGuire
Rosen
Trotter
Evans
W. C. Sullivan
Tele
Ingram
Gandy

Los Angeles has requested permission to immediately interview Cole to determine his willingness to furnish information regarding his communist activities.

Observations:

We have received no information indicating that Cole has had an ideological break with the communist movement. If interviewed, the possibility exists he will attempt to claim cooperation with the Government in an effort to clear his name. However, in view of the wealth of information he could furnish concerning the CP, particularly the Professional-Cultural Section, SCDCP, and the movie industry, it is believed this interview should be conducted.

100 — 2230 — 83

RECOMMENDATION:

In accordance with the above observations, it is recommended that the attached radiogram be sent to the Los Angeles office granting permission to interview Cole.

100-2230
Enclosure
1 - Mr. Belmont
1 - Mr. Bland
1 - Mr. Parsons
1 - Mr. DeLoach
1 - Mr. Mohr

(7)

~~CONFIDENTIAL~~

( )

F B I

Date: 2/9/61

Transmit the following in _____
                                (Type in plain text or code)

Via ____AIRTEL____ _____ AIR MAIL - REGISTERED
                                (Priority or Method of Mailing)

TO: DIRECTOR, FBI

FROM: SAC, LOS ANGELES (100-8864)

SUBJECT: LESTER COLE
         IS-C

ReBurad 2/3/61.

On 2/8/61, LESTER COLE was contacted in the vicinity
of his residence, 7765 Firenze, Los Angeles, by SA's ███████
███████ and ███████ COLE was found to be cordial
and not at all hostile toward the interviewing agents.

He stated, however, that he knew of nothing whatsoever that he cared to discuss with the FBI even before the
interviewing agents were able to explain the purpose for the
interview. He asked whether any charges were outstanding
against him; and when advised to the contrary, he stated that
he had nothing whatsoever to discuss with the FBI. Accordingly,
the interview was terminated.

The results of the interview will be incorporated
in the next semiannual report due concerning captioned subject.

P
(3)- Bureau (AIR MAIL)(REGISTERED)
1 - Los Angeles
    (4)

REC- 50 100-3230-84

FEB 13 1961

57 FEB 15

ALL INFORMATION CONTAINED
HEREIN IS UNCLASSIFIED
DATE 3/13/79 BY 2333

Approved: _____ Per _____
        Special Agent

acquainted with me concluded that he "never heard Cole teach or advocate the overthrow of the government by force and violence." That, of course, was hardly enough to conclude any investigation, since another informer (name blacked out) reported that from 1939 on, as executive board member, treasurer, vice-president and president of the Screen Writers Guild, I "worked with the C.P. to capture the Hollywood trade unions."

It wasn't until February 1961 that I had the first inkling of the FBI's interest in me. The foregoing items are from the files finally turned over to me under the Freedom of Information Act.

My one FBI interview wasn't terminated as claimed. I recall it well. There were two agents, both well-dressed in three-piece suits and straw hats, one in his twenties, the other about fifty. The latter did the talking. When the interview was "terminated," the older one then asked to speak to my wife. It was eight in the morning. Kay was still asleep, and I told him she had nothing to say to him. He wanted to know how I could speak for her. Did I really have the right to make such an assumption? I said yes, I did.

Whereupon he looked at me with something akin to haughty condescension, shook his head sadly, then tsk-tsked: "Male chauvinist." They walked away. *Then* the interview was terminated.

From then on I suppose I was aware of the possibility of surveillance. Aside from suspecting my phone to be tapped, I was followed all over the U.S. and when in Europe was under the scrutiny of the CIA. My mail was observed, if not opened, and it continued, according to the report, for thirty-two years. Suddenly it stopped. Why then, when my activities became politically more open than ever before? Or had it stopped? Was it just that for the eight years since the report ended they had failed to send me the documents?

I wrote to the Chief of the Department, David G. Flanders; I wanted its report on me for the past eight years, and if they didn't send it, I wanted to know why not. Within two weeks, I received the following reply:

UNITED STATES DEPARTMENT OF JUSTICE
FEDERAL BUREAU OF INVESTIGATION
WASHINGTON, D.C. 20535

MAR 10 1980

Mr. Lester Cole
Apartment 4
741 Kansas Street
San Francisco, California 94107

Dear Mr. Cole:

This is to acknowledge receipt of your letter dated February 20, 1980, which was received at FBI Headquarters on February 26, 1980.

Your letter indicated that the FBI had stopped pursuing your activities in October, 1942. [sic]

As we stated to you in our letter of February 1, 1980 you were the subject of a Security Matter investigation which began in August, 1940, and continued until October, 1972. This investigation was closed on October 27, 1972, since you were no longer believed to constitute a potential or actual threat to the internal security of the United States.

One of the documents we forwarded you dated October 27, 1972, contains information which is classified "Confidential" according to the FBI's current classification guidelines.

For your information, a copy of the Federal Register pertaining to the FBI's system of records is enclosed. The criteria as to why your Security Matter Investigation was closed has been circled in red.

If you remain dissatisfied with the classified information, you may appeal to the Associate Attorney General as we stated to you in our letter of February 1, 1980.

> Sincerely yours,
> [s] David G. Flanders
> David G. Flanders, Chief
> Freedom of Information-Privacy
>   Acts Branch
> Records Management Division

Enclosure

"This investigation was closed on October 27, 1972 since you were not longer believed to constitute a potential or actual threat to the internal security of the United States."

Thirty-two years! Myself and how many others like me, for how long, tracked, trailed and tailed. Hundreds of thousands of citizens' tax dollars paid to agents and informers, all to end in nothing. What frustration it must have been for them!

You will notice that Mr. Flanders signed his letter "Sincerely." This was one year, of course, before his new President leaked the story, in March 1981, of a plan to "unleash" the FBI and CIA and resume widespread wiretapping, "black bag" break-ins, infiltration of citizens' groups and every manner of harassment of lawful political activities. When public opposition blew too stormy, Ronald Reagan backtracked — the plan was just a "proposal" under consideration.

But has the plan been abandoned? Just a few weeks ago, in May 1981, the *Los Angeles Times* reported the latest version, this time confined to the FBI (is the CIA too busy elsewhere?). It would authorize the FBI to employ illegal methods to harass individuals and groups who carry on constitutionally protected activities. Then, without waiting to be asked, or even looking at the trial record, Reagan rushed to give a presidential pardon to two top FBI officials who were convicted of widespread abuse of the rights of wholly innocent and unsuspecting people. This is a clear signal that the political paranoia of the current administration prevents it from seeing anything wrong with "official" lawbreaking.

This lawbreaking began in 1936, under J. Edgar Hoover and President Roosevelt, and has only periodically abated when public opposition grew too much.

Most Americans have little recollection of the dark decades of HUAC. From 1938 to 1975 it traveled like a carnival throughout the country, breaking up families, turning friends into enemies, destroying reputations and lives. Public revulsion to this shameful period of our nation finally caused the elimination of the Committee in 1975. Congress sent several rooms full of HUAC files to the national archives to be sealed for at least fifty years. Now the administration's right-wing ideologues have revived the Senate Internal Security Sub-committee and are doing their best to reinstall another HUAC in the House of Representatives. Congressman Don Edwards has asked "Will we move those miles of records — rumor, gossip, innuendo, yellowing clippings — back to Capitol Hill?"

It *can* happen here; when bigots are permitted to burn wooden crosses, how long will it be before they start burning paper documents, old-fashioned documents like the Constitution and its Bill of Rights?

1

Comic Contradictions

It was March of 1932 and the country was fast approaching the bottom of the deepest depression ever known. And, suddenly, ironically, I was about to become rich and, for those times, very rich. Ten million bewildered men and women — as yet too stunned to be angry — found themselves without work. The hungry, starving with their children, were forming endless breadlines in cities and towns all over the land; hundreds of thousands were being thrown on the streets because of their inability to pay rent. I had not yet fallen into that seemingly bottomless black pit, but I was dangerously close to the rim when the unexpected change came.

My good luck called for a celebration and a farewell party before I left for Hollywood. I bought bottles of the very best bootleg gin, cooked pots full of spaghetti — for this occasion with meat and mushrooms in the sauce! — and shortly after noon good friends and well-wishers began to gather at my scrubby little Manhattan flat at Fifty-first Street and Lexington Avenue.

Gathered to congratulate me and wish me luck were friends

from my earliest theater days, one or two from childhood, as well as more recent friends, men and women I had come to know during the last two years. I had met my newest friends while working as a free-lance story reader in and out of the editorial departments of Fox, Paramount, RKO, and Universal film companies.

Most of the theater people were out of work, and the play readers were making from three to six dollars a day — when they could get the work. For such sums we read a play, gave a judgment on its suitability for a film, and wrote a fairly detailed synopsis. Five dollars was the pay for novels, and six if they ran over five hundred pages. Some of us were experienced in theater, others had college degrees, and all were hovering on the poverty precipice.

Despite the long and wearying hours of this drudgery, I somehow had managed — a combination of will and inspiration (well, maybe just desperation) — to write my second play. It sold under the most auspicious circumstances with such a splash of publicity that I instantly went from a young has-been to a writer wanted by three of the film companies for whom I was at that very time working as a free-lance, three-dollar reader. I accepted the Paramount offer: two hundred fifty dollars a week, with six-month increases of fifty dollars, for five years. Of course, there were six-month options that it was their privilege to take, not mine to refuse. But I knew nothing about such inequities at the time.

The play had been completed less than a week, submitted but a few days before, when Frieda Fishbein, my agent sold an option to Rosalie Stewart, probably the most prestigious independent producer then on Broadway. For years she had presented the plays of George Kelly, twice Pulitzer Prize winner with *The Showoff* and *Craig's Wife*. His last two plays were poorly received by critics and audiences alike, and that winter, disgusted or disheartened, he announced he would write no more plays. Brooks Atkinson, the presitgious drama critic, had just interviewed Rosalie Stewart on the drama page of the *New York Times.* When asked what her plans were, she replied with finality, "Not to produce again until I find another George Kelly."

When, six or seven weeks later, she announced the purchase of my play—foɪ which she would seek the services of Helen Hayes and Jean Dixon—the memory of her statement was still very fresh. I was suddenly catapulted from three-dollars-per-synopsis obscurity into theatrical headlines and a Hollywood contract. I was on my way to fame—

The Twentieth Century Limited to Chicago left Grand Central around 6:00 P.M. My friends poured me on the train with embraces and kisses. I assured them that I despised movies. The theater was my only love, and I would be back for the opening of my play, to write another, and another, and—

The conductor warned the most sober amongst us that the train was about to leave. In went my bag, and somehow I followed. The next thing I knew it was daylight, and I was dazedly peering out of the window of the drawing room. There was Lake Erie, and a knock on the door told me we would soon be in Chicago. I missed breakfast, but I managed to get a cup of coffee which I finished as we rolled into the terminal. I changed train stations, and by this time I was clear-headed enough to look around.

I was standing beside the sleek Santa Fe Chief—ten or twelve long, shiny, streamlined cars. The deserted platform made me uneasy. It was only fifteen minutes before departure time, but there weren't any passengers to be seen. Could this be the right train? I asked the conductor, and he assured me it was. "Then where are the passengers?" I wanted to know.

"They're already aboard. Both of them." He paused. "You're the rest." A porter took my bag and I went up the steps.

This train, the pride of the country, would travel two

thousand miles with three passengers. The bottom had certainly fallen out, and I knew that the three of us on this train weren't the only cross-country travelers in the United States at that time.

Hundreds of thousands were hitting the roads and rails with bundles of clothes and only the most necessary possessions, leaving from where they had neither food nor heat nor shelter to take their chances elsewhere. Homeless men, women and children were wandering from nowhere to nowhere, begging and stealing to stay alive. And here I was, in a first-class compartment, de luxe.

The porter put my bag down and I suddenly felt ashamed, guilty, as if my good fortune were a caprice of fate that was separating me from all I belonged to, making it unreal. "Buddy," I heard myself saying to the porter, "I'm a working stiff just like you. Me being in here is some kind of joke. So tell me, what does a *real* high-class guy with a private room like this usually tip you?"

He was obviously uneasy. "Whatever he wants to, sir!"

That made me furious. "None of that 'sir' crap," I said, and handed him a dollar. He started to reach in his pocket for change. "No, keep it." I don't know what came over me, but I quickly reached for my wallet and took out a couple of more bills. "And these are for the high-class guys who never got on board to tip you today. Okay?"

I could see that his eyes were studying me to discover just what kind of a nut or drunk he had here, but slowly he smiled and nodded. "Okay, mister. Gonna see you have a good ride out. Two nights and most of three days. You need some booze?"

"Got some."

"Whatever you want, just buzz."

"Thanks."

He nodded and left.

Two nights and three days, then Los Angeles. I tried to think ahead. Archie Leach had invited me to stay with him until I found a place. He was an old friend, once a juvenile in Shubert musical road shows, now called Cary Grant at Paramount. He was sharing a house with Randolph Scott, the western movie star, somewhere out in Westwood, and I'd accepted the very kind offer.

But thoughts of pleasures and luxuries of the future were mixed with memories of the past. It was my father's voice I thought I could hear. I hadn't seen him in ten or twelve years, but I could hear him both congratulating and warning me now. His words would have been like this, as if a reminder of my working-class background: "Remember, son, a royal flush comes once in maybe ten million hands, but for workers there's almost never even a pair of deuces. So don't forget, however much they pay you, you will have earned more. That's what profit is — the part of your labor the boss keeps for himself." It was as if it were not twenty years ago, but last Sunday that I stood listening to him talking Marxism to his friends from the bench in Claremont Park.

My mother had a gloomier vision — and it was far from my thoughts right now. She somehow took my success as a sign of her defeat. She had predicted, over a twenty-year period of conflict at close quarters, that without a college education I'd end up digging ditches, organizing trade unions, and spending my life on a soapbox preaching socialism "just like my father." She went on insisting that my current success was just a temporary stroke of luck, and I'd land back on earth, a loud-mouth working stiff like my father. Without an education I'd get nowhere and would always come back to her for help. All she hoped was that someday I'd be man enough to admit my mistake.

I had quit school in 1920, following years of quarrels. We had been moving from one city to another as that ambitious little steel spring of a woman sought to make the fortune my father couldn't or wouldn't. All the while, my love for the theater was intensifying, and I was determined to overcome all obstacles on the crooked road to reach my goal. When I finally got my chance, it came in an odd way.

My mother had opened one of her countless business ventures — she'd had at least half a dozen since divorcing my father when I was ten — and this one was another lunch-room in New York on Twenty-seventh Street between Third and Lexington Avenues. I was again out of work — as she always predicted when a job ended for one reason or another — and I helped her put the place together and advertise it. I handed out leaflets on Lexington Avenue, came back in time to serve lunch, and then washed the dishes. My mother was the cook; and I was the rest of the staff.

One afternoon a few days after we'd opened the lunchroom, my sister returned from school and hurried excitedly into the kitchen where I was doing the dishes. "Do you know about Butler Davenport's Theater?" she asked.

"No," I answered, "what is it?"

"A theater, two blocks away, right on Twenty-ninth, the other side of Lexington. I'm coming home, just off the El, and as I'm passing an old guy comes out — boy, you could spot him as a ham the minute you looked at him. You know, handkerchief sticking out of his sleeve and —"

I interrupted. "So what happened?"

"Well, he stops me, and says he's putting on a play and needs some young people, boys and girls, in one scene, and would I care to play in it."

"How much?" I asked.

"Nothing. I said my mother wouldn't let me out nights alone, but I had an older brother, and if he were in the show she might. He said to bring him over. Come on!"

We ran. The theater was a converted four-story brownstone, not unlike the one that housed our lunchroom, with kitchen and bedrooms behind. But Davenport had converted the first and second stories into the theater and stage, with perhaps one hundred ninety-nine seats, or whatever was under the required Equity minimum. We hurried through the lobby, were promptly "engaged" and ordered to rehearsal the next afternoon.

Butler Davenport was a dandy: haughty, evidently wealthy. The actors in his company were Broadway professionals, out of work and also out of funds. He supplied them with no cash. In payment he let them use their dressing rooms for sleeping quarters and supplied a cook to prepare their meals. The understanding was that when they found a paying job on Broadway, they could leave with a week's notice.

Soon after the first show closed, Davenport asked me to stay on as his stage manager. He promised to teach me what to do. And he did. He knew theater. I not only operated the curtain and the lights from his small switchboard, but also handled props, worked as a stagehand and did anything else he needed. The actors helped change the scenery.

Davenport's theater was forced to do plays in the public domain because he couldn't afford playwrights' royalties; his theater enjoyed considerable status with Broadway people. As a result, there was a delightful bonus for us; courtesy tickets were available to us for all the Broadway theaters that were not sold out on our night off. Cook and dishwasher from eleven to three, stagehand at night, and Broadway theater-goer once a week. Life was full.

My career with Davenport ended abruptly one night after the performance of a play titled *The Polish Jew*, an obscure drama written in the nineteenth century. As stage manager, I had the curtain, the lights and, in this play, much more to keep me busy. There was a carefully contrived scene in which the leading man, Davenport of course, was driving through a snowstorm. Above the proscenium we rigged a tightly webbed basket filled with white confetti which, when I jiggled a rope, off-scene, would gently sprinkle down and create the illusion of falling snow. At the same time, while one hand was thus employed, I held the "reins" of his sleigh in my other. The sleigh's gliders were on small wheels, so the "horse" off-stage had little trouble pulling him from center stage into the wings.

Nothing to it. But this one night, for some reason, the rope attached to the basket of confetti got stuck somewhere up above, and the snow didn't fall. I slowed down pulling him; he declaimed about the snowstorm, but it wasn't snowing; his speech would soon be over and I was desperate. I gave an extra hard tug on the confetti rope and succeeded — alas, too well. Something up there tore, and the equivalent of a sackful of confetti poured down on his head.

The audience howled, of course, and I quickly pulled the curtain. Davenport strode off stage, controlling his rage and humiliation. He shook himself free of most of the confetti, ordered me to clean it up quickly, and stepped out in front of the curtain to apologize to the audience.

In the most nonchalant, airy tone, he said, "An unexpected blizzard. (Laughter) It will cause only the briefest delay in communications. As soon as we sweep up, the show will go on." They applauded. We did go on, but after the final curtain fell and the cast had responded with applause, he almost ran to me, quivering. "Get out! Idiot!" I left depressed. Could my career in the theater have ended on Twenty-seventh Street and Third Avenue?

In the "Help Wanted" advertisements in the newspaper the very next morning was an offer for a swimming counselor at a boys' camp in Maine. Woods, lakes, fishing, rivers. How marvelous! The job paid a hundred fifty dollars for seven weeks, with room and board. I would be rich! I instantly applied, lying about having two years of college education. I also enclosed proof that I had been a lifeguard the previous summer at Far Rockaway Beach and had given swimming instruction. I was accepted.

"Luck, always luck!" My mother said it with disgust. "If it wasn't for luck — and me giving you a roof over your head — you'd be in the gutter, a Bowery bum. A ditch digger."

On board the train to Maine with me and eighty to a hundred youngsters was a man a few years older than myself,

Abe Finkel, the dramatic counselor. When he learned of my interest in the theater, of my experience with Butler Davenport, of my ambitions, it instantly bound us together. Finkel had been Finkelstein, and he was related to the famous Yiddish theater Thomashevskys, rivals of the Adlers and Maurice Schwartz, the big three "Belascoes" of the Yiddish Broadway, which was on Second Avenue below Fourteenth Street. Abe's sister was married — or soon would be — to Muni Weisenfreund, later to become the film star Paul Muni, but then just a well-liked talented juvenile on the Yiddish stage.

At camp Abe, who had never learned to swim, wanted me to teach him, and of course I did. In return he lent me many of his books on stagecraft, and as he trained and rehearsed the boys for the Saturday night campfire shows I spent as much free time as I had watching and learning from him.

Like myself, Abe had little formal schooling, but he had been in the Yiddish theater since childhood. At the end of summer, he was to start his first job on Broadway as an assistant stage manager for Morris Gest's super-spectacle, *The Miracle*. The play was an importation from Germany, directed by Max Reinhardt, the recognized European theater genius of that time.

On August 1, Abe received a long-distance phone call. The schedule for pre-rehearsals had been set ahead; an enormous cathedral setting designed by Norman Bel Geddes was being erected in the theater, and he was needed at once. Abe explained to the camp management. They were unsympathetic. He had a contract with them, and they expected him to fulfill it. But he told them — to my astonishment — that I was equally if not more experienced in the American theater than he, having just finished a successful season with the prestigious Davenport Theater in New York. He insisted that I could easily handle the balance of the program that he would outline for me, and they reluctantly agreed. He was damned lucky they knew nothing of the New York theater!

To my astonishment, and with not a little pride, I actually did well, staging the final, lone one-act play Abe had selected from Harvard University's 47 Workshop, then under Professor George P. Baker.

During rehearsals Abe wrote me, expressing his confidence, and making me promise to visit him when I returned to New York at the end of August to tell him all about it. When the final play was a success, the camp management offered me a job for the next season, either again as swimming counselor or in Abe's job if he were not available. I felt very good indeed; I had a skill that could get me somewhere, somewhere I wanted very much to go.

Back in New York, I immediately looked up Abe at the Century Theater. He took me backstage, and it was a moment of breathless awe. The theater was being converted into a huge cathedral, and even in the early stages of construction the genius of Norman Bel Geddes was apparent. But I had little time to admire it then. Abe introduced me to Langdon West, the stage manager. The casting had begun, and Abe told West he would like to have me hired as an extra, maybe even play the small part of the executioner, since my physique was excellent. West nodded; no question about being an extra, but to get the part of executioner he would have to take me to the director. I couldn't find enough words of gratitude for Abe, but he good-naturedly shut me up, saying I'd done him a great favor that summer. West brought me into the easy presence of Max Reinhardt, who then ordered me to take off my shirt and show my muscles. Reinhardt nodded approval, asked my name again, shook my hand, and wished me good luck. I thanked him and all but floated away.

The role of executioner was something less than a feature role requiring any particular histrionics. But it did require muscles. In one of the later scenes, it was my job to pick up the sinful nun, throw her over my naked shoulder — I wore only a loin cloth — and rush her off to her execution. That meant carrying her while the orchestra played a screeching crescendo, from the stage down a long aisle through the theater, out a door behind the last row in the orchestra before I set her down. When not doing that I was one of the crowd, at times reaching more than a hundred fifty costumed people on the stage. For this I received two dollars a performance, sixteen dollars a week.

At last I felt myself started; the humiliating experience with Butler Davenport was all but forgotten. Now I was working with Max Reinhardt, a man considered one of the world's finest directors, and associating — however distantly — with such famous people as Lady Diana Manners, who played the Madonna and alternated as the nun, with Iris Tree, daughter of the famous British actor, Sir Beerbohm Tree; and there was Germany's most prestigious actor, Werner Krauss; a lively young German, Fritz Feld, a little older than myself, who understudied Krauss; Schuyler Ladd, a prestigious American performer; and Rosamond Pinchot, a lovely young woman who was the daughter or niece of the Governor of Pennsylvania. I felt myself touching the famous, the world-renowned; it was fame by association.

As rehearsals progressed, the stage manager needed more assistance. Abe suggested me. That brought a weekly increase of four dollars and I had, among other new assignments, the job of starting the crowds down the aisles on cue, of announcing to the stars and principal players their calls for appearance on stage. I'd knock on their dressing room doors and call, "Half hour," "Fifteen minutes!", "Five minutes to Curtain!" I was helping run this great show! I still cherish a lovely photograph of Iris Tree, who played the Wayward Nun. Her photograph is inscribed: "To Lester, who so often swept me off my feet."

It was a time when there was little happening for me in the outside world that wasn't theater. Life was the Century Theater; theater was my life.

I had long-since become acquainted with the leading players

beyond the knock on the door and the polite "half hour"
call. Lady Diana Manners was a woman of great beauty and
cool charm, and it was all but impossible not to fall in love
with her. Somehow I managed to conceal this unrealizable
passion, and she treated me with warm friendliness which
was almost destroyed later when she suspected that I had
played a devilish trick upon her husband.

I had not, of course. Captain Duff Cooper, later Lord
Cooper, had arrived from London to see his wife's now world-
hailed performance, and at my usual "half hour" call, she
asked me into her dressing room, introduced me, and asked
if I would take him out front and guide him to his seat. She
gave him his ticket. I led him past the man who tore the
ticket and pointed to the stairs beyond the elevator. I explained
that his wife had chosen a seat in the first row of the balcony
because it had the best view of the stage. After starting him
toward the stairway, I hurried back to work.

Sometime after our performance ended, I was near her
dressing room when he came back. I noticed the puzzled
look on his face, and as I was about to pass by she called me
into her dressing room. Apparently his first words told her
something had gone wrong, and she had him wait until I
reached the room. "Now tell it," she said, looking at me very
queerly. He seemed as puzzled as I. "Well, old girl, it was a
jolly show —"

"Jolly?" she bit the word.

"Quite. And the girls' costumes were, well, a bit naughty,
but the songs and dancing were quite clever, I thought. What
I don't understand, my dear, is why I didn't see you."

She turned to me. "Where did you send him?" My heart
pounded wildly. I already knew what had happened. Atop
the Century was a small second theater, for intimate musical
reviews, called the Century Roof. I could only mumble, "I
pointed to the stairs, Lady Diana, leading to the first balcony."
"Then how could he have gotten to the Roof and seen the
Heywood Broun Revue?" she demanded.

Curtis Moffat, London

Iris Tree as the Wicked Nun in *The Miracle*. She inscribed the photo:
To Lester Cole who so often swept me off my feet — Iris Tree

He came to my rescue, suddenly realizing what had happened. "I say, Di, it really isn't the young chap's fault. He did direct me to the stairway, but before getting there I noticed the elevator. And with my arthritis, you know. . . . Devilish sorry, old girl."

She nodded and asked him to step out for a moment. When he was gone, she smiled and gave me a little hug. "All my fault, Lestah deah. I should have told you, if he were going to get to his seat, you'd actually have to put him in it." The next night I did.

A short time later her mother, the very aristocratic Violet, Duchess of Rutland, arrived to learn why her daughter was creating, as she put it, "such an international commotion." Tall, head with its aquiline nose held high, she surprised everyone by belying her appearance and actually being a very genial, outgoing person. When I met her in Manners' dressing room before a performance and was introduced, she looked at me through her lorgnette, smiled, and turned to her daughter. "Is this handsome young creature your leading man?"

Diana laughed and said humorously, "Unfortunately not, Mother."

The Duchess seemed ruffled. "How dull of them; he should be." She turned to me and smiled. "Can you be at our hotel tomorrow morning for coffee? I should like to do a pen portrait of you." It turned out the Duchess was an extremely talented, if overly romantic artist, and the sketch she made of me indicates she thought I should have been, if not her daughter's leading man, at least someone's. She sketched a Barrymore-ish profile, with delicately waved hair and a bit on the feminine side; but I cherish it nevertheless. At the time I wondered whether reprints shouldn't be sent around to producers considering young actors for leading roles. That idea never got beyond the fantasy stage. The sketch never left my flat and to this day is framed and hanging in my study, an incredible reminder of someone who existed only in someone else's eye.

After another season in New York the show closed in May, to start a road tour in September, and I sought jobs in the theater in New York. That year the confidence of the Duchess of Rutland came close to reality. Broadway producers Al Woods and William Brady had started casting a new play. Dick Findlay, a young actor who'd been with *The Miracle* from the start, suggested I come with him and try to get a stage manager's job. He was after a part as the young leading man. He'd heard it hadn't been cast.

I went reluctantly. Woods and Brady undoubtedly had an over-supply of stage managers, and the chances were slim. But I went and stood behind the actors when they were asked to line up, waiting for a chance to inquire about an opening for a stage manager. Alice Brady, Brady's daughter, a recognized star on Broadway, was to play the lead, and they were looking for a young man to play opposite her in the first act. I was standing behind Findlay when Bill Brady, Jr., who was to direct the show, beckoned in Findlay's direction. Delighted, unbelieving, he started forward, but to his dismay and astonishment Brady snapped impatiently, "Not you. The man behind you."

The juvenile lead opposite Alice Brady? Me? Impossible! But they handed me a script, I read some lines with her, they liked the way I handled them, and I was hired. The part was something less than leading juvenile. I was playing a young Jewish motion picture producer at a time shortly after the turn of the century. Somehow I dropped dead between Act I and Act II. But it paid a hundred twenty-five a week. Certainly at last I was on my way! Four weeks of rehearsals and we left for a tryout in Atlantic City. We died. The critics were merciless, but in a way I was considered lucky; they didn't even mention me. We closed at the end of the first week.

Always Abe Finkel, my good friend Abe, was there. He had a close pal named Lou Lusty who, to this day, now past eighty, remains a dear friend. Lou, a man of sardonic wit, was then head usher at the Rialto, a movie house still on the corner of Forty-second Street and Seventh Avenue at Times Square (recently a porno house). Abe persuaded Lou to hire us as ushers. I could then make it through the summer until we were once again on the road. The musical conductor at the Rialto was Dr. Hugo Riesenfeld, a master musician, whose twenty-odd-piece orchestra accompanied the films. Seeing the same film two, three, four times a day for two weeks or more, I began to know soon after the film started whether the opening was "right" or "wrong," whether the action developed logically, growing out of the characters, or whether it was tricked by the whim or phony ego of the director. I began to understand motivation, character, conflict, and suspense without ever being aware of those words themselves.

It was a seven-day-a-week job, ten to eleven hours, two dollars and fifty cents a day. Of course, there was no union, and no one counted the hours except one's weary self. Lou Lusty could always be counted on to let one of us slip out on a slow afternoon to catch a theater or movie matinee. For me, the dull routine job was only a means of survival that made possible a life of intense excitement. I remember an affair with a lovely young woman who had been in *The Miracle* the past season, striving as I was for a career in the theater. In free time, along with more intimate pleasures, we read, talked of the marvels of Shaw and Ibsen, saw current plays such as *What Price Glory?* and *Desire Under the Elms.* We knew the writers and players intimately, it seemed, even if from afar; we lived close to them because, I suppose, their characters became people in our lives.

I was becoming conscious of myself in a new sense, one that strove to fight off the feeling of low self-esteem that my mother had earlier instilled — that without a formal education I would become a "nothing," a "Bowery bum," a "ditch-digger." I was beginning to see that it was possible to be a person of learning, self-taught, without ever knowing quadratic algebra, trigonometry, or the physical sciences.

Perhaps the work that moved and inspired me most at that time was Maxim Gorky's revolutionary novel, *Mother.* I lived and breathed the role of her son. When the mother, who had fought him so bitterly, saw him killed while leading the workers, she at last awakened and took his place in the struggle. I suppose I wanted desperately to be that young striker and for that mother to be mine.

What a romantic fantasy, what a dream of transference I so desperately wanted within my own life! But I felt I would never have the courage of that young worker, nor would my mother and Gorky's character ever become one. From then on, along with the American writers such as Jack London, Hawthorne, and Dreiser, I read all the Russians, the French, the Irish and the English. Here were writers who at that very moment, as for years before and many to come, were changing the minds and hearts of people all over the world.

They changed mine. During that late spring and summer of 1925, when not ushering at the Rialto, I was completely absorbed, living, laughing, crying in the world of literature and drama, feeling joy and fear and love and envisioning the nobility of fighting for a socialist life for all, along with the sense of agony that was the lot of most people struggling to survive in a world of hunger, cruel torture and pain. It was then I knew and felt my first determination to give to others if I could — to tens, hundreds, thousands, millions if possible — some compensation for what these magnificent writers were giving to me. I, too, would write.

I think now it was Gorky's writings that led me to Communism more than did, at a later time, Marx, Engels and Lenin. For me, life's essence emerged through the novel, the play — then, potentially for the most part — film. This feeling seemed to saturate my consciousness so that without any particular intellectual or scientific understanding of the connection between art and politics, they had somehow merged in me. It had happened, and it would never leave me. Without

at all realizing it, I was in a process of change when I started
rehearsals again for the next season on the road with *The
Miracle.*

Sketch by Violet, Dutchess of Rutland. I considered
sending it around to producers seeking young actors
for leading roles.

2

Cecil B. De Mille, Master Teacher

It was late in September of 1925 that we started out again. By then I liked to think of myself as a "seasoned trouper," and with the changes in cast and staff I rose from sixth assistant stage manager to third. That year Morris Gest's general manager, a heavy-set, genial man named William Oviatt, brought his lovely wife and their eighteen-year-old son along on our travels. Bill Jr. was unmanageably wild, warm and generous, and adored by parents who had absolutely no control over him. He soon chose me as one nearest his age and interests, and Bill Sr. suggested he'd be pleased if I'd share a room with him and sort of keep an eye on him — to the degree, he hastily added, such a thing was possible. It turned out to be more a pleasure than a chore, although young Bill certainly was never controlled by me. I didn't even try.

It was the jazz age, the Clara Bow flapper era. The "superior" part of me scorned it, but the rest of me lived it day and night. At that time it was a way of life, particularly in show business. One might scorn it, but there was no way

to shun it, especially since Bill and I had so much in common
— a love of jazz, bootleg gin and, of course, "dames." Chicago,
our last stop that season, was the wildest, with Louis Arm-
strong playing a trumpet at a speakeasy cafe called Kelley's
Stables where theater professionals were invited free on Monday
nights, and where the cast of a Mae West play would gather
along with Louis Wolheim's wild men from *What Price Glory?*
Abe Finkel and Teddy Thomas (nee Thomashevsky), another
assistant stage manager, were somehow related to George
Tobias, who played Lipinsky in *What Price Glory?*.

It was a season few of us wanted to see come to an end —
but our wants obviously had little to do with it. I was back at
the job of ushering at the Rialto just briefly when Bill Oviatt's
father turned up something more attractive and remunerative.
Young Bill and I were put in charge of the checkroom at the
Cosmopolitan Theatre on Columbus Circle at Fifty-ninth
Street, where Leon Errol opened in a musical farce called
Louis the Thirteenth. I worked much shorter hours, and
once again I had a chance to catch up through Walter Cowan
and other friends with what was going on in the real world.
Back to Greenwich Village each night after the show closed
and into the controversies about the expatriates in Paris —
Hemingway, Henry Miller, Gertrude Stein scorning the philis-
tinism of the U.S. And those who scorned *them*: here at
home didn't we have H.L. Mencken, George Jean Nathan
and their *American Mercury*? We read every issue cover to
cover, and devoured such marvelous satirical novellas as Joel
Sayre's *Rackety Rax* and *Hizzoner the Mayor*.

But we had more. The burning issue of the scandalous,
inhuman frame-up of Sacco and Vanzetti in Boston, their
trial and death sentence aroused worldwide protest in distinguished circles. Who could not help feeling pride in being
associated, however distantly, with such famous people as
Heywood Broun, Dorothy Parker, Theodore Dreiser and scores
like them? They were indeed renowned leaders. Walter and I
and our friends were part of the rank and file but however

distant, we were part of the same fight. And new names came into my life, writers who spoke at meetings of protest, men such as John Howard Lawson, Francis Farragoh, Emjo Basshe, at that time non-Communists of the intellectual left. And Mike Gold, Communist writer and critic; until then I'd never heard of him. These men were also planning a Workers' Theater, and again I dreamed desperately of writing. But now tortuous doubts assailed me.

"Workers' Theater." What did I know about the exploitation of workers? Only what I had learned from my father, a trade unionist and militant Socialist. What kind of worker was I, using the theater as a way of having fun? What could I write about? Nothing! I hated the job at the Cosmopolitan cloakroom and was enormously relieved when August came and I could quit; rehearsals were to start for the final year of *The Miracle*'s road tour.

It was September 1926. I was twenty-two. Many of the old cast of minor actors had dropped out, and new people were hired. A member of the stage crew, the head of props, was Dick White. Over the years we had become friends. He always saw to it that his wife, Helen, was engaged in a minor role so that she could travel with him. This year they brought into the cast a friend of Helen's age, thirty or so, named Florence. She was tall, handsome, bright and easy to be with and talk to. We soon found a friendship developing, and by the time we went to Philadelphia for the opening of the road tour I found for the first time a woman who was as attractive the next morning as she had been the night before.

We decided it would be worth it to try and live together. Her salary couldn't have been more than fifty dollars a week, so there were economic advantages for both of us. But mainly there was an attraction that continued as the weeks passed and, without any vows or commitments, we found a warm, closer-growing relationship. The fact that she was eight or ten years older than I never caused a problem; in fact, it had the opposite effect on me. The extraordinary experiences of her life seemed to give me a new sense, emotionally, and I warmed more and more to her as we learned about each other's past.

Florence was the first person I'd found in the company to whom I could speak about my too-oft-forgotten radical ideas and of my doubts about capitalist society. She was a respectful if skeptical listener. Abe and all the others had no interest in what was going on in the Soviet Union or in the Sacco-Vanzetti frame-up — beyond making cynical wisecracks. When I tried to discuss these things, they soon shut me up. But not Florence. She'd had an extraordinary life, a childhood almost too painful to tell. Somehow she'd gotten through high school, went into training as a nurse and, through a friend, learned of a man of means who required a live-in nurse. She went to him, was interviewed and hired. This man, Wilson Mizner, was about fifty then, and she was in her early twenties.

Mizner was something of a celebrity in his time, much in demand as a wit and raconteur among the "smart set." As a youth, in 1898, he'd gone to Alaska and had wittily reported to newspapers and magazines about the gold rush, the wild and weird characters, the gambling and thievery, more than hinting that he was not above partaking in all the activities available. When he hired Florence, it was apparent he was in dire need; either alcohol or drugs, or both, had just about done him in. She nursed, fed, watched over him, and soon became his mistress. This relationship went on for a few years, but broke up in the middle twenties when he went to Hollywood to try writing for movies. At that point, Mizner just dropped Florence.

Philadelphia, Kansas City, and then the long, exciting ride to San Francisco. The publicity men who preceded the show to each city created enormous interest, so it was like a Barnum and Bailey circus coming to town. The announcement that, shortly after our arrival, over a hundred men and women would be engaged to play in the show, heightened interest everywhere.

San Francisco was no exception. And for most of us who had never been there, the place had magic. We played in the huge auditorium, which seated four or five thousand people and was in the Civic Center, a block from the Opera House and City Hall. Almost every performance was sold out. The city was like home — a miniature New York. But, unlike New York, everything was within a stone's throw. We took the cable car to Fisherman's Wharf, then really a wharf, and ate shrimp and oysters pulled from the unpolluted bay. The two months there were a holiday.

Los Angeles, our next stop, promised to be even more exciting. Many of the actors hoped to find movie work, and we knew the show would receive great attention from the film industry because of a publicity ploy Morris Gest conceived. He announced that Professor Max Reinhardt had been summoned from Germany personally to direct the show for the Los Angeles run to make sure it had the freshness the author had originally given it. There were headlines and follow-up stories even before we arrived.

Of course, everyone in the crew and cast knew Gest's motive in spending that kind of money to bring Reinhardt from Germany. It was not, as the press was told, to make sure the play still had its freshness and original touches after all these years. Langdon West had kept the play alive and well. His careful eye preserved the vitality of the work. Gest had a different purpose: the proper ballyhoo could sell the play to a major film company. We guessed that he might have persuaded Reinhardt to come by telling him there was more than a possibility that he could direct the film.

Whatever the reason, Reinhardt accepted. We had been in Los Angeles about a week, going through the routine of casting the extras, beginning to outline the action roughly for them. The enormous set was being constructed in the huge

Production staff of *The Miracle*. Lester Cole, second from left.

Shrine Auditorium when Reinhardt arrived. Along with dozens of reporters and photographers, Gest, Oviatt and the half dozen stage and assistant stage managers were at Union Station to greet him. I was elated when he remembered me from New York and warmly shook my hand. Gest then took over, and we all went our several ways.

When I came home to the very decent little apartment Florence and I had found, she wasn't in. It was a one-bedroom, kitchen and bath in a pseudo-Spanish courtyard around which were eight or ten similar bungalows, called, in Hollywood's habitual hyperbole, Firenze Gardens. But the courtyard was on Sunset Boulevard, a few blocks east of Western Avenue where Fox Studios then stood, and a few blocks west of Bronson Avenue where Warner Brothers made their films at the time. We felt "in," with shopping close by and the Shrine Auditorium only a half hour away.

Florence came in shortly. She'd been shopping and telephoning; we didn't have our own phone yet.

"I called Wilson."

"What for?" I was ruffled, actually jealous, I guess.

She laughed, kissed me. "I told him I was bringing you over. He wants to meet you." And she pleaded, "Please?"

I nodded. It occurred to me then she probably wanted to show Wilson Mizner that she still was desirable, even to a reasonably good-looking young man. And I was curious about this eccentric celebrity.

It was late in the afternoon when we arrived at his very fashionable apartment in the Chateau Elysee.

He was good-naturedly drunk and jovially introduced us to a young friend, who would soon become a well-known film director. Mizner greeted Florence with an affectionate kiss. Then he shook my hand as if we'd been close friends for years. I took an instant dislike to him.

"Listen, you," he said with friendly gruffness, "you're new here, and I don't know how long you expect to stay. But remember this: Hollywood ain't dog eat dog, it's man eat

man. Never forget." And then he went into the story he'd
been saving for our arrival with great relish:

His agent had taken him to Jack Warner, to whom he
told one of his much treasured tales, an incident that occurred
during the gold rush in the Yukon just before the turn of the
century. Fun, skullduggery, himself in the center of it, of
course. A story Mizner felt his agent could sell for a fortune
— at least twenty thousand dollars.

"Warner had listened poker-faced," said Mizner. "No
mean conniver himself, he said it was little more than an
incident and a couple of pretty good situations, but not enough
to make a screenplay. And since I had no experience writing
screenplays, someone of high caliber *and* high salary would
have to be hired for that. So he asked the agent the price
and, when told, offered him 25 percent of what he asked for.

"I was so mad at that chiseling bastard I could've punched
his big Jew nose right then. Imagine, five thousand bucks for
a Wilson Mizner story! Then I got an idea. I told him okay,
I'd take it half down on signing the deal and half when I
turned in the story. The agent made the deal, picked up the
twenty-five hundred the next day; they gave me an office,
and I went to work. One week later I had the thing down,
about twenty-five pages, and I called the bastard for an appointment. He couldn't believe I was all done. Wonderful!
Here was a writer who didn't waste a producer's time for a
change.

"So I put the story in my briefcase, took twenty-five sheets
of blank paper and stuffed them in, and a couple of minutes
later I'm in his office.

"When Jack reached for the manuscript I took from my
briefcase, I held up my hand and said, 'Jack, you're a smart
man. When you said a week ago there wasn't much meat to
this —' I took the blank pages from the briefcase, 'I didn't
know how right you were. One hundred percent. It stinks. If
I took that other twenty-five hundred from you, it would be
stealing. This isn't worth your while reading.' And with that,

I tore up the blank pages and threw them out the window, reached over and shook the flabbergasted bastard's hand, and said 'We both took a chance and you're a hell of a good sport.'"

Mizner grinned. "I walked out. That cheap Jew crook sat there with his mouth open. I think I've got a real deal now for the story at Paramount."

Mizner poured another drink. He was quite drunk now. Florence, looking at me concerned, thought we'd better leave. Outside she said, troubled and compassionate, "I'm sorry. He's right back where I left him, only older. That horrid anti-Semitism. It's a sickness." I could hear what she was telling me; she felt he needed someone to take care of him.

The next day rehearsals with Reinhardt were due to start at eleven, and by ten-thirty we stage managers and assistants were hustling the newly engaged and regular extras into their places in the huge rehearsal hall where chalk lines were drawn for aisles and stage. As a rule, at this early stage of rehearsals, understudies were used for the leading roles; but today Gest had called out the leading players, and they were not in the best of moods.

The rehearsal hall had something not ordinarily seen; on one side, against the wall, were a dozen upholstered chairs and a second row of them two steps higher. We were too busy to be more than casually curious, but the answer soon came, very impressively.

Enter Morris Gest, beaming, and behind him more than a dozen well-dressed, well-fed men, imposing and important in appearance. I immediately recognized Sam Goldwyn, and Abe pointed out Louis B. Mayer; then Jack and Harry Warner in the front row, followed by other notables we didn't know, and bringing up the rear, majestically, Cecil B. De Mille and a subservient assistant.

Bowing and scraping, Gest beamed and purred. "We'll

start in a moment, gentlemen. I'll call Professor Reinhardt."
He darted for the door.

If Gest could put this over, maybe we'd all be back after
our last stop, which was Dallas, and start making a movie!

It was less than a moment before our impresario was
back, his arm through Reinhardt's. He led him to the guests
and introduced him. No one could fail to see the astonishment
and embarrassment on Reinhardt's face. Was he outraged at
the indignity of being put on display? He was talking in an
undertone as Gest led him to the director's desk and chair.
Gest was protesting, as in earnest explanation or humble
apology. Reinhardt said something to him which caused Gest
to turn abruptly and walk quickly to seat himself with the
guests. Slowly, Reinhardt mounted the single step of the
platform, stood behind the chair at the desk, very calmly
surveyed the scene. It was a long pause, and the silence was
heavy and respectful. Suddenly I heard: "Lester, vill you
please come here?"

I looked around, uncertain. Then, a little more forcefully,
"Herr Cole, *komm!*"

"Yes, sir!" I hurried to his side. He shook my hand, and
I felt the nervous pressure. Then he turned to the honored
guests.

"Gentlemen, zis is vun of my assistants, Lester Cole."
His voice was calm as he went on: "He has been viz zis
production from *drei jahren* now, and I'm zertain you vill
enjoy greatly seeing him conduct zuh rehearsal." He turned
and smiled at me. "First, Lester, describe the setting, zen
proceed." With that he sat down, folded his arms, looked
over smiling at Gest, and waved for me to start.

I didn't dare look toward Gest or anyone. It was true, of
course, that after rehearsing this show scores of times in the
past three years it was routine stuff. Any of the assistants
could have done it, and most certainly our chief stage manager,
Langdon West. But that wouldn't carry the sting he wanted
for Gest, and he chose from among the lowliest.

For the cast and crew the joke was clear enough, and as I described the set I could see the cast grinning, nodding; they doubly appreciated Gest's mortification. Then, instead of walking through the rehearsal, they played their parts as if in an actual performance.

When at last it was over, Reinhardt applauded. This cue was humorously taken up by the cast and seriously by the celebrities. Reinhardt motioned me over. He shook my hand and, in an undertone, said, "Thank you, Lester. You haff saved me great embarrassment und transferred it vhere it belonged." He indicated Gest. "How do you say — 'venal'?"

A young man waited patiently behind me. When I turned, he said, "Mr. De Mille would like a word with you — at your convenience," he added with hasty respect.

Reinhardt indicated for me to go. Standing at the door was De Mille. He spoke so the others would be sure to hear. "I liked your work."

"Thank you." I was a little awed by this tall, arrogant man.

"Do you have a run-of-the-play contract here?"

"No, sir. Standard Equity. Two weeks' notice either way."

"How would you — no, first, if I may ask, what does Gest pay you?"

"Seventy-five a week."

"I'm making you a firm offer now. One-year contract, three hundred a week, as my first assistant director. Finish the run of the show here. I don't want to deprive Gest of your services. When will this be over?"

"Well, another ten days of rehearsals, then a five-week run."

De Mille nodded, took out his card. "Be at my studio — the De Mille Studio in Culver City — the Monday morning after this play closes. Nine o'clock." He then wrote on his card, handed it to me, and was gone. On the back he had written: "Bring this man to me as soon as he presents this card." He signed it " C.B. De M."

I stood there, speechless. Illustrious guests gone, my friends began to gather around, curious. What was there to say: that this kid, twenty-three, was about to start a career in the movies, not at the bottom, but on a rung close to the top of the ladder, with the most prominent director in the business? A man with a studio named after him — well, that he named after himself, let's put it that way.

I don't remember much about the next six weeks except that the show opened, played its five-week run, and on the final night we had a party at Firenze Gardens. Florence and I had all our friends, a gallon or more of bootleg gin, a table piled high with food. Again, for me, tears. I'd said my good-byes earlier that evening to Fritz Feld, Diana Manners, Iris Tree, and other members of the cast, and now it was breaking with friends of years. I don't remember how the night ended; I guess I passed out early.

But Monday morning, bright and early, I was sober, excited and impatient. I took a bus out to Culver City, where the De Mille Studio was located, five or six blocks from the enormous MGM plant. It had a facade like a Southern mansion — tall, two-story columns — with beautifully manicured lawn and shrubs around its curved driveway.

Nervously I stumbled off the bus and all but ran to the entrance. I presented the card to the young woman at the desk. She smiled, asked me to sit down, and picked up the phone, announcing to someone that I was there.

"It will just be a moment," she smilingly assured me. I thanked her.

It was forty-five minutes later when a man of about forty came through a door. I was the only one there, so he assumed it was I for whom he was looking. "Mr. Cole?"

I nodded.

"Terribly sorry to keep you waiting, but there's some sort of most unfortunate mix-up. You say Mr. De Mille asked you to come today?"

"Yes."

He shook his head. "I've been trying to get through to

him since you were announced. He's on location in the desert
— " Before I could say anything, he went on. "It will be at
least a month before he's back." He went to the desk, took
the card De Mille had given me. I reached for it, but instead
of returning it he put it in his pocket. "Why don't you call
him in about six weeks? I'm sure he'll be back by then." He
started to turn away.

"You don't understand," I said, desperately. "I'm supposed
to start working today, as his assistant. First assistant. He
said —"

"Terribly sorry. Mr. De Mille left no instructions," he
said, already through the door which quickly shut behind
him.

Fourteen years later, under quite different circumstances,
Cecil De Mille and I would meet again.

When I returned from the studio, numbed, outraged,
and told Florence what had happened, she tried to comfort
me and make light of it. "Remember what Wilson said? This
joint is a human jungle — men eat men here. We're animals."

"But we animals eat food," I cried, "and that takes
something we haven't got."

She refused to take it too seriously and actually laughed.
"Don't tell him," she said.

"Who?"

"Wilson. He'll blame it on the Jews."

That stopped me. "How could he? It was De Mille."

"He's so idiotically prejudiced, that wouldn't stop him.
He'd say the bastard changed his name from — Demilsky,
or Demilovich."

I had to laugh, and she embraced me, hoping I felt less
heavy-hearted. "You'll find something. Call Jerry Daniels."

"You're not only beautiful, you're smart." I kissed her
and went to the phone. Daniels was a young fellow we'd met
during the run of the show who worked at Warner Brothers
in the accounting department. When I reached him, I told
him what had happened.

"Wait a minute. I read somewhere this morning, or yesterday, De Mille returned from Location this weekend and
will be winding up his flick on the back lot in ten days. He's
right here!"

"Shall I sue him or shoot him?" I asked.

"Forget him. He was showing off that day. Just another
bastard. The town's lousy with them."

"I can't let him get away with it!" I insisted.

"Unless you've got it in writing, a contract, there's nothing
you can do."

Florence was listening, her ear against mine at the phone.
"Jerry, I need a job. Bad. Anything. We're broke. I've got to
start right away."

"You serious? Any kind?"

"Damn right."

"Hold on." In two minutes Jerry was back. "You know
where this studio is?" I did, of course. It was only three
blocks away from our bungalow court. "You mean I really
got work, a job?" I was astonished.

"You said 'anything,' and I'm taking you seriously. Be at
the back gate on Bronson at 7:30 tomorrow morning. Day
labor. Fifty cents an hour, eight hours a day. Okay?"

"Christ, yes! Thanks, Jerry, we won't forget this."

"You and Florence come over for dinner tonight, okay?
I'll call Annie. And we'll talk things over."

Florence was already getting dressed. "Where are you
going?" I asked.

"Fifty cents an hour, eight hours a day, six days a week is
twenty-four dollars. How far do you think that's going to
take us?" She adjusted her lipstick. "I'm going to see Mizner."

I should have mentioned that in the past year Mizner
somehow had bought or conned his way into a part ownership of
the new top restaurant in town, The Brown Derby, then the
first of three, located on Wilshire Boulevard across from the
Ambassador Hotel. That afternoon when she came home she
said she was starting work the next day, too, as a cashier in

his restaurant. It was never said, or even hinted, but I assumed Mizner had given her the job with the usual string attached.

"I found a place," she said a few days later, "nearer to where I work."

I nodded. We knew from the beginning that what we had would not be forever and that this was as good a time as any to make the break. It had been fun for us both, but now she needed what I couldn't give and he could. Security. We kissed goodbye, tenderly. When the taxi she had phoned for honked outside, I helped her out with her bags. We kissed again, wished each other good luck, and she drove off.

Cecil B. De Mille, who gave my first lesson about Hollywood: It's not dog eat dog, but man eat man.

Mother, 1905

3

From Below the Ground Up

The next day I started my Hollywood career at Warner Brothers from the ground up. To be precise, from about four feet below the ground's surface. I reported for work at 7:30 and was sent with a pick and shovel gang on the back lot to dig ditches for only they knew what. We were about thirty men of all ages. Soon the foreman showed us where to start, and as I swung that pickaxe a mean rhythm developed: with every swing to the earth, my mother's voice kept time with the movement: "I *told* you. . . . *Make* something of yourself . . . . *mule.* . . . *mule.* . . *mule.* . . Like your *father.* Your mother knows *nothing.* . . . Say I'm *right.* At *last* say I'm *right.* No?. . . Okay, so you got a *socialist* pickaxe *union.*"

This tiny woman, hardly five feet tall, weighing less than a hundred pounds, was a human of superhuman persistence. Back in Poland, her father had been a small businessman, a bookbinder, who planned to bring his wife, son and two younger daughters to this country. He didn't believe that the streets were lined with gold, but he was confident that he could underprice his competitors and become prosperous.

He arrived first with his son Joe, then fourteen, and together they set up the business. A year later he sent for his wife and two daughters. Fanny, my mother-to-become, was then eight or nine, her sister Lena six. Without passports they had to escape across the border, as so many immigrants were then forced to do. After the girls' father left, their mother became ill with tuberculosis, and in the dash across the border to the harbor where their ship lay, she became worse; she died three days out to sea. The two little girls arrived alone.

For Sam Rosengarten, my grandfather, the grief may even have contained a measure of relief. For shortly after he and son Joe arrived, a young woman came to work in his shop. Just the week before his daughters' arrival, this woman announced she was pregnant. By my grandmother's death, an awkward situation was averted. Grandfather married almost at once, and six months later my mother had her first half-brother.

Fanny and her stepmother did not get along from the beginning. With the coming of the first child, to be followed within less than a year by a second, and then a third, all sons, the girls were made into household drudges and given little thought by their father who, if not prospering, was finding his skills in demand. By working with Joe twelve to fifteen hours a day, he was getting by.

My mother's size disguised her iron will. At twelve years of age she had a fierce fight with her stepmother. And when she discovered she could get no support from her father, she made up her mind. Early one morning she and Lena left as usual, but instead of both going to school, this twelve-year-old girl went in search of work. She found it that day in a shirt-waist factory — cheap child labor was always in demand. That afternoon, while her stepbrothers were out playing, and her parents and brother Joe were working in the shop, she packed her own and her sister's meager belongings in two pillowcases and walked to a tenement nearby. There she had already arranged for the mother of a girlfriend from school to take them in. Mother would make enough to pay for their room and board.

How she managed she never told me. When her father found her by following Lena home from school three days later, Fanny refused to return and kept Lena with her. The stepmother liked the arrangement. Little financial help was given them. Her stepmother saw to that. But her brother Joe helped them get by.

Fanny continued to work and keep Lena in school. When she was sixteen, she met Henry Cohn. For herself she saw little chance of achieving the American dream of success, and her marriage to my father, twelve years her senior, could have had little to do with love. But she saw him as bright and learned — he not only could speak good English already, but along with Yiddish spoke Polish and German. He read poetry and philosophy. This was a man with whom to have children, one who believed in a good education and would make a success in this country. Doctors, lawyers; where else but in this land were such accomplishments possible?

My father was a Jewish boy of sixteen when he arrived in this country from a small Polish town outside Warsaw. In 1895 his parents somehow saved or borrowed enough to pay his passage to America so that he could escape being drafted into the dreaded Polish Army. His one overriding task upon arrival was to pick up enough of that gold that paved the streets to send for his younger brother, Abe, in time to help him also evade the draft. He had about three years in which to do it.

Shortly after arriving and finding a room, he found a job as a cutter's apprentice in a men's necktie factory. His wage was two dollars and fifty cents a week, which left little toward his brother's boat fare. After a month or so, he wrote home explaining that either his parents had been misinformed about the gold in the streets or he had arrived too late; look as he might, he could find none. It was eight years before he saved enough to bring Abe over.

Henry was a hard worker and became a skillful one. When he met my mother in 1900, he had risen to assistant cutter and his wage was fifteen dollars a week. He was the shop's union organizer (although the union was not recognized), and he was a Socialist. He read Marx and Engels: their books were his bibles. He was a member of an organization called the *Arbeiter Ring* (Workmen's Circle), which raised money from workers to open a sanatorium in a little village called Liberty in the Catskill Mountains. The *Ring* bought an old house for workers and those in their families who contracted consumption, as tuberculosis was commonly called then. Rest and fresh air were the only hope at that time; there was no medical cure.

Soon Henry and Fanny were married. They took Lena into their home, and continued her schooling. In 1904, three years later, when my mother was nineteen, I was born. I could not know then, of course, but she took her vow that Lester, this precious son whom she loved more than anyone else in the world, would get everything America had to offer. My father would provide the means for an education; she would provide from her overflowing supply the needed will power, the driving spirit that could not be conquered by any obstacle or adversity. Who was better qualified than she? Was she not one hundred pounds of steel, 100-percent American steel? Well, she would later admit, just a little imported, and she'd add, "In America, what isn't?"

I can remember nothing of the years before we lived on 149th Street and Columbus Avenue, when I was perhaps five or a few months younger. We lived in a rough slum neighborhood, then mainly Irish. My mother was on her way to her dream of her first million. Where they got the money to buy the store, I don't know; maybe her brother Joe helped her. There, three or four shops down from the corner saloon, was her candy store with an open counter to the street in warm weather, from which she served ice cream cones and seltzer water for "one cent plain, two cents strawberry or cherry flavor."

We lived behind the store in three rooms, of which only

the back bedroom had a window looking out into the dark alleyway. The kitchen and dining room were one. I shared one room with my sister Blanche, then two. My parents had the other room and Aunt Lena a couch in the kitchen-dining room. There was a toilet and bath, and in the corners, for heat, were steam pipes which went from the cellar below us to the tenants above. The flat was gas-lit.

It was a good business corner because the Ninth Avenue El station was there. By then my father was a head cutter, earning twenty-five dollars a week, which was enough in those days for any family to live on, but not for Mama. To add to Pop's wages and the income from the store, she acquired a paper route and somehow induced him to make the early morning deliveries. So before he went to work he was out of the house a little after 4:00 A.M., winter and summer, seven days a week, delivering papers, adding another two, maybe four or even five dollars a week. Fanny's children were going to have the best. I guess Henry had no argument against that.

So out at 4:00, back at 5:00 or 5:30, and my mother would be up and have his breakfast ready. Before he left, Lena would wake me up and dress me for kindergarten. My mother would already have opened the store, selling papers, cigarets and chewing tobacco to men going to work. Blanche would also be awake by that time, and Pop would kiss us both goodbye and hurry off. The factory he worked in was on Broadway and Twenty-fifth Street, more than an hour away on the El. His day there started at 7:30.

The exciting memory for me at that time was late summer and early autumn, the year 1909, when the New York City mayoral elections were approaching. Where Henry's energy came from one can only guess, but at 6:00 P.M. he'd come running into the store, grab a wooden soapbox, and hurry to the corner, near the El stairway. I can still see my mother looking after him, shaking her head hopelessly, muttering, "What *narishkite, narishkite*" (foolishness).

In a flash he'd be on his soapbox, and as the workers came down from the train platform above, he'd start exhorting them to unite, to organize, unionize, to be men and not slaves. And the only way to do that was to vote Socialist, and elect Morris Hillquit the Mayor of New York. With a Socialist mayor they would have unions, an eight-hour day, a forty-hour week, they'd have a share of the profits — on and on, passionately. Some few people would stop curiously to listen, take one of his Socialist leaflets, but most would hurry by. What astonished and impressed me then (as now!) was that even when there were only two, or even one interested, he would not be discouraged. He would just keep talking.

"But you're talkin' to nobody," I once said.

"Time, Lester, *mein kind.* Time. Socialism will come. You'll live to see it."

Most evenings when my mother sent me out to say his supper was already cold, Murph, my friend, a kid who lived in the tenement flat above us, would be coming out to get *his* father. They were both at the corner. As I pulled my father's coattails to get him home, Murph was getting his father, and I could hear the voice snarling from inside the saloon behind me: "Get away from them swingin' doors, goddammit!"

But his pop would come out, and my pop would pick up his soapbox and say hello to his pop, who would kind of nod, which was about as close as any self-respecting Irishman could get to admitting the existence of a Yid Socialist.

I'm not sure when or why we left the candy store on 149th Street. Certainly one reason must have been that it was far from prospering, but another could have been my mother's concern about the tough neighborhood. My friend Murph's older brother, then about twelve, had just been sent to a reformatory, a common enough occurrence in the neighborhood. She worried about me.

Actually, she had reason to. The most fun I had with Murph was stealing. Murph was very clever at it, and it was high adventure. It was something less than grand larceny, but it was cruel, and in typical kid fashion, vicious.

Here's the way we worked it: Our victims were the Italian pushcart vendors who slowly made their way up Columbus Avenue and the side streets, stopping to call out or sing operatically to the windows above of their fresh fruits and vegetables.

While waiting for the customers from the tenements to come down, I would stand unobtrusively in a doorway near the vendor's cart. Then, when one or two women would come to buy his fruits and vegetables, Murph would suddenly appear, come close and taunt the pushcart man. He'd start yelling, "Don't buy from him, he's a dirty wop, his stuff is rotten, he's a robbin', lousy guinea. Don't buy from crooked dirty guineas!"

The vendor would try to shoo him away, but Murph would circle his pushcart, push the women, frighten them away, and finally the poor man would become so enraged he'd chase after Murph down the street, cursing wildly in Italian.

When they were fifty feet or so from the pushcart, my time had come. I'd run a few feet to the cart, fill a paper bag with apples, pears, or whatever was closest, and dart off in the opposite direction.

The day the cop brought me home to the candy store by the scruff of the neck — Murph had escaped — was a day I'll never be allowed to forget. After a gruff warning to my mother, he left. Whether, in her rage, it was accidental or intentional, I'll never know. In any case, she never expressed regret. She screamed her curses and smacked my face while holding my hands. As I pulled away, I struck the steam pipe in the corner of the room. I screamed in pain, and almost instantly a blister the size of a quarter appeared in the curve between my right thumb and forefinger. Only then did she let go. My pain was unbearable. But the only pain she was aware of stemmed from her shame. The blister healed, but left a small permanent red scar.

By the time my father came home that night she had

already made up her mind. She told him what had happened. "It's our luck he's too young to go to jail. We should live here and next year he should go to the reformatory like the Irisher upstairs? With such a reputation, he could become a lawyer? He would *need* a lawyer. For this I'm working my fingers to the bone? For my son to become a thief?"

The next thing I remember we were living in a fairly new tenement house on Belmont Street on the northern edge of Claremont Park in the West Bronx. It was a beautiful park, with green grass and trees; I'd never seen that before in my life. And tennis courts, and places to play baseball and soccer. A different world, and this time a Jewish one.

Perhaps the rent was low because of the difficulty the men had getting to work. My father and the others had to walk more than half a mile across the park, then down a steep hill for another quarter of a mile. Out of the park then, at Webster and Wendover Avenues, there were still six or seven blocks to the Third Avenue El station. Going to work couldn't have been too bad, but the walk home in the winter darkness up the slippery, frozen hill after standing nine or ten hours on his feet must have been exhausting for my father. I guess even that was better than the paper route at 4:00 A.M. I never heard him complain.

The tenement was across the street from the park, and beyond the first twenty feet of sloping grass were perhaps a dozen benches lining a gravel path, and it was there on summer evenings and Sundays that my father soon made friends. They were mostly working men, but also a lawyer or two, and a dentist. They would talk and argue about unions, socialism and religion. My father was an atheist. Often I would listen and hear of the 1905 Revolution in Russia, and the names Marx, Engels and Lenin were soon familiar. I knew what they stood for even before I could read, and the way my father was able to beat those college-educated lawyers and dentists! My father, with his Marxist philosophy and ideology, could take on all comers. What a source of wonder to me! It could be that then in my mind the importance my mother put on education and a profession diminished. Certainly the way Pop demolished the professionals in debate made me very proud. Part English, part Yiddish, always aggressive, eventually he had even his most formidable opponents saying, "Enough, Henry, enough already!"

Aunt Lena, always quiet, helpful, somewhat retiring by nature, and loyal to my mother, announced one evening that at night school she had met a man who worked in the post office, and before we knew it she was married and gone. My mother was pleased, and I suppose my sister and I were, too, although we missed her kind and helpful ways. My mother had her social life, too. The hot subject among the women of the neighborhood was not socialism; they were suffragettes and regularly would hold Kaffee Klatsches where they'd organize for demonstrations.

I started first grade at P.S. 28, on Anthony and Tremont Avenues, about eight blocks away. School was very exciting for me, with few problems, but as soon as I grew taller, within a year or two, I found coming home a dangerous business. Along Anthony Avenue the "goyish" kids would lie in wait for the "Yids." All would be quiet; then suddenly from behind fences and hedges would come half a dozen or so of these kids. They would hit us with fists and sticks, call us kikes and lousy sheenies. I'd come home from school crying and bloody, my clothes dirty and torn, almost every day. My mother went to school to complain, but there was little that could be done.

It was my father who found the solution. With the other fathers on the park bench, he outlined his plan. It was simple enough. All the Jewish kids from six to fourteen would, he said, be "organized." We'd have cut-off broom sticks, our school rulers, and small stones. We'd meet in the schoolyard after school, make sure all of us were together, and then start home in a group. Of course it worked; when three or four kids saw more than a dozen of us with rulers, sticks, stones and ready for them, they still called us dirty sheenies, but while running away. I still remember our pride, our feeling of power. We didn't know the words and music of the song, "Solidarity Forever," which I doubt had yet been written. But its words and music were already seeded in my heart. Wasn't my father wonderful? And life was good: school, baseball, soccer, my friend Walter Cowan.

Before I knew it I was ten. It was 1914. World War I had started. My father lectured his friends on the bench about the reasons and the consequences. The Americans were not fighting "Huns," he would argue hotly; there was no difference between the Russian Czar and the German Kaiser and the King of England. These rulers were fighting over colonies in Africa, for the riches they were stealing from the *"Schvartzes"* (Blacks); so the rich would get richer, and millions of poor men whom they would conscript into their armies would be killed. The men would listen, and most of them would nod their heads and agree. It was a capitalist war. They'd say, "Henry's right!" Of course he was right; he was my father!

My mother didn't share my admiration. To her he was fast getting nowhere, and, she demanded to know, if *he* got nowhere in this world, where would his *children* get? Our house became heavy with harsh words and long silences. I was very uneasy, and I felt estranged from my sister, Blanche, who during the arguments held on to my mother's skirt and half hid behind her, while I stood on my father's side.

Finally, one day she made her demand, an ultimatum. His brother, my Uncle Abe, whom he had brought to this country a few years before, had already found a wife with money and was flourishing in the dress business. My mother demanded that Pop borrow some money and start his own neckwear business. He refused; his brother had already paid him back the boat fare. Abe owed him nothing. And Pop did not want to become a boss. He was a working man and would remain one.

One night, at the peak of an argument, she made her

final statement. "All right, Mister Cohn, Socialist mayor bench number three in Claremont Park. With your unions and *Arbeiter Ring.* You have your world out there on the bench, and at the tie factory, but for me and my children that is not America."

Our neighbor, a lawyer named Bernstein, was called in by my mother to arrange a divorce. A few weeks later I learned that she had custody of both kids. My father kissed Blanche and me goodbye and left, promising to visit on Sundays. We moved a few miles away to a smaller apartment, near Crotona Park on the East Side of the Bronx, and I transferred to P.S. 44. I saw my father on Sundays. He rented bicycles and taught me to ride.

Although she always complained bitterly, he must have provided something out of his wages, which were his only source of income. Because when summer came, somehow there was always enough money for her to take us to the country for "fresh air." Every summer it was the same place, a tiny cottage in the Catskill Mountains in a village called Halcott Center, about ten miles by horse and carriage from Fleischmann's Station, the nearest railroad stop.

Over the next few years we shared the cottage with friends, often with Walter Cowan and his mother. Walter, three years older than I, an avid reader, soon had me fascinated, overwhelmed, by Joseph Conrad, and during the fall and winter introduced me to friends, some of whom were in their later teens in high school and who would hold forth on Oscar Wilde and Bernard Shaw, while others would challenge them with the works of Gorky, Chekhov and Tolstoy. I remember one brilliant, embittered young hunchback, Tommy Deutsch, later Tom Van Dyke, who could not only recite "The Ballad of Reading Gaol" by heart, but most of Wilde's epigrams. At twelve it was a new world to me. In that rarefied environment I rarely expressed an opinion. I never opened my mouth, except perhaps in awe to say, "Yeah?" or "Jeez!"

My mother, it seemed, became more of a dynamo than

ever. Different jobs in different towns and in 1917, six months before I was fourteen, we moved to a little town in New Jersey, Roselle Park, about twenty miles from New York.

She found a place to live, bought second-hand furniture, and we discovered that she had bought a small notions shop, selling pins and needles, crochet and knitting materials, thread and yarn, and bolts of cloth — cotton, wool, silk. By that time I began to wonder about her. Far from unattractive, she seemed to have absolutely no interest in men. The lawyer Bernstein wanted to divorce his wife and marry her; she rejected him. Her children were all she thought of or loved, and she tried to dominate our every move. I think one of her greatest disappointments was her inability to change my thinking. This, of course, she blamed on my father, and she was correct. His way of thinking of himself, of working people and a socialist world made sense to me. Her driving ambition for wealth did not.

I missed Pop, and it would be a couple of years before I saw him again. He had moved to Baltimore, which seemed thousands of miles away. We received birthday cards and presents, but it was for those summer evenings and Sundays on the benches in Claremont Park, hearing him talk — I longed most for those times.

Come the spring of 1917 I would be graduating from the eighth grade in a few months. The U.S. had entered World War I a few weeks before, and patriotic fervor was rising everywhere, supporting President Woodrow Wilson in his vow to "Make the World Safe for Democracy." I remembered three years before, when the war started, what my father had said. But I could find no young friends in Roselle Park that I could talk to. Then, surprisingly, I discovered that while my mother disagreed in many areas with my father, she was opposed to the war. This was gratifying and brought me closer to her than I had felt in years.

Home was the haven. The fever of patriotism that swept

the school gave me a strange feeling of being alien and alone. I was afraid to speak out, to oppose so many who felt so strongly, and I had no intention of doing so. Unexpectedly, in a very frightening way, it happened. I was a good student, particularly in English. The teacher liked my compositions and often had me read them to the class. One morning, her face aglow with pride, she announced, "I want a two-page composition today about our glorious soldiers, telling why we are proud of them, and how these heroes are going to save the world for democracy."

Dutifully the students set to work, but I found myself paralyzed. I simply could not write what she asked for, nor could I put down what I truly felt. I just sat there, numbed, hearing only a voice inside me hiss the warning, "Run, run. Get out of here."

Then an idea hit me. I would raise my hand to go to the toilet, suddenly get sick there, and ask to be allowed to go home. Pleased with the strategy, I raised my hand, only to find her standing over me smiling. Usually I was the first to finish an assignment. When she saw I was not writing, she assumed I'd finished; but when she picked up the blank pages she was puzzled. "What's wrong, Lester?"

That was the time to say my stomach ached, my head ached, I had a fever, but instead something totally unexpected happened. Hot tears started down my cheeks, I started to tremble, and before I realized it I was shouting something like this: "I don't believe it. It's all a lie. They're going to get killed for the profits of rich people. That's what happens in war. The poor get killed and the rich get richer."

The poor woman was stunned. It took her a moment to get into action. "Did the class hear what Lester Cohn said?" she demanded in cold rage.

Of course they did. They started yelling. "Cohn, Cohn!" "Dirty Jew German Hun!" "Jew traitor!"

"Apologize!" the teacher said, grimly, clutching my arm

with all her strength, pulling me to my feet. I wanted to scream or hit her. But I stood silent, and then she made her decision. "Come with me!"

She dragged me to the principal's office, told him the story, and instantly he rang the school bell for general assembly in the auditorium.

When he dragged me there five minutes later, onto the stage, there were already five or six hundred children seated in the auditorium, excited, knowing something unusual was going to happen; my sister was somewhere among them. Holding my arm, the principal turned to the assemblage.

"We have here in our school one traitor, a boy who is opposed to our soldiers, to this patriotic war which will save mankind from the savage Hun." He turned to me, let go of my arm, and pointed to the flag on its stand at the side of the stage. "I am now going to ask you to retract your statement and pledge allegiance to your flag."

I stood petrified. "Retract, apologize and pledge allegiance," he repeated in the severest tone.

It was then I became aware he had let go my arm. Swiftly, I scampered off the stage, through the hall and out of the building. Instantly behind me I heard the screams of the girls and the hysterically furious boys. Dimly the voices of the teachers could be heard trying to stop them, but I knew they'd pay no heed.

They chased me, all the eight or ten blocks to my mother's shop. They were less than a hundred feet behind me, shouting curses familiar to me for years: "Sheeny, kike! Go back where you came from!"

The cries of the kids had already attracted my mother and she was at the open door when I stumbled in, breathless. "Lock it," I managed to say.

"What did you do now, you idiot?" she screamed. But I didn't answer. She locked the door and I hid behind the counter. By this time the police were already on the scene, along with the school principal, and soon the children were herded back to school. Then she grabbed my wrist and yanked me from behind the counter, and suddenly I remembered and looked at my hand, where the red scar between my thumb and finger was as bright as ever.

What happened after that I cannot recall. I must have bowed to her insistence, returned to school, and apoligised. My few friendships had vanished, and I felt more alone than ever. It is a dim, grey period; without remembering how it came about, I graduated with high grades and played the leading role in the final school play about the history of our country, in which I narrated the Declaration of Independence. My first theatrical performance! My mother was there, of course, feeling proud; she loved me and must have felt that all she now needed was the technique, the method, to control me, to mold this child, her very own and favorite, into a dream realized.

Henry Cohn. My father was an ardent socialist and trade union advocate in my youth.

4

Revolt and Revolution

Less than a week after I graduated, at the end of June, 1917, Blanche and I were told to pack our things. We were moving to Washington, D.C. An old friend of my mother's, whom we called Aunt Ray, had a good job in Washington. She not only convinced my mother that there was money to be made in a boarding house there because of the thousands of civilians coming to work in the newly established war offices, but had actually found her the house, furnished and ready to go. By nightfall we were there.

Washington was exciting—the places to see, the feverish activity. In less than a week all the rooms in my mother's boarding house had filled. She hired Black kitchen help and maids to clean the rooms. She herself was the cook. Those who boarded at the house had excellent food for breakfast and dinner. She prospered and was happy: I would go to college with that money.

In the fall I started at McKinley High School. The feverish war propaganda had gotten to me; it had become so much a part of life that I seemed to live with it quite apart from any previous feeling. Along with others, I hoped we would win, that "the Huns who killed little Belgian babies" would be shot down by our soldiers, and that — who knew? — maybe it really would make the world safe for democracy.

Within a few months the papers were full of the Bolshevik Revolution. I followed the news stories with interest in the papers and read that it was really the Communists who were the enemies of democracy. The Bolsheviks' peace treaty with the Huns meant more of our soldiers would have to be killed before we won. Once again my home education and what I was getting in school were in conflict.

McKinley High had a swimming pool, and I soon became an expert swimmer and learned fancy diving off the three foot board. I made the freshman swimming team and won a life-saving certificate. That summer, already fourteen, I was ready for my first job; the need for help was so great I was taken into the War Department as a messenger boy, in an office that supplied athletic equipment to soldiers. Raymond (or was it his brother Howard Emerson?) Fosdick was head of the office.

I don't know what was in my mother's mind when the Allies won the war the following November. Her boarding house emptied within two months. But as always her motors were running. She had found a small restaurant not too far away, on the second floor of a two-story building, with a furniture store below; behind the restaurant were the usual two bedrooms and a bath. It was there I learned to cook, helping her late in the afternoons after school. But she was unlucky, and this time unprepared. The restaurant failed quickly.

Against her will, my mother sent me to Baltimore temporarily to live with my father, who was the head cutter in a neckwear factory. I shared his small room and continued high school. There I stayed six months. It was a very uncomfortable living arrangement, but gave me an opportunity I had long been waiting for — to talk about socialism and what was happening in Russia. My father was excited by the events, but gloomy. He said "They" would not allow the country to live. The capitalists would invade Russia and destroy the workers' socialism before it could get going. I was surprised at his pessimism; I had expected a feeling of great victory and a greater future.

I made one friend at school whose name I shouldn't have forgotten because, in a way, it was he who introduced me to what was to become the greater part of my life's work. His father owned a little movie theater on East Baltimore Street called "The Blue Mouse," and every time the movie changed he would sneak me in and I'd see the picture for nothing. Whether it was D.W. Griffith's Ku Klux Klan riding against its Black enemies or Theda Bara seducing and ruining some innocent young man, it was an excitement that could be found nowhere else. I watched excitedly — and far from critically.

It came as no surprise to me to learn that my mother had returned to New York and acquired a new business. She soon sent for me. The legal arrangement was such that neither my father nor I had any choice. Despite the discomfort of living in one room and the small allowance he could afford to give me, I didn't want to go. Not only was there The Blue Mouse, which had become like a drug, but I enjoyed the freedom I had living with my father. And we talked about the books I'd read, the movies, and socialism. Once when I told him about the disastrous day in school at Roselle Park, he nodded and only said, "Tactics and strategy. There's a time to talk and a time to keep your mouth shut." That was a sage bit of advice I never mastered.

When I reached New York, I found the situation worse than I thought. The new business was not in the city, but sixty miles away, a country vacation boarding house, on the edge of beautiful Lake Mahopac in Dutchess County. The idea was for me to come right up and, during the Christmas holidays, start getting the place in condition through the winter for a spring opening. That was my first hard-fought and successful rebellion. I saw the school, didn't like it (there was no swimming pool), and so I told her flat out I was leaving.

In the end we compromised. I would go to school in New York and return to help her summers. She arranged to have me live with our old friends and neighbors on Belmont Street, the Toorocks. The old man was a close friend of my father's, an ardent Socialist, a worker in a men's clothing factory. They had three sons, and the oldest, already out of college, an accountant, was gone, so I had his room. The middle brother, Abe, was a salesman, and Meyer, nicknamed "Chiefie," was a football star at New York University.

That first night when I came in for dinner Mr. Toorock came home. He had aged so much I hardly recognized him: thin, worn-out, weary. I remember when he took me in his arms I started to cry. But I quickly brushed the tears when Mrs. Toorock called us for dinner. I had not been in the dining room for some years and now, behind Mr. Toorock's chair, was a print of an old man with white hair and a long grey beard. Perhaps to hide my feelings, or maybe just because he actually did look funny, I started to laugh, and I said, "Who's that funny-looking old geezer?"

There was a sudden stiff stillness. Nobody moved. I knew I'd said something wrong. "I'm sorry," I said to Mr. Toorock. "Is that your father?"

That broke the silence. The small, emaciated little man suddenly lost all his weariness, and his voice was strong, but it quavered. "Yes, Lester, that's my father." His voice rose. "And he's *your* father, and your *father's* father! He is *mankind's father!*" Whereupon he lowered his head to his soup and started to eat.

It was Chiefie who relieved me of my bewilderment. "That's Karl Marx," he whispered. Almost immediately I found my voice.

"I'm sorry, Mr. Toorock. I know who Karl Marx is. Papa loves him. I just never saw his picture before, that's all."

He looked up and smiled, and everybody was relieved. It was Evander Childs High School in the winter, my mother's boarding house in the summer. I worked for my keep. Not only did I rent out rowboats (where did she get the money for this place?), but I gave swimming instructions and acted as lifeguard.

My mother had a successful summer. So did I; I fell madly in love with a beautiful girl named Cecil Schultz, whose mother kept much too close an eye on us, to our full-time frustration. As before I helped in the kitchen, waited on tables. Still there was time to fish in the lake. I rigged a sail on a canoe with outboards, which was a thrill, and swam at least a mile a day. I grew inches taller, four or five more than my father, who was five foot four, and my body grew strong.

But with the end of summer, after Labor Day, with Cecil gone and everyone back in New York, there were the day-long chores of putting boats and canoes away for the winter, and lonely, empty nights, and a longing for Cecil, an urge so strong as can only happen to a teenager certain of his one and only great love.

School began in less than a week. I wanted to go back to the Toorocks' and the swimming team at Evander Childs — and Cecil. My mother flatly refused. She couldn't afford it; I'd go to school here, as Blanche would. It was then I decided.

With my mother at the market, Blanche at school, I quickly packed a bag, and laughingly included a toothbrush. Leaving a goodbye note, I promised to write "before I become a lawyer, doctor or dentist." I hitched a ride to the railway station.

I found the rooming house in Greenwich Village where my friend Walter Cowan lived — I seem to remember it was 10 Bank Street. I rented a room for a week and waited for Walter to come home from work. He was delighted to see me and insisted on taking me to dinner, to a place called "The Pirate's Den," and he pointed out the celebrities. I'd never heard of them but was nonetheless impressed. It was like the hold of a ship, the waiters dressed like pirates — it was wild. In a few days I discovered I had a job problem. My name, Cohn, was acceptable in no Gentile places, and only some Jewish establishments — perhaps those with no Gentile clientele. I was getting nowhere. Answering advertisements, door-to-door, no jobs.

I had started lying about my age and claiming to have graduated from high school. Now I had to choose a new name.

Walter and I set about choosing one. It was clear enough: with no family or financial support in an anti-Semitic world such a name as Cohn was an obvious handicap. Especially when I didn't believe in any of the things Jews did, from God to Kosher. Why have a name that was like wearing a yarmulke and the Star of David on my forehead? As we pondered a suitable name, I suddenly remembered a story my father once told me: my name really wasn't Cohn at all!

Laughing, I told Walter the story. When he was my age, sixteen, my father had arrived at Ellis Island, frightened and eager. The official looked at his papers, frowned, and tried to pronounce the boy's name. "Kolitnyvesky," my father said it for him. The official shook his head. "You'll never get nowhere in this country wid a tag like dat, kid. Think up something simple. Names is free in dis country. Somethin' easy to say."

"Short?" my father asked, showing off his English.

"Yeah."

In a moment he had it. His almost agnostic rabbi teacher, a socialist and lover of poetry and philosophy, who taught him English for a year before he left, a man he greatly admired, was named Cohn.

"How about Cohn?" he asked.

The man behind the desk nodded approvingly. "Good. A simple Jew name. Nobody could miss it."

"Kolitnyevsky!" Walter shouted triumphantly. "Cut off the last two-thirds and you've got it. With a *C*. Cole."

"Great!" I agreed. All I had done was to go back to one of my roots and cut part of it off, and three days later Lester Cole had a job as a shipping clerk in a Jewish-owned shop called the American Gear Company on the corner of Fifty-third Street and Broadway, directly under the El, which crossed from Sixth Avenue to Ninth along that street, rumbling and shaking the old building all day long.

I worked in the basement. When crates of auto parts — transmissions, differentials, clutches and axles — were delivered from Fifty-third Street, I opened the iron doors on the sidewalk, rode up the freight elevator, helped unload on the street and again unload in the cellar. The swimming the past summer had put me in shape for this grueling work, but not for cockroaches, which were two to three inches long and had taken over the basement, along with the rats. But I was started on my own. Twelve dollars a week, which didn't seem bad for a Cole of eighteen, who really was only a Cohn of sixteen.

After work a new world was opening up for me. With Walter and friends I met through him, I would go every Monday night to LeBlang's cut-rate theater ticket office in the basement under Grey's Drugstore on Forty-third Street and Broadway. Times Square, White Lights. I was hooked. For seventy-five cents, or at most a dollar, seats could be had on the second balcony; and after the first act, one could move down when the theater wasn't crowded. The excitement! Here was O'Neill's *Emperor Jones*, with Paul Robeson; Tarkington's farce, *Clarence*; the mind-boggling *School for Scandal*; Joseph Schildkraut and Eva LeGalliene and Helen Westley in Molnar's *Liliom*. This was the world I wanted. I watched in awe the romantic shenanigans of Lou Tellegen in a dimly remembered play called *Blind Youth*. In my wildest fantasies I could not imagine that within ten years I would become a stage manager for Joseph Schildkraut and his personal friend — and write a play about him that would star Lou Tellegen.

But then, in 1920, working in the filthy basement of the

American Gear Company, my thoughts were closer to those of my father; I began to understand what a member of the working class really was. There were, of course, no unions for shipping clerks, or stock clerks. I worked ten hours a day, eight to six, six days a week. By June, the heat in that basement and the stink of the rat dung seemed more than I could endure. But endure I did. I had to eat and pay rent.

Somewhere around that time I had my name changed legally, and some years later Blanche and my mother followed. I worked at Lake Mahopac one more summer. No day passed when my mother did not urge me to ask my father for money to finish high school, go on to college and become a *mensch*. Around this time word came from my father that he had remarried. His wife's family had insisted he accept as a dowry sufficient money to start his own neckwear business in Baltimore. He accepted but he still worked as a cutter and his new wife took charge of the office and the bookkeeping. I was glad for him, but this development gave my mother added force in her acrimony. Pop was no longer a poor working man. "In business for himself, with a 'wealthy wife,' he is a miserable dog if he does not help his son." Over and over, every day. What a bombardment! Finally the summer was over.

It was a troublesome time. Among those running the country, panic set in: if the workers in Russia could take control what was there to prevent radical workers like the IWW from trying it here? There was reason for concern, if not panic. Led by White Generals and the remnants of the Czar's army, aided by six or eight European and Asian armies — more than 80 percent of the new Soviet Union land mass came under hostile control. How did these peasants and workers, all but destroyed in World War I, actually drive the invaders back beyond their own borders and into the seas? Ignorant, illiterate peasants and workers!

So, starting in 1919 U.S. Attorney General A. Mitchell Palmer was taking no chances. With his young, trusted, eagerly ambitious assistant, J. Edgar Hoover, he began what became infamous as "The Palmer Raids." Although the stated goal was to wipe out the newly organized Communist Party USA, they did not spare Socialists, Anarchists or anyone else who raised questions in their paranoid minds. Workers clubs were left in a shambles, union meetings disrupted, and records stolen. Finally, in 1920, the hysteria mounted to the point where five legally elected Socialists were thrown out of the New York State assembly.

I cannot recall his name, but it was for one of those five ousted Socialist assemblymen that I was working at the time. He owned a small auto parts business, and I qualified as a shipping clerk. At American Gear Co. I had come to know about pistons, rings, transmissions and differential parts. He had an assistant but when the assemblyman was thrown out of his job in Albany, he was forced to let the man go. I became his sole employee — and his friend. But with J. Edgar Hoover whiplashing his way through progressive forces like a wild cowboy with the slogan, "Out With the Reds," my employer's customers, themselves afraid of guilt by association, dropped off. He had to close. It was a tearful farewell; we had become very close in those few months.

The next summer I found myself with a job as a lifeguard on the beach at Far Rockaway, twenty or so miles out of the city. I only had to lie about my age, display my lifesaving certificate, go through the tests, and I was hired. It was a summer of sun and fun — of laughing, happy kids and attractive women. But I began to wonder how right or wrong my mother was in her insistence upon an education. Summer can be three happy months, but nine uncertain, unhappy ones inevitably followed. Were they to be as a stock or shipping clerk for all the years I could already see stretching ahead?

When the summer ended, I returned to New York. My mother had sold her boarding house in Lake Mahopac for reasons she never explained. Now she was prepared to open a lunchroom on Twenty-ninth Street near Lexington Avenue. I had two friends, commercial artists, whose studio was a short distance away on Broadway, and they inspired me to my first "published" work, my very own idea. One of them gave me a large old palette. In his studio I dabbed a dozen bright colors around the edges, attached a couple of brushes in the hole reserved for holding the palette with one's thumb, and had him letter the name I had created for the restaurant: "The Palate." When I explained the pun to my mother she accepted it, and I proudly hung the sign outside the entrance.

It was a few days later that Blanche came home and told me about Butler Davenport's Theater. Thus my Theatrical career began. The world I dreamed about for myself was about to start. That was, I think, 1921.

Now, six years later, the dream seemed over. My reality now was digging ditches on the back lot at Warner Bros. with the future my mother warned me against still pounding my ears, heavy with scorn and pain. "A ditch digger, a Bowery bum? All my life I worked for you to be something. But you knew better. So now dig, dig. It gives you muscles, everywhere but in your head."

5

Show Biz

Living alone, determined to find a way out, I would dress after work, visit theaters, look for jobs. It was then I learned of Stanley Rose's Bookshop on Hollywood Boulevard near Cherokee Street, next door to the famous Musso Frank's Restaurant.

Stanley's was a haven for Hollywood's screenwriters, novelists, poets, actors and journalists, employed and unemployed. He was generous, gave more than he took from those in need, relying on more prosperous clients for material benefits. He was rewarded by the admiration and gratitude he received when he could be of help to any of us. His business flourished along with his philanthropies.

A rebel, a cynical radical, Stanley attracted notables — as well as unknowns like myself and Cedric Belfrage. A young Englishman my age, Cedric was a stringer for the *New York Sun* and British movie fan magazines. He and I hit it off instantly, and one evening, sitting around the reading table in the back room of the bookshop, someone caustically mentioned Sid Grauman and the new monster movie palace

he was building five or six blocks west of the shop on Hollywood Boulevard. Cedric and I looked at each other; my first
lead to a job!

In Los Angeles Sid Grauman could not be challenged.
With one large house downtown, he then built the Egyptian
Theater on Hollywood Boulevard just below Highland Avenue,
and was soon to complete the acknowledged most luxurious
and splendiferous of all movie palaces, Grauman's Chinese
Theater. His prologues, as he called them, were luxuriously
inventive; they supplemented the films and drew crowds as
large as those the films themselves attracted.

I phoned Grauman's office for an appointment and was
told to appear the following evening at his office in the Egyptian.
When I arrived, I was ushered in by the house manager with
surprising and quite unexpected cordiality. To my astonishment, Grauman greeted me with great warmth and told me
he had been in the audience with L.B. Mayer and Warner
and De Mille when Reinhardt had me direct the rehearsal of
The Miracle. Why had I left the play, he wanted to know. I
didn't mention the De Mille back-stab. In an off-hand manner I
managed to say that Hollywood attracted me, I planned to
do some writing, needed work, and it occurred to me that he
might need a stage manager for the new Chinese Theater.

He did indeed. I was just the man! "Seventy-five a week
to start and I'll bill you as my Assistant Director." And he
added quickly, "That's just for a start until we see how it
works out." We shook hands.

He immediately phoned his publicity man, and the next
day the ditchdigger of the past six weeks had items in the
dailies and the trade papers reporting his engagement for
this "most important post." Grauman built it up, explaining
that I was also finishing a play which was soon to be optioned
for Broadway production, in which he planned to invest. A
complete invention, but it read well.

I was overwhelmed, but Cedric was not taken in. At twenty-
three, like myself, he was as much a veteran of flak in news-

papers as I was of the ways in the theater. To build himself
up, Cedric said, Grauman would do anything — including
build me up. I took Cedric to lunch at Musso's. It started a
tradition: whenever either of us had prospects for more than
the rent, we'd treat the other to a meal there. Also, being
next door to Stanley Rose's Bookshop, it was convenient.

Cedric's career as a dedicated journalist was as precarious
as was mine in the theater. But we were both aware of the
real world around us; we worked and made enough for rent
and food and found life full.

The job with Grauman was interesting. I was doing it
well, and the night the first picture opened he raised my
salary ten dollars. I should have known better than to write
of my rise in the world to my mother; three weeks later she
was in Hollywood, and in two days living in my cramped
quarters. Most regretfully I was forced to evict a lovely young
woman who was sharing it with me; my mother soon found a
large place suitable for mother and son. I needed taking care
of, she insisted. Blanche came out that summer after receiving
her B.A. at Hunter College in New York.

I worried about the opening night at the theater; not
about my work, but because the first film to open the house
was none other than Cecil B. De Mille's *King of Kings.*
Would he and I meet? Would Grauman introduce me if and
when he brought him on the stage after the film? Would I
punch the bastard in the nose?

Not that I had much time to think about it. Preparing for
the prologue required complete concentration. With a cast of
sixty or more singers, actors and dancers, the performance
lasted perhaps forty-five minutes. The entertainment was
devised to enhance the film that would follow. Song, dance
and atmospheric scenes, hopefully, would put the audience
in the most receptive mood possible. There were tableaux of
"The Last Supper" and other scenes from Christ's life, as
well as appropriate music and dance. My job was to see that
everyone was in place at the proper time, that light cues were

given — in short, to make the show go smoothly.

It did and was enthusiastically received. Grauman came back when the film began and took me out front to a seat he'd reserved for me. When the film was over, to my intense relief, the applause merely brought De Mille to his feet in acknowledgment. He bowed, and the evening was over. Cedric had been there, of course, to review the film for his British paper, and we left quickly. Around the corner from the theater on Franklin Avenue, an Italian shoe repairman was secretly famous for his homemade wine, which he made in a room above his garage. With a jug we went to Cedric's apartment, a few blocks away on Highland Avenue, a pseudo-Spanish bungalow court, with red-tiled roof and palm trees, there to talk the rest of the night away.

When I think of those years in Hollywood, Cedric always comes clearest in my mind. Our youthful visions of an equitable, socialist world in the future made him the one person I could talk to. We discussed books, films, movies, the revolution in the Soviet Union, the Sacco-Vanzetti frame-up, where all appeals had failed, and it seemed certain they would be murdered by the state. And when the execution did happen on August 23, 1927, their executioners ignoring the strikes, protests and demonstrations all over the world, I wondered then how long such criminal injustice would be tolerated. In Paris, 150,000 persons marched on the U.S. Embassy and fought the police from behind barricades. And we all but wept in helplessness when we read that in Boston, despite the downpour of rain, 250,000 men, women and children marched in the funeral procession. And those 250,000 people became a half-column story on the inside pages of the L.A. newspapers. How many million would it need to reach the front page? How many million more to change the people's indifference and concern for only themselves into a nation of brothers and sisters?* Such were my youthful thoughts, and I remem-

---

*Fifty years later Massachussets' Governor, Michael S. Dukakis, proclaimed them innocent, called their execution a "Grievous miscarriage of justice," cited abuses

bered Gorky, and I knew once more I must read, I must learn, I must write, and have an effect on the minds and hearts of others.

We took consolation in foreign films, which forced admiration and aroused enthusiasm. In the few art houses in existence, it was possible to see Soviet films of Eisenstein and Pudovkin, and those coming from Germany, from directors such as Murnau, Pabst and Fritz Lang. We marveled at Murnau's *Last Laugh* with the magnificent Emil Jannings. How Murnau had completed that entire silent film, perfectly told, without *one title* to describe the action or replace the dialogue! It was the ambition of every director to do just that, and up to then he was the only one to have succeeded. (I had yet to learn, in the coming years, as a writer demanding recognition for all writers, that it was not Murnau's art that created the film without titles, but the art of the consciously ignored screenwriter, one Carl Mayer, who had indeed written the perfect silent script from which the film was made!)

Following the run of *King of Kings*, or shortly before it ended, the new Douglas Fairbanks film, *The Gaucho*, was announced. Since most or all of the cast of the *King of Kings* Prologue were white, and the new picture had Argentina as its location, we could use little if any of the De Mille prologue cast. An advertisement announced that we sought Latin-American dancers and singers, some partly skilled as well as headliners.

The next day it seemed hundreds, if not thousands, of the loveliest women and handsomest men appeared and lined up for blocks outside the stage door. Many were talented singers and dancers, genuine artists, who rarely had an opportunity to exhibit their talents except in small Chicano clubs downtown in the Los Angeles *barrio*, "spic-town," as it was referred to.

---

by the prosecution, including "appealing to the jury's prejudices and biases" in the midst of a nationwide campaign against Communists and radicals. He designated August 23, the 50th annivesary of their execution as Sacco and Vanzetti Memorial Day. (*Facts on File Notebook, 1977.*)

I had helped Grauman conceive this prologue, which we decided to call "Argentine Nights." It was elaborate, diverse and featured some of the finest Latino artists available. Grauman couldn't help adding, for sheer diversity, the wonderful mouth organist, Borah Minnevich and his newly titled "Latin Rascals," the only non-Latinos in the show. But the rest were genuine: a wonderful La Jota dancer, dancers with castanets, a Gaucho chorus, a Marimba band, a musical genius who played the Gourd, Mariano Del Gardo and twenty or thirty background dancers and singers, their names not listed in the program other than as Gauchos, Senoritas, Padres, Indians, etc. The theme was the celebration of their country's freedom and annual Fiesta. Conrad Nagel, hardly a Latino, was the Master of Ceremonies.

I go to this length to give some idea of the time, care and creative energy Grauman put into his shows, along with money, to indicate why he had no peer. A special choreographer was engaged for the dancers, and Grauman and I staged the show. The prologue was the talk of the town and all but overshadowed Fairbanks' film. It played to full houses for many weeks.

The cordiality and friendly collaboration between Grauman and me began to show an abrasive strain when we started hiring the Mexican-Americans applying for work. The featured players like Borah Minnevich and his Rascals had their price, and of course it was paid, as were the demands of the well-known dancers and singers from the Spanish community. But the small-time players, the "spics," were bought at miserly wages. The chorus in *King of Kings* had received, if I recall, about thirty-five dollars a week; Grauman was conning these eager people who could sing and dance at least as well, if not better, for twenty dollars.

"There's a time to talk, and time to keep your mouth shut," my father had said. Maybe this was the time for the latter, but it was just too much for me. I told Grauman he was taking advantage of them; if they were good enough to perform on his stage, they were good enough to receive what he paid his white performers in the previous show.

Astonished, Grauman was then furious and said coldly that I was his assistant, not his financial advisor. He walked away. And as we started rehearsals, he barely spoke to me. I knew the end was at hand when *The Gaucho* programs appeared. My name as his assistant was there, but at half the type size as on the previous program.

At the proper time I gave two weeks' notice in writing. It was acknowledged by the bookkeeper. I never saw Grauman again. This could have been the birth of my reputation as a "troublemaker."

Backstage, 1930.

J.L. Milligan, L.A.

6

A Writer Is Born

For the next three years, jobs came easily. I was soon working for Franklin Pangborn, a local favorite, acting a small part in modern light comedies. Then I moved on to Edward Everett Horton for *Springtime for Henry*, followed by Dion Boucciault's *Streets of New York*, a melodrama of the 1850s. Boucciault was one of America's first dramatists, and Horton had an eye for the unusual. I was his stage manager and played small parts. I really learned for the first time the way plays are put together and saw the skill and knowledge required to put them on successfully. Horton had them. It was the beginning of the talking-picture era, he was in great demand, and all too soon chose films over the theater in which he had spent all of his professional life.

By this time well-established in the local theater community, I almost immediately received an offer from Joseph Schild-kraut. Shades of *Liliom* seen years before in New York! Since then Joe had become a De Mille star, and his father, Rudolph, a star of the Yiddish theater in New York, also played big supporting roles in silent films. Joe, if memory serves, was

Judas in *King of Kings*. Apparently, he tired of films and, with Frank Reicher, a fine German actor and director who spoke perfect English, he invested in a lease on the Hollywood Playhouse on Vine Street just above Hollywood Boulevard.

Schildkraut asked me to be his general stage manager, paid a hundred dollars a week (a fortune), and had his press agent fill the papers with stories about me. Headings ranged from "SCHILDKRAUT NAMES GENERAL STAGE MANAGER" to "FORMER GRAUMAN AIDE NEW SCHILD-KRAUT EXECUTIVE." It was wild, and I would have been embarrassed were it not that Cedric again assured me it was par for the course.

Soon we were rehearsing the first play, quickly cast, entitled *From Hell Came a Lady,* by George Scarborough, which very shortly went back whence she came. Joe's next venture, directed by Frank Reicher, was the charming if bland nineteenth century English comedy, *Pomander Walk.* But even with Lionel Belmore in the leading role, supported by a fine cast, Joe's lofty dream of giving people "real theatre" ended quickly in economic disaster.

One person's dream ends in agony; a glorious one comes into being for someone else. During our many months together, I got more out of it than I could possibly expect. Joe's father, Rudolph, famed for Shakespearean roles, and Joe's wife, the former Elise Bartlett, had befriended me. An actress herself, Elise was not only beautiful, but also a most sophisticated woman with a biting sense of humor. She was divorced from a New York publisher. Joe, although some years past the stage and age of a matinee idol, had his vanity intact. He still tried desperately to enjoy the adoration and easy conquests of his faded youth. This of course was not unknown to Elise, try as he might to deceive her. Her scarcely concealed, scornful amusement infuriated him. All this under a veneer of affection, consideration, and words of love, played out in front of me as if they were on stage and I was the audience.

I was. After dinner on those nights I would go home,

realizing the potential of this comedy being played out by them for me. I made notes. The play was just waiting to be written. I put aside the one I was working on, and less than two months after Joe had closed shop at the Hollywood Playhouse I had a first draft. My first completed three-act play. I called it *Words Without Music.*

But what to do about Joe? I knew from our months together he had very little sense of humor, even less, if possible, where he himself was concerned. This mockery of him as a fading matinee idol could infuriate him, yet I was certain he was ideal for the role and could make a great comeback in it. To the extent he was slipping in films and had no plays lined up for the foreseeable future, I thought he might be tempted; a man who can laugh at himself is almost always endearing to his audience.

I finally decided to show it to his father, with whom I'd become good friends. The next day old Rudolph phoned and asked me to hurry over, and when I came into their little house I saw his wife, Joe's mother, in the kitchen. He hugged me, then rubbed his hands gleefully, and said in very torn English, "My boy, this is very good. But I urge you not to let Joseph see it. Get it to New York, and get it on."

"But —" I wanted to explain how I thought Joe might use it to his advantage.

He cut me off. "No buts. You don't want to hurt him, yes?"

"Yes. I mean no."

"Just remember. Not even God can keep the truth from hurting. You think maybe you can?"

What could have been added is that neither God *nor* I could keep it a secret. Less than a week later Joe called; he'd read in the paper I'd just gotten a job in the Galsworthy play, *Escape*, which would play both L.A. and San Francisco. He congratulated me, and said Elise and he missed me, and wouldn't I come to dinner.

I accepted, and he cordially insisted I make it that evening.

A drink or two and Joe got to the point. "The play's finished? When am I going to get a look at it?"

I suspected he knew and wasn't pretending he didn't. "Oh, that long-awaited working-class drama." I shook my head. "Still struggling with the climax of the second act."

He smiled, "No, no sweetheart. I'm talking about the new one." Elise, sitting a few feet away, smiling, her eyes darting from one of us to the other, started to talk, but he cut her off. "Something about words and music," he said.

So Rudolph had talked, after warning me not to. I felt trapped. I must have turned several shades of red. It was Elise who came to the rescue, evidently reading my mind.

"Joe's mother overheard you and Rudolph talking," she said. I felt better about Rudolph, but that was all.

"Why did you give it to that old bastard and not to me?" he demanded, the smile icy now. "What's this *Music* gambit?"

"Oh, Joe!" She was becoming impatient. "Your standard bait was, 'Would you like to come up and see my etchings?' and Lester changed it to 'Would you like to hear my records?'" To me she said, with a mocking smile, "Some disguise! But Rudolph was forced after Joe's mother spilled it, to tell us about it. Sounds funny; can I read it?"

"No!" Joe yelled. "Not until I get this straightened out. I don't know whether it's slanderous, or libelous, but goddam it, I'm willing, sight unseen, to make a deal. I'll take an option on it. One thousand dollars."

"Will you play in it?" I asked. Maybe it would still turn out for the best.

"Two thousand," he said, not answering my question.

"For six months?" I wanted to know; it was the standard option time.

When he said nothing, Elise laughed. "For life, silly. He wants to buy it and bury it." Then she corrected herself. "No, cremate it!"

"Very funny! Shit on you both!" He stormed from the room.

Elsie laughed, came over and hugged me. "Rudolph says it's very funny. And good. All the best of luck!" And she kissed me. I looked worriedly toward the room where Joe had gone, but she shook her head. "He'll get over it. If the play is a success he'll get himself headlines telling how he gave you all the material." She laughed, amused, and I wondered how long a marriage like that could last.

Then I shuddered as I realized that at the end of my comedy the actor's wife approached his prostrate, pleading body calmly, stepped over him and walked out. (It turned out to be prophetic; about a year later, that's about what happened.)

Off the manuscript went to New York, to Frieda Fishbein, a highly recommended agent. She liked it, and I signed up with her.

Waiting for an interested producer was torture. Fortunately, rehearsals on the Galsworthy play started and that helped.

Before the play opened, Cedric had to go to New York on an important business matter, and he would miss reviewing what had promised to be the most important — meaning expensive — film of the year, Howard Hughes' *Hell's Angels*. It would open at the Chinese Theater in three days. He asked me to review the film for his London paper, *Film Weekly*. I consented, but apprehensively because I knew before seeing it I'd be prejudiced. Stories of some of the horrors that happened during production could not be kept quiet, and Hughes already had an unsavory reputation. Word had gotten about that an autographed picture of Mussolini hung behind his desk and that Hughes was an anti-Semite. On the less political side, he was criminally careless with the lives of the people who were making his film.

The film was, of course, a smash hit. Ben Lyon, James Hall and Jean Harlow were the stars, and the flying scenes, for that time, were spectacular. But young Hughes was not an easy man to work for. He tore the story apart, so mutilating it that during shooting the director, Lewis Milestone, quit, to be suceeded by Luther Reed, who soon followed Milestone and, of course, the real director then took over — young Mr. Hughes himself. He was new to films, but he had his father's millions.

My review was favorable in some respects, but I included a story that until then he had suceeded in keeping out of the press.

Word had come from location during the shooting of the film about the death of a mechanic, which happened this way: Hughes had insisted that one of the largest planes in which the two heroes supposedly were flying go into a sensational tail spin, come out at three thousand feet, right itself and land.

The professional pilots he'd engaged said the plane would never do it and refused. Working on the theory that his money could accomplish anything, he paid a pilot an enormous bonus. The man accepted, but not without a plan of his own. He took along a parachute. The mechanic who accompanied him evidently was not told by Hughes, but the pilot, just before going into the spin, gave a second parachute to the mechanic, who was afraid of it; he'd never used one. The pilot tried to put it on him when the plane was in the spin, a second circling plane photographing it all. Desperate at three thousand feet, the pilot leaped to safety, unable to help the frozen-with-fright mechanic, who crashed with the plane in flames. (What a scene *that* would have made!)

As I watched the screen, I saw what had been done. Before the pilot parachuted, the film editor cut away to some action later shot on the ground, then picked up the falling plane at one thousand feet and followed it to the ground as it crashed in a burst of flame. Then, of course, another cut; in a close shot our two smudged but unhurt heroes step out of a smoldering plane. I wrote the truth in the review, which ended with the following thought after revealing the criminal act: "In *Hell's Angels,* Mr. Hughes reveals what a strange sense of humor he has. He would have us believe that Angels may come either from Hell or from heaven, but with enough money they come from Hughes Studio." Hughes was furious.

No name appeared on the review; the English paper stated, under the title, "From *Film Weekly*'s Special Hollywood Correspondent." Hughes could not blame Cedric, who proved he was in New York at the time; *Film Weekly* did not really know who wrote the review and refused to push Cedric into telling. I was later to have one more anonymous, less gratifying, brush with Hughes.

During the run of the Galsworthy play in San Francisco, I received a call that *Words Without Music* had been optioned by one Murray Phillips who, Freida Fishbein assured me, was a quality independent producer on Broadway. A letter followed, along with the Dramatist Guild contract and his five-hundred-dollar option (less her 10 percent) for six months, and an assurance he would tell me when to come East for the rehearsals, which would begin as soon as he cast the play. He claimed he had a big star lined up for the part, but would not tell me his name until the deal was signed.

I was elated, of course, but not knowing how soon rehearsals would start, and having little more than the four hundred fifty dollars, as usual I had to go to work immediately. With the news that I had sold a play for Broadway, three agents tried to sign me up for film-writing jobs — but only in the future, and only when the play was produced and, of course, *if* it was a hit.

But the sale of the play did help. I got a job at MGM as a play reader at fifty dollars a week. They gave me a desk in a large office with a dozen or more people, all readers. A young, lively Lillian Hellman had a desk near mine, doing the same work, and we met for the first time.

The speed-up was incredible. They'd want a novel read in hours; they pushed on to the next and the next. I tried to organize the readers to make a collective protest. Someone snitched before I reached half of them; I was out of MGM in just two weeks.

Still no word on the play, so I took a job with a stock company, a small, almost unknown group headed by an actor named David Callis who, together with his leading-lady wife, took their group to play a season in El Paso, Texas. He played comedy roles in plays I'd helped stage previously. Amusing, unexciting stuff, which might have been endurable had the social atmosphere in El Paso not been stifling. The town was ultra conservative; in a suburb sprawled the Army's Seventh Cavalry Regiment. With rehearsals every day for the weekly change in plays, a miserable hotel room which I could barely afford, I was somewhat less than ecstatic.

After a couple of weeks, I was at the point of giving two weeks' notice. Then, luckily, I struck up an acquaintanceship with Emiliano Fernandez the cellist in the four-piece theater orchestra that played overtures and entre-act. He was a young Mexican who lived across the bridge on the other side of the Rio Grande in Juarez. He was bright, knowledgeable, a fine musician, and a passionate proletarian; we soon discovered we had much in common, and I had much to learn about Mexico from him. He introduced me to his family: mother, sister, brother-in-law, and their two lovely children; he showed me the bullet-pocked side of his house, reminders of the revolution almost twenty years before. His father had died fighting with Pancho Villa. He was named Emiliano after Zapata. It was all new and wonderful to me, and they enjoyed this gringo's eagerness to learn their ways. In not more than a few days, his mother asked if I cared to share room and board with them. I happily accepted.

The immediate consequences were hardly what I'd expected. I casually mentioned the move. When the owner of the theater heard about it, Callis was called in and given orders for me to move back to El Paso. Suddenly the prejudice, never visible to me before, snarled and sniped from all sides. Callis, in a spot, assured me he did not share the bigoted views, but he had no choice. The company could easily be boycotted. I would have to move back to El Paso.

Callis had no choice. Neither did I. The Fernandezes had become friends; we were like kin. It would be a betrayal to give in to this bigotry. I gave Callis two weeks' notice, and told Emiliano and his family what had happened. He wanted to quit his job in protest. I begged him not to; he was the major support of his family.

It was a tearful departure two weeks later. The entire family came to see me off on the train for Los Angeles, the children hugging me and whispering, "Adios, adios." Embraces all around, tears in Emiliano's mother's eyes and my own about to flow, and I was gone.

The day I got home the phone rang. It was Frieda Fishbein in New York. She had tried to reach me in El Paso, learned I'd left and was calling me to say that Murray Phillips, my producer, had found a star of first magnitude. Phillips planned to start casting in three months, then open in Chicago for the tryout, tour a couple of cities to smooth it all out and into the Belmont Theater, Forty-eighth and Broadway, in late September or early October. He'd want me there a month before rehearsals started to discuss changes.

"To hell with changes," I remember yelling impatiently. "Who's the star?"

"You're going to like this, Lester," she replied, maddeningly. "One of the biggest. Perfect casting for the part."

My god! Did he actually show it to Schildkraut, and did Joe have the sense of humor to do it? "Who is it? Come on, come on, his name!"

"Lou Tellegen," she finally said.

It *was* perfect casting. Tellegen had only to be himself; a womanizer of notoriety, a fading leading man as age raced to overtake him. And his publicity had been good. Recently he had published his memoirs, which were reviewed in the dailies everywhere, and in the *New Yorker* by Dorothy Parker, who titled her review, "Kiss and Tellegen."

I tried Central Casting for extra work in films — at five dollars a day. I didn't pick up much. My money was going faster than I expected it to, as when does it not. With a month to go before rehearsals started in New York, I either had to borrow or go back and live with my mother and sister, a prospect I did not relish.

It was then I heard a bit of sensational scandal that could be written into an outline for a movie and earn me a small fortune; a sure-fire gamble if ever there was one. Ah, Hollywood! Had I already been infected?

Once again, it was Howard Hughes who offered a beautiful opportunity for me to vent my animosity and get paid for it — a multiple pleasure.

There was rage and concern in Hollywood against Hughes, and he was enjoying every moment of it. He had bought a vitriolic, anti-Semitic novel and announced he was making it into a film.

The book was a satirical novel about Hollywood, written by two Englishmen, the Graham brothers. Titled *Queer People,* it was an amusing tale of Hollywood's clownishness, corruption, chiseling and cheating, which would have been fair enough, except that the clowns, chiselers and cheaters were *all* Jews, and the main characters were easily identifiable as Carl Laemmele, head of Universal Pictures, and a few others. Laemmele, of course, was furious, and there was talk of libel suits and other threats, all of which Hughes reportedly read with great delight.

It was then I heard the story which I knew would stop him and at the same time make a fistful for me. Somewhere — how and why I cannot recall — I met Billie Dove, who, when she heard I was a writer (the story of my play-to-be-produced had traveled), hoping to avenge herself and her husband, told me the story.

It seems Ms. Dove, one of the most glamorous and voluptuous of the current stars, had become the object of Hughes' cravings, and he was determined to have her.

Miss Dove was married to William Seiter, a fairly successful director of silent films, who was having no luck breaking into the talkies. At some social gathering the Seiters had met Hughes, and apparently in moments she became his obsession. At any price, of course, since price was his yardstick. But it was not hers. When he discovered that money didn't buy her he showed the crafty side of his nature.

He came up with a pretty good scheme, arrogantly figuring he need only get Seiter out of the way to make some progress. A week later Seiter received a phone call from a couple of producers in New York, offering him a job to direct a talkie in their studio there. Could they send him a script? Delighted, he said yes, and soon the deal was made and he was on his way.

No sooner had he gone than Dove got a call from the casting director at Hughes Studio. She replied she hadn't made a screen test in years; when she was wanted for a part a company contacted her agent. Hughes then personally called her; wouldn't she at least come to his office and talk about the script? He wanted to rewrite it for her. With every reason to suspect his motives, she declined and phoned New York to tell Seiter what was going on.

Seiter was having related problems there. The studio was an empty loft in a factory building, the producer-partners were shiftier than the makeshift studio. He had been shooting only a day with an unknown leading man, a miscast leading woman and equipment so inadequate no film could be properly made. He decided, with Billie's uneasiness at home, to quit. The partners were frantic; they doubled their offer to him. He gave it one more try. But in one scene an actor walked through a door and the entire wall fell down. Seiter had had it.

Furious, he grabbed one of the partners by the neck. Seiter was a husky man and, when angry, could be menacing. He demanded to know what was going on; whose money was behind this production? Intimidated, they told him. Now it was all clear. He phoned home and took the next train back.

Whether or not he confronted Hughes and beat hell out of him, I never found out. But in the eight- or ten-page story outline I wrote in four days, with fictional names but easily recognizable characters, I had my outraged husband do just that. He tore the office apart, after beating up "Derrick Johnson," who lay cringing in the corner, bleeding from nose and mouth. To make sure there would be no mistaken identity, I had my hero take a picture of Mussolini off the wall from behind the desk and crash it over "Johnson's" head. The portrait was left hanging like a ragged necklace, as the husband stalked out of the office.

As soon as the story was written and copies were available, I called one of the three agents who had courted me when my play was sold. I picked the Jewish one, figuring his sympathy for the "cause" might overcome customary agent practices. He was enthusiastic: we would send it only to Laemmele and Hughes, marked "Urgent, Personal." The accompanying note said briefly that after reading it, they would understand the need for hasty action.

It came. The next morning Laemmele called and offered five thousand dollars for it. I was overjoyed. Laemmele would hold it over Hughes' head to retaliate should he make *Queer People*. The agent said he'd be right over to sign the papers. His phone rang. It was Hughes, personally.

"Who's the author of this slander, this libel?" he demanded to know.

"A British author," my agent replied. I had, of course, used a pseudonym (as I would years later, out of sheer necessity).

"One of the Graham brothers!" Hughes was screaming. "The double crossers. I'll sue them for —"

"Mister Hughes," the agent cut in, "it was not the Graham brothers. And, incidentally, I've just had an offer of ten thousand dollars for the story!"

Shocked, I started to protest. The agent quickly covered the mouthpiece.

"What the hell are you doing?" I yelled. "We agreed to give it to Laemmele for five thousand and stop Hughes from making *Queer People,* didn't we?"

He waved for me to shut up, lifted his hand from the receiver and said with a smile: "You'll go fifteen thousand? No, I can't close the deal. I'll get in touch with the author tonight and let you know the first thing in the morning." He hung up, leaped to his feet, and hugged me.

"Kid, you're in the chips!" he shouted.

"Fifteen grand?" I was stunned. "But —"

"But that's only the beginning." Greed was gleaming in his eyes. "Listen, he knows Laemmele's bidding for this. Now I tell Laemmele about the bid I got, and he'll know who it's from. Baby, this is only the beginning! No telling where it's going to end. Laemmele'll go to thirty, forty grand to stop that bastard. You're made, baby!"

I didn't like it. But there was no stopping this maniac. I demanded he sell it to Laemmele at once; this was highway robbery, crooked, criminal. Nothing I could say stopped him for long enough than to say, "Kid, you're learning about the movie business right here and now."

I don't know who learned the greater lesson. When he called Hughes the next day to say he had a bid of thirty thousand, I was standing next to him and saw him go white. "You're no longer interested? Then I'll have to give it to the other guy." He gulped, then managed to say, "Go ahead?"

We both knew it was dead. He called Laemmele, gave his name and was told Laemmele was not in. He was also told Laemmele was no longer interested in the story.

The next day the trade papers and the dailies carried a prominent story saying Howard Hughes had dropped all plans to make *Queer People.*

The agent was horribly shaken and genuinely puzzled.

"Who'd ever believe a Fascist and a Jew could make a deal?"

I was furious. "Business, you stupid bastard! Jesus and the devil would have made deals if they were businessmen." How I wanted to punch him in the nose! "You ought to pay *me* 10 percent," I yelled. "Five hundred bucks, for the five thousand you pissed away. And you were going to teach me something about the movie business."

Two days later, while I still had the fare, I left for New York.

Almost immediately upon my arrival, Frieda Fishbein took me to Murray Phillips' office. He was a short man, with lively eyes (or do I mean shifty?), energetic and smiling. He was brimming with confidence.

"And the best news of all," Phillips chirped, "is the title." When I stared uncomprehendingly, he added, "We've changed it. Beautiful."

I stiffened. "I suppose eventually I'll hear what it is."

Phillips laughed. "Sorry, of course. Lou thought of it; perfect. Oh, and about the —"

"Title," I cut in.

"Sorry, I'm just so excited about this play. We're calling it *Love Technique.*"

Good god! I don't know why the thought went through my mind about the title, *The Light That Failed,* and I said as sourly as I could, "Why not *The Love Technique That Failed?*"

"I'm coming to that," he chuckled. "You see, it doesn't. We changed the ending. When she's about to leave, he seduces her all over again."

"That's not the way I wrote it," I managed to say.

"I know. We appreciate that. But you see, Lou simply can't, won't, play a part where he loses out in a love affair with his wife, or anyone. It's not the public image of him." Again he chuckled. "Don't worry, Lester. It's in the bag, I assure you. My word of honor." He reached on his desk and grabbed a few pages. "Here. Read it today. The rest of the play is yours, practically word for word. And I want you to come on the road with us. We open in Chicago. Then Cleveland, Indianapolis, maybe Pittsburgh, then the subway circuit here in New York and into the Belmont. Beautiful. Forty-eighth just east of Broadway. Rehearsal at ten."

I had one more question. "Who's directing?"

"The best in town," he grinned, tapping his chest. "Me."

We left his office. I told Frieda that since 1927, under the new Dramatist Guild contract, as she well knew, I had the final word on any changes. She urged me to read it. We went back to her office, I did, and those five pages changed the whole meaning of the play.

That night, meeting with Abe Finkel, Teddy Thomas, and Lou Lusty, I read the play aloud and then read them the changed ending. They all urged me not to pull it away. The play was pretty good, no masterpiece by far, and it was 1930, the depression was on us. The ending was not as bad as I thought, just conventional. I reluctantly agreed.

We opened four weeks later in Chicago, at the Studebaker Theater, a large prestige house on Michigan Boulevard. Phillips had done a good job of directing, to my surprise. Tellegen was very skillful, the supporting cast first rate. But as I expected, the notices in the Chicago papers ranged from poor to fair to almost good; it was Tellegen who drew them in. We opened August 7, 1930, and played to almost full houses for six weeks. Then on the road for three weeks we played to big crowds, before hitting New York and the subway circuit. Instead of playing all the houses — Bronx Opera, Riverside, a Brooklyn theater — Phillips said we were ready with one more week in the theater in Queens.

Advertisements announcing the opening at the Belmont were appearing daily, with my name as author prominent and quotes from the critics in Chicago and elsewhere. The anticipation in the cast was intense. None of us could wait for the week to be over, for the opening on Broadway. Even my mother was less grudging in her compliments when she came to Queens to see the play. Tellegen had given a long interview to the *Times*, which would appear in the theatrical section on Sunday, the day before the opening.

Saturday night, awaited so impatiently, came at last. The curtain fell, and all anyone could think about was opening Monday at the Belmont. My royalties were paid monthly, but of course the actors received their salaries on Saturday night and were surprised when Phillips didn't come around as usual to their dressing rooms to hand them the pay envelopes.

They dressed, waited. We chatted, waited. No Phillips. Calls went out, to his office, to his home. No Phillips. The woman who answered the phone at his house said she was his wife. She had been out, and she thought he would have come over here to pay salaries. But when she came back, she noticed that his wardrobe was cleaned out, his clothing and shirts and everything gone. Mrs. Phillips had called the police.

Lucky we were stranded in New York! He could as easily have done it in Indianapolis. Curtain on *Love Technique.*

Because of the publicity, I was not long in finding work. I was now a playwright, and I had years of experience in the theater on the West Coast. I had also been a reader for MGM (two weeks). Now I made the rounds of story editors in the New York offices of Paramount, Warner Brothers, RKO and Fox — avoiding MGM. I was immediately engaged by them all, on a free-lance basis. As described earlier, the pay for that work then was three dollars to read a play, write a synopsis of no less than five pages, and then evaluate its suitability for a film. For a novel up to five hundred pages, five dollars. Over that, six dollars. So by working ten, twelve, fourteen hours, I could make thirty-five dollars, and sometimes even forty dollars a week, which wasn't bad in depression-doomed New York. I could even have a spaghetti dinner once a week or so for out-of-work friends.

By this time there was no doubt in my mind that I was going to be a playwright. After work at night, I struggled hunting for a theme. I wanted something to say, just what I wasn't quite sure of, but it had to be "important." It would be about workers. But who, when, about what — and why? I searched for a premise, something with the current cruelties of the depression at its core. Late one night two small items, side by side in an evening paper, gave me the story. One item related the story of a wealthy woman who lived on the upper East Side who had lost a beloved dog, and she was spending two hundred and fifty dollars a day on radio and newspaper advertising offering a reward for its return. The other story, by editor's design or coincidence, told of two unemployed men, one of whom found a temporary job, and then by luck another for his friend. They quarreled over one dollar. They fought, and one killed the other.

In my play, the dead man was buried in Potter's Field, the public grounds for the impoverished. The little dog was found at last but apparently had been raped in an alleyway by some huge mutt. She died despite the efforts of three veterinarians and was given an ebony casket and buried in the posh Scarsdale Pet Cemetery. What unsubtle fury!

I called the play *Still Life,* the title suggested by the seeming immovability of the wealthy characters' feeling for the suffering of the poor. It was somewhat awkward in its construction with eight scenes and four sets, yet manageable. In 1932 such plays could be considered "box office," as a reflection of our life in those times. That was the play Rosalie Stewart bought.

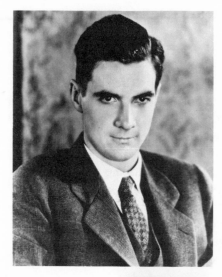

Howard Hughes earned an unsavory reputation at an early age. Billie Dove revealed one reason. The author used her story to scotch an anti-Semitic project Hughes started.

7

The Good Life, Hollywood Style

The train was speeding across Nevada toward the eastern slope of the San Bernardino Mountains. We'd soon be there. What was I letting myself in for? Certainly I had dreams of fame and glory in Hollywood. I knew the industry was as corrupt and inhuman as any business on the face of the earth. But I would get two hundred and fifty dollars a week and save at least half of it. Perhaps I'd stay as long as a year. I'd make enough to return to New York and write more plays. How unprincipled, how normal.

As I sat at the table in the dining room, having coffee, the conductor approached with a deferential, "Good morning, sir" and said he'd brought me the compliments of the engineer, who wanted to know if I'd enjoy watching the train cross the border into California from his cab window.

It was more than a break in the monotony. It would be a new experience. At one time in my life—as what kid didn't—I must have wanted to be an engineer on a locomotive (as well as a fireman), so I told him I'd enjoy it very much, gulped down my coffee and walked through the empty cars to the front of the train. The engineer didn't have to poke his head through a side window to see that the train stayed on the tracks. He had a large, clean, glass window in front of him, and he sat in a comfortable swivel chair with his instruments in front of him and the speed regulator at his left hand.

We were introduced. He thanked me for coming up. It was getting lonely aboard; since the last two passengers got off at Santa Fe and no one got on board, I was the sole passenger. "See there? Top of the grade? That's the California line." Then he grinned. "How'd you like to drive this crate across the border?"

I laughed, sure he was kidding. But no! He got off his swivel seat, sat me down, put my hand on the throttle, and then said, "See there? The speedometer? It's at fifty. That's top speed on this grade. Now you keep your eye on it; if it goes below that, advance the throttle to keep it at that speed. Simple?"

I was scared to death, gulped, and managed to nod. But before we got to the top of the grade I was exultant. I was doing it, driving the Chief! Somewhere in my complicated psyche, I remember shouting, whether aloud or inside myself, I don't know, "De Mille, you dirty bastard, watch out. Here I come!"

Cary Grant and Randolph Scott lived in Westwood in a large, sprawling downstairs flat with perhaps eight rooms. One of them was prepared for me, and I received a warm welcome. Cary was just finishing his first picture — I think for Ernest Lubitsch — and was living modestly. Like myself, he might soon be back on Broadway, going once again on the road for the Schuberts. Who knew then?

There were few pretensions in their life-style. A Filipino "boy" was assumed a necessity, of course; but the friends

Archie Leach, an old friend now known as Cary Grant, shared a flat with Randolph Scott. They fixed up a room for me.

who came most often were studio working people: secretaries, set dressers, the "ordinary people" on the lot. No big shots. It was a pleasant, easy atmosphere. A party was thrown for me as soon as I arrived, and to my astonishment and delight Cedric Belfrage was there. He was in for a brief visit from London and was interviewing the most famous young man from Bristol in the West of England, Archie Leach — now Cary Grant. It was a memorable night.

Without a car, which I could not yet afford, the trip by streetcar or bus from Westwood to the Hollywood studio on Marathon Street, below Gower, took more than an hour. I could have driven with Cary or Randy, but they didn't work every day. When they did they left before 6:30 A.M. After a short time, I found a small apartment near the studio and soon made a down payment on a second-hand car.

At the studio I was assigned to an office in the Writers' Building. An amiable scenario editor put me at my ease, telling me to relax until they found an assignment for me. I could wander about the sound stages, introduce myself to the directors, and watch the scenes being shot. Not all directors would be cordial, he warned me, but I was not to take a rebuff seriously. Just leave the set and think nothing of it.

Perhaps it was on the second day that I saw Sylvia Sidney playing a scene. I hadn't been struck so hard by the mere appearance of a woman since age sixteen at Lake Mahopac. Short, with large brown eyes and a seductively curved body — it was lust at first sight.

A problem of the greatest importance was to learn how to meet her. Introduce myself? Impossible. But there had to be a way!

In the lunchroom there was a writers' table, and I soon became friendly with Brian Marlowe, also a New Yorker, which immediately gave us much in common. Right then I wanted to know how I could meet Sylvia Sidney, and he laughed and asked if I didn't know it was said — he wasn't sure — that she and one of the executives at Paramount were

Paramount Studio

Sylvia Sidney, object of all my desires — briefly.

friends. I didn't know, and said I didn't care. In which case Brian introduced us.

She was cordial, almost friendly. When she learned I was a playwright, that my play was sold and that Jean Dixon and Helen Hayes were being sought for the leading roles, I imagined (I was ready to imagine anything, everything!) her eyes lit up with interest. She said perhaps some day I'd have a leading role for her. She wanted to divide her time between Hollywood and New York, etc., etc. I only half heard, but I passionately promised she would have a play of mine.

Soon I received an assignment, but my mind was only on Sylvia. After many lunches, she finally invited me to dinner at her home the following week. Punctual to the minute, I arrived and noted with slight dismay the large, beautiful car standing in the driveway behind her little runabout, and wondered who else she had invited for dinner. And why?

I rang the doorbell. Very soon it was answered by a uniformed maid. I gave my name, and she replied, "Miss Sidney is not expecting you."

I was astonished. "But she is! I wrote down the date. I—"

"Sorry, Mr. Cole, there has been some misunderstanding. She is not expecting you." And then, as if out of pity, she pointed to the big car. "Do you know whose car that is?"

I guessed, nodded, went out to the curb and got into my little Ford and drove off. From then on I made sure to keep a distance between us in the studio lunch room. I quickly got her out of my mind, probably with some malignant characterization of Hollywood actresses or some other convenient rationale — a lonely young man should never be without one.

My first assignment totally occupied me then. It was almost too easy, an episode in a film starring Lionel Barrymore, called *If I Had a Million.* There were ten episodes in the film, and as many writers and directors. The picture made use of all Paramount's featured players. It was star-studded, as they liked to say. The story was about an eccentric millionaire, played by Barrymore. About to die, the rich man decides to give away his wealth, and bestows a million dollars on a dozen or more characters chosen haphazardly. Mine was a man accused of murder, played by Gene Raymond, whose million-dollar check arrives just before the time of his execution. I forget what happened then.

They accepted my episode for the screenplay, and once again I waited. I began to become acquainted with some of the writers, meeting them at the writers' table. Along with Marlowe was Claude Binyon, a former writer for *Variety,* a jovial guy who had a passion for trout fishing in the High Sierras. When he mentioned it, I had a sudden rush of memory of my days on Lake Mahopac and asked him if I could go with him the next time he drove up. He was delighted, took me to a sporting goods store, and helped me pick out the rod, line, reel and flies I would need.

The next Friday we left the studio around four and started the two hundred sixty-mile trip to June Lake. It then took more than ten hours (today on super-highways, six) across the Mohave Desert to Bishop, then up into the mountains. I was overwhelmed by the beauty, and Binyon was pleased to find a kindred soul. Thereafter it became obsessive. Whenever I had at least three free days, off I'd go with Binyon, later with my close fishing friends, Carl Dreher and Arthur Strawn.

My next assignment was too good to be true. The scenario editor phoned and said I was to see Barney Glazer. As I entered his office in the Producers' Building, he greeted me cordially and told me he was to make Paramount's most important film of the year; he was acting on a hunch that I was the man to write it. He had seen a rough cut of the Gene Raymond episode, and it "had something," something he wanted in the leading man in his film. Smiling, he then handed me the book he wanted adapted and asked if I was familiar with it.

It was Hemingway's *A Farewell to Arms.* I stared, stupefied. He seemed to understand and smiled. "I just know you can do a good job; Gary Cooper and Helen Hayes are going to star in it, and it won't hurt your reputation to get a screen credit on it."

Helen Hayes! I had received a letter from Frieda Fishbein saying production of the play had been postponed because Hayes had a film commitment. Rosalie Stewart had exercised a second six-month option, to wait for Hayes. Was this the reason for the postponement? A good enough reason, I was forced to admit.

"And Cole," Glazer was saying, "keep this quiet, about your getting this assignment. Not a word to anyone. As you may have already gathered, writers are a strange bunch. Cutthroat, back-stabbing, jealous — you know. And giving it to a young newcomer — you know. So just say nothing to anybody, personal friends included. And when it's done, then it can all come out."

I promised. I thanked him and said I hoped his faith in me would prove to be justified. Back in my office, I could feel the sweat running down my face. I went to the washroom for some cold water. Then I came back and started to read.

Glazer phoned. "I forgot to tell you. What I want first is a treatment, about fifty, sixty pages. All the major scenes, indicate the main dialogue, you know?"

"I know." I didn't, and went to the Story Department and asked for a couple of treatments to read, to understand the form.

I read the treatments. The job, technically, was simple enough: but how to transform literary prose into visualizations was a different matter. I worked day and night, thinking of nothing else. When I was perhaps twenty or so pages into it, my energy and enthusiasm at their peak, there was a knock on my door and a tall, thin, hollow-cheeked man with his hair parted in the middle, 1920s college style, walked in. I'd seen him at the writers' table occasionally; quiet, retiring, seldom smiling.

"Lester Cole?" I nodded. "I'm Joe March," and he offered

his hand, which I took. So this was Joseph Moncure March, a favorite writer of mine who may not be remembered by many today, but who was quite famous in the twenties for his sardonic humor in narrative poems. The two best known were "The Wild Party" and "The Setup." Joe had worked for Howard Hughes, I believe, on *Hell's Angels* and had come from there to Paramount. Later I learned his salary at Paramount was a thousand a week.

Had he dropped in merely to say "Hello"? I was flattered, but it soon became clear he had another purpose. He looked at me a little quizzically, smiled thinly, and then said, "I know what your assignment is; what you're working on."

I didn't know what to say and muttered something like "Really?" How did he know?

"And I know that Glazer wanted you to keep it secret, to tell no one."

That surprised me. "How did you know that?"

He grinned. "Because he asked me to do the same thing." When I stared uncomprehendingly, he went on. "Yes, I'm working on it, too. What Glazer hoped would be one of his best-kept secrets has become one of the bastard's worst." I was speechless, and he went on. "There's something else you should know. This is not a contest between us, in which he will judge who wrote the better script. No matter how good or bad either of them is, he won't use them. He won't even *read* them!"

"You're over my head, March."

"I'll help you to the surface. You're new in this business. Do you know the word, 'business'? Glazer, of course is — I'll save the foul language — not much different than a lot of others. In the whole industry you can count the decent producers on the fingers of one hand. In our case, this is what happened: with Gary Cooper under contract, drawing salary and not working, and Hayes's contract soon to begin, the front office is pressing Glazer to get a shooting script. To show them his willingness, he has not one, but two writers working their asses off to turn one in as fast as possible; a race. But he's really stalling. There's only one man he wants to write this script, and that's Oliver H.P. Garrett.''

I knew the name, of course. A former journalist, he had written many hits for Paramount. Garrett was one of their top writers.

"Garrett is working on another script. How soon he'll be finished I don't know. But the minute he is, you and I will be dumped, and he will be assigned to the job.''

"Then why should we break our skulls on this?" I wondered aloud.

"I'm not. Working on a new book of my own.'' He grinned. "Relax,'' he said, and left.

At lunch I asked my friend Brian Marlowe what he thought of March's story and he said, "Better believe it.''

I didn't know what to do. Confront Glazer? Raise hell with the scenario editor? Both could deny it. And Glazer called writers back-stabbers! It stank. The industry stank. The episode was degrading. And soon enough I was to learn the degree of degradation to which most working writers were subjected. Mine was everyday, routine stuff.

It went according to Joe's prediction. In about two weeks Glazer called me and asked that I bring him what I'd done so far. When I handed it to him across his desk, he didn't look at me for a moment, then brazenly smiled and said, "Thanks for your effort. I'm sorry, but I was forced to put another writer on the job. We'll try again some time!''

It was too much. As he reached out to shake hands, I turned and walked out of the office. I went to Joe March's cubbyhole, and he told me he'd already been down there. Same story, almost word for word.

We went to lunch together. Joe knew Marlowe because his wife's sister and Marlowe's girl were friends. Joe got up from the table, went to the phone and came back in a few moments. "Are you busy for dinner tonight?" When I said,

"No," he went on: "My wife asked if you'd come over." I was more than pleased.

Evidently Joe had told her about me and the Glazer episode. He'd also reported that I was single, without even a temporary attachment. Peggy March thought there was no harm in trying to find out if Jonnie (as her youngest sister Jeanne was called) and I might not find each other attractive. Jonnie, when I saw her, looked sixteen, but that was misleading. She was nineteen and had been married shortly and unhappily to a stage director who didn't make it in films and returned to New York — without her. The divorce had just become final. She was on the rebound, I on the lookout. Jonnie was a simple, sweet and unpretentious young person, with a warm, lovely smile. The evening wasn't half over before we were making plans to meet again.

So with Marlowe and Marsha Wood, his girlfriend, we soon were a foursome, and it couldn't have been more than a month before Jonnie came to live with me. I told her I could make no serious commitment, that I planned to stay only for six months, a year at most, and go back to New York. She accepted the arrangement, and life was pleasant.

I had no assignment at the studio and spent my time there working on a play of my own. Despite my idle time, to my surprise, they took up my option for another six months. I learned why: they were interested in buying my play for a film after it opened. But they wouldn't give me the fifty-dollar increase stipulated in the contract, saying the depression had brought about a policy of no raises for anyone. Waiting for the play to appear, I accepted, secretly delighted.

During this period I began to hear the complaints of writers; the practices of the producers went far beyond such petty perfidy as Glazer's. One could be writing a script and a fellow writer would be put on the same assignment without either's knowledge. When finished, each would discover that he was sharing credit with another writer with whom he didn't

work and whose changes in his script he often felt were disastrous and damaging to his name, to say nothing of his dignity
and creative conviction. The complaints seemed universal; it
was in Stanley Rose's back room at the bookstore that writers
would let loose with their beefs. Some were cynical, but I
don't think I met one writer in that first year who didn't
swear that as soon as he could afford to he would leave, go
back to writing plays, novels, or short stories.

In this time of depression, money, only money, held them,
except for the elite in upper echelons. But for the "working"
writers it was all but intolerable. They were cheated, and lied
to. Their work was slashed. The resentment kept building. I
remember one night in Stanley's, a man I later discovered to
be an early Communist Party member, paraphrasing the slogan
at the end of the Communist Manifesto, suddenly shouted,
"Writers of Hollywood, unite! You have your manhood to
gain, and nothing to lose but your salaries." There was laughter,
but little else — at that time.

The months passed quickly and otherwise delightfully.
Jonnie proved a wonderful and loving companion. I taught
her to cook, but she soon was teaching me. She was a country
girl, born in Chico, in Northern California. She grew up near
the Sierras, and loved the mountains. Soon Jonnie began to
accompany me on fishing trips.

The assignments handed me at the studio were tripe,
bottom-of-the-double-bill western melodramas, and I spent
more and more time on my new play. Then, without warning,
near the end of my second six months at Paramount, a situation arose which put all thoughts of plays out of my head.
Suddenly my life was to change; reality was to take over.

Following Franklin Roosevelt's election and promise of a
"New Deal," the reaction among the conservative executives
was one of retreat and recover. The conservative label applied to
practically every studio owner in Hollywood. Shortly after
FDR's inauguration, the president declared a bank holiday
in an effort to bring the economic chaos into some semblance

of order. The producers saw an opportunity to utilize this crisis to their advantage.

It is important to bear in mind that Los Angeles was an open shop, non-union town. The only union of any importance in the film industry was the IATSE (International Association of Theatrical Stage Employees). Their home base, of course, was the New York theater, but they had spread into the movie houses by organizing the projectionists. They had power — especially their leadership, which was soon to be controlled by the Mafia.

That union leadership had long since found its way into the producers' pockets. They accepted a no-raise and wage-cut contract for their membership and handsome kickbacks for themselves. Irving Thalberg, the brains behind L.B. Mayer at MGM, had created the Academy of Motion Picture Arts and Sciences in the late twenties, an organization that accepted only the highest-paid and most esteemed actors, directors and writers. The academy honored them with dinners and annual affairs where it presented awards for the best films, performances, direction and scripts and hailed them all as "artists." Thalberg made it clear "artists" would never deign to organize or become members of a trade union.

But Hollywood unions began with the advent of talking pictures, when the personnel of Hollywood began to change so dramatically. The technological revolution had within it the seeds of one far more political. Broadway actors, playwrights, novelists and journalists were needed for "talkies," and they arrived by the Pullman carload. Actors began talking of an actors' union, or a branch of Actors' Equity, the theatrical union. Playwrights soon were seeing what was happening to their work and recalled that in 1927, through the Dramatists Guild in New York, writers had won control of their material from the Broadway producers. The situation was beginning to simmer with the influx of these "outside agitators," so much so that, in obvious alarm, on June 21, 1932, *Variety* reported that MGM's Thalberg was urging the Academy to strengthen its organization to keep "artists" free from trade-union domination.

By the time of Roosevelt's announcement of the Bank Holiday in January 1933, the Academy did the producers' bidding and called upon the industry to do away with all contracts as they expired. For the first time the higher-salaried creative people saw themselves in jeopardy; those Rolls Royces, Pierce Arrows, Cadillacs and many-acred estates in the Beverly and Holmby Hills Gardens of Eden were in jeopardy. And none breathed easier when Fox announced a cut in *all* salaries, including those of the grips, electricians and members of the IATSE.

The first revolt took place. The membership of the IATSE defied its leadership and voted against a wage cut. They won. Determined to counter this success the companies made their big move. Simultaneously in all studios, writers, actors and directors were called to an important conference — each group to a separate projection room. When the forty or more Paramount writers gathered, Ben Schulberg, head of the studio, introduced a man we'd heard of and known about, a sort of general manager of the business aspects of Paramount named Emmanuel Cohen. A very small, slight man of about fifty, with just the right unmistakable New York accent for the occasion, Cohen seemed to personify the Eastern investors he appeared to represent.

Cohen immediately took us to his heart and into his confidence. This art of film, this industry we all loved, was in jeopardy. The depression was going to get worse, and while box office receipts had not fallen disastrously yet, we must prepare for it, all of us, fellow artists, together. The people of America are depending on their artists to make the sacrifice. And the sacrifice need not have been as great were it not for the foreign element in our studios, the trade unions. Because the IATSE members had contracts which they forced the producers to sign, the producers had no alternative but to turn to the artists.

"Therefore," he continued, his voice choking a little, "it is with deep unhappiness but in the interests of the country we all love that we are asking you, contract writers and those who work week to week, to immediately accept a 50 percent cut in salary."

Cohen knew we would understand and keep Paramount's flag flying and join with the actors and directors. As we walked out, men and women in various stages of bewilderment and indignation, Brian Marlowe looked at me and almost smiled. "The silly sonofabitch. He actually told us what to do, didn't he?"

I nodded. "Laid it out."

Good old Henry Cohn, my pop! I could see him proudly looking at me. Whoever thought twenty-five years after I'd carried his soapbox at 149th Street and Columbus Avenue, I would be carrying one of my own in Hollywood!

"This must be happening in every studio in town," I said.

"Sure. Thalberg set it up."

"Okay. Where do we start?"

"Telephone. Get some likely names."

For more than twelve hours that afternoon and night, we phoned around; we had prepared a preliminary statement which we read to each prospective sponsor. Finally we had signed up ten writers. We met at Musso Frank's the next day at lunchtime, went afterward to the back room of Stanley Rose's Bookshop and rewrote our original statement, which was then mimeographed and circulated throughout the studios. In the intervening decades, page 3 has disappeared. Some years ago I sent a copy of my three surviving pages to the Screenwriters' Guild, where they can be found in the archives. My mimeograph original is the only copy left. Those remaining pages read this way:

For the purpose of discussing the betterment of conditions under which writers work in Hollywood, the following motion picture writers met on February 3, 1933:

Kubec Glasmon
Courtney Terrett
Brian Marlowe
Lester Cole
Samson Raphaelson
John Howard Lawson
Edwin Justus Mayer
John Bright
Bertram Block

The meeting was prompted by the fact that there has probably never been a more propitious time in the history of the motion picture industry for the writers — acting in concert and presenting a determined and vigorous face — to take the place to which they are entitled. It was pointed out, when the present chaotic conditions have subsided and order has been restored, the task of enforcing any demand for improvement of the writer's lot would be immeasurably more difficult. It was pointed out also that the task to be done here in Hollywood is far less difficult than that successfully carried out by the Dramatists Guild in taking command of the theater at the height of its prosperity and at the time when there was a strong association of managers and producers.

All present agreed that the only possible hope for obtaining any demands from the producers lay in building a powerful organization among the writers — one sufficiently powerful to back up its demands by shutting off the source of supply of screenplays. It was decided that this could best be done by holding a series of meetings to which each member enrolled should bring one guest at the next and subsequent meeting, selecting those best fitted for membership by their reputation as craftsmen in sympathy with such a movement and their courage to fight through to a successful conclusion.

Several important suggestions were made. One was — through negotiation with the Dramatists Guild of America, to be carried on in New York, the now moribund screen writers' subsidiary of the Dramatists Guild be revived and turned over to the authority of this group, and that the Dramatists Guild lend us its utmost support even to the extent of prohibiting its members to sell plays to the motion picture producers who contest our demands.

The second suggestion was brought forth with a great deal of highly favorable criticism, that of placing screen writers' remuneration on a royalty basis. The consensus of opinion was that this could best be done by embodying in a standard writer's contract a minimum percentage of the gross receipts of the picture, the writer to have a specified drawing account against such royalties. Royalties should be paid one year after the release of the picture and semi-annually thereafter, and the Writer's group should have full access to the books — full right to audit them for the purpose of determining the accuracy of gross figures.

The meeting drew up the following tentative demands as a basis for a program of action.

1. The membership of the Guild shall be limited to writers who have received screen credit for writing motion pictures. New members shall be admitted as they pass this. . . .

[The document continued on page 3, which, as I said, cannot be found. But to the best of my memory, it included a detailed description of minimum salaries, a statement against unfair practices of putting writers on scripts without notification of the writer already employed, and, most important, a demand writers, not producers, would control their material, as in the theater.]

Then followed page 4 with the final tentative demands:

7. If the producer desires to employ some other writer to work on the script, this writer shall be paid by the producer and whatever sum paid him must not affect the original writer's royalty agreement.

8. The writers shall have the sole right of saying what their credits shall be in such cases.

9. The writer's credits shall be included in all advertising.

NEXT MEETING: Friday, February 10, 1933, at Hollywood
Knickerbocker, Ivar Street.

Included also on page three must have been the unequivocal statement that the writers rejected completely the producers' "recommendation" that we cut our salaries 50 percent.

Our document produced a major upheaval, a rebellion that stunned the producers and was immediately called a "Revolution." Those writers who called the meeting were, of course, labeled Communists in the trade papers, Bolsheviks who were seeking to overthrow the motion picture industry by force and violence *and* subversion (nothing was left out).

But such was the mood of the majority of writers that these labels meant little or nothing to most of us—then. Instead of twenty writers appearing at the Knickerbocker Hotel the next week—remember, each of us was to bring one qualified, trusted writer—more than fifty appeared to greet the ten signers.

We were ten, the organizers of this writers' guild. The first "Hollywood Ten." Our "crime" was identical to that of the Ten who were to come fourteen years later: we organized a trade union among creative workers, a "revolutionary" action, and later some of us organized and actively participated in anti-Fascist organizations, raised money nationwide for help to the International Brigade, aiding the Spanish people in their war against Franco, Mussolini and Hitler. But I knew no Communists or anyone even remotely connected with the Party were among the members of that first "Hollywood Ten." There was indeed a Communist Party in California, undoubtedly with an office in Los Angeles, and it put out a paper known as the *Western Worker*—but I knew no Party members then. I had never even seen their paper.

The meeting at the Knickerbocker Hotel was militant. Playwrights like Louis Weitzenkorn, who had just recently written the Broadway hit, *Five Star Final,* Edwin Justus Mayer and Samuel Raphaelson, already established Broadway playwrights, spoke eloquently, telling how they had won the fight for recognition of the Dramatists' Guild in New York. John Howard Lawson spoke; then others, including myself, spoke for the lower-salaried "working" writers. Our nine points were accepted in principle, to be voted upon finally when we had sufficient membership to give us the necessary strength. The principle was set that no one present would accept the 50 percent cut; each person present would attempt to bring in at least five qualified writers to the next meeting, which would be held in the old Writers' Club Building on the corner of Cherokee and Sunset Boulevard in Hollywood.

Noticeably absent from the first meeting were those we might call the high-salaried "old timers": the ultra-conservative writers from MGM and Paramount and Fox, men like Rupert Hughes, Howard Emmett Rogers, Fred Niblo, Jr., John Lee Mahin, George Bruce, and a score of others in their camp. Our first meeting had alarmed them. They now came to our second one with no good purpose in mind. The old Writers' Club had as its president one Howard J. Greene, who presided that night. More than three hundred writers were present.

As motions were offered to set up a committee to write a draft constitution, substitute motions flew from the conservatives: as artists we should not become part of "red unionism," but should fight for liberalization of the Motion Picture Academy of Arts and Sciences, led by many of those present. This, of course, was Irving Thalberg speaking through his mouthpiece, James Kevin McGuinness. He was hooted down. Other attempts were made to divert us, but to no avail.

I then offered a motion that everyone there in favor of the new Screenwriters' Guild pledge a week's salary toward the financing of the initial costs of organization, and that we agree to a ten thousand dollar fine for any member who broke the agreement reached. I argued we must have money to hire a secretary, start an office, print stationery, and engage an executive secretary. But Howard Greene countered that the sum suggested was outrageous.

I asked him how much he earned a week. Greene replied that it was a private matter. "Not to me," someone yelled. "You get a thousand bucks a week."

I could see that at this early stage no one was eager to put up that kind of money and quickly offered an amended resolution. "How about a hundred dollars a member now, with dues and assessments to start with the membership's acceptance of a constitution?"

This proposal was unanimously accepted. The word "union" was avoided by all who sought to unify such a diverse political and economic group. A "guild" was acceptable, and the name "Screenwriters' Guild" was adopted. Checks were already being written and collected from almost all of the three hundred who attended the meeting. A press release would go out to include the notice that any writer not a signatory would be fined ten thousand dollars when the Guild was recognized if he or she accepted the 50 percent cut in salary. We spoke of enrolling more members. There were perhaps six to eight hundred writers in Hollywood then, most of whom qualified to be brought into the ranks.

Elections of officers were held. John Howard Lawson was nominated for president. So was Greene, by the conservatives, and Oliver H.P. Garrett, who withdrew in favor of Greene. Then Louis Weitzenkorn who, because he was one of the signatories to the original organizing announcement, was nominated and seconded. He withdrew in favor of Lawson, whom he spoke of as a true liberal, a middle-of-the-roader, and a unifier. Although many who now read this characterization of Lawson as a "liberal" may laugh at Weitzenkorn's seeming naivete, he was absolutely correct. In 1933 Lawson *was* a liberal, a middle-of-the-roader, and a unifier. A strong member of the Dramatists' Guild in New York, but by no means a leftist, Lawson was certainly not then, as he became known later, the leading Communist in Hollywood.

Recently Cedric Belfrage was going through some ancient

files and came across the following item on the theater page of the *New York Sun*, dated November 12, 1927, from the days when he was a stringer for that paper. Under the heading, "What Is a Worker's Theatre?" John Howard Lawson described the goals of the recently organized New Playwrights' Theatre. Lawson wrote:

> We regard partisanship and dullness as capital dangers. We trust our spiritual limitations are not those of the soap box. I can imagine being tremendously excited by a Fascist play or a Catholic play or an anti-red play — if it contained the precious spark of exciting theater. I don't think I am exaggerating when I express my grave doubts that such a play will ever happen. . . . But suppose it did happen — a play defending big business or Nordic superiority or the Fascist state or the Ku Klux Klan or the Methodist Church, defending any of these things with the hot passion of genius? All right. I for one believe that such a play ought to have its place in the most revolutionary theater imaginable. Your professional agitator will unquestionably disagree with my statement, but it is not the business of a theater to be controlled by any class or theory.

It is no wonder that Jack Lawson was regarded as the most liberal of all liberals when he was unanimously elected as president of the Guild! Undoubtedly changes were taking place in him during the six years between that statement in 1927 and his election in the Guild in 1933, but he did not join the Communist Party until 1936.

At our first meeting of the Screenwriters' Guild, of the three hundred writers attending, 102 signed up and wrote checks for one hundred dollars each. By April 7, ten days later, we had 173 signed. Ten months later there were 343 paid-up members.

At a later meeting of the new Guild, a motion was passed that all members of the Academy resign and the former Writers' Club be officially dissolved. It was not without hard work on the part of those who devoted themselves to this cause that our strength grew in numbers and with it our determination to get a contract. The 50 percent cut in salary was finally abandoned by the producers. With this first victory, our reputation grew and our growth accelerated; by July, 1934 we had 640 members; by October, 750. That was about 85 to 90 percent of the working writers in Hollywood. The hold-outs were mainly at MGM — McGuinness, Rogers, Rupert Hughes and others, who had led the fight against the formation of the Guild as patriots against the "Red Menace."

It must be emphasized here: it is my conviction that Capitalism gave birth to Socialism, not the other way round. So it was industry that gave birth to trade unions, not trade unions to industry. That was the historical process. Thalberg continued to vilify the writers, saying, "They live like kings — but join a union like plumbers and miners." At that time there existed in his own studio writers who were more exploited than working plumbers and miners. They were called Junior Writers. In the main, they were college graduates, and these young professionals worked for thirty-five dollars a week creating stories which, when acceptable, would be passed on to Thalberg's high priced favorites (McGuinness and friends). The favorites would turn the stories into screenplays and receive thousands a week, and *all* the screen credit. For the "miners and plumbers" there was a pittance and utter anonymity.

That anonymity had been successfully preserved over the decades, and I would like to break it in two cases I know of personally. Fred Rinaldo and Robert Lees were two such "junior writers." In 1933 they each earned thirty-five dollars a week. In the next six years they wrote the screenplays for about seventy-five short subjects, of which a half-dozen won Academy Awards (for which they received no recognition), and in 1939 their salaries had risen to eighty-five dollars per week. It is important to note that they were leaders among the junior writers and were pivotal in the Guild's winning the MGM vote in the National Labor Relations Board election in 1938.

Shortly before the end of my contract term at Paramount, as I pondered "What now? And where?" and how could one develop enough reputation, if ever, to be free to write what you feel and control its journey to the screen, two newly arrived young writers on the lot appeared in my office and introduced themselves.

I'd heard of them; collaborators on a couple of good, left wing plays in New York, off Broadway, they were engaged for three months, with options to eternity, to do a treatment on a detective novel. They were passionate young revolutionaries, at least the spokesman for them both seemed to be, and they had been sent to me to help them. (Why? By whom? What kind of expert on revolution had they been told I was?) Well, someone so misinformed them, and they stated their plight.

"The story is junk."

"What else is new?"

"We need your advice. How to put a truly revolutionary movement, some real content into it."

I knew the novel. I told them I thought it was impossible, since it wasn't in the material the company bought.

The spokesman looked at me pityingly. "If it were, we would not be asking information from someone we were told was an expert." Before I could ask him the source of his information he went on. "We recognize, of course, that the producers, to say the least, are not interested in that sort of thing. Our problem is to get it in without them noticing."

I couldn't believe it. I tried to be polite. "You are aware, of course, that whatever their political and intellectual limitations, the majority of them read English."

He ignored that. "I'm thinking of something like this: There's a street fight, at night, under a lamp post. That's in the foreground. In the background hungry workers are picketing, and have signs, banners, to strike, to fight, to struggle, to demand jobs, food for their kids. Things like that. In the *background*," he emphasized.

I nodded. "You realize, of course, that what is in the background on film is originally in the foreground in your script. Right up front."

Again the look of pity, this time with contempt. "We know that! What we want to know is how to do it. How to get it into the picture." When I shook my head he shook his, sadly disappointed. "Just another Hollywood hack."

They finished their three months, and didn't return from New York for six years.

Were they Marxists, Communists? Would they be the kind I would be working with if I joined the Party? I would have to find out, and I did. Yes, some like them, some worse, and some better. All kinds, just like anywhere else. What I had to find out is where did I belong, if anywhere, and what kind among all kinds was I?

In general, the work and excitement of the formation and growth of the Guild seemed to fill most of my life. Shortly before option time at Paramount, a long-awaited letter arrived from my New York agent, Frieda Fishbein. *A Farewell to Arms* had long since finished shooting, Helen Hayes was back in New York, and I was waiting for a call to come for rehearsals of my play, *Still Life*.

Fishbein's letter killed all such hopes. She reported that both Hayes and Dixon wanted major alterations in the play before they would sign contracts. It was not a question of the play's content, thought by many to be a bit too radical for those who bought the more expensive seats. No, it was that Hayes, undoubtedly the star, was dissatisfied because although hers was definitely the more sympathetic role, she was in but two of the eight scenes, while Jean Dixon was in six, practically the entire play. And Dixon, for her part, said quite bluntly that she certainly would not, night after night, work her ass off in six tough scenes while Hayes ran off with the show in two.

Obviously I had a lot to learn about "show biz." (Who hasn't?)

Rosalie Stewart was discouraged, and Fishbein gave me

the feeling that she would not pick up a third option at the expiration of the second.

And, as was to be expected, probably because of my Guild activity, Paramount did not pick up my option when it came due a short time later.

But my new play was almost finished. The little bungalow Jonnie and I lived in was cheaper than anything we could find in New York, as was food, some of which we supplied from our little vegetable garden.

It made no sense to go back. Jonnie's aging mother lived in Los Angeles, as did her sister and children; her father, long divorced, lived with her brother and his family up north in Chico. Separation without a genuine necessity would be too painful for both of us, so we dug in.

And then came the good news! Jed Harris, Broadway's leading director and producer, had optioned my play, *Still Life*. All was far from lost. Just sit tight and it would all work out. Paramount, hearing of it, offered five, then ten thousand dollars for the film rights. I had my laugh then; they'd pay ten times that after Harris had put it on.

At the time I had a Hollywood agent with the quaint name Homer Lovelace, and to my astonishment less than three weeks after I had left Paramount, he found an assignment for me. Not only that, but somehow Lovelace had managed to get three hundred dollars a week, which he stated was my free-lance salary. That started my work at William Fox Studios, located at Sunset and Western Avenue, just before the time Twentieth Century Fox was formed in West Los Angeles.

Word had gotten around that some of the organizers of the Guild, myself included, would never work at MGM. That was the beginning of the blacklist. But it was far from industry-wide: the producers were not that organized, and they all competed for the writers they thought could be most profitable to them.

The boss of Fox then was Sol Wurtzel, a man with a strange tick that turned up a corner of his mouth, which I took for a smile until I learned better. During the year and a half I spent at Fox I wrote, alone and in collaboration, five screenplays for low-budget epics like *Charlie Chan's Greatest Case, Pursued, Sleepers East,* and *Wild Gold.* They were all learning experiences, and I developed a skill which was to become one of my greatest assets — the ability to make sick scripts well. I became a "doctor" who could diagnose the ailment and prescribe the cure. Only one incident in that year is worth recording, but it illustrates not only the power of the producer, but his ego, and one of the strange ways in which it could be displayed.

I think it was my second of the six assignments. I can't recall its name, but the story had appeared serially in either the *Saturday Evening Post* or the *Ladies Home Journal.* It was a sentimental, sticky story by Kathleen Norris, sister-in-law of the well-known and worthy writer, Frank Norris. Their work showed no family connection. I do recall that the great silent film star John Gilbert, whose voice made him unsuitable for talking pictures, was standing by, without salary, hoping to learn direction and start a new career.

Neither the director nor I took this trivia very seriously; for both of us it was just a job, but there was one scene in the book so outrageously sentimental that I simply eliminated it from the screenplay, after which I turned it in. A few days later I received a call to come to Wurtzel's office. The corner of his mouth twitched (by then I had learned that this was not a smile but a sign of annoyance). He told me that I had eliminated the very marvelous scene for which he had particularly bought the story. I could hardly believe what I heard, but said merely that I couldn't agree with him and, then, the habit I have never shaken, blurted out, "It's outrageously sticky, nonsensical, Mr. Wurtzel."

"I hired you to write, not to tell me about the values of

what I buy. I know my audiences. Now will you, or won't you, put that scene in?"

I shrugged. "Sure, if you want it. But I don't want my name on the script. And I can say right now, if it's in, this picture will get notices in the trade papers as the worst of the year."

"I said I know my audiences. You just write it."

I did. Director Kenneth McKenna started shooting. To my surprise, I was given another assignment. I watched the shooting and became friendly with John Gilbert, who invited me up to his fabulous mansion high above Beverly Hills, with its swimming pool that was placed against a rocky hill, from which he had the water run down, waterfall fashion. Gilbert was never to make it as a director. Rumors were that Louis B. Mayer had sent out word to ruin him — for some personal reasons never explained. Certainly he was a fine actor, and I never thought his voice was unsuitable for talkies.

The Kathleen Norris film was finished. I had written a script Wurtzel liked and was on my third assignment when it was previewed. My prediction was correct; the trade papers called it the worst, or one of the worst, of the year. They ridiculed the particular scene he insisted upon. And the next day I received an envelope from the desk of Sol M. Wurtzel, with the reviews in it, the damning parts underlined and a note from him saying the enclosed slip from the accounting department will explain what he does when his orders are obeyed. It was notification that my salary from that day on would be increased fifty dollars a week.

The irrationality of it was beyond me, and there was nothing to do but take Jonnie, Marsha and Brian to Musso's for dinner to celebrate the sometimes gratifying irrationality of this "dreamland."

Not all the pictures on the Fox lot were cheap "B" films. Dudley Nichols and John Ford were there; we often had lunch together. Nichols' interest in the Guild had increased to the point where he became one of the most active and influential members.

At about this time, my mother decided my career in Hollywood had some permanence to it, came from New York, and dropped in on us. Jonnie seemed to her some sort of intruder in her son's life. My mother worked on me, questioning the suitability of my choice, not only a *shiksa,* but a woman with little education (had she forgotten mine?). I could think of only one way to put an end to what began to grow from bickering to bitterness.

A few weeks after she arrived, I invited Joe March and Peggy to come with Jonnie and me for the weekend to Agua Caliente, the posh resort but a few miles from Tijuana. And there we sprung it on them: Jonnie and I would get married, and they would act as our best man, witnesses, and bride's woman (since no longer a maid). When we returned on Monday, I introduced mother to Mrs. Jeanne Cole. She moved out that day.

Fox in Westwood was now built and already known as Twentieth Century Fox. I was engaged again as a "doctor" on my first "A" picture, something called *Under Pressure* with the two big stars of *What Price Glory?,* Victor McLaglen and Edmund Lowe. The film had already been shot and, when rough cut, re-cut and finally cut, it still made no sense. How many additional scenes would be required was impossible to calculate from the mess seen on the screen, and I asked to see the original script.

Raoul Walsh, the director, who probably to this day has the greatest contempt for writers, said, "I threw away the Goddamned stupid script. It made no sense. Here's what I worked from." And he handed me a twelve-by-sixteen inch piece of grey cardboard, the kind around which they fold men's shirts at the laundry.

I was forced to go to the front office for a copy of the script, from which I did my rewrite. It was considerable. I cannot recall whether Walsh was retained to do the retakes, although he is credited as sole director. But what I had written was shot, and I shared screenplay credit.

With the success of *Under Pressure,* which received excellent trade paper notices, my reputation as a "constructionist" spread in the industry, and Columbia Pictures offered me a fifty dollar increase to rewrite something called *Too Tough to Kill,* about which I haven't the faintest recollection other than the files that show it was done, and I shared screenplay credit with the previous writer.

If my career as a writer in Hollywood had become a reality it certainly had not on Broadway. Without giving any reasons, Harris dropped his option. Frieda was trying to sell it to the Schuberts, but that seemed hopeless. And, in a sense, the play outlived itself without being born; the depression, though far from over, was no longer a theme that interested producers.

There would be other plays, I knew. The theater, I still believed, was where what I wanted to communicate would and could be heard. There was the Theater Guild, the new Group Theater, and there was talk of a federal theater. I vowed to myself I'd never stop trying.

To Lester:
Your severest critic who understands and loves you.
                                        — Mother

8

FDR's Mystery

Sometime in late 1934 after I had achieved notoriety if not recognition for militancy in the Guild, I was visited by two members of the Communist Party. They invited me to join a Marxist study class for the purpose of learning the philosophy of Marx and Engels in the belief that with such understanding I would want to join the Party.

It was the time Hitler had risen to power, the time of the Reichstag fire and the frame-up trial of the Communist Dimitrov, by the Nazis. Dimitrov's call for a worldwide United Front Against Fascism was one for which I had great sympathy. Soon thereafter a Hollywood anti-Nazi League was forming, led by film director Herbert Biberman. I joined immediately.

One of the two Communists who visited me was Melvin P. Levy, a plump, genial man of about my age. I mention only Levy's name here for reasons which will become clear later.

I told them I would think about the class. I talked it over with Jonnie; she agreed that I should join, and said she would join with me. At the first meeting of the study group, I was impressed: the writers in attendance were known to me as hard workers for the Guild. None was a "star," but many were well-known. They were well-paid, competent, serious people. I felt at home almost immediately. Marxist theory is not easily absorbed and understood, and many of the words and phrases were new to me, if not literally foreign. But once I read the *Communist Manifesto of 1848*, nothing seemed strange or unfamiliar. It was as if I had been brought up on this way of thinking from childhood. Memories of my father, whom I had not seen or heard from in more than fifteen years, came vividly back to mind. I had found one of my traditions, connected concretely with memories of the Toorocks and my father, who had been a militant Socialist, but never a Communist. By now the Socialist Party, I believed, had weakened and was no longer effective. The Communist Party seemed to have inherited the legacy of the earlier militants.

A month or so later another man of about my age dropped by to see us. He introduced himself as the organizer of the Party's Hollywood section and asked us to join. Jonnie and I were not unwilling, but there were a number of questions we had to ask. One of them was about dues, and suddenly I remembered a practical question which then was most important: How much *time* would my obligations to the Party take? I had recently decided it was time to pursue my long-awaited education, and I planned to go to UCLA Extension the following semester and take courses in English and literature. It was high time, and I thought my mother would be pleased that at last I was getting some sense.

I liked the organizer's answers: clear, concise, without flourish or red-banner waving. The dues proved to be reasonable enough, and regarding time spent in Party activities, there was no limit. You gave of your time what the situation demanded, and what you were capable of contributing. It was not a club, but a Marxist revolutionary party. The writers had perhaps the greatest obligation to give as much of their time and ability as humanly possible. The struggle ahead to consolidate the union meant a brutal fight to gain recognition. People were going to get hurt. There was talk of the producers forming a company union to combat us. There was a strategic maneuver under way to give control to the IATSE, which, under its present corrupt leadership would mean destruction for the writers.

I knew about this, of course; I was in the middle of it, whether in the Party or not. But then I had a sudden fear.

"Would I have time to take English and literature courses at the University Extension?" I wanted to know again.

The organizer said frankly he didn't know; that sort of decision would be up to me. I explained I had been waiting years for a chance to study English, never having gone past the second year of high school. He grinned, "Sean O'Casey never got that far."

Okay, Mom, it's me and Sean. All I have to do is write a fraction as well as he does — and be half the man. I paid my new Comrade the one-dollar initiation fee, was assigned to a branch, and notified when and where the next meeting would take place. Jonnie went through the same routine.

Meetings were held twice a month, rotating from one member's house to the next. The "business" I confess, seemed less than exciting. We took turns giving "educationals," which for us were mainly on literature and art. In my branch, made up mostly of film people, we discussed how to increase membership and how we could support, both in activities and financially, the organizations fighting Fascism: the Hollywood Anti-Nazi League, and the League Against War and Fascism. Soon to come was aid to the International Brigade fighting Franco in Spain. The discussions were time-consuming, and many of us felt impatient that we weren't moving fast or effectively enough. But then, who was moving faster? Who was moving at all?

Meanwhile, much was happening in my working life. Following the stint at Columbia, I returned to Twentieth Century Fox, where I was given an unlikely assignment — an untitled original someone had written for Shirley Temple. I wasn't doing very well when a lucky change took place.

S.J. Perelman was working there at the time, on a musical he found impossible, and under working conditions he felt were worse. His collaborator was John Bright, a witty, sardonic guy who was spending many of his nights and early mornings in the Black jazz spots down on Central Avenue. He had a habit of wandering into work around two in the afternoon. Perelman, morning after morning, arrived for work by 9:30 A.M. Finally Bright was taken off the assignment and I was transferred to it. It was to be one of the big pictures of the year, a favorite of the head of the studio, Winfield Sheehan, who had personally bought it on a recent trip to London where it was a big hit. Buddy De Sylva, of the songwriting team De Sylvia, Brown and Henderson, was the producer. How being a songwriter qualified him for producing films is known only to those who engaged him. But here he was, our boss, and we told him the story needed drastic changes, to which he replied Sheehan didn't want a line changed, so just write it as it was, putting it into script form. We did the equivalent of a duo shrug; it was their money. And we were certain it never would be made, so our names would not appear on this atrocity.

Through S.J. Perelman I met and became fast friends with his brother-in-law, Nathanael West, with whom S.J. had gone to Brown University. West's lackadaisical manner in college earned him the nickname of "Pep." By the time we met, West had written two critically acclaimed novels, *A Cool Million* and *Miss Lonelyhearts*, but neither had sold as many as a thousand copies.

Among the writers then at Twentieth was Samson Raphaelson, a nice guy who was one of the Guild's co-founders. But his recent Broadway hit, *Accent on Youth*, seemed to S.J. to have swelled Raphaelson's ego to outsize proportions. At the writers' lunch table, perhaps it was Raphaelson's insistence on telling the story of his assignment, and how he expected a smash hit to result, that most irritated S.J. So when an opportunity came to bring him down, he didn't let it go by.

A rather odd situation existed in the building where we worked. Directly above us was the office of Colonel Jason Joy, the booming-voiced scenario editor who did the hiring and firing of writers. The building was heated by steam pipes in the corners of the rooms, and the round cap that concealed the hole from our ceiling to Joy's floor had fallen off, making his voice on the phone clearly audible most of the time. His dull routine talk was distracting in the extreme. We were even thinking of asking for a change of office when one morning we heard his booming voice say, "You don't like Raphaelson's script? Let him go?"

The look of pleasure on S.J.'s face was instant; we were on our way to Samson's office.

Sam was rather surprised to see us. His feet on his desk, reading a magazine, he waited for a reason for this intrusion. Not for long.

"Finished your script, huh?" S.J. said.

"How d'ya know?"

"We know more than that. It stinks!"

Sam was on his feet, indignant, but before he had a chance to get a word out, S.J. went on.

"So bad, it's hopeless. You just can't write screenplays, Sam. Go back to New York."

"What the hell are you talking about?"

The telephone rang. S.J. then worked on a hunch. "There's your answer." Sam picked up the phone, and we could hear the Colonel's boom. After less than ten seconds, he nodded and hung up.

"How did you bastards know this?" He was as curious as he was furious.

"Figured it out," S.J. lied. "The way you kept talking about how great it was at lunch. We figured, 'He doth protest too much'." S.J. waved jauntily. We walked out. Sam didn't come to say goodbye when he left the studio that day.

From then on we listened more carefully to our source. And a few days later when we learned our fate, it was not hard to take — we knew it had to come.

The Colonel's voice had boomed, "Perelman and Cole? Really? Okay. Right away."

"Let's beat him to the punch," S.J. said. I nodded, and we hurried upstairs, not to Joy's office but to De Sylva's. We didn't wait for permission from his secretary but barged into his office. Buddy seemed startled. S.J. wasted no time. "Buddy, we quit. We did our best, but this thing stinks. It's dead and it stinks. Bury it," or something like that. I won't attempt to recall his precise words; they were always distinctly his own.

"Where can we pick up our checks?"

"See the cashier. . . Oh, thanks for trying."

S.J. went back to New York. Somewhere during this time I had finished a play, hopefully a comedy, called *Sauce for the Gander.* Someone optioned it and raised the money to put it on at the Hollywood Playhouse. I had high hopes, but it wasn't much of a play, and it never made it to Broadway. Failure was hard to take, and I kept muttering that the Hollywood Playhouse was a jinx for me, as it was for Schildkraut. Childish stuff, wounded vanity. The truth I was unable to reconcile was the contradiction between the box office demand for light comedy and the cruel tragedy all around us. There were millions of homeless and hungry here in the United States. Fascists and Nazis roamed through Europe, while England, France, and the United States made their perfidious accommodations. Politics entered our courtrooms in the trials of the Scottsboro Boys and Tom Mooney. In this vicious turmoil, what was this trivia I was writing? Somehow I knew there was a deep split between what I felt deeply and what I had learned to do well in order to earn high pay.

That is, until then. Now, after the job with S.J. ended, weeks and then months began to pass without an offer of an assignment. Jonnie and I moved to a very modest little bungalow on Fuller Street near Santa Monica Blvd. on the "wrong side of the tracks" in Hollywood. Fortunately, my mother opened another of her lunchroom ventures, and it was going well. At least I didn't have to worry about supporting her.

There were three ways of earning a good living as a writer in the studios. One was to sell an original story and one's services to write the screenplay. Another was to get enough assignments on a free-lance basis to work thirty-five to forty weeks a year. The third was to be in such demand that a studio placed one under contract. Now I found myself with savings dwindling rapidly toward zero, and I was beginning to worry. My agent hinted that my Guild activities certainly were blocking me at other studios besides MGM; no scenario editors came out and said just that, but he sensed it. In fact our drive for recognition was failing, and writers were dividing along class and economic lines. For many the question of ownership of material — which meant control — became a prime issue. In films it was complicated, quite unlike the solutions found by dramatists and novelists in their organizations. They owned their copyrights and received royalties. Screen writers just sold their labor. For us, where writers' work was collaborative, and one writer so often followed another, who would have control? The novelist or playwright from whose work the screenplay was adapted? The writer of the screenplay? It would be simple enough where the screenplay originated from a story written by the screenwriter; otherwise knotty problems faced us.

Among us, many of those who earned two or three thousand a week felt that for such sums the producers could do whatever they wanted with the script. But others disagreed. Some felt the deepest mortification when their work was tampered with. And for lower-priced writers like myself, the question of royalties was a bread-and-butter issue — indivisible from the question of control. A writer could turn out a script for a few thousand dollars that would make over a million in profit. His share could be less than 1 percent of the *profit*, whereas had it been a successful play or novel his percentage would have been 5, 7.5, and finally 10 percent of the *gross*.

In the end, we had to face the issue with the membership. But our attendance had rapidly dropped. At a meeting called in 1935, only forty members appeared. It was less than a quorum. No resolution could be offered.

Many were discouraged. It looked as if the years of work, the belief that we could rally the writers into a strong organization, was a dream. And with it the unemployment situation for me was becoming serious. During the period of unemployment, I wrote a play, *The Honorable Johnsons*, sold it, and it was tried out in a summer showcase theater in New Jersey. Again a comedy. It died quietly. I wrote two film stories. Neither of them sold — then.

Blanche, with a B.A. degree that made her a laboratory technician, found little work at her profession. She managed a cram course in stenography and typing and found a job as a secretary at Columbia.

Finally, after about five months without work, I received an offer from Republic Studios, then a quickie studio. Republic made mostly cheap "B" Westerns, for the second half of double bills in neighborhood movie houses. They offered me a job at two hundred dollars a week, which they claimed was the top money they ever paid. It was a cut in salary of 40 percent, but I had no choice.

Republic was owned by one Herbert Yates, whose main business was Consolidated Laboratories, a giant film-processing plant which had a practical monopoly in Hollywood. Republic for him was either a toy or a tax shelter, if such things existed in those days. He appeared at the studio only occasionally to see one of their Westerns. All other business, such as costs and distribution, was discussed in his office at Consolidated.

But the current executive producer at Republic was a shrewd, ambitious man of about forty, Nat Levine, an experienced manager of small movie house chains. This job was a step up for him. He was eager to learn and did so more quickly than most. Astutely, he hired as an associate producer Burt Kelly, a man who had a real feeling for film and decent human instincts. Over the years loyalty and a capacity for friendship developed between us which lasts to this day.

Even before I started my first assignment for him, Kelly told me he knew how they'd slashed my salary. If we could make one or two good pictures together, he'd get me back up. The first one was a charming, unusual story called *Hitch Hike Lady*, based on an outline from the unlikely pen of an actor, Wallace McDonald, perhaps fifteen or so pages. I wrote an acceptable screenplay, Burt got Alison Skipworth for the lead, a good supporting cast, including Mae Clark and Arthur Treacher, and Aubrey Scott as director. The script was written in six weeks, the film shot in two: another "quickie." But the results astonished Levine, and he proudly showed it to Yates.

The trade papers were laudatory. *Variety* said: "Best effort from Republic in a long time. Good entertainment on any double bill and should gain fair grosses in some houses soloing." And it did succeed, as no other Republic film had ever done before. Kelly had made it on a low budget, perhaps seventy or seventy-five thousand dollars, and was highly praised. And while I had my name on the screen for the screenplay, no credit was given in the *Hollywood Reporter* review. The omission marked the beginning of their attempt to make me a non-person in that producer-oriented trade paper.

But I was somebody at Republic. Burt got me a raise for the next script, and there was more. I told him about Nathanael West in Hollywood and out of work. He had read and admired West's novels. I introduced them and Burt put him to work on the next one with me. It was a silly thing called *Follow Your Heart*, on which Sam Ornitz had struggled manfully for some time. We had it no easier, but somehow it was written, made and released. My salary went up again.

West and I remained collaborators, and our next assignment turned out to be most gratifying. There is an unusual and amusing background to this story and the effect of this film on Yates.

It was early in 1936, many months before the election which swept Roosevelt back into his second term. *Liberty Magazine* had a bright idea for a serial. It was common knowledge that Franklin D. Roosevelt, when finished with a long and arduous day's work, would relax at bedtime reading mystery stories. An enterprising editor from *Liberty* went to the President: if he gave them an idea for a mystery story, they would put eight or ten of the top mystery story writers on it, make it a serial to be run in weekly installments, and call it "The President's Mystery." Roosevelt no doubt saw little harm in that kind of publicity and gave the editor an idea. The central character should be a corporation attorney in Washington who had become disillusioned by the corrupt practices of his firm. He leaves on a fishing trip and disappears. His wife is found murdered that night or the next day. Who dunnit? "You take it from there" is all Roosevelt is reported to have said.

Liberty took it from there, with enthusiasm. They engaged Rupert Hughes (a violently anti-Roosevelt man), Samuel Hopkins Adams, Anthony Abbot, Rita Weiman, S.S. Van Dine, and John Erskine. Perhaps because of the time pressure these fiction writers, among the most popular and well-known of the day, did not work together. One of them took the idea, wrote an outline, and divided the work into six parts. Each contributor wrote his or her part without much further consultation. The result may be imagined: incongruities and contradictions, as well as a lack of continuity, suspense or clues in a mystery where these elements are of the greatest importance.

The advance publicity was tumultuous; certainly the name Roosevelt and the fame of the writers made it seem as if this story would sell to movies for a top price. But in every studio — MGM, Warner Brothers, Paramount, RKO, Universal — where competitive bidding was expected to be wild, there was a distinctly negative reaction. Opinion was unanimous: the story made no sense. Whatever merit Roosevelt's original idea might have had, it was no longer visible in this badly mangled editorial paste-together yarn. So the story, for which *Liberty* had expected a minimum of a hundred thousand dollars (a vast sum in 1936), found no buyers.

Except one. Republic. Burt Kelly convinced Nat Levine that he could get a hell of a screenplay out of this with Pep and myself writing it, and now it could be bought cheap. I think the studio paid fifteen hundred or two thousand for it.

We wrote it.

As I recall, we retained the mystery and the way it was solved, but little else except the principal character and his dead wife. We started with the corporation lawyer who leaves Washington disillusioned, goes off on a fishing trip, and learns the next morning that his wife has been found murdered. From then on we were on our own. I saw an opportunity for a politically oriented subtext, which eventually took over. The newspapers those days were full of accounts of big corporations closing down their fruit and vegetable canning factories. Tens of thousands of farmers found their crops rotting, and cannery workers were thrown out of jobs. Ours became a story of solving the problem of hungry workers and farmers, not just of solving the mystery. Kelly bought the idea, but our work was shunted aside for almost a week by Pep. On the first day in a new office — it was the season, I guess — Pep saw something in the tree branches twenty feet from the window, and the next morning he came to work with a BB gun. Like myself, Pep was a fly fisherman. But he was also a duck hunter, and this morning he had a grim look on his face. He opened the window, gun on his lap, and waited.

"What the hell do you plan to do with that?" I demanded.

He made a motion for silence, like a wild duck hunter sitting in a blind. Finally he said, "There are shrikes around here."

I was exasperated. "What the hell are shrikes? C'mon Pep, let's get to work."

"You start. I hate shrikes. You know what they do? Rob little birds' nests of eggs, and eat the little newborn things. I hate them!" Then he took careful aim, shot, and his exclamation of pleasure brought me to the window. On the ground, just inside the studio fence, was this rather large greyish bird, with a heavy beak, curved and ugly. "Shrike," he explained to me, "is a kind of thrush, but a bully. I think its name comes from the German, *Geshreih*, or shriek. Anyway, they get their prey, insects or little baby birds, and to eat them they impale them on thorns. They're Nazis." And with that he took another shot at a shrieking shrike and found his mark.

Three days later he gathered up the now-putrid mess of perhaps a dozen birds and put the corpses in a trash bin. We heard the shriek of the shrikes no more and went to work.

The story developed beautifully once we saw our goal; the desperate farmers and the cannery workers get together, form a cooperative, illegally take over the cannery, and start production on their own. The conflict, of course, was with the big corporation, which sought to drive them off the property. Their defiance led to a fighting, action showdown and a victory for the farmers, the workers — and the program of Franklin D. Roosevelt. It was into this conflict that the corporation lawyer had come only for some trout fishing, but he found himself becoming an enthusiastic supporter of the farmers and cannery workers. Played with a flair by Henry Wilcoxen, he of course meets beautiful Betty Furness, daughter of the cannery owner, and with the solution to the farmer/cannery worker/corporation struggle, they fall in love, the mystery of the murderer of his wife is somehow solved, and they live happily ever after. Mystery, romance, and a generous dash of Rooseveltian propaganda.

Kelly was pleased, Levine delighted. Phil Rosen, the director, did a sympathetic job and brought the film into the can in twelve shooting days at a cost just over one hundred thousand dollars. It was Republic's first (and I think only) "super-special." For that studio, a big gamble.

Proudly, Levine called in Herbert Yates to see what he felt was Republic's best film to date. Pep and I were invited to attend the showing in the projection room, an honor and a sign of appreciation.

The film was run. The lights came up. I can still see Levine looking eagerly at Yates for praise, for words of commendation. His expression altered when he saw Yates' face; jaw set, fists clenched, so enraged he was for a moment unable to speak. Finally it came out in a roar. "Who's responsible for this propaganda, this Roosevelt communist crap?" He looked around wildly.

Levine was startled. I'll say this for him; his name was on the credits as Executive Producer, Kelly as Producer. Levine took full responsibility. That must have saved our jobs. But Yates had more to say:

"Put that communist shit on the shelf. We're not releasing it."

Levine attempted to protest, but now Yates' rage was mounting. "You goddam fool! You put a hundred and five grand in that commie crap; if we released it, it would be worth God knows how many hundred thousand, maybe millions of votes for Roosevelt. I've got one hundred thousand in that film." He was shouting, out of control. "But I've got *two hundred thousand on Governor Landon in this election*! Can you do simple arithmetic?" Trembling with anger, he strode out.

The film was shelved, of course. Yates was the boss. Two months later Roosevelt won his second term — by a land-slide — somehow without help from Kelly, Pep and myself. Following the election, Yates did some simple arithmetic, and ordered Levine to have the picture previewed and put into distribution.

The trade papers had high praise for the film. The *Hollywood Reporter* headlined its review, "PRESIDENT'S MYSTERY B.O. [Box Office] Properly sold can prove a clean-up." In the course of its praise, it did say,". . . leaning a little heavily toward sociological propaganda at times." But it added, "A serious demonstration of class advancement of the Republic product." Screenwriters' credits were eliminated from the review. The *Film Daily*, which reached distributors and movie-houses all over the country, called the production "a timely subject presented in an exciting, interesting manner that should attract the masses." This paper noted that the script "was carefully prepared for the screen by Lester Cole and Nathanael West." All in all, they saw it as "excellent." And Yates muttered unbelievingly.

In New York the dailies praised the film highly, and one spoke of it as among the best ten films of the year. The film went on to make back for Yates far more than he lost backing Landon.

After writing three more pictures for Republic, I received another raise, bringing me to what other studios had paid me more than a year before.

It now began to seem the life of the Guild was at stake. The red-baiting was having its effect; writers were being cautious. Thalberg was reported in *Variety* as threatening to shut down MGM, lock the gates, and stop making films. He said the writers would give him no other choice if they got what they wanted — a union to control production. Not that anyone believed him, but writers not working at MGM saw no advantage in coming under its threatened ban of Guild members.

Our one hope lay in something the government had proposed, and which would come before — we hoped — the current session of Congress. It was a bill that would legalize collective bargaining, give workers the right to decide whether to affiliate with the newly born CIO, the AFL, an independent union or no union at all. The pressure for this legislation was enormous throughout the industrial cities — the depression was now in its sixth year.

To make sure writers were not tied to MGM-type contracts, the Guild passed a resolution that no member could sign a contract that went beyond May 2, 1938. This was the date felt to be practical by our most pessimistic members; the National Labor Relations Act would surely become law by then. With that the battle became fierce and ugly.

Our action to limit the length of contracts brought swift reaction from the growing opposition. It also brought doubts to the meek and more quiescent members of our Guild. Emboldened, MGM had its dutiful, high-salaried robots set up a rival organization; they called themselves the Screen Playwrights. Glowing praise came from Wilkerson and his *Hollywood Reporter*, the Hearst press, and of course, Chandler's then open-shop *L.A. Times.*

It must be remembered that the motion picture industry moved to Los Angeles for two reasons, and it is difficult to state which was the most important. One, of course, was the proclaimed reason, the months of continuing sunshine. The unspoken reason was the crushing of trade unionism in the city decades before, which made Los Angeles one of the nation's chief citadels of the open shop.

The Screen Playwrights must have been months in secret preparation because shortly after the announcement of this company union's formation, they called a meeting, open to all writers, at which they had ready for approval a constitution and by-laws, as well as recognition and a first contract from one studio — MGM, of course. Despite thorough publicity and advertising, the meeting was sparsely attended. Only forty-five writers, besides those from MGM, attended. From all reports, the constitution sought to make this "union" elitist; the qualifications for membership were very stringent. But it gave Thalberg an opportunity to send a telegram of congratulations, stating that his approval and recognition of the Screen Playwrights proved that MGM was not anti-union, just anti-*communist* union.

Rupert Hughes rose to denounce the Screen Writers Guild

as a communist front, intent on taking control of the industry by subversion. Those present passed a resolution to strengthen the ties with the Writers' Branch of the Motion Picture Academy, which writers had weakened when they left it and denounced it as a producer-dominated organization. Our departure was highlighted by Dudley Nichols, one of the Guild's most esteemed writers, among whose credits were the famed films, *Stagecoach* and *The Informer*. Nichols publicly spurned their award for the best screenplay at their annual award-giving dinner.

Despite temporary setbacks in Guild growth and strength, we were actually making a genuine contribution to trade union growth and consciousness not only among actors, but among clerical workers and the story readers, both in Hollywood and in New York. It has been said, and I believe it to be true, that our Guild inspired reporters and editorial writers and our own members who were also newsmen and women, to be in the forefront in the organization of the Newspaper Guild. Cultural workers, creative people, were coming to union consciousness. Wages might go from seventy-five a week to thousands, but they were still wages.

In an attempt to quell the rising resentment and organizing impetus among artists as well as workers, Roosevelt put through various public works projects, which included one for writers — the Federal Writers Project. This project put hundreds to work in every state. A common goal seemed to be writing the histories of their states, valuable books still extant, if not too well-known. Better known was the Federal Theater Project, under the guidance of Hallie Flannigan, which brought hundreds, perhaps thousands of playwrights, unemployed actors, directors, set designers, musicians, and stage technicians together at a low but living wage. "Living newspapers" — performing plays such as *One Third of a Nation* and other documentary dramas of the current social realities — were shown at low, popular prices. The effect upon the American people was enormous; the difference between this work and most of the trash being shown in movie houses had its effect. Certain producers began to see profit in film topics other than sheer escape and inane fantasy. Even though the ideas expressed and social realities depicted caused some of them extreme uneasiness, the magnetism of new fields of profits conquered most misgivings. To show poverty, joblessness, hunger and homelessness in movies not only awakened the consciousness of the millions who saw themselves represented realistically on the screen, but it aroused their consciousness and stimulated what was most dreaded by the producers who made the films — a sense of the dignity of the common man and woman, their courage and strength to fight back.

It was a heartening, vibrant time. All around appeared the creations of those who but a year or two before seemed without hope. In new government buildings, such as Post Offices, great artists were painting the history of our land in provocative and inspiring murals — Anton Refregier, Bob Gwathmey, Phillip Evergood, the Soyer Brothers, Ben Shawn — for the first time people saw historic depictions of labor's struggle from the Molly Maguires to the heroic fight of and for Joe Hill.

This cannot be said too emphatically: we were attacked for "attempts to subvert, to overthrow the government by force and violence" when actually we were organizing and fighting for democratic trade unionism, against Fascism in Hitler's Germany and Franco's Spain, against racism here and everywhere and for man's movement toward an understanding of how to make this a better world for all. Over the years, yesterday's "subversion" has become accepted reality: Social Security, Medicare, the United Nations, the reinstatement *in fact* of the First Amendment. (And how ironic it is that today we are fighting a desperate right-wing government that seeks to end all of that and rather than seek peace, risks the destruction of civilization on this earth to restore a system which is beyond repair.)

Every action then taken by the Hollywood Anti-Nazi League

and the League Against War and Fascism, every campaign to raise money for ambulances for the Abraham Lincoln Brigade in Spain brought intensified accusations against the Screen Writers Guild, which of course in no way participated organizationally in any of these activities, although many of its members did as individuals.

The reason was clear. While the Screen Playwrights was the "recognized" Guild (by MGM), the Screen Writers Guild was pressing for NLRB elections, which we felt confident we would win, thus forcing the producers to negotiate with us. There is little doubt that members of the Playwrights slid into our Guild, playing the role of informers for the FBI. To our horror, we discovered the infiltration went far beyond the Guild; we discovered our own Party county organizer was an informer, if not an actual FBI agent.

Hollywood was the world historic scene in miniature; they could not stop us nor could they stop trying to. It would be ten years before they tasted the fruit from the seeds they had then planted, in a garden obsessively cultivated.

All through this period I worked, in the Guild, in the Party and, most gratifyingly, successfully in the studios. My credits, although mainly on "B" pictures thus far, were not unimpressive. My salary had gone up another hundred a week. I worked forty or more weeks a year and could accept or turn down assignments. I was a "success."

9

The Tumultuous Thirties

Burt Kelly accepted an offer to produce at Universal, and he brought both Pep and me along, getting raises for both of us. With the intensification of Guild organizing, the NLRB elections expected in the near future, work in the Anti-Nazi League and the meetings to create support for the Spanish Republic against Franco, some people asked when and where did we find time to "live"? The answer, of course, was that *this* was living; it was indeed our lives.

It was about then, to my delight, that Cedric returned from England with a wife, Molly, and their first child. His recently published book, *Away From it All,* an account of his travel around the world, won critical acclaim and sold well for a nonfiction title. Most important, it won him a high-paying job for one of the British papers as their Hollywood correspondent. Molly was lovely, and their baby daughter Sally a dream. Jonnie looked away longingly, as if to say, "When, darling, when?"

Late one afternoon I returned from the studio to find our friends, Brian Marlowe and Marsha, tremendously excited.

They insisted we hop into their car at once and ask no questions; they wanted to show us a miraculously beautiful "something."

Over Cahuenga Pass we sped at sunset, into the San Fernando Valley, soon to turn off the highway and past cultivated fields and occasional farm houses, still less than ten miles from Hollywood. Brian abruptly turned off Burbank Boulevard onto a bumpy dirt road bearing the sign "Ranchito Street," and suddenly pulled to a stop before an immense, fully grown walnut grove.

It was Brian's way; he loved to tell his stories as he was telling us this. On the way out he and Marsha talked of all kinds of matters: personal, political, trivial, everything but the reason for this drive. We waited, playing the game he so enjoyed. Suddenly he swept his arm over the entire walnut grove and said casually, "Five acres, five thousand bucks. A thousand an acre. Whaddya say we split it?"

"Yes, yes!" It was Jonnie's instant cry of assent, and we all knew why.

Her childhood memories of farms and orchards were vivid. She loved the country and here, ten miles from town, we could have it. The walnut trees, branch to branch, let little sunlight to the ground, so along with cutting some out for where the house would stand, we would clear a few more for a vegetable garden and some citrus trees.

At that time we had only about thirty-five hundred in the bank; I felt we couldn't strip ourselves, even though I was working. Brian, who then was in a far better financial position, offered to take three acres and we'd have two. We agreed and bought the land outright the next day.

We found an architect, and plans were drawn up for both houses. Caution — was it a premonition? — made me suggest to Jonnie that we wait on the house and first build a double garage with a guest room, kitchen and bath, leaving out the wall separating the garage until we built the house itself. And so it was, the garage became our bedroom-living-dining-room, and we had a small kitchen and bath. It was soon completed, and almost immediately after moving in we started having the big trees removed from the area where we planned our vegetable garden and our citrus trees, which were quickly planted. Then, of course, we built a chicken coop. I was up at six each morning, working for at least two hours before going to the studio. Jonnie spent every spare moment working and planning.

Our garden grew beautifully, enough for us and the Marlowes, who preferred the shade and an evening drink to farm work. Jonnie and I were never closer. Only Pep West, close friend and constant visitor, worried us. He had no permanent relationship with a woman, and it bothered him. He tried many, many tried him, nothing lasted.

And then it happened. Ruth McKenny, an old friend, who had the year before written the best seller, *My Sister Eileen*, was out for a visit to Hollywood, probably in regard to the sale of the dramatic rights. With her was her husband, Richard Branston, and of course we invited them and Pep to dinner. How it happened I don't know, but Ruth failed to mention that her sister Eileen was there and coming with them. Imagine our surprise and delight when Eileen and Pep looked at each other, a long, inquiring unmistakable look. Jonnie's eyes found mine: was something happening?

It was, and three months later they were married. Eileen, jovial, easy and outgoing, seemed to enjoy Pep's lackadaisical manner. She was an admirer of his writing, which of course was essential for perfect companionship. Jonnie and I had a strange sense of accomplishment; irrational, since it all happened so accidentally. But it did happen in our house and we felt triumphant. From then on we spent much time together, and among Jonnie, Eileen and myself we energized Pep enough to take an interest in at least joining a Marxist study group; slowly, we felt, we would bring him along.

At the studio, work was going beautifully for me. It was

there, at Universal, that my reputation for being a script "doctor" was further established. From April 1932 until February 1935, three years, I had received six screen credits. But at Republic in a little over a year I had four, and at Universal from late 1937 through April 1940 I wrote two original stories and ten screenplays, some alone and some in collaboration.

In 1939 I sold a story to Burt Kelly at Universal for George Raft. Pep did the screenplay alone — his first — since I could not resist an offer from Walter Wanger at United Artists. The inducement was a good raise in pay with which, once achieved and established, I could return to Universal, or go elsewhere.

Wanger bought a story called "Winter Carnival." The authors were Budd Schulberg and Maurice Rapf, two youngsters just out of Dartmouth College, in revolt against their fathers (one head of Paramount, the other an executive at MGM). The two took a holiday in the USSR, fell in love with Russia, and returned determined that the next generation of studio heads (themselves?) would have a more radical outlook! Their fates, rising and falling, are another story, but Schulberg does come into this account briefly and tellingly later on.

I collaborated with them, both inexperienced but talented young men, and shared the screenplay credit. I then went off to write an original with Carl Dreher, a dear friend who escaped the blacklist years later by giving up as a chief engineer of sound at RKO and becoming Science editor for *The Nation* until he died many years later. Universal bought the story, and I wrote the screenplay with one Brown Holmes (both story and collaborator completely forgotten). From there I went back to Burt Kelly to write the screenplay with Kurt Kiodmok on a sequel to the popular film, *The Invisible Man*, appropriately titled *The Invisible Man Returns*. I had to admit that, while my bank account was increasing and my financial security strengthening, what I was writing was little more than junk stuff.

But I consoled myself, or tried to, by rationalizing; I was

becoming more skilled, better known, higher paid. Yet I continued to feel unsatisfied, strangely unfulfilled. And here I was, already thirty-five!

Was it possible for a Marxist — which by then I felt I was — to make a creative contribution to films, aside from trade-union work? For years, of course, our opponents claimed we sought to subvert the industry and the country by "sneaking in" lines of revolutionary propaganda.

The truth is that if anyone were foolish enough to try something that silly it would immediately be discovered and eliminated. The other truth is that "politics" are expressed in every film. An escapist "entertainment" is political to the degree that it denies the existing social realities and, as in the film, *The President's Mystery*, I sought to inject such reality when the subject called for it. My politics, pro-union and pro-socialist, were never "injected" into films, yet I believe often the feelings were represented in attitudes of the characters. In future films this became more evident, but by then it was historically more acceptable.

In 1936 John Howard Lawson returned to Hollywood. Two plays produced in New York had not been financially successful, and with growing children and an offer to work, he came back, but a very different man. Always brilliant, with the keenest intellect, during those four years away he devoted himself to a study of Marxism, challenged, he told me, by Mike Gold. He returned a changed man from the one who wrote about the philosophy for a workers' theater in 1927. It was not long before he was recognized as a leading Marxist scholar, particularly in the field of creative writing.

At the time of his death in 1977, he was still being accused, in the *New York Times* obituary, of having been "the cultural commissar of Hollywood," of "giving his colleagues tips on how to get the Party viewpoint across in their dialog."

In a letter to the *Times*, Ring Lardner exposed this slander. He gave Lawson's true position, which I quote:

Actually he regarded anything of that sort as a puerile approach to the politicalization of screenwriting. More revolutionary movies, he said, would come from the interdependence of form and content and the deeper penetration of character, especially in neglected sections of the population.*

Lardner then goes on with this bit of ironic whimsy: "To his younger, less philosophical disciples, his counseling sometimes seemed remote from the immediate struggle."

Jack Lawson was a man of great learning and intellectual power. After his years of rethinking his philosophical position, his first theoretical book was published, coincidentally with his return to Hollywood in 1936. Titled *The Theory and Technique of Playwrighting* (years later to be revised and include screenwriting), it was a Marxist work of acknowledged scholarship and intellectual perception, and it was widely read in Hollywood. As it was the first work of its kind in English, he was immediately labeled by the opposition as the "Red leader" in the film industry and he was a principal target for abuse. His later works, over the years, included *Film, The Creative Process,* and *Hidden Heritage.* The reputation as a leading Marxist scholar was well earned.

On April 12, 1938, Jonnie's immediate struggle was to give birth to our first child. Labor lasted all day and night and, finally, on the thirteenth, Michael was born. We had prepared for the big event. The house had been built, a beautiful bungalow with walls of adobe brick twelve inches thick against the heat, an insulated roof with redwood shakes and handsome hardwood floors throughout. It cost twelve thousand dollars, but at the salary I was then receiving it would soon be paid off. Yet it did seem a luxury; in those days construction at $3.50 a square foot was very, very upper class.

*New York Times, August 16, 1977.

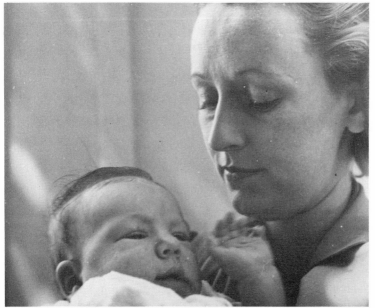

Jonnie and Michael

The immediate political victory in 1938 was the decision of the NLRB to permit writers to vote for the union of their choice. With this decision the Guild came back to vibrant life. As we started organizing for the crucial vote, a legal struggle intruded itself. The Screen Playwrights claimed that since it had a contract, no vote was required. But on June 4, 1938, the NLRB determined that writers were entitled to vote for the collective bargaining representation of their choice, ignoring the obvious "sweetheart" contract between the Playwrights and the Motion Picture Producers Association. A secret ballot was ordered held within twenty-five days.

The producers, frantic, had the Screen Playwrights sue the Guild for libel in the amount of two hundred thousand dollars. What the libel could be about, nobody figured out, but I think they sought to prove that with the Screen Writers

Guild a victor — which was a foregone conclusion -- their members would be blacklisted.

Blacklisting was already an acknowledged weapon. Dalton Trumbo was prepared to testify that in 1936 Jack Warner fired him, bluntly stating his Guild activity as the reason. When Trumbo said that was blacklisting, Warner replied, with his famous grin, "Sure it's blacklisting. But you can't prove it since we got no list; we do it by phone." There were others, including myself, ready to testify that we were warned by McGuinness that we would be blacklisted at MGM in 1933 if we didn't stop our work in the Guild. Our preparation for defense against the libel suit was needless; the case was preposterous and promptly thrown out of court.

The excitement was intense; after five years, at last we would make a test, supported by the government, which would determine the issue of representation: Screen Playwrights, Screen Writers Guild, or none. The election was to be held on June 28. The Producers Association did everything it could to sabotage it. Its stooge, Wilkerson, gave the "Communist Takeover" of the industry scare headlines in his *Hollywood Reporter*. The Hearst newspaper and the *L.A. Times* were in there pitching, and a spokesman for the producers announced in *Variety* that the voting was futile, since the Producers Association would not accept the elections as legal and intended to resist them in every way possible. Contrary to and in defiance of the law, no voting was to be permitted on studio property. Immediately the NLRB threatened legal action, and the producers backed away from that confrontation.

We had allies, too; top artists in the industry. Director Rouben Mamoulian came out in strong public support for our Guild. Robert Montgomery, President of the Screen Actors' Guild, did the same, urging uncommitted writers to vote SWG: "Anything else," he said, "including staying away from the polls, was a stab in the back not only to the writers, but to the Actors and Directors," the latter then just having formed the Screen Directors Guild.

June 28 came, the election took place, and it was a stunning victory. First, of the 773 eligible voters, the turnout was *100 percent*. And the way they voted at some of the studios was astonishing: at MGM, the birthplace of the Playwrights, the vote was 63 to 33 in favor of the Guild; at Paramount, 60 to 14; RKO registered 30 to 0; Universal, 22 to 2; Warners, 38 to 1; and at the independents, Hal Roach, Monogram, Selznick, Int., Goldwyn and Republic, not a single vote for the Screen Playwrights. The final tally, as reported in *Variety*, which included those eligible but not at studios, was Guild 615, Screen Playwrights 158.

Producers and their writer-allies screamed, "Communist control." Of course, that was nonsense. "Communist control" was neither a possibility nor our goal. Party members could not have constituted more than 3 percent of the Guild membership, if that many; and we had few if any influential "stars." We won because of the inspired leadership of many fine, liberal, dedicated writers — Dudley Nichols, Ernest Pascal, Phil Dunne, Jules and Philip Epstein, and scores of others who believed in the Guild and were among its most effective members. But there is little doubt that the few of us who were Party members played a vigorous and effective role in explaining the issues, organizing and getting out the vote.

Party membership was secret, but writers couldn't be prevented from speculating. Many of us in Guild leadership were simply assumed to be members. By putting ourselves and our jobs on the line, speaking out publicly on controversial issues, we were later called, in the generous war years, "premature anti-fascists." There was general contempt for the MGM-Thalberg clique; among writers, we were respected and interest in the Party began to grow. More Marxist study classes were formed, and with other organizations which sought broad, democratic participation, a "Democratic Front" was formed. The League of American Writers had come into being. With many notable writers in the East, such as Theodore Dreiser, taking a leading role and joining the Party, the Left's prestige grew.

With our winning of the Guild election, other elements began to affect the opposition of the producers. Resistance to Roosevelt's domestic economic programs in the arts was becoming poisonous. It was generally assumed that the defeated Screen Playwrights was part of the power group which brought into being the House Un-American Activities Committee, with Martin Dies, the Texas Congressman, as chairman.

Under the leadership of Earl Browder, the Party supported Roosevelt in most of his domestic policies, but opposed him when he accepted Britain's appeasement of Hitler at Munich and condemned his "neutrality" in the Spanish War. Millions of Americans joined in opposing these decisions; the Party was, in fact, leading a growing anti-fascist coalition.

But, as always, for producers, box office receipts were the primary consideration. The audience could take just so much of the Busby Berkeley musicals and the Crosby-Hope gambols. The success of the political plays of the Federal Theater Project, which at its bargain prices was becoming a real or imagined threat, made them realize that a qualitatively new demand had been created. Warner Brothers had led the way. Discovering early in the depression that such films as *I Was a Fugitive from a Chain Gang*, made with much trepidation, were a great financial success, they started looking for other social subjects. Along with their realistic gangster films, in which James Cagney and Edward G. Robinson were great attractions, Paul Muni became an overnight star in *Fugitive*, and subjects of equal quality were eagerly sought.

Then, in 1937, a truly revolutionary film appeared: a Warner Brothers production of *The Life of Zola*, starring Paul Muni, with Gale Sondergaard and Joseph Schildkraut; the screenplay by Norman A. Raine, Heinz Herald, and Geza Herzeg and directed by William Dieterle. They held nothing back. The power elite and the military were mercilessly exposed as corrupt tyrants, immoral, deceitful and willing to go to the most inhuman lengths to preserve the power of the explicitly described ruling class. Prior to *Zola*, Dieterle directed *Louis*

Pasteur, written by Sheridan Gibney and Pierre Collins, and then *Blockade*, written by Lawson, the film of the Spanish people's war against Franco (Mussolini and Hitler supplying arms and men); then *Juarez*, written by John Huston, which like the others, pussyfooted nowhere, and showed the revolution in mid-nineteenth century in which the people overthrew the European colonial despots.

One would be in grave error to imagine that the themes exposing those in power had any effect upon the people *producing* the films, however inspiring and enlightening they were to those seeing them. A notorious example of this dichotomy is an incident that preceded the production of *Zola*. Matthew Josephson had written the book, *Zola and His Times*, which Dieterle wanted to film. Jack Warner attempted to make a deal for the rights to the book. Warner reportedly offered Josephson a preposterously low figure, which Josephson rejected. Warner was indignant and offended. After all, Zola was long gone, the Dreyfus case was history, and these matters were all in the public domain, merely recorded history in Josephson's book. Warner threatened to have his research department do the necessary historical investigation, put a film writer on it, so that it would cost him nothing but the one salary. He was proud of his acumen and the righteousness of his position; the film was researched, written and made.

Shortly after it was released, Josephson's lawyers sued for plagiarism and, to his chagrin, Warner discovered that his researcher used none other than Josephson's book for parts of the research.

The basis for the suit was a fictionalized scene that Josephson had created to help cover some time lapse for narrative continuity. Warner was asked to produce the "historical basis" for the incident and try they did, but the nearest his researchers could come was Josephson's fictional version. Josephson won, and the damages were more than twice as much as the price he had originally asked for his book.

Harry Cohn at Columbia had a New Deal winner, *Mr.*

Deeds Goes to Town, to be followed by a beautifully rewritten
and socially important adaptation of the Kaufman-Hart farce,
You Can't Take It With You. Where the authors of the play
hinted at the corporate control of the country, the writer Robert
Riskin and director Frank Capra played it out, ironically,
satirically, and with telling left jabs. And when this was followed
a year later by *Mr. Smith Goes to Washington*, the script
written by Sidney Buchman, again for Capra, there were few
companies that could ignore the trend.* But MGM, with stars
like Greta Garbo and Clark Gable were able to — there were
also profits in anti-Soviet films like *Ninotchka* and *Comrade
X* — and the comedies of Bing Crosby and Bob Hope found
big audiences for Paramount.

Yet the swing was toward socially aware, New Deal ideas
for which more liberal-minded writers best qualified. Right-
wingers and members of the defunct Screen Playwrights began
to scream that *they* were being blacklisted by the Communists
who were overpowering the producers with their propaganda.
This opened them to ridicule. John Ford, acknowledged as
one of the leading directors, made not only *Stage Coach*, but
the greatly admired *The Informer*, written by Dudley Nichols.
It was impossible for them to cry "Red" at *Grapes of Wrath*:
whose screenplay was written by one of the conservative screenwriters, Nunnally Johnson.

In a real sense the late thirties was a time of belated New
Deal awakening and recognition of the menace of Fascism.
It was the time of the "progressive," the anti-fascist, anti-
racist, which we felt best described us. We did not advocate
force and violence to overthrow the government; we did not
engage in subversion; our task was to convince, when possible
through logic and with persuasion, that man could create a
better world. Some of us were eloquent, others not.

In other ways signs indicated that this too was "our time."
In the 1938 California race for governor, we were among those
forces who rallied behind Culbert Olsen, the liberal candidate.

---

*Rarely are these socially relevant classics included in the movies shown on TV today.

One of the issues for us, one that started long before I became politically involved but one for which the struggle never ended until is was won, was the fight to release Tom Mooney and Warren Billings, two active San Francisco trade unionists who were accused of throwing a bomb into a patriotic parade in 1917. Now, at long last, the Communists and the progressive elements in the labor movement, the Upton Sinclair backers of the previous election and supporters of the farm workers in their fight against the Associated Farmers in the lettuce fields in the Salinas Valley, were unified. What we sought from Olsen, as previously we did from Upton Sinclair, was a pledge that if elected he would pardon Mooney and Billings from their life sentences.

He promised, and on the day he was sworn in as governor he kept that promise.

Cedric and I could not miss that moment on January 7, 1939. Twenty-two years in prison on a frame-up constituted an outrageous injustice that made Mooney's cause as much our concern as the Scottsboro Boys and Sacco and Vanzetti killings. We set off in Cedric's car for San Francisco. With scores of others, many non-Party members who had long served on "The Committee to Free Mooney and Billings," we gathered at a hotel for an initial celebration.

The next morning we drove to San Quentin across the recently completed Golden Gate Bridge, a half hour's drive. We were permitted through the gates and waited at the door through which Mooney would come. It was tense. I had a camera ready; this was a moment to record. And when suddenly, unaccompanied, Tom Mooney came through the door there was a wild and joyous cheer. Dozens of people raced to embrace him. I didn't manage to get the perfect pictures I'd hoped for, but got some. We shook hands and embraced, but along with the sense of victory was the feeling of sadness. Mooney had aged grievously. He was heavy, trembling, as he came out. A sick man, surely, but marvelously one who could still smile, accept and give warmth, and even laugh after twenty-two years in prison for a crime he did not commit.

The day was planned. We left immediately in a caravan
of cars for Sacramento, where Governor Olsen was sworn in.
As promised, his first formal act was to announce the pardon
of Tom Mooney. Before the year was out he did the same for
Warren Billings. Tom didn't live to see that day; within a few
months he became seriously ill and died.

But on that day of his pardon we drove back to San
Francisco where a parade was led by the Longshoremen's
Union. At its head walked Tom Mooney with Harry Bridges.
Mooney pointed to the building where he'd really been on the
fateful day — some six blocks farther up Market Street from
where he was accused of being at the time the bomb exploded.

Next morning Cedric and I drove back to Los Angeles,
still tingling with a sense of triumph from the knowledge that,
however minor, we did play a part, we were in and of the
movement that helped bring about Mooney's freedom. It was
food for the soul. It gave me, for one, a renewed determination
never to stop struggling to alter a system that could so criminally deal out injustice.

Growing unity between Communists and left-liberals —
Roosevelt supporters — developed rapidly between 1936 and
1939. The increasing opposition to the Screen Writers Guild
by the producers and their company union, the Screen Playwrights, made red-baiting a popular fad, but proved stunningly
self-defeating when the Guild won the NLRB election and
was designated the legal bargaining agent for film writers.
The strife in the auto industry, the violence, the sit-down
strikes and the failing economy — more than ten million unemployed — brought about a Republican victory in Congress
in 1938, and with it the creation of the House Committee on
Un-American Activities, with the ambitious, violently reactionary Martin Dies, Democratic Congressman from Texas, as
its first Chairman.

Dies wasted no time in attacking his prime target —
Hollywood. He was after headlines, and there weren't many
to be had out of people like Sam Ornitz, Herbert Biberman,

Out at long last! Tom Mooney (l.) with Robert Minor, editor and cartoonist for the Party paper.

myself or even, at that time, men like John Howard Lawson. Although a Democrat, Dies was of the extreme right wing, and his target was Roosevelt and such New Deal "subversions" as the Federal Theater Project. In that time of unemployed millions there were thousands of actors, actresses, playwrights, designers and theater people of all crafts out of work. Hollywood people supported the Federal Theater in every way possible, and those who did became Dies' targets; were they or were they not Communists, subversionists? Writers like Phillip Dunne, a middle-of-the-road liberal, actors such as Cagney, Bogart, Melvyn Douglas, went before Dies to deny any support for his smearing methods. It was clear to the most powerful film people, including many producers, that although Dies' purported purpose was to investigate all "un-American activities," he had no intention of looking into the growing fascist organizations, the Nazis, the Ku Klux Klan, or the American Christian Crusade, headed by the notorious anti-Semite, Gerald L.K. Smith. There was such unity in the industry that Dies, despite the urgings of the embryonic right-wing groups (soon to become organized into the "Hollywood Alliance for the Preservation of American Ideals") could not get the support of the producers, and never came closer to Hollywood than San Francisco.

Radio broadcasts and newspaper headlines on August 24, 1939, caused an earthquake around the globe whose shattering tremors recorded high, frightening marks on Hollywood's political Richter scale: a non-aggression treaty had been signed between Nazi Germany and the USSR.

It just about shattered what had become an informal coalition between Party members and progressive-minded, liberal writers, actors and directors. The Hollywood Anti-Nazi League, in which so many had been active and influential, lost its most important members and was forced to change its name, which only proved to the opposition that it was nothing but a political front for the C.P. from the very beginning. Members of the Party, too, were thrown for a loss, if not out of the ball game, by this sudden decision.

Yet for some, like myself, the treaty was far from incomprehensible, and the disarray meant only that we had more work ahead of us than ever. How to make it clear to those who felt injured, betrayed, that this non-aggression pact was not a military alliance, that it was necessary for the USSR to buy time, since it was now clear that the Western Allies were trying to turn Hitler around against their common enemy, the Soviet Union. It was clear to me and countless others that the Soviets needed time to prepare their defenses. Moscow's tactical move was a response to many events: the "neutrality" of Britain, France, and the United States in 1936, when the Nazis and Mussolini's forces helped Franco overthrow the legally elected democratic government of Republican Spain; Prime Minister Neville Chamberlain's sell-out of Czechoslovakia at Munich; the takeover of Austria without a murmur of protest from the Western powers. So we argued — forcefully, far from always successfully.

Suddenly the Soviets attacked the heavily fortified border between themselves and Finland. Up went the scarcely concealed gleeful cry of the opposition: "Poor little Finland!" And there we had another formidable task. How could it be made clear that the open fascist, Baron Mannerheim, head of the Finnish Government, would open another major avenue of invasion of the USSR similar to Czechoslovakia. History told it, but not the press of the Western allies: following the 1917 Bolshevik Revolution, the new Soviet Union gave Finland, long a Czarist colony, its independence. Then, during the Civil War and the aid given the White Generals by the Western Powers, Germany and Britain moved into Finland and installed Baron Mannerheim as its "fuehrer." He then proceeded to build the most heavily fortified border in the world between the two countries, all paid for by the Allies. After which, Mannerheim became Hitler's ally.

It all seemed so gruesomely simple; Finland was an avenue into the Soviet Union and had to be blocked. And if indeed the Hitler-Stalin pact was for the purposes its critics claimed, why would the Soviets attack their ally's ally? So we tried to make clear, but ours were whispers in a storm.

In 1939, before that storm broke, Burt Kelly offered me the most exciting assignment since *The President's Mystery*, three years and ten screenplays before. He had been given Nathaniel Hawthorne's classic, *The House of the Seven Gables*. Why Kelly had the assignment was never quite clear: perhaps because the book was in the public domain and therefore did not have to be purchased, or maybe because of a new star, Vincent Price, who had just been successful for Universal in our potboiler mystery, *The Invisible Man Returns.* A young writer, Harold Greene, had done a treatment and Burt wanted me for the screenplay. Universal grumbled; my salary was now up to perhaps six hundred a week.

Burt had the power, and I went to work. Deep changes in the character relations were required, and I changed one of the principal characters, Holgrave, from one Hawthorne described as a "radical" with only abstract philosophical tendencies, to an active Abolitionist. *The House of the Seven Gables*, in 1940-41, showed Northern capitalists of 1850 engaged in illegal slave trade; it was a radical bombshell. With Front Office trepidation, the film was made, despite fears of a Southern states' boycott. Joe May was director. Because he was a refugee from Germany, and had made only one film in this country (the aforementioned *Invisible Man Returns*), it was felt that his command of English had not yet been established and I was assigned as his dialogue director.

When the film was finished and ready for release, the executives at Universal became even more alarmed upon seeing it. They accused Kelly — and me, of course — of writing radical politics into the film and emphasizing them in the shooting. Their anxiety was caused by the abolitionist's role, and the villainous Northern slave trader. Yet in the main the reviews were excellent. Margaret Lindsay as Hepziba was eloquent; Vincent Price and the rest of the cast were outstanding; and, to our astonishment, no critic had apparently read the book — either before or after seeing the film. No reviews that I saw remarked upon the changes from the original. So much for critical scholarship.

But what were such studio problems or even the Nazi-Soviet Pact and its impact upon the world to me at that time? Fifteen months after Michael was born, Jeffry emerged on the scene, causing a joyful dispute between Jonnie and me as to which of the two was the most beautiful boy in the world. Two babies sharply curtailed her activities and I'm afraid I was not of much help. Although in the Party we were supposed to have more enlightened *views* regarding women than "the bourgeoisie" — and perhaps we did — in practice I'm afraid there was little difference between our male-female relationships and the sharing of duties that existed among those we considered "less enlightened." Jonnie did most, if not all, of the domestic chores.

This is perhaps as good a place as any to introduce a subject that must be in the minds of most readers — whatever their own political affiliations or involvements. Even the readers who have been active Communists themselves are probably unacquainted with the special — indeed unique — situation that existed in Hollywood in the thirties and early forties. Obviously, the Communist writers, actors and directors in the film industry worked and lived entirely differently from Party members in the working class. We were not part of the working class in any ordinary meaning of the term. While some lived modestly because their incomes were limited, at Party meetings in the film industry one met men and women who were earning thousands a week.

The competition among writers for jobs — four, five or

six writers of comparatively equal skills for every job available
— could not help but create destructive competition. The
Party membership was not immune. How did this situation
affect us morally, ethically, politically? To what degree did it
create conflicts between principle and opportunism? How
could it be avoided?

It couldn't. While holding as fast as we could to our political objectives, it was still necessary to engage socially with
those in power, or those close to the powers that can give
assignments.

I was certainly not immune. I was invited to the homes of
prominent directors like Norman Taurog, at whose tennis
court I met producers and directors and entered into limited
areas of their social life. It was common, everyday practice.
In between sets of tennis there were always drinks and shop
talk, and if one recently had written a film that received good
notices, actors and producers were always interested: "What
are you doing next?" It was a common enough way of life
everywhere, but perhaps much more intensely so in this "Film
Colony," as the industry was all-too-accurately described.

But the jungle environment led to far less innocent incidents
than tricky job hunting, rubbing elbows and other parts with
important people.

In such an environment, along with opportunism, sooner
or later comes corruption. That critical year 1940, Communist
Party member Martin Berkeley was accused and brought up
on charges of attempting to steal another comrade's story
and trying to sell it. I was on the committee which heard the
evidence. The committee found him guilty.

To my astonishment the majority of the "jury" let him off
with a severe verbal reprimand. I was in the outraged minority
which had demanded his expulsion from the Party. The
majority's reply to my stand frankly stated it was based upon
fear. Were he expelled, Berkeley could do great damage by
naming perhaps as many as fifteen or twenty members. I
argued that this was short-sighted, and that I wanted my

vote for expulsion recorded wherever such things are filed.

This "trial" could not be kept secret in the Party and created a great deal of controversy. And our fear would return to haunt us a dozen or so years later. In 1951, Berkeley was one of the first "friendly" witnesses to name former comrades to government investigators. Whether he started in 1939 when the Party let him off so lightly, or sometime later, it is impossible to know. But Berkeley evidently sometime started a systematic search, in ways unknown, to collect names of Party members in and out of the film industry. By 1951 he claimed to identify 153 members, of whom sixty-odd were writers. Callously he named them all. I cannot help but wonder whether the Party, out of fear that perhaps twenty members such as myself might have been named by him then, did not make the tragic mistake of permitting him to remain and become the informer who started the landslide for the congressional committees a dozen years later.

There is another theory held by some about Berkeley. There was a rumor that he was subpoenaed to appear before the Un-American Activities Committee in 1951 and replied by telegram that he was not then nor had he ever been a member of the Party. According to this theory, the government confronted Berkeley with proof of membership. His telegram then became possible evidence of perjury. Threatened with at least three years in prison, he caved in. Perhaps so, but this theory still doesn't account for Berkeley's list of 153 names.

The two years of the "Nazi-Soviet Pact" were trying times. Along with philosophical and ideological differences, there were many problems, conflicts, clashes of personalities. One of the difficulties during Party leader Earl Browder's "Democratic Front" period was that people joined the Party not so much out of deep intellectual and humanist motivation, but on the basis of personal friendship. In his memoirs, Dalton Trumbo confesses that this was one of his main reasons; he wanted to be with his friends.

And some must have believed the stories of the opposition: that we controlled not only the Writers' Guild but writer employment. There were a few who opportunistically joined in the misconceived belief that Party members had the power to get them jobs.

It was many years later that I learned that sometime in 1940, the FBI placed spies — agents and informers — on my trail. That they were working closely with the Motion Picture Alliance and the Un-American Activities Committee is now clear from their records. When expelled Party member John Leech publicly named members to a Federal Grand Jury, we knew something like that was going on, but there never was any proof until many years later.

Despite the attempts to keep membership secret, as I have said, it was not difficult for the opposition to make some pretty accurate guesses. The conflicts, personal and political, were not all that well-concealed. Lawson and I became objects of open opposition in the Guild and he, brilliant intellect and fearless activist, seemed to me to go overboard in what I considered his dogmatic projection of Earl Browder's line. John was not merely 100 percent for Browder's "Democratic Front" line; he was 120 percent for it. At the end of the war, Browder published his political philosophy in a book called *Victory and After*, which practically abandoned Marxism for social-democratic collaboration with capitalism. This, followed almost immediately by a letter of criticism from a leading French Marxist, Duclos, ended Browder's leadership. But until then John seemed to hold fast with Browder. There was sharp, at times bitter, conflict. It was something less than a harmonious period.

It would be a serious error to rely solely upon such generalizations as the above to describe that and other periods. There was harmony in the Party, and there was conflict. Many examples of autocratic, or bureaucratic, attempts to impose a "line" could be given, but this is one I recall vividly, since I played a central role.

During this period, when writers in Hollywood were experiencing the euphoria of victory following the NLRB elections, we were visited by the Central Committee Cultural Director. He was sent from New York to speak of the strategy we should consider following our recognition by the producers and the signing of a contract.

About twenty-five writers — all of our Party people — were called to a meeting. This soft-spoken, learned man gave an Educational, as it was called, on the role in trade unionism intellectuals and creative artists must play. He concluded that, following the signing of the contract, we must educate and organize the screenwriters to take their union — our union — and join the CIO.

Those present looked at each other in astonishment. This man, whatever his erudition in Marxism, knew nothing of the social and economic status of Hollywood writers! It was utopian to imagine that men and women whose salaries ranged from thirty-five dollars a week to thirty-five hundred, whose life styles and reasons for organizing into a Guild were so varied, could actually take on the task of organizing not only their own colleagues but lead the various craft unions into one industrial union. It was utopian!

Objections were raised; the reality of the industry was pointed out. Nothing fazed him. This was the line, and it must be followed.

Soon it was eleven o'clock; people began to leave. A motion was made; it was seconded. The question was called. I objected. There had not been sufficient discussion.

I voiced my objections, obvious reasons why this industry could not be arbitrarily seen in industrial union terms.

As the pros and cons were argued, the membership left until there were only four of us left. It was perhaps one o'clock when the chair again called the question. The vote

was taken. Three in favor, one (myself) against. Carried. I
was angry. I said this was railroading of a leftist, dogmatic
position. There was shock at my speaking this way to a member
of the Central Committee. I was rebuked for my tone and
words. Had there not been ample discussion? Was that not
democratic?

"Yes," I replied bitterly. "Reducing the voters from twenty-
five to four. It was democracy — by exhaustion." And I left.

The next day I learned that our Comrade from New York
was furious. He believed I was a Trotskyist; he would bring
the matter up with the top leadership when he returned; I
would be expelled. I shrugged; if that's the way it was, let it be.

But it wasn't. Whatever happened in New York I don't
know; that was over forty years ago. The motion that was
passed never saw the light of day. Neither it nor my expulsion
was ever heard of again.

But for me, by then all this had become part of a way of life.
I was embattled in many ways, and I felt the stronger for
being in the thick of it.

The defeat of Finland and our defense of that mini-war
brought fury down upon us from the America Firsters and
their allies; they particularly tried to destroy the progressive
movement in the Guild. As late as 1941, more than three
years after we had won the right to bargain collectively for
the writers, the producers still used every known method to
stall negotiations. Red-baiting was the principal weapon.
Liberals inside the Guild were faltering, fearful of their association with us. We knew it was then a question of using
organized labor's most powerful weapon. With the industry
doing well in the theaters, anticipating greater and greater
profits, which meant more and more films, those of us on the
Executive Board won a resolution to strike, and a date was

set for the membership meeting at which the vote would be taken.

Professionally, those were busy and successful days for me. I had completed a screenplay, a mystery-comedy at Warners for Errol Flynn, called *Footsteps in the Dark*, which had been started by John Wexley, and we shared screenplay credit. And during that time Brian Marlowe had a stroke. As he partly recovered, I went to his house and we wrote an original story called *Among the Living*, which we sold to Paramount. Brian could not get out of bed, much less work at a studio, and when I finished the assignment at Warners I immediately went to Paramount to do the screenplay on our story. It was part of the deal that along with the price for the story we would do the screenplay. They put one of their contract writers on to work with me. I missed Marlowe, but the times were so critical for the Guild I was grateful to have Garrett Fort, an experienced film writer, to share the work.

Strike, strike! There was strike talk everywhere: on every studio lot and lunchroom, in Musso Frank's, in Stanley Rose's. Many writers were fearful, justifiably so. If we struck and lost, the leaders and those who supported them would certainly be blacklisted; the warning of this eventuality had already been widely publicized.

It was this fear that brought a prominent young writer, Dore Schary, a proudly self-proclaimed liberal, to my Paramount office one morning. He told me how influential I was, and begged me *not* to use that influence in favor of a strike. He was at last getting somewhere in the industry; he had children to support, a mortgage to pay off; he could be ruined. I replied there were many children and many mortgages, but if we stuck together we could win. It was then he said something I remember well because he lived by that philosophy to his end. "Why stir up a stinkpot? You're doing okay. So am I."

The meeting hall for the strike vote was packed, the atmosphere taut. Many spoke for, few against. Some of us expressed confidence that a near-unanimous vote would force the producers to sit down and bargain. If those in the room refused to write, the producers could not survive with the handful of Screen Playwrights. Five or six hundred writers a year out of our more than a thousand members were working. *We* could close them down. And we could bargain not only for the obvious rights, which we had announced almost eight years before, but for more — for pensions, for royalties, for control of our material, for the protection from the butchering of that material at the hands of incompetents, many of whom were not even writers.

The strike vote was overwhelming in favor, almost unanimous. A strike deadline was set, a bargaining committee was nominated, and I, as one of the Executive Board members was elected to it.

Our estimate of the producers' loudly professed declarations that they would never bargain with us was correct. A few days before the strike deadline the Executive Board received official word from the Motion Pictures Producers Association that they were prepared to recognize us and start collective bargaining.

But even then, with the date to start negotiations set, Y. Frank Freeman, former head of Coca Cola Corporation in Atlanta, now inexplicably the Chief Executive of Paramount Pictures, urged the producers to bring Martin Dies out to investigate. Being from Georgia, Coca Cola Freeman didn't understand why Hollywood producers didn't take him seriously. Dies was not invited.

10

Hollywood Discovers an Ally

That first night of writer/producer negotiations found some of our committee of five — certainly myself — tense and uncertain. Not that the demands we sought to achieve were unreasonable: minimum wages, writers to arbitrate screen credits, a 90 percent Guild shop, and, the toughest of all, control of our material. We ourselves were divided on the control issue, not in principle, but on the complicated machinery we'd have to use if it were granted. When the producers might employ two, three, four or more writers to complete one script, whose work of the four would be controlled, by which writers? Yet the principle was something some of us believed paramount to achieve; the way to implement it was still unclear.

We met for dinner at Dave Chasen's restaurant in Beverly Hills, in a private dining room upstairs. When I arrived some of the producers and a few of our members were already there at a small bar, chatting amiably enough. I sauntered over and one of our group introduced me to a man whose head was partly turned.

"Lester, meet Cecil De Mille." He turned. "Mr. De Mille, Lester Cole."

De Mille, of course, didn't recognize me or my name. He smiled, extended his hand. I kept mine at my side. There was an awkward pause, and the Guild chairman, Sheridan Gibney, looked at me inquiringly, embarrassed. Not De Mille. He eyed me keenly and said, "Have we met before? I'm afraid I've not a very good memory."

My answer came almost instantly. "About on a par with your conscience." I turned my back, walked to the bar. Later I explained to Gibney.

Our bargaining committee quickly decided negotiations might run more smoothly if I were replaced by someone whose relationship with a member of the other side did not have a hostile personal past. I agreed and resigned. For the next meeting if I recall, none other than Dore Schary, of all people, replaced me. The negotiations were extensive, but there was no strike. We won our first contract.

Schary, of course, did even better. Sometime after we won the contract, a brief item appeared in the corner of page one in *Daily Variety*, announcing that Dore Schary had been engaged in an executive capacity at MGM.

Jeffry and Michael

Meanwhile, our Ranchito Street farm flourished with beautiful fruits and vegetables, fresh eggs, more walnuts than we could give away and, of course, our two sons. They grew rapidly, were healthy, and Jeffry, always trying to catch up with his fifteen-month-older brother, had already begun to show his envy. Mike could walk, and at six or seven months all Jeff could do was crawl. To demonstrate his frustration, he would sneak up behind his unsuspecting sibling and take a ferocious bite out of the calf of his leg. Screams, flying fists, bloody noses, soothings and comforts and scoldings. He soon learned to walk and that crisis was over.

In that period the situation in Europe was becoming dis-
hearteningly tense. The USSR had issued clear warnings about
what it believed would be the consequences of the Munich
Pact. The League of American Writers called a meeting in
New York to determine policy in this international crisis and
other matters. Between assignments, it was possible for me,
as a member of the National Executive Board, to go to New
York and participate in the discussions. Once I made the
commitment to go, I had a sudden pang of guilt. I'd be so
close to Baltimore, and it was almost twenty years since I'd
seen my father. I'd never met his wife and never seen my half-
brother, Jerry, who was by then eighteen, a freshman at
Johns Hopkins University, ambitious to become a doctor. I
wrote and said I was coming East and would like to stop off
on the way.

By return mail came a joyous letter, perhaps thirty pages,
handwritten. Pop had followed my career, and the family
had seen all my pictures. He knew of my trade union work,
and couldn't wait to see me. The letter went on and on.

It was mid-afternoon a week later when I arrived in Baltimore and went straight to his factory. Up a flight of stairs in
a shabby old building, I entered the shop, where, his back to
me, Pop was standing at a long table covered with the layers
of material, a cardboard or wooden pattern on them and his
knife skillfully cutting through along the edge of the design.
There were six or perhaps eight Black and Puerto Rican
women sitting at sewing machines.

I had entered the shop through the office and was greeted
by a small, pleasant woman, about a dozen years older than
myself, who introduced herself as Clara, my father's wife.
She led me into the shop, called "Henry!" When he looked
up and saw me, he came running, and it was the warmest
embrace, along with kisses on my lower face and neck — I
stood six or more inches taller than he.

Into the office we went, talked about my children, and he
eagerly looked at the snapshots I'd brought. Proudly, they

showed me a picture of Jerry, whom I would meet at dinner that night. At the mention of dinner, Clara excused herself and hurried home to prepare it.

There was, among the women at the machines, one who was in charge, and my father told her to close up that night; we were leaving. And then suddenly he reminded himself of something and hurried me over to a small showcase where his latest product was on display. "Pick some, Lester. What you like. As much as you want."

They were handsome, stylish ties, and I selected a few. But on turning them over I suddenly realized something was missing and looked up at him, stunned, as if demanding an explanation. Perhaps he'd forgotten to mention it or hoped I wouldn't notice; he started to tremble and was on the verge of tears.

"Lester. I can explain. Yes, no union label. You see Roosevelt, this New Deal, it's wonderful for workers in big factories, but this little place, so small, just six women, if I had to have a union shop, I couldn't keep going." He took my arm and forced me toward the women at the machines. "Come, ask them how I treat them. Like a father. Ask them if they want a union, ask them!" I tried to turn away. It was too much. His eyes beseeched me to understand.

So this was the once-militant union organizer, the stump speaker for socialism. All that went through my mind was the old song, "Look for the Silver Lining," which the garment workers' union had paraphrased, "Look for the Union Label." And it wasn't there. I don't know what made me say it, or why I thought of my mother at that point, but impulsively, as if sympathetically, I said, "And of course it costs plenty to send Jerry to college."

"No, no!" He was tearful. "Jerry has a scholarship. There is no way a small business like this can be a union shop. No way!" He reached to the showcase, "Here, take." I selected three ties. I had to. It was as if his life depended on it. Then we left.

Jerry was a nice boy, eager to know about movies, and the evening passed pleasantly enough. But I left the next morning no less disturbed. Was there something I had to learn? Or unlearn? Did time do this to a man? Business? Was it inevitable?

Burt Kelly had moved from Universal to Paramount, again as an associate producer, and again called me for work. The film was called *Night Plane from Chungking*, and, if I recall, Donald Ogden Stewart and three other writers had preceded me. Once again, a stitch and a patch, another routine job. My salary increased again, but what did it really mean? Jonnie and I in those days of "Poor little Finland" felt anything but secure. Her fear for the boys, then still toddlers, was real enough. True, our Ranchito house and acreage were paid for. We had some money in the bank. But unemployment was always on the horizon. There was no security. Who could tell? Unable to work at MGM for all the years I'd been in Hollywood, my agent now told me word was out that RKO was barred to me. We decided to find a haven.

In more recent years, Oregon has become a favorite fishing area. We loved the Cascade Mountains, Diamond and Crater Lakes, and the rivers — the Santiam, McKenzie, Rogue — whose tributaries were filled with trout, and, in season, steelhead and salmon. Why not a modest farm up there, near the fishing? A place that would be self-supporting, which we could buy with the money from the Ranchito place. We hoped to find a farmer to run it for us, share the profits, and live independently, however modestly it may have to be, should the necessity arise.

We talked to friends about it. Michael Blankfort, who had been the film and theater critic on the *Daily Worker*, the Party paper in New York, had come out and was working in films. One evening, speaking with him, we told him of our plan, and he became strangely enthusiastic. It turned out Blankfort had a close friend who was the district organizer of the Party in the Salem, Oregon, area. The man was both a carpenter by trade and a marvelous dairy farmer; he had been in the area for some time and would certainly help us find a place. He might even want to work it and share the profits with us. We asked Blankfort to write and say we were coming.

If anything hastened our decision, it was the heightening of the political tension in the Guild. I was running for a second term on the executive board. An accelerated campaign to oust us in favor of a liberal-conservative coalition had taken shape and was pressing hard. Each year, prior to elections, a nominating committee was selected by the executive board to choose candidates. This year, in the spring of 1941, three members of that committee wrote a letter to the executive board complaining of an attempt of some committee members to breach the constitution of the Guild. They wrote:

> At the opening meeting of the nominating committee when the names of Lester Cole and John Howard Lawson were proposed for re-nomination, the five members who voted against their re-nomination were unanimous on two points. The first was that these two members had served the Guild well and faithfully. The second was, because of the political opinions held by these two members, they were not fit to hold office in the Guild. To further augment that argument, they stated a certain percentage of the membership felt the same way, and that they therefore were justified in removing these two names for consideration for renomination.*

The letter continued by quoting from the Guild constitution, showing the argument to be clearly illegal. The executive board instructed the minority on members' constitutional rights. We were nominated and elected by large majorities. I became treasurer.

---

*Screen Writers' Guild files, 1941.

But the conflict would continue, the opposition would never cease, and their success would come when the time in history made it almost inevitable. This I firmly believed, and I had to be ready.

It was with the wind blowing that way that we drove the boys to Oregon and met Blankfort's friend who indeed was knowledgeable and already had five farms for us to look at. We were delighted to learn of his experience and willingness to run the place and share the profits, if there were any. We soon found a farm we liked nine miles out of Salem, the Oregon capital, on the edge of a little village called Turner. Forty acres, thirty-five in cultivation, a house for us, a cottage for the organizer and his wife.

June 22, 1941 was a day of great rejoicing for the America Firsters, Father Coughlin and his fascist radio report from Detroit, Gerald L.K. Smith and his American Christian Crusade. At long last their prayers were answered — the Nazi invasion of the USSR had begun. Almost immediately, leading generals and statesmen in the West were predicting, with scarcely concealed glee, that those Russian peasants would go under within six weeks before the mighty Wehrmacht. And with that glorious conquest, the politics in this country could turn out President "Rosenfeld's" pro-commie mob, and the wholesale clean-up of the undesirables could begin in earnest.

But in some incomprehensible fashion, those "stupid peasants" and their "godless" leaders, with their women and children mangled and slaughtered, bombed to fragments, retreated but never gave up. Instead of the war being over in six weeks, six months later Pearl Harbor was bombed and we were at war, and *allied*, for God's sweet sake and humanity's everlasting shame, to those very same atheistic, communist bastards! As heroic resisters, the industry leaders now saw the Russians differently. There was pressing work to do. We had to show the true nature of the enemy. Anti-fascists, even those who, like us, were "premature" understood the nature of this enemy. We could write about him. Those in jeopardy before were now in demand. Patriotism and profits once more went hand in hand.

A pressing and irritating matter of a personal nature hit at the same time. The next spring between jobs, on a visit to the farm, from which we had received glowing reports from our comrade-partner, we discovered it to be in a shambles. The man was an alcoholic; it was apparent immediately upon his greeting. His wife's nervousness showed. Three cows had died. The fields had not been planted. It looked a total ruin.

It was Jonnie who saved the situation. Her older brother, Dick, an all-around farmer-mechanic-builder-handyman, still lived in the little town of Chico with his wife, three children, and Jonnie's aging father. To our astonishment, Dick was eager to take the place over. I fired the comrade. Dick and his family moved up within two days, during which Jonnie and I struggled with the milking machines. Who was more astonished that we could work them — the cows or ourselves — we never discovered, but the arrival of the Prior family was a superb relief. From then on all went well. The farm prospered. Within two years we bought the forty acres of excellent pasture land that lay beyond the wooded hill on the edge of the farm, and as long as the war lasted the place afforded Dick a good living and us a wonderful holiday headquarters. Jonnie's father tended the beautiful vegetable garden. Dick's wife canned fruit and vegetables and berries. Even the old man's death, a few years later when he was well past eighty, was peaceful; he simply went in his sleep.

I was called back shortly to an assignment at Warner Brothers to rewrite a script written by John Wexley, a fine playwright and film writer. Wexley's credits included such notable plays as *The Last Mile* and such films as *Confessions of a Nazi Spy,* and the Bertolt Brecht story, *Hangman Also Die*, about the murderous Nazi, Gauleiter Heydrich. He had been assigned then to a frivolous comedy murder mystery called

Footsteps in the Dark, which was to star Errol Flynn. It was hardly his style; I rewrote it; John and I shared screenplay credit.

Around that time Pep West's new novel, *The Day of the Locust*, was published. When he gave me an autographed copy with the words, "Just don't hate me, will you?" I read the book with some uneasiness. Anticipating my criticism when I'd finished, he said, "I can only write one way. If I were to put into it, along with those stumblebums and phonies, the sincere, honest people who work here in Hollywood, and are making such a great fight, the whole fabric of this peculiar half world I attempted to create would be badly torn apart."

"Okay, Pep. But if you want to know what I think. . . ."

"I knew what you'd think months ago. That's why I didn't show you the manuscript. You would have convinced me, and I wouldn't have written anything."

We laughed. Nothing could break our friendship, we were certain. Not so. A week later he and Eileen drove off with their second love, a hunting dog, in the back of the station wagon on a duck-hunting trip at the Salton Sea. Pep promised us a feast; word was out the ducks were there.

They never returned. A notoriously bad driver, Pep was so absent-minded and careless behind the wheel I would never permit him to drive when I was in the car. They shot their limit and were speeding for home. At a "T" in the road, Pep simply overlooked the "STOP" sign and zoomed out into the highway. A speeding truck crushed them; they were killed instantly. It was an incredible shock to us all. The grief weighed mightily on Laura Perelman, Pep's sister, but no more than it did on Ruth McKenny at this sudden loss of her sister Eileen. We all grieved. Jonnie added to her sadness a feeling of guilt; knowing what a poor driver Pep was, she felt she had not sufficiently impressed upon Eileen the danger we knew existed.

During the next year at least half a dozen of the first pro-

Soviet war films were in production. At MGM, where anti-Soviet films such as *Ninotchka* had been the style, they were preparing a script titled, *Song of Russia.* Jack Warner had happily agreed to Franklin Roosevelt's request that he film a popular, current book by the American Ambassador to the USSR, *Mission to Moscow.* Even Paramount's Y. Frank Freeman caught the spirit for our new ally. He bought German refugee Stefan Heym's book, *Hostages,* a series of exciting stories of the Czech underground during the Nazi occupation.

I was brought in to write the screenplay, my first of three films about the war. I knew the book; I was excited. Buddy De Sylva, whom S.J. Perelman and I had the pleasure of beating to the punch six years before at Twentieth Century Fox, was now a Paramount producer. When I arrived at the studio he sent for me. He was alone in his office, and his greeting was surprisingly cordial. He told me to sit down because the story he was about to tell me might knock me off my feet. He could not tell it when S.J. and I were at Twentieth, he said, but now with Winfield Sheehan dead, or what amounted to the same thing, out of the industry, he could.

The story was this: Sheehan was visiting London in 1934 (the year before Sid and I worked for him at Fox). He was, of course, entertained nightly, heavily dined, and even more heavily wined, and in that condition saw a number of musical comedies. There was one he particularly liked — or thought he did — and ordered the company's London man to buy it. It cost a fortune, but he planned to make it his major picture of the year. Back at the studio, Sheehan waited eagerly for De Sylva to deliver our script, and when finally we had it ready for him, he read it and exploded: who dared to change not only the lines but the whole goddam story? It was unrecognizable. Buddy, who we knew had followed the script, much as we disliked it, brought him the original libretto of the musical he had bought. It was only after looking at it that he realized that, perhaps a little drunk, he had given his

London man the wrong title, and he had bought the wrong musical. Embarrassed, he swore De Sylva to silence. The project was coffined and quietly buried.

So now, Buddy said, this belated apology. I laughed with him and was sent off with his best wishes. Obviously I had judged him wrongly; he really seemed a decent sort of guy.

Frank Tuttle, a director of comedies and melodramas since Paramount's days of silent movies, was assigned to the film. I knew him as a member of the Party and felt, should any political problems arise with De Sylva, I'd have an ally.* Assigned to the script with me was one of the studio's most experienced writers of comedies and melodramas, Frank Butler, a very amiable, completely apolitical man. Butler's salary was at about two thousand a week, and the common practice then, a purely business matter, was to make certain no contract writer was ever unassigned. Put him on anything whether he was right for it or not, so long as his salary could be written off on the picture's budget and not charged to studio overhead.

We went to work. Butler, experienced, certainly contributed to what was a difficult problem of construction, selecting from the eight short stories incidents and characters that could be woven into a single, coherent dramatic narrative, and to our gratification each sequence we turned over to Tuttle and Sol Siegel, De Sylva's associate producer, met with warm approval. At the end of perhaps ten weeks, we'd completed the rough first draft of the screenplay and promptly submitted it to De Sylva.

The next day we were called to his office. He was exuberant, lavish in his praise, congratulated us warmly. In fact, he said, it was perfect, absolutely perfect, with the exception of one minor detail, which in the course of polishing in the final draft we could take care of with our hands tied behind our backs. Siegel, as usual, nodded vigorous assent. But Tuttle's

---

*I mention Tuttle's Party affiliation for reasons which will become clear later.

averted eyes gave me my first sense that something was wrong. It was "political."

Buddy made it seem as if the change were so trivial he'd first tell us the good news. They had signed Luise Rainer for the starring role. She had recently finished *Good Earth* at MGM, for which she won an Oscar. Real box office. And then he went on about the rest of the cast, and I sat waiting for the bad news. It came as the conference was about to end, an all-but-forgotten triviality.

"Oh, about that little change. It goes this way: Now you have the dame, Rainer, the daughter of a wealthy Czech industrialist who collaborates with the Nazis, right?"

I nodded, waiting.

"Okay, so on this night like you got it her old man is giving a party for the Nazi bastards. The way you have it now she can't stand them. She hates them; to her they're murderers, bastards, criminals of the lowest kind. She can't stand to even talk to them, right?"

"Right!" chimed Tuttle, Butler and Siegel. I nodded, sensing with dread what was coming.

"So the next morning you have her go out and secretly make connections with the underground. At first they're suspicious because they know how rich she is, but she proves herself to them, and they take her in. And there, working in the underground, she falls in love with one of these resistance guys. Right?"

Again the chimes. Again my heart sank lower.

"Okay, fellas," he grinned triumphantly, "here's the change. Simple as ABC. At that party her old man gives for the Nazis — we keep that, of course; it's great — in comes this well-dressed, high-class, handsome sonuvabitch, a collaborator like her old man — we *think*. She knows nothing from politics and couldn't care less. Nazi-Shmazi, a man is a man to her, and here is this gorgeous hunk of meat who looks at her in a way that she melts. Like hypnotized. Before she knows it she's in bed with him, and he is *something*.

She's hooked, and I mean *hooked*! Completely. And it is then, only *then*, that we learn he was *posing* as a collaborator and is really a part of the underground. Great switch? And she's in love, she's never had a lay like with this guy, so what the hell does she care about his politics? Got it? Love, sex, politics, the works. We got it all in one package. It's just that sex hooks her into the underground, not that intellectual political crap. That's all. The only change. The rest is perfect. Whaddya say?"

"Nothing wrong with that," Frank Butler said, and indeed, for him, there wasn't.

I looked at Tuttle. Obviously he was struggling for an answer and looked toward me to take the lead. Christ, I thought, is this guy, who's been here almost twenty years, one of their top directors, afraid to open his mouth?

So it was up to me. I tried to keep calm, and I think I managed to. "Buddy, it doesn't *hurt* the story but, forgive me, it kills it. You see, I'm trying to show that not only men, but also women have the courage inside themselves to rebel against cruelty and injustice. We'll have a heroine that way, Buddy, not just another dame who can't resist a good lay."

He was patient with me. "Be realistic, kid. That's the way dames *are*. Look, fer crissake, let's not get idealistic about dames having principles."

There was silence. I didn't know what to say. It was still up to him. "Agreed?" he asked and looked from one to the other.

Butler was first. "Agreed, Buddy," he said amiably. And Sol Siegel was quick to back him up.

Tuttle was really tortured. "I — I — let me have a little time to think it over, Buddy. There is a point to what Lester is saying."

Buddy then looked at me. "Agreed?"

I knew it meant the job. But the idea seemed so indecent, so obscene, I couldn't go along. "Nope, I don't go for it."

DeSylva was genuinely astonished. "You mean you're

walkin' off it, over this little thing?''

Now, for the first time, on a story that to me was of utmost importance, I alone, not the Guild, was being put to the test. Did I mean what I had said so many times at membership meetings? I felt the eyes of hundreds of writers looking at me.

"Yeah, Buddy. I guess that's what I mean. The story as it is makes sense. Your way it's the same old hack job.'' By the time I got to the door, with Tuttle looking the other way, Buddy stopped me.

"Wait a minute. I know you put your guts into this, kid. Let's put it this way. Maybe I'm wrong, maybe you're wrong. Let's take twenty-four hours to think it over. Each of us.''

I couldn't believe my ears. In all my years, with dozens of producers, Burt Kelly being the only exception up to that time, this was the most reasonable statement I'd heard. I was genuinely touched.

"Thanks, Buddy. That's fair enough. We'll both think about it.''

"Good!'' And he came from behind his desk and shook hands.

The three of us left, and Butler said he'd never heard anything like it, and Tuttle congratulated me and said he'd stick with me now to the end. I glowed inside. I had to hurry home to tell Jonnie. Nothing like this had happened before. Not that it was settled, but that it was even debatable!

The next day I waited nervously in my office, and it wasn't until after lunch that the phone rang. I lifted the receiver.

It was Buddy. "Make up your mind? No, don't answer. I have. We're gonna do it your way.'' It was hard to find my voice.

"Now you and Frank get busy and give me a polished shooting script in a coupla weeks. We're startin' on the sets today.''

"Thanks, Buddy. A hundred times. This is great.''

I got to Tuttle and Butler. They congratulated me. Tuttle said, "And with all due apologies to you, Frank, this is Lester's kind of stuff, and Buddy knows it."

"And I know it," Frank replied generously.

I literally worked day and night. It had to be the best. We turned it in about three weeks later. Buddy promised a great production and Sol Siegel, at his side, also thanked me and hoped I'd be back soon on another assignment.

I walked off the lot on air. A triumph, I told myself, an example of what one can do by being firm, principled, willing to put one's job on the line. I couldn't write about this in the Guild Magazine, but I could talk about it to show writers that it could be done!

A few weeks later I ran into Frank Tuttle at a meeting. He was there with Tanya, his wife, who greeted me. But Frank seemed uneasy, and, after a hasty greeting, started away, as if looking for someone. I looked at Tanya. She knew something and seemed unhappy. Before I could ask her, she said:

"Go speak to him. Make him tell you." I nodded and went to him.

"What's up?" When he tried to excuse himself, I stepped in front of him. "C'mon, out with it. What have you done to the script?"

"Not me, Lester, nothing, I swear!" But he was trembling. "Buddy, it was Buddy. He conned you, but I didn't know it then. He needed you to finish the script, but once it was done, he just had Frank rewrite those two sequences. The way he wanted them."

"And you stood by?"

"What could I do?"

"You're going to shoot it the way they're screwing it up?"

"What can I do?" He was pleading, and he actually meant it.

"I said I'd quit. Why can't you?"

"Sure!" Now he was righteous, indignant. "What would

it have cost you, a free lancer? Three weeks' salary? But my contract has three years to go, no options. There's a little difference there."

More than a little. To a degree, I know now how money ruled all of us there. But there was a stop line for some of us, as time would show, and no dismal depth to which others wouldn't sink.

He seemed triumphant over the point he felt he had just scored.

I suddenly remembered. "Don't you have a right, like any director, or writer, under your contract, to refuse an assignment if you feel you're not right for it."

He tried to speak. Nothing much came out except, "Yes, but, except, maybe —"

"Except maybe," I spit out, "you're a stooge, comrade, or a mouse. Or could it be a louse?"

It was predictable. When the pressure was on some years later, even though he was far from financially pressed and was practically retired, Frank Tuttle sang to the Un-American Activities Committee with the other canaries, and my name was a high note in his song.

Banjo lesson for Michael

Photo by Cleo Trumbo

11

Hollywood At War

From the days in 1933 when we first started organizing the Guild, we were accused of subverting film content in an effort to take over the industry. Following our victory in the NLRB elections some five years later, the opposition to the Guild added another note: The Guild had become a "tool" of the Communist Party, and it would use its power to blacklist all who opposed us.

I can think of only one case during my decades in the industry when a few of us consciously used our influence. It is worth telling because it illustrates the limited extent to which Party members even thought of exerting what power they possessed.

From the late thirties into the World War II years, *New Masses*, the leading cultural/political monthly of the Party, sent an art exhibition to Los Angeles as part of its annual fund-raising drive. There was nothing concealed about it. The publicity made Party auspices clear. These annual affairs were managed by the late George Willner and his wife Tiba. (George was the business manager of the magazine.) They usually exhibited at a no-less-elegant hotel than the Beverly Wilshire. Many fine works by leading left-wing artists were brought out: those of William Gropper, Robert Gwathmey, the Soyer brothers, Raphael and Moses; Phillip Evergood, Anton Refregier and many others.

The exhibits attracted people of all political coloration: wealthy collectors from the film industry, as well as the financial and professional world of Los Angeles. Each year was more successful than the preceeding one.

After more than half a dozen of these annual jaunts, the Willners decided to move with their two growing children to Los Angeles. The best job George could find was as a used car salesman. They were barely getting by. It was the one and only case, to my knowledge, where we attempted and demonstrated "Red Power" in Hollywood. Nat Goldstone was a writer's and director's agent. Perhaps ten of us were signed with him. John Howard Lawson, a few others, and I figured out that between us we were bringing Goldstone quite a few hundred dollars a week in commissions and we'd see what leverage there was in that. We approached Goldstone, told him what an intelligent and knowledgeable man George Willner was, and requested that Willner be hired to become one of Goldstone's assistants and represent us. We had faith in Willner — we trusted him — which, we made pointedly clear, was more than most writers could say about most agents. The leverage was clearly implied.

George was put to work. We had not misrepresented him to Goldstone. He soon earned a reputation in the industry. Enterprising, soft-spoken, intelligent, Willner quickly got to know which writers would be good for what kind of story or script. Soon other writers began to hear about his successes and switched to the Goldstone Agency. Nat saw his business growing and, in a few years, to protect himself against competitors, he offered George a partnership in his firm, which George accepted. He became one of the top writers' agents in Hollywood. That, to my best recollection, was our one and only attempt to show the clenched fist. Just imagine, had we failed, we would not have had one "Red Power" play to our credit!

The people of Leningrad were withstanding the Nazi siege under conditions that aroused admiration the world over, and now the battle for Stalingrad had begun. The Second Front had finally opened with the landing on the beaches of Normandy; at last a feeling of victory was in the air. Admiration for the Russians was widespread; they had become, in the eyes of the majority of the American people, our most valiant ally, and already some producers were looking forward to the bucks to be made out of "victory" pictures.

With the progressive forces once again working together in Hollywood, bringing all their talents to the war effort, some of us felt we should shed the cloak of secrecy regarding party affiliation. During the bleak years, in 1941, Dalton Trumbo had done it: when he finished his eloquent antiwar novel, *Johnny Got His Gun*, he gave it to *The Daily Worker*, which ran it serially. It created a furore, but it didn't hinder him in terms of work (he became one of the highest salaried writers in Hollywood).

Now in 1942, others, including Ring Lardner and myself, wanted to come into the open. Our position on so many political issues made our association obvious, and our silence when accused by the opposition, we believed, weakened our cause. But the Party ruled against it. I was by then Vice President of the Guild. It was argued that acknowledged membership would harm my effectiveness. My reply was that my very effectiveness would prove they had nothing to fear from my membership. I lost the argument. In my second term as Vice-President, Mary McCarthy, Jr. was forced by pregnancy to resign. I succeeded her as president.

It was then held to be even more unwise to go public. Open identification would provide more ammunition for the enemy propaganda against us. Maybe so. When the next Guild election came around, the same cautious attitude prevailed. It was decided I should not run for a second term, since this might create a center-right coalition. After all those years I wanted to win an election like that, but I saw the wisdom in the position and agreed. Emmet Lavery, on a left-liberal coalition, demolished the opposition and I became again First Vice-President.

At Columbia Pictures, its president, Harry Cohn, considered himself a gambler. A conservative, to be sure, but a gambler. One of his executive producers, Sam Bischoff, found a story for which he felt he needed Burt Kelly, then still at Paramount as an associate producer. Kelly liked the story and, with the inducement of a substantial increase in salary, made the change. When George Willner heard of this and the nature of the story, he was in Kelly's office in minutes, offering me for the job. He knew that here was one of the few chances to get me a film that was important. As had become the pattern in such cases, when the film was considered daringly political — meaning historically realistic — the right wing howled "Subversive!" and pointed to it as another example of how the Reds controlled employment among writers. They knew, of course, that this was false, that writers were "cast" for assignments, even as actors and actresses: did they understand the subject; were they familiar with the social forces involved? So when it came to the current vogue of anti-Nazi, anti-fascist films, it was natural that, for example, John Howard Lawson would be "cast" to write *Sahara* and not a rightwinger from the erstwhile Screen Playwrights.

Burt Kelly needed no convincing; he quickly gave me the story to read, but Harry Cohn was not so sure. My reputation as a Red bothered him, and he was afraid I would go politically overboard. It would be a waste of money; they'd have to rewrite. Kelly insisted, and Sam Bischoff backed him up. With great misgivings, Cohn finally assented.

The story was called *None Shall Escape*, by two European refugees, one Alfred Neumann, an established German writer of short stories, and the other Joseph Than, about whom I knew nothing. But they had written a tale of the Nazi occupation of Poland and the extreme torture and human degradation to which the Jews were being put on their journey to the gas chambers. The story was projected into the future: following the Allied victory the Nazi Gauletier was on trial in a Polish court. His accusers were those victims and witnesses who had survived.

From my point of view, the story lacked something: the Jews were passive; they went to their deaths without a struggle. True, some did, but others did not. Kelly agreed; passivity was horror but not drama. A climax was required.

In the story Harry Cohn bought there was a rabbi, an intelligent humanist who, before the occupation, had friendly discussions on freedom and justice with the town's Catholic priest. Now, rounded up with the other Jews of this town, herded on a cattle car, he began to ask his tortured conscience whether all that talk with the priest about fighting for freedom was only that — talk.

When the train (in the screen story) came to its destination, the Nazi guards ordered the prisoners down a ramp to waiting trucks that would take them to the gas chambers. The rabbi's moment of decision had arrived. He turned to his fellow victims — men, women and children — and with what eloquence I could achieve and what passion I already had, I had him exhort them in what might be their last hours not to be herded like cattle to slaughter — but to resist. Then happily, for I could not find the required eloquence in my own vocabulary, I plagiarized. In the course of the speech there was no way to attribute the words I used to their true author. I stole a line made famous by Dolores Ibarurri, known in Spain as *La Passionara*, an idolized woman who inspired tens of thousands of Spanish people and the International Brigades in the thirties. Unforgettable was a speech in which she said these words: "Fight, fight, for freedom, for justice. It is far better to die on your feet than to live on your knees!"

With those same words, the rabbi exhorted his people.

Inspired, exalted, the Jews in the film fought, catching the Nazis by surprise, seizing guns, killing some of them, wounding others by throwing stones. They fought and died, standing on their feet until the end, and some escaped to join the partisans.

The script was accepted by both Kelly and Bischoff and quickly made.

By the time it was shot and edited, I was long gone from Columbia, but Kelly invited me to the studio projection room to see the final cut. I was pleased with what I saw; the script was shot as written and two fine performers, Marsha Hunt and Alexander Knox, were supported by such excellent actors as Henry Travers, Richard Hale and many others. Andre de Toth, a Hungarian who himself fled the Nazis, brought passion and deep understanding to the direction.

Cohn, who rarely if ever bothered reading scripts, was of the "old school" of top executives. With the power of the "final cut" of the film, he could alter a film in any way he pleased, despite writer or director. This was a hangover from the silent film days, when with a subtitle such as "Two years passed, Mary's mother died, but she was blessed with a baby boy," an executive could change the entire meaning of a film. But those days were gone; to change talkies meant to re-shoot, and that meant money. The cheapest way was just to cut.

So when Cohn watched the rabbi, heard his speech, and saw the action it inspired, he was horrified. "My God, this goddam thing is *controversial!* It would be okay if *goyem* (gentiles) made it, but for Jews to blow their own horn on how they're standing up to the Nazis is *chutzpah,* absolute *chutzpah.* It ain't true. Where the hell did Jews ever stand up to the Nazis?"

Then he eyed me and turned to Bischoff. "I warned you not to hire that goddam red troublemaker." It took Bischoff, Kelly and Sidney Buchman, who was present in the projection room, to calm him down. Buchman, one of Cohn's top writers, soon to become a writer-producer, assured him that if it did create controversy, it was of a good kind, and if the Jews did not stand up and fight as I had written it, goddam, they should have, and this picture was showing them in their best light. Not only that, he added, but hundred of thousands of Jews *were* fighting, in the armies of the USSR. That stopped Cohn, almost. "Them Commies, they're suddenly Jews? Atheists, for crissakes!" Then Buchman asked how about the Jews in the U.S. Army fighting Nazis. That finally shut him up.

When the picture was previewed, he was stunned. *The Reporter* review headline read, "Bischoff Picture Magnificent Job." As usual, I received no mention in the review or even in the credits. This omission was made idiotically ironic by this sentence in the review: "One actor is entitled to singular mention. . . his name Richard Hale. The thrilling speech in which, as the Rabbi, he calls to his fellow Jews to fight and die rather than bow another inch will long be remembered." Who wrote that speech? Richard Hale? Sam Bischoff, Harry Cohn? Or *La Passionara*, via this humble admirer?

When the film was released, the *Los Angeles Examiner* saw it as "forerunner of a cycle that will hit the screen; it is a neat, compact and interesting film dealing with the problem of retribution." This review also pointed out: ". . . the speech of the Rabbi is one long to be remembered," and concluded that while it was not a "big picture" (meaning an expensive "A" picture), "its theme promises much and its ideas are sure to bear fruit in every mind."

The film, under Kelly's supervision, was shot in fourteen or sixteen days for under two hundred thousand dollars. We had the pleasure of seeing it get top billing on double bills across the country.

And, as Cohn feared, there was indeed controversy. In some sections of the country where Nazi sympathizers existed in an underground fashion, such as ethnic German areas of Brooklyn and the Yorkville section of Manhattan, stinkbombs were thrown into the theaters. Fights started. There were some arrests. But elsewhere the film was well-received, and in many places when the rabbi called upon his people to resist, and they did, audiences cheered.

This controversy actually helped the picture become a money-maker, which was basically what Cohn cared most about. Then, to his astonishment, the story was nominated for the Academy Award.

Buchman laughingly told me how the day the nomination was announced, in the small studio dining room where the top writers, directors and producers lunched daily, Cohn boasted about the kind of guts he showed in making the film, and he wanted to see more of this kind of stuff from his writers and producers. "Guts, controversy, let's not run away, fer crissakes. We gotta fight like them friggin' Jews did in the pitcher!"

Reviewers may conceal your name from the newspaper reader, but the animosity of a trade paper had little effect upon the producers' eye for profits. In the event your name didn't appear in a review, which might be headed: "Bischoff Picture Magnificent," producers knew what part producers had played in making it so. While publicly they went along with writer anonymity, privately they knew it was the writer who made the difference. And if they didn't, a smart agent was there to tell them so. And Willner told those who didn't know: I had made my last "B" picture.

Two weeks later I was at Warner Brothers to write the screenplay for an important Errol Flynn picture, *Objective Burma*. Alvah Bessie had been assigned to write the story, but after a brief outline of a dozen or so pages he was pulled off by Jerry Wald, the producer, to work on something else, and I had the story and screenplay to struggle with. There was haste — as when wasn't there — and a talented young radio writer, Ranald McDougall, just out from the East, who had never written a film, was assigned as my collaborator. By this time it had become a habit for studios to give me young writers to "break in." Ranald was a pleasure to work with: bright, eager to learn, a facile writer of dialogue; we got along famously.

Raoul Walsh, whose contempt for writers I have already described, was the director. Perhaps all that remained of his former habit was his contempt. For here Jerry Wald held the reins tight, held him to the script, as did Errol Flynn.

This film had its own built-in controversy. It was obvious from the start that Jack Warner had read a synopsis (never the book — heaven forbid!). It was an historical account of the British Army's attempted invasion of Burma early in 1941. The book was called *Merrill's Marauders*, and Warner rationalized that since it was history why pay money for it? (Had he already forgotten his experience with Matthew Josephson and the suit of plagiarism which cost him a fortune on the Zola picture?) Well, he saw Errol Flynn as the ideal American counterpart of Major Merrill, handed Bessie the book, and said change it to American. Bessie objected, told him it was plagiarism. When I read it, I said the same. To no avail. And it was only the location, Burma, that McDougall and I now used; few, if any of the incidents. But when the film was shown in England there was outrage, and Warners paid, in British contempt and box office boycott.

The film was made with the tropical marshes and jungle-like trees in a Pasadena park as the wilds of Burma. Everyone was pleased with the results. When the final script was typed for production, Jerry Wald had put on the cover, "Story by Alvah Bessie; Screenplay by Lester Cole and Ranald McDougall."

McDougall protested, and I found myself in a dilemma. Actually, Bessie had made some contribution to the story, but was it sufficient, considering our changes? McDougall wanted to bring the matter before a Guild Credit Arbitration Board, but Bessie was a friend of mine, a comrade who had fought with the Abraham Lincoln Brigade in the Spanish Civil War and returned to work as a film critic on *New*

Masses. He had come out West only a short time earlier and had but two or three minor screen credits. I was strongly urged to get him a credit on this important film. It was wrong of me; I knew it then, and feel it even more painfully now, almost forty years later. But I did it. I talked Ranald out of going to arbitration. I offered him top credit on the screenplay — his name before mine — if he'd not bring the matter to arbitration, where I suspected we would win over Bessie. I tried to assure him that the story credit was of minor importance, and with the greatest reluctance he went along.

But when the Academy announced that the "Original Story" by Alvah Bessie for *Objective Burma* was nominated for the Oscar, I was afraid to face McDougall!

Well, the Flynn picture didn't win the story award. I think it went to *The House on 92nd Street*, which far more deserved it. McDougall's resentment was close to rage; he was convinced that had we demanded "Original Screenplay by Lester Cole and Ranald McDougall," we had a very good chance of winning not merely the nomination, but the award itself. He blamed me for political favoritism. It *was* political favoritism. I swore to myself it would never happen again.

I had by then been in the Party about ten years, and it had become a way of life. Over the years deep and lasting friendships developed, as did cool acquaintances and actual dislikes. But I think by then I had come to realize that for myself, unlike some others, liking or disliking a Comrade was secondary; the Party was not a social club. I was held far more firmly by the conviction that Capitalism not only is inhuman (or *pre*-human, as Engels had put it) but that the contradictions made the movement toward Socialism, and eventually toward Communism, inevitable, however slow and painful the awakening of consciousness and the struggle. The concept of a world in which no one would profit from the labor of another, was a goal worth struggling for. We thought we'd eventually achieve a state of brotherhood where each would contribute according to his ability, and each would receive according to his needs. To reach these goals required organization, and the Party, whatever its weaknesses or strengths at any given time — and I was aware of both — remained the only viable organization through which to make the struggle.

Perhaps it was this deep feeling that made it possible for me to be less enticed by fame and fortune than many of my colleagues. I was established now. I felt able to speak out and make a front line fight for democratic trade unionism in Hollywood, and I never stopped writing articles and talking at Guild meetings about the need for writers to gain control of their material, to forsake illusory high salaries and opt for a royalty basis of payment, such as the dramatists had in their Guild contract and the novelists in the Authors' League.

The USSR was astounding the world by its resistance. Leningrad, under siege for nine hundred days, with more than a million men, women and children starving, freezing and being bombed relentlessly, was successfully resisting. And the Nazis were stalled on the outskirts of Stalingrad. They were unable to carry out their plan to cross the Volga, turn north, and surround the European part of the country.

It was soon after this real war began that the Party played a major role, along with liberal and progressive film writers, in organizing the Hollywood Writers' Mobilization, whose stated purpose was to aid in winning the war in every possible way that writers and actors could, including enlistment. As writers we were sponsored by, among others, the University of California at Los Angeles, and with them we published *The Hollywood Quarterly*. Dalton Trumbo was its editor for an extended period: our hope was that through the articles published we would both enlighten and inspire others to make a maximum effort toward the winning of the war.

The mini-war — against us — continued unabated. Our enemy was not just the producers, our traditional foe, but also the union which had come to dominate labor in the film industry. This union was the International Association of Theatrical Stage Employees — commonly known as the IATSE. Its leaders were the darlings of the right-wing rags when they proclaimed their unrelenting war against Communism and "subversives" in Hollywood. What all the press ignored was the story of how IATSE's leaders subverted the union by accepting illegal bribes from the producers. Corruption was the name of the game, and these characters were corrupted by Organized Crime as well as the moguls of Hollywood.

The full story of IATSE's corruption didn't emerge until 1949 — and even then, it emerged only because of the dogged efforts of Father George H. Dunne, a Jesuit priest who taught social science at Loyola University in Los Angeles. Had it not been for Dunne's painstaking and courageous research, the truth might never have been known. In 1945, the priest-professor became interested in the strike of the Conference of Studio Unions against the IATSE. He spent the next three years researching the hidden history of the IATSE. The resulting study, *Hollywood Labor Dispute*, was aptly subtitled "A Study in Immorality."

According to Father Dunne, the story began back in 1932, with a bribe in Chicago. The money came from men named Barney Balaban and Sam Katz, who owned a chain of movie theaters in the Chicago area. They were worried about a strike and decided it was worth a twenty-thousand-dollar payoff to eliminate that anxiety. The recipients of the bribe were George Browne and Willie Bioff of the Motion Picture Projectionists Union, a part of IATSE. When Browne and Bioff found themselves twenty thousand dollars richer, they couldn't keep from bragging about it, and their drunken boasting soon caught the attention of another speakeasy patron, Frank Nitto, then a top associate of Al Capone.

Father Dunne reports that by 1934 Capone had taken over the union — with George Browne as national president and Willie Bioff as his right-hand man in Hollywood. Balaban and Katz, as pioneers in labor-management relations, soon found themselves with high-salaried executive positions at Paramount and MGM, respectively, and they continued to pay Browne and Bioff, who in turn cut in Capone and Nitto, who reportedly sent a cut back east to Lucky Luciano and his "family."

In 1941, Browne and Bioff were indicted for accepting bribes from the producers. Nicholas Schenck, president of Loew's Inc. (MGM), was the "bagman" who delivered the money each year. The producers screamed their innocence, and then tried to prove that they were the victims of extortion. But the evidence told the story. Browne and Bioff were sentenced to eight years in prison. They appealed over a three-year period, but without ultimate success. Schenck received a one-year sentence for his role in the scheme.

Press coverage at the time minimized the extent of the corruption — conveniently ignoring the mob connections. A few scapegoats went to prison, but the overall reputation of the union was untarnished. Richard Walsh took over as president of the union, with Roy Brewer in charge of Hollywood. They immediately pledged "union unity" and a continuing fight to root out "Communist subversion." The plan was to bring rebellious unions into line by merging them into the IATSE, and to destroy any union they couldn't control. Among the IATSE's targets were the Painters Union (then under the leadership of Herb Sorrell), the Carpenters Union, and the Writers and Actors Guilds.

The producers' corruption of the union and the mob influence in the industry should have made headlines, but the press didn't consider this scandal worthy of investigation. Instead, the focus was on efforts to root out "subversion" in Hollywood. Guild activists were smeared, and personal attacks began to appear in the *Hollywood Reporter* against progressive individuals. The American Legion was quick to support them, and of course Gerald L.K. Smith, leader of the openly anti-Semitic National Christian Crusade, spoke everywhere about the "Communist-Jew control of Hollywood." They were joined by the Detroit Fascist "Radio Priest," Father Coughlin, whose tirades poisoned the air. The Hearst press, alarmed at the war-forced alliance with the USSR, joined when it saw the hopes of a quick Nazi victory over the Communists fade.

Roy Brewer was relentless and powerful. How influential he was in the formation of the right-wing, defeated Screen Playwrights' new organization, the Hollywood Alliance for the Preservation of American Ideals, can only be surmised, but what is known is that once they *were* organized, they and Brewer were allies.

Brewer went after all the independent unions and in 1945 Herb Sorrell, the leader of the Painters Union, organized with the Carpenters the Conference of Studio Unions to break the attempted stranglehold. It was clear that the IATSE control meant the death of democratic unionism; its constitution stated that only the national president has the right to order a strike regardless of any membership vote. It was for that reason the studios paid the enormous bribe annually. It was against this that the Conference at last called a strike.

The writers were in a predicament. Many did not support, or want to support, the strike, and among Party people it was far more than a predicament; it was a dilemma. The Party, under its then national executive secretary Earl Browder, had adopted a no-strike position for the duration of the war, and here was this man Sorrell needing our help — even more, in a way, we needed *his* to maintain *our* independence — and we were helpless in any formal way to help. At that time I was either first vice-president of the Guild, or had already become acting president; and the responsibility weighed heavily. We simply could not desert Sorrell in his fine fight nor could we push against the no-strike position of the Party during the war. We believed in it. To this day I am not sure, had the membership voted to support the Sorrell strike, what we in the Party would have done. When it didn't pass, many writers, as individuals, not as Guild members, supported Sorrell and even marched in his picket lines, myself included. Warner Brothers was one of the main targets. Armed guards were on the roofs of Warners' studios, but not to prevent violence in the streets; if anything, their presence encouraged it.

The strike was won, then lost. The Cold War played its part with the arrival of the Un-American Activities Committee. But the record is clear. As Father Dunne describes it with documented evidence, the conspiracy widened and deepened over the years. His study reproduced excerpts from the steno-graphic minutes of the Tax Fraud Hearings in Chicago in 1948 and 1949 against Nitto, Capone and Nick Circella, alias Nick Dean.*

Leo Spitz was the attorney for the Producers' Association, acting as liaison between Bioff and Schenck. A deal was made, as the records of the tax court reveal.

Nitto, Bioff and U.S. Tax Attorney:

Q. What arrangements were made between you and these motion picture executives whom you mentioned?

A. Well, we were to receive $50,000 a year from each major studio and $25,000 from the smaller studios.

Q. By the "major studios," what companies do you mean, Mr. Bioff?

A. Well, such companies as Twentieth Century Fox, Metro-Goldwyn-Mayer, the Paramount Company and Warner Brothers.

Q. And who were the minor companies?

A. Columbia and RKO.

Q. Now, did you convey this understanding and agree-ment to the other heads [of studios; L.C.]?

---

*Father George H. Dunne, *Hollywood Labor Dispute: A Study in Immorality,* (Los Angeles: Conference Publishing Company, 1949).

A. No sir, I did not do that. It was done by Mr. Schenck.

Q. All right. Now the day following the conclusion — or directing your attention to the day following the conclusion of the basic agreement meeting, did you receive a visit from Mr. Nicholas Schenck?

A. Yes, sir.

Q. Do you recall where that was and what happened, Mr. Bioff?

A. I think it was at the Warwick Hotel in New York.

Q. What happened?

A. Well, he brought $50,000 with him.

Q. Nicholas Schenck visited you at the Warwick Hotel and brought $50,000 with him, is that correct?

A. This is right.

Q. Was there anyone who came along with Nicholas Schenck at that time?

A. Well, Sidney Kent.

Q. What did Sidney Kent bring with him, if anything, Mr. Bioff?

A. I think it was $25,000, if I am not mistaken.

Q. Did they give that money to you?

A. Well it could have been to me or Browne. We were both there. I just don't remember.

Q. And these two gentlemen left $75,000 in the room, is that correct?

A. That is correct.

Q. Was that in cash?

A. Yes, sir.

Q. And what did you do with that cash?

A. Well, Browne and I split $25,000 between us, and we gave $50,000 to Circella. [Al Capone's man. L.C.]

Q. Now what about the $50,000 that was to come from Paramount? Do you recall how that was paid, or how it was to be paid?

A. It was in smaller amounts. I think the first payment there was from Mr. Austin Keough, at the Warwick Hotel, he delivered $10,000 or $20,000.

Q. All right. Were there any other payments made, do you know?

A. Well, I don't recall whether at that time we collected from Warner Brothers, but eventually we got all the money.

Q. The entire $200,000 from the four major companies you mentioned was paid, is that correct?

A. That is right.

Q. What was done with that money, as far as you know, Mr. Bioff?

A. Well, Browne and I got one-third and Circella got the balance with the exception of some money I delivered to Paul and Campagna at different times.

Remember, the theater owners, Balaban and Katz, who started in 1932 paying off Browne and Bioff, paid only for the union in the IATSE that controlled the theater projectionists throughout the nation. This new payoff was for Hollywood control, and the two hundred thousand dollars was an annual bribe. For it the IATSE would seek to control the writers, directors, musicians, grips, carpenters, painters — bring them all under IATSE control. The hearings further revealed that Nick Circella dutifully turned over the two-thirds he received to the syndicate. It was against this control that the Painters Union, under Sorrell, sought to break out of the net, organize the Conference of Studio Unions and bring democratic unionism to Hollywood. Yet despite the exposure of Nick Schenck, after Browne and Bioff were jailed, the IATSE held on. Its control over the projectionists in the nation's theaters was its unbreakable power over the Hollywood industry.

It might reasonably be asked: Despite the apparent co-operation and seeming collusion among Browne, Bioff, the Capone-Nitto mob and the Producers' Association, wasn't two hundred thousand dollars a year for all those years really extortion? Wasn't that an awful lot of money just to keep the Hollywood unions under control? The simplest arithmetic will show how profitable that annual pay-off was for the producers and why they willingly paid a seemingly enormous sum.

The number of people steadily employed by the industry ranges between twenty-five thousand and thirty-five thousand. Were they to be well enough organized to seek raises of, let us say, ten dollars a week every two or three years to keep up with the rising cost of living, that would be $250,000 to $350,000 a *week*. Multiply that by fifty weeks a year and the Producers would be paying out in wages somewhere around $150 *million* additional every two or three years.

It is obvious the crime syndicate and the IATSE gave them a very generous deal.

With the birth of the informal partnership between Roy Brewer and the Motion Picture Alliance, the same people again were in conflict. We on the one side, and on the other MGM's McGuinness, Mahin, Rogers, Niblo, Jr., and for additional financial support aging Rupert Hughes brought in his nephew, Howard Hughes, new owner of RKO. John Wayne joined and in the early fifties became its president.

Almost immediately as a result of this informal alliance a statement appeared announcing that its principal goal was to root out communist subversion from the motion picture industry, their euphemism for their intention to destroy democratic trade unionism. They had the aforementioned support from the press once again.

But by now, however ugly their propaganda, the producers saw future markets in Europe only in the event of an Allied victory, and the Alliance was unable to enlist their cooperation. Jack Tenney, a former musicians union leader, was elected to the California legislature and promptly, in classic renegade style, abandoned liberalism to head a California Un-American Activities Committee. Even with that assist, the MPAPAI and Roy Brewer could not convince the producers to support the state witchhunters in an "investigation of Communist subversion." So the opposition contented itself with campaigns of personal slander, of exposure, either through informants within the Party, or the FBI. Most of us, unfortunately, were confident that their time would never come; the period of oppression had passed. That wasn't "revolutionary optimism"; I'm afraid it was closer to Utopianism. It was just that their time had not yet come, and most of us could not see that it would. We firmly believed there would be a total victory, there would be democracy; the Party would come into the open and function as a political party for Socialism.

We were such optimists. I remember a wonderfully cheerful writer, the late Michael Uris, whose living motto was "Socialism by next Tuesday." But for reasons not easily explainable, I didn't share the feelings of my comrades. It would never be that easy; the U.S. and the Soviets were partners to defeat the Japanese and Nazis, not for an era of peaceful co-existence.

And for us the conflicts were not over; they were just beginning. My gloomy prediction was laughingly dispelled a short time later when George phoned to say Jimmy Cagney's office had called and said they wanted me for a screenplay.

"I told them your salary was up a hundred. He said okay. Then I said," George added with wicked glee, "It's not okay until Lester reads the story and *he* okays it."

Such were the illogical swings, the contradictions and the anarchy in the industry at the time, 1945. Greater ones were still to come.

Jimmy Cagney had left Warners and, with his brother Bill as his producer, had gone to United Artists to produce independently. He had bought a story by Garret Fort titled,

Blood on the Sun. Michael Curtis would direct, Sylvia Sidney would play opposite Cagney and, of course (one of the reasons for wanting me), they needed the shooting script in a hurry.

I was more than willing. It was a good story and an important one. We had conferences before I began; I suggested changes, some of which were accepted, others not, but a new ending I proposed was enthusiastically agreed upon. Within a short time my revised outline was completed, approved, and I began work on the screenplay.

The film was completed in December 1944. It was a time, as I've said, of fervent patriotism and tremendous effort for winning the war. The Russians not only had broken the siege of Leningrad, but had routed the Nazis from the fields surrounding Stalingrad and were driving them westward. The Second Front in Normandy had been achieved, and the combined American and English forces were winning major battles in Europe. Victory was in the air, on the land, and in the hearts of hundreds of millions. There was pride and joy — and deep compassion for the families of the dead.

But there was still Japan. And this Cagney film was about Japan in a most provocative fashion. It told the story of an infamous historical document dating back to 1927 that would become known as the Tanaka Memorial, so named because its author, Tanaka, had been the Emperor's military minister. The document sounds incredible today, but it is a historical fact: a carefully conceived plan to conquer the world. The film told of an American reporter (Cagney) in Tokyo in 1931, who learns of the plan, gets the cooperation of a beautiful Eurasian woman (Sidney) and together their mission becomes one of stealing the Tanaka Memorial and getting it out of the country to the League of Nations. *Variety*, in reviewing the picture, said: "It has been years since James Cagney has had a role so beautifully tailored to his talents. . . nor has he ever had better femme support than that provided by his co-star, Sylvia Sidney." They gave me credit, along with Garret Fort, "for major contributions to the successful whole."

The *Hollywood Reporter*, as usual, ignored the other writer's name because of mine, but praised the film. At the preview, the picture shocked me. And after I read the *Reporter* notice the next morning, I suspected something had been said between Wilkerson of the *Reporter* and Bill Cagney prior to the preview.

First shock: on the screen the credits read: Screenplay by Lester Cole, added scenes by Nathaniel Curtis! I had not been informed that anyone had followed me, had written any "added scenes." As I watched the film I saw only my script; I wondered when the changes would come. They finally did; a substitute for my ending had been written, the revised ending they had so enthusiastically approved. Why the change?

At that time, with the War close to victory in Europe, William Randolph Hearst was putting on a campaign for a ne-gotiated peace with Japan as opposed to the U.S. official position for unconditional surrender. My ending of the film attempted to fortify the government decision. I had Cagney and Sidney escape to Geneva where the League of Nations was in session, triumphantly turn over the Tanaka Memorial to the delegates (including, of course, the Chinese, who were to be the first victims of the worldwide plan of conquest). The two pro-tagonists wait eagerly for the debate to start. The Chinese delegate offers a motion; the Japanese delegate asks that the Chinese motion be tabled (which is also a historical fact) and the motion is buried. The Chinese were placid, accepting — they had made a deal.

Cagney and Sidney walked out stunned, defeated. All their efforts defeated by the Chiang Kai-shek government. Bitterly he berates the U.S. for its failure to be a member of the League of Nations; our country, he believes, could have forced the issue to the floor. As they are leaving, three American tourists at the entrance are trying to get in — a man, woman and their son of about fourteen. The guard refuses them admittance, and when the man indignantly says he is an American, Cagney bitterly informs him that the U.S. is not a member of the League. Then he looks at the youngster and says, nodding glumly, "Good luck, soldier." The father frowns. "What do you mean?" Cagney replies, "In the next world war, he'll be just about the right age." They walk out. The couple stares at their son, not understanding. FADE OUT.

It was the elimination of this final scene that produced Curtis' credit. In his ending the Japanese police discover Cagney's possession of the document, and the chase begins through the streets of Tokyo. (Back lot) He slips the document to Sidney, then speeds toward a neutral nation's embassy. Just before he can get through the gate he is shot (only slightly wounded, of course) and falls down. At that point the embassy guards rescue him. The Japanese say, "So sorry. Big mistake. Very sorry. Excuse, please!"

The guards help Cagney to his feet, and the final line went something like: "Yeah, I'll excuse, when we get even."

It all became clear to me then. For months Hearst editorials had been pounding away with that very line; we can negotiate when we've evened the score. Bill Cagney wanted nothing "controversial" such as a hint of our government's demand for unconditional surrender. Evidently Hearst's politics were Bill's. He had gotten to Wilkerson before the preview and that was why, though the *screen* all-too-clearly credited me with the screenplay, Wilkerson's review had these two lines in it, ". . . avoiding all but a hint of delivering a message" and a "thoroughly satisfying ending." Bought and paid for.

But I was furious. After the preview I told Jimmy Cagney that it wasn't just me he sold out, but the American people, and he would hear more about it. Always a decent guy, he seemed embarrassed. I went home that night and started an article for the publication of the Hollywood Writers' Mobilization, the *Hollywood Quarterly*. The preview screened April 26, 1945; my article, entitled, "Unhappy Ending," was published in October, six months later. It exposed the duplicity.

No sooner had it appeared than the following splashed and smeared itself on the front page of the *Hollywood Reporter*:

TRADEVIEWS *by* **W.R. WILKERSON**

• COMES now the HOLLYWOOD QUARTERLY, A "literary" magazine, published by the University of California Press. The first issue of this publication indicates that the motion picture industry is about to take another beating from the many volunteer critics who will take advantage of any outlet in which to vent their spleen against the producers who make the films.

There is a noticeable political drift in this magazine, too, since it is being published under the joint sponsorship of the University of California and the Hollywood Writers Mobilization. Prominent among the editors of the magazine are such well-known defenders of "causes" as John Howard Lawson, Emmet Lavery, Edward Dmytryk, Dudley Nichols, Abe Burrows, Boris Ingster, Sam Moore and Earl Robinson. Lawson, as could be expected, is one of the five top editors. The other gentlemen are on the "advisory Committees."

An "Editorial Statement" gives the tipoff on the true purpose of the Quarterly. It reads: "The war, with its complex demands for indoctrination propaganda, and specialized training, emphasized the social function of film and radio. One of the first casualties of the conflict was the 'pure entertainment' myth, which had served to camouflage the social irresponsibility of much of the material presented on the screen and over the air."

Doesn't that sound familiar?

And sure enough, there is a five-page tribute to the motion picture "genius" of Communist Russia's Eisenstein. In the midst of his glowing praise of Communism's fair-haired boy, the author, Ben Maddow, does a little sneering at such great American films as "The Sign of the Cross" and "Marie Antoinette."

Then there is a honey of a little piece by a left-wing writer named Lester Cole, in which he attacks the Brothers Cagney for making a whopping boxoffice success of "Blood on the Sun." We recommend this article to every producer in town as a good example of the strange workings of the left-wing mind. Any producer who reads the piece will also realize he will find himself the subject of similar bitter criticism if he should employ the services of Lester Cole and then not make the picture EXACTLY as Cole wanted it made.

After damning the Cagneys for editing his political ideas out of the script, Cole then fulminates against the entire motion picture industry. He writes:

"It should go without saying that the desire to make motion pictures of merit and the desire to make a profit are not mutually exclusive. But the right to extract profit at the expense of quality has been repudiated by the American people, and has resulted in laws designed to protect the consumer from industrial misrepresentation. Even Wall Street has an S.E.C., but as yet the bucket shop has not been outlawed in Hollywood. To be reputable or not to be, that is the question. Along with Hawaii and Alaska, Hollywood should make application to join the Union."

We recently took note of the fact that the Hollywood Writers Mobilization is partly supported by the Community Chest. The motion picture industry gives a lot of money to charity and it has a right to demand that none of this money finds its way into the coffers of a political, left-wing group like the Writers Mobilization.

Our people, who really love this industry and want to see it grow from greatness to magnificence, should also remember that the HOLLYWOOD QUARTERLY is being published by the University of California, an institution supported by public taxation. Our tax money is as good as that paid by the left-wingers and, besides, there are more of us.

Legislators who have been investigating some of the irresponsible behavior that goes on at the University of California at Los Angeles might very well probe into the real reasons why a state-owned institution is helping to promote anti-Hollywood and Communistic propaganda.

If anyone thought they weren't out for scalps, this column had to make things perfectly clear. Yet many seemed to feel that since their names had not appeared, the problem didn't apply to them.

Michael (l.) and Jeffry at the farm in Oregon.

Jonnie had just returned from Oregon when the article appeared. Her father, then past eighty, had died peacefully in his sleep, and following his burial her brother Dick Prior told her he had been thinking for some time of finding someone to take his place at our farm. His daughters were ready for high school, and he wanted to come to L.A. And, he told her, not to worry about the farm, he knew we depended upon him. The farm was prospering, and he had received two offers to sell it at a slight profit.

Jonnie was all for selling. She felt the blacklist, so long unofficial in so many places, would certainly now directly affect me. We had by then bought a very modest old farmhouse on a lovely acre in North Hollywood, and she would feel more secure without the worry of the farm in strange hands. And she too felt she did not want our sons to go to a country school. So we sold to the highest bidder, came out a little better than even; I felt the pressure slightly ease. And by that time we had a business manager who had placed us some time before on a very modest budget. Now with the sale of the farm and our savings, which by then appeared substantial, the foreseeable future seemed more secure.

Most friends and many comrades felt I had gone too far in my article against Bill Cagney. One doesn't make that kind of fight for the control of material individually. I argued it was not individual, but our goal in the Guild since its inception. There was nothing "heroic" about my taking it on. I'd been preaching it for years; how could I do other now than practice it?

George kept plugging away for me as if nothing had happened. Carl Dreher and I had been talking about a story we had in mind. I haven't the faintest memory now of what it was about, but my old records show we sold it, again to Universal. Before it was sold, George got me a job on a screenplay, also at Universal, and the world was not quite so bleak. But it lasted only a month. Then nothing.

This was 1946, a year after Roosevelt's death, and the winds of politics had chilled to freezing. Truman, under pressure from growing reactionary forces in Congress (the Democrats had lost sixty seats) opposed them verbally while accommodating them in practice. He signed Executive Order 9835, the "loyalty" oath, which at first ostensibly applied to government employees only, but soon was to spread through industry and the entire educational system. And by that act, which he claimed was to "take the ball away from his opponents," he actually put it into their hands, and it let loose such cagey crooks as J. Parnell Thomas, Republican of New

Jersey, member of the Un-American Activities Committee (HUAC). Truman invited Winston Churchill to speak at Fulton, Missouri, where he made his notorious "Iron Curtain" speech, and the Cold War gathered momentum at frightening speed.

The Motion Picture Alliance for the Preservation of American Ideals was urging HUAC and then Chairman John S. Wood to pay Hollywood an investigative visit, but the producers stalled; they were afraid of that kind of publicity. Besides, Wood was an outspoken anti-Semite, as was John E. Rankin. his committee henchman. Both were Southern racists as well.

So far, Hollywood seemed an island in all the national turmoil. True, I'd been out of work, but other comrades with credits and good screenplays were hard at it; perhaps I *had* stuck my neck out just a little too far in the Guild fight. There had to be *some* casualties!

And the one morning George called. He tried to keep his voice calm; in fact, he spoke so softly I could hardly hear him.

At last it was clear. Jack Cummings, MGM producer, wanted me for a picture. All I could do was scream, "Jonnie! Me! MGM! Tomorrow morning!"

Now, at this time, when I was the target of an industry fast going to the right, the most right-wing company of all wanted me. After Thalberg's vows (true, he was dead), L.B. Mayer's openly stated position, the power of the Hollywood Alliance at MGM, the villification in the *Hollywood Reporter* . . . what happened? It was impossible! I called George back.

For him it was almost simple: "First, your pictures make money. To them that means only one thing; you're good. Trumbo is working there, isn't he? Don Stewart is there, right? And besides this guy Cummings is very special. He's got his own axe to grind. I'll tell you about it on the way out tomorrow."

With all the excitement — big raise in salary, success, esteem, overcoming all obstacles, who could ask for more? Or who could be that gloomy and pessimistic to believe that this was just another contradiction and it would crumble all too soon? My years of uneasiness vanished. But not Jonnie's.

12

Triumph, The Peak

On the drive out to MGM the next morning, I learned about Jack Cummings. He was L.B. Mayer's nephew. In the ironies that can so easily occur in that jungle, the nepotism had a reverse effect. Cummings had started at the bottom years earlier, as a lowly production assistant. He was very intelligent and really learned the craft, but he made his way up only slowly, painfully. He was resented and put down as "the boss's kid nephew," despite his skill. Finally, because his keen sense of story selection and production ability could no longer be denied, he was given an opportunity to produce two-reelers, shorts. In the course of seeking new talent in Oregon, he came upon Esther Williams. He made a swimming short and she was sensational. He followed it with her first feature, *Bathing Beauty*. It was an instant financial success — well-produced, at minimum budget. Others followed, but Jack really commanded their respect when he made MGM's smash of the year, *Seven Brides for Seven Brothers*. He had come into his own and was looking around for broader fields than escapist musicals.

When we came into his office, George and I found a man of about my age and build whose smile was pleasant but searching. He had a scissor's-sharp mind and, I was to learn, a supreme scorn for the right-wing element that had so dominated the studio. Whether his purpose was to employ me as a gesture of defiance, I never discovered. He told me only that he had seen me at a writer-producer meeting, which he attended as an observer, and liked the way I stood up to the producers. Then he saw a couple of my pictures and decided I was the kind of man he wanted to have working for him.

He handed me a slim hard-bound novella by Mackinlay Kantor, *The Romance of Rosy Ridge.* I liked Kantor's lyrical, romantic style. He was one of the more popular and widely read authors of the time.

Cummings suggested that since it was short, perhaps I could just sit in his office and read it and give an opinion. I did and quickly saw serious problems of adaptation. It was but ninety-six pages in length, the type widely spaced, with a dozen pages of illustrative sketches. The lyrical writing was as much descriptive as narrative. In little over an hour I realized it contained some well-drawn, arresting characters, from an interesting period in American history; but there was far from sufficient dramatic material. To make this a film required not adaptation, but a major invention.

George had gone. I would take a bus home from Culver City. I was sick with disappointment. After being blacklisted for thirteen years at MGM, I simply couldn't take an assignment unless I felt confident I could write it to the satisfaction of the producer. To be fired at MGM as a failure was something I could not allow to happen.

I looked at Cummings. "I wonder if you would agree to an arrangement like this —" but I got no further.

"Look, I know it's only a long short story; there are only two real actions in the thing. It goes nowhere, except the love story. But it was an exciting time in our history. That's why I thought you'd be the person for it. The whole thing's got to be filled out, detail, dramatic incidents. . . ."

I nodded. "What I was going to say was this. I appreciate your faith in me. But I'd like to study it and see whether or not I can come through for you."

"Sure, sure. Of course." He got up from behind his desk, and we shook hands. "How about tomorrow, same time?"

I somehow managed to keep from panic. "No. I mean something else. As you've said, it has a warm love story, a couple of melodramatic actions. And it has something else. The residue of hatred and prejudice at the end of the Civil War —"

"Right!" he nodded vigorously. "Right now there's maybe thirty minutes of film there. We need at least a hundred and twenty. That's what I want you to supply."

I took a deep breath. "Mr. Cummings, I'm going to level with you. Since 1933, a dozen years ago, I've been unofficially blacklisted at this studio."

"I know," he said quickly, "and I'm about to put an end to that."

I was touched by the man's sincerity. "I don't know why you're doing it. I'm not asking, only grateful. My problem is, I'm not sure I can find a way to solve the problem this story poses. and I won't work here unless I can find solutions you like. I simply can't come here under salary, grapple with this thing for six weeks, and have to leave. I couldn't take it. Can you see the item in the *Reporter*? 'Cole flops at MGM.' If I come to work here, I've got to know that in my mind and yours, I've found what's needed."

He said nothing. He just studied me and waited. I went on. "If you're not in any great hurry, I'd like to make this suggestion: give me three weeks, at home, on my own time. No salary. If I can come up with an idea that you like, and one that you want me to do into a screen play, great. If what I do is no good for you, it's a private matter between us. Nobody need know. Maybe something else will turn up

here that we can do. Together. I have this strong feeling I'd
be happy to work with you. It would be more than a job."

After a moment, he said, "What is it you will be looking
for that you feel isn't there?"

"The heart of the story. The 'why' of it is missing for a
film. *Why* does this young man come to that family that
night? There must be a reason for his coming and staying,
aside from falling in love with the girl. That's a cliche. He
comes, he stays. He helps with the crops. Why? It's what
makes old Gil suspicious of him from the beginning, and
since the question of whether he fought for the Union or the
Confederate Army is settled half-way through, that's not what
bothers old Gil. And the fact that Gil lost two sons and a
brother in the war and is a dyed-in-the-gut hater of Yankees
is not enough. When bushwhackers who have been burning
barns and buying up land are shot and hanged, Kantor's
story is finished. For him. And for a novella, okay. But not
for a full-length film. Why did this young man come? Without an answer we have no movie. If I can find that, I think
we will have."

I could see I had hit a responsive chord. He said, enthusiastically, "Right, right! You've said what I've been trying to
think through and never got to. Okay, do it! Let's go!"

"Give me three weeks on my own. No pay."

He nodded slowly. "I know. The Alliance guys; McGuinness, Rogers. . . " He stopped pacing and came to me, a warm
smile on his face, one I'll always remember. "Go ahead. I
know you'll do it."

I did. Whether he'd like it or not, so far I liked it. I felt
I'd solved the problem. It was dramatic, even tragic in its
way, but not enough to stop audiences from freely allowing
tears after suspense, relief and a test of a man's courage.

Jack liked it. He notified George he was putting me on at
two-hundred-fifty raise in salary; I now hit one thousand a
week, and at MGM! Among friends in the writers' ranks and
comrades, it was a subject of excited speculation. Dramatists,
playwrights, they were asking the same question of MGM

that I had asked of the motivation in Kantor's book: Why? Why had MGM taken me in?

I had been happily working less than a month, just finishing a detailed outline which would become the basis of the screenplay, when Cummings came to my office visibly upset. He was supposed to start shooting a film called *Fiesta*, to star Esther Williams (her first non-swimming role) and Ricardo Montalban, a handsome young Mexican actor who, Jack was certain, would become a star as a result of the film; Mary Astor and Akim Tamiroff were also in it. Dick Thorpe, an old pro, was the director. The problem: no acceptable script and shooting had to start in Mexico in six weeks. He tossed a script on my desk and said, bitterly, "Over a year the guy's been working on it; six, maybe eight versions. This last one had to be it." He shook his head. "It just isn't there."

I looked at the name of the author. George Bruce. I knew him only too well as a member of the extinct Screen Playwrights, of the Motion Picture Alliance for the Preservation of American Ideals, a man I'd passed half a dozen times in the hallways during the past month, neither of us glancing at the other.

"You want me to work with him?" I was incredulous.

"No, no! Christ, no! Over a year, it's no good Lester, I need a complete rewrite, ready to go in six weeks." He sounded desperate and didn't attempt to conceal it. "I can't blow this; there's already over a million in it; costumes, sets in Mexico, the salary commitments to the actors. . . ."

"Just so I don't have to work with him," I said.

He was relieved. "Just give me a rush, rough draft in a month. Then we can start shooting, and you can write final dialogue ahead of the camera, down there."

I went to work. Day and night. A rewrite, with the story reconstructed, the characters drawn and in conflict, the narrative flowing. It wasn't anything outstanding, but it was shootable. Jack was overjoyed.

"Pack up. It's great! We're leaving the day after tomorrow."

"Where to? What about *Rosy Ridge*?"

"It'll wait. We're going to Mexico. I'm going to need you on the set. Lester, I told L.B. about this; it's not going to do you any harm, believe me."

I was too caught up in the excitement to figure out what I had let myself in for.

The picture was going well. The cast was contented, the director pleased, Jack proud and delighted. He spoke of assignments after *Rosy Ridge*, of getting me a contract, even of the possibility of directing: "Why not? You've got what it takes. We're going to do things together."

Now I was really in a world that was moving away from my origins. Would more personal wealth and power give me greater authority in the working-class struggle, or would I drift away? With the excitement of the work, there was little time for thinking through those matters.

The film was shot, and I was back in Hollywood, joyfully, with the family. A holiday, high in the Sierras. We hired horses, packed in, and went fishing. It was unforgettable. Arthur Strawn, writer, good friend and fishing companion, came along. High up Rush Creek at ten thousand feet altitude, close to the pass where the lakes had golden trout, an unsurpassed California native fish. When Mike, then nine, caught his first, a twelve-incher, it was a rare celebration. We smoked our limits every day, on a contraption rigged from an old abandoned stove, some grates, and the pipes that carried away the smoke. Plentiful trout, both broiled on charcoal and cold smoked, the gourmet delight of the rich, seemed an ironic symbol of my way of life then. But Arthur warned me, "Don't look for symbols. You are *rich*, and you *are* a Marxist. That's not ironic; it's just a contradiction — or, shall we say, dialectical?"

Upon returning home, the most gratifying of all surprises awaited me. George Bruce, who had written the original story and screenplay of *Fiesta*, had read my script and protested my sharing of screenplay. He already had solo story credit, but he still demanded Guild arbitration. The customary arbitration procedure was followed and, to his consternation and

Bullring, Mexico City. Between shots while making *Fiesta*. Producer Jack Cummings, center, author far right.

my almost fiendish delight he lost even more: it was determined the credit should read, "Original screenplay by George Bruce and Lester Cole." It wasn't often a score could be chalked up against a member of the Motion Picture Alliance for the Preservation of American Ideals by a "subversive Red!"

Something even more extraordinary occurred in this first MGM experience. After the thirteen years and over thirty-five films, the *Hollywood Reporter* for the first time had my name printed among the credits when they previewed the film. No world-beater, *Fiesta* got passable notices and was a fairly profitable film, making an American as well as a South American star of Ricardo Montalban. But why, suddenly, did they credit me along with Bruce for the screenplay? In

the past, not only my name, but even the names of my collaborators were obliterated. Was it MGM that they feared? I
never found out, but on my three MGM films, printed credit
was given me in the *Hollywood Reporter* reviews—and at a
time when the campaign they were mounting against me was
reaching a climax.

I returned to *Rosy Ridge*. Looking at it afresh, after ten
weeks, I reexamined the changes and additions I planned.
Some were major, most importantly the "*why*?" I would like
to illustrate the filmwriter's task by going into some detail
regarding the writing of this script to show that the job is
actually more than writing "camera angles." It is a dramatist's
creativeness in visual terms and in dialogue not found in the
book. This is one of the reasons I have always fought to have
control of our material, as the dramatist does in the theater.
I had it in this film, thanks to Cummings.

In Kantor's book, Henry, the stranger, fought with fist
and gun, shot three of the barn-burners, and proved it was
not Yankees burning in hatred, but both sides burning barns
to force farmers west and buy their land cheap. Henry was
acclaimed a hero, and Lissy Anne was delighted when her
poor prejudiced daddy could no longer oppose their marriage,
whatever color Henry's britches, blue or gray.

This was no climax for a film. It offered no answer to the
basic question raised: *why had Henry come*? Why, after politely
being invited to stay the night, had he then so busied himself
on the farm that he never left? He worked like a horse without
pay through the planting and harvesting seasons, with never
a word of explanation. I had farmer Gil McBean torn between
gratitude and frustrating suspicion. The central question for
Gil *and* the audience had to be answered before the film was
over.

The book opens with the McBeans sitting on their porch
in the dusk with a warm spring evening when the sound of

music is heard a short distance away on the road. Curious, they find the stranger, Henry, singing through a thin piece of paper wrapped around a comb. Hospitable, they invite him in for a meal.

I open quite differently, on a map of Missouri in 1865 which bursts into flames, over which in montage are a series of barn burnings, masked horsemen, killings and impoverished farmers leaving the state for the West. The state, divided by the Civil War, cannot heal its wounds; supporters of North and South are in violent civil strife. It is only then that I introduce the McBeans, whose barn is partially burned. They are sitting gloomily on their porch in the dusk. Gil McBean, home from the war, is contemplating with little pleasure rebuilding his barn, and planting the corn without his sons, Ben and Will, killed in the war. Suddenly they hear music, the music of a mouth organ, a harmonica, a tune *they know to be Ben's! His mouth organ!* He wasn't killed, after all, and has come home! They run across the field, wildly, joyously calling his name. Arriving at the fence, they find not Ben, but a stranger named Henry Bohun. After their shocking disappointment, Sairy McBean reminds her husband of his manners. The stranger is invited in and offered a place in the barn to sleep that night. But next morning Henry doesn't leave; cheerfully, he starts to haul water from the creek for Sairy, plant corn with seventeen-year-old Lissy Anne and twelve-year-old Andrew. Afterward, he begins repairing the half-burned barn. Why? Why is he staying, day after day? Gil becomes more and more suspicious of Henry's working like a horse without pay. And then casually, one day, Henry tells Gil he's decided to stay on and help with the harvesting that fall.

Gil goes into a state of frustration. Why, why? What's goin' on? Ah, it's Lissy Anne, all the time sweet-talkin' her and playin' them spoony tunes on his mouth organ. That's it. Gil vows, as in the book, that no damyankee's ever gonna get a daughter of his. Then follow the melodramatic incidents from the book, in which Henry fights, gets beaten, then shoots three villains, and the other two, captured by townsfolk, are hanged. Henry's a hero, and he's proved that the thieves wore *both* blue and gray pants; it had nothing to do with the color of britches.

With that, Kantor ends his book with a brief paragraph: Gil sees the light, permits the marriage, and the wedding takes place with half an acre of dinner tables set out under the trees.

That was the ending I had to change before even starting the assignment. Here is what I did. The scene following the hangings of the barn-burners takes place on the farm. The Yearys, for generations close friends, but Union folk during the War, come to visit for the first time in years. Now that Henry has settled the barn-burnin', they drive up to the fence and say there's good news: "Henry is a schoolteacher and folks has invited him to stay. They will build a schoolroom, and that night there's going to be a play party to raise money for books. Ain't you McBeans acomin'? Ain't Lissy Anne and little Andrew goin' to get some of that there book larnin'?"

What happens then is best told by the screenplay itself:

> Gil just stares, dumfounded, but Sairy manages to nod her head. Old Man Yeary slaps his reins, and the team starts off. His young folks start to sing a song.
>
> INT. CABIN — SHOOTING OUT THE DOOR
>
> The McBeans stand stunned, as the song grows dim in the distance. CAMERA PULLS BACK AS THEY ENTER THE CABIN. There is a long silence. Gil sits down. Lissy Anne watches him. Sairy goes to the fire.
>
> > Sairy (tentatively)
> > Don't reckon there'd be any harm in goin' t' the school, do you, Gil?

Gil (suddenly roaring)

No, by Jackies! I don't keer how many whackers he's kilt, or
if they pin a ribbon on him like a prize bull at a county fair!
We ain't agoin' t' *him*!

Lissy Anne (pleading)

But Pa! Why couldn't we —

Sairy (at the same time)

If we —

Gil (thundering)

I said *no*! He came to this house apurpose. He tol' you that
hisself, didn't he?

(Lissy Anne nods unhappily)

Alyin' about wanderin' the hill when he was lookin' for our
house an' no other. What for? C'n you answer that?

(no answer)

If he's got some truth to him, he'll come here to this house
and say it.

The women find no answer to this, and are startled, as
is Gil, to hear a voice agree with him.

Henry's Voice

That's why I've come, Gil!

They turn.

MEDIUM SHOT — ANOTHER ANGLE

Henry, cleaned up, but with bruised and battered face,
is standing in the doorway.

Henry

All right for me to come in?

Lissy Anne is breathless, her eyes darting from Henry
to her father. Gil nods slowly.

                              Gil

If yer ready to speak out the truth, reckon it is.
        (a grim warning)
But mind yuh, no slick talk, arguin' me into things. I wanna
know straight an' simple; yuh came for a purpose; well, what
was it?

                            Henry

I made a promise.

        Suddenly there is tight stillness; no one of the McBeans
        dares to breathe. It is as if they know the answer, dread
        it, yet demand it now.

                            Henry

I promised Ben.

        That's what they knew. In that moment of silence it
        stabbed into all their minds and hearts. They wait in
        painful silence for Henry to go on. Henry looks at them
        with great tenderness.

                            Henry

I just couldn't tell you when I first came here — with you
feelin' the way you did about Northerners. Maybe you won't
even believe me now; but I hope you will.
            (they wait, and Henry seems to pull himself together
            for the task)
I'd been teaching school over to Lorn Widow Crossing, about
fifty miles north an' west of here. To join up I had to cross
the hills — not far from here — where Agony Creek spills
down from Black Mountain — I hadn't met a soul all that
day an' I was singin' as I always did to keep myself
company —

FLASHBACK   **DISSOLVE TO:**
MOUNTAIN SIDE TRAIL

        A beautiful day. The hillside is a mass of flowers, and
        the creek sparkles like pouring brilliants in the sun. In
        the distance is a small figure, swinging down the trail.

It is Henry. His bundle of belongings is hanging from
a stick held on his shoulder, and at the end of the stick
a pair of shoes dangle from their laces.

MEDIUM CLOSE SHOT

Henry pauses in his tracks and hums quietly as though
he imagined he might be hearing something. And sure
enough, somewhere not far off, the sound of a harmonica playing has joined his tune. Henry grins, sings
four bars louder, and sure enough, the harmonica
swings into the chorus. Henry looks about, then hurries
along to meet the harmonica player.

FULL SHOT — FORK IN TRAIL

Shooting out on the angle of the trail, from the place
where it meets. Although neither can see the other yet
because of the brush and the trees, they are coming
swiftly to the place where the meeting is inevitable.
Both are enjoying the episode, and looking forward to
the meeting. They arrive at the fork, where they become
visible to each other just as the song ends. They stare a
moment, sizing each other up, and their faces break
into friendly grins simultaneously.

The lad who faces Henry is not more than seventeen,
rangy, with a thatch of tousled hair. His cheeks are red,
and like peaches what with their unshaven fuzz,
bleached blonde by the sun. And his name is Ben.

                         Ben
Y' shore make right tuney music, stranger.

                        Henry
Thank you, stranger. Where you headin' for?

                    Ben (grinning)
Where the fightin's thickest, I reckon.

                        Henry
Looks like we're goin' the same way. . . be glad to have yer
company.

                              Ben
Don't mind a mite.
          (curiously noticing Henry's dangling
          shoes)
Ain't them wearin'-shoes?

                    Henry (laughing)
Best wearin' shoes I ever did have. That's why I'm not wastin'
'em walkin'. S'pose the army don't give out any shoes; what
then?

                    Ben (impressed)
Now that's right smart thinkin' —

                                        DISSOLVE TO:

CLOSE MOVING SHOT — TWO PAIRS OF SHOES
DANGLING FROM BUNDLE STICKS

They seem to be swaying in time with the song being
played and sung at the other end of the sticks. ANGLE
WIDENS and SHOWS the two lads swinging happily,
easily along the trail. Henry is singing lustily, and Ben
is playing with verve.

                         Henry
How about some food?

                    Ben (attempted lightness)
Ain't hungry.

                    Henry (shrewdly — having
          noticed the boy carried nothing but what he wore)
Left home in kind of a hurry, didn't you?
                    Ben (uncomfortably)
Don't know what you mean.

                         Henry
Oh nothin', 'cept when people leave in a hurry, sudden-like,
they're liable not to think much about food.

                         Ben
          (grinning — a little shamefacedly)

Well, y'see, Ma — she was down t' the far end of the field, an' I didn't want to bother her none with little things, so I jes' tol' my sister — I was walkin' down the road a piece.

Henry (nodding soberly)
Must've 'spected to meet up with someone like you, 'cause I've got enough food in this bundle for six.

Ben (grinning appreciatively)
Now that's right smart thinkin' —

DISSOLVE TO:

A CAMP FIRE — THAT NIGHT

Beside a creek, the two boys are finishing off their meal, tired, and satisfied.

Ben
When do you reckon we'll git to the main road?

Henry
'Bout noon tomorrow.

Ben (nods, stretches out on his back, and looks up at the stars)
Shore is a pretty night. Good fer corn growin'.

Henry (studying the boy)
'Bout now yer Ma's goin' to be wonderin'.

Ben (matter-of-factly, but with genuine feeling)
It was jes' that I — wal, sayin' goodbye she an' Lissy Anne'd sure start cryin', an' — jes' as soon not see that fer the last thing.

Henry nods understandingly.

I'll get someone t' write Maw a letter fer me.

Henry
I can do that.

                              Ben
                    (with boyish gratitude — grins)
Say, meetin' up with you didn't harm me a mite. Eatin-food,
an' letter-writin'.

                              Henry
Never been to school?

                              Ben
Ain't none in our hills
                    (curiously)
You sound like you got right good larnin'.

                              Henry
Well, enough to teach school. That's what I do.

                              Ben (astonished)
Schoolmaster?
                    (then, impulsively)
You ain't got no right goin' to war.

                              Henry (curiously)
Why not?

                              Ben
                    (wishing he hadn't been so forward)
Course you have; a man's gotta right to do what he thinks
best, but —

                              Henry
But what?

                              Ben
Well, Ma says the most important thing in the world is
school larnin', an' —
                    (again with boyish conviction)
If it's the most important, reckon it's more important than
fightin' wars.
                    (defensively)
That's what Ma says, an' Ma's right smart, even though she
cain't read none herself.

                              Henry
                    (impressed, drawn to the boy)

When they burned down my school, I couldn't see no other
way but to go. Sooner the fightin's over, the sooner we'll put
up another school.

Ben (excitedly)

Same reason I'm goin'. I don't keer a hoot which side
wins —

Henry (sharply)

I do!

Ben (quickly)

What I mean is, that ain't what counts mos'; we got folks
fightin' on both sides. All I'm goin' for is to help get it over
quicker. Fer Ma t' git Paw home; she's worn t' bone amissin'
him.

   Henry nods, moved by the simple way the boy tells his
story — after a pause, Ben looks at Henry shyly.

S'pose you'n me're together — in the same company, Henry.

Henry

Don't see why not.

Ben

I mean —
(hesitantly)
Would it wear you thin larnin' me word-writing? Not much
— jes enough words fer one letter.
(laughs a little)
Ma sure would be surprised to get a letter from me — myself.

Henry (touched)

I'll teach you, Ben.

Ben (gratefully)

Will you? I'll find some way to faver you fer it. I sure will.

Henry

I'll tell you what — you can teach me how to play the mouth
organ.

> Ben

Sure will. Now here — just blow in it — that's all y'
gotta do —

EXT. WOODLAND TRAIL — EARLY MORNING — HIGH ANGLE FULL SHOT

The early morning stillness is shattered by a harmonica
playing. CAMERA PANS DOWN to find the two lads
walking along, their arms locked. But it is Henry who
is playing.

> Ben

You sure learn fast.

> Henry

There's the road.

They swing down the remainder of the trail to the
roadside.

MEDIUM SHOT ON DIRT ROAD

It is little more than a double-rutted wagon trail. As
they arrive at it, Ben holds back, suddenly thoughtful.

> Ben

'Round that bend in the road a way there's a fork. I'll
footrace you to it.

> Henry

Goin' t' teach me footracin' too, are you?

> Ben (grinning)

Sure. Ready?

Henry tucks his bundle under his arm, and Ben does
likewise.

Go!

And they're off.

Ben is in the lead, by about four strides, and both boys
are pacing themselves for a half mile.

CLOSE TRAVELING SHOT — BEN

Confident, running with easy grace.

CLOSE TRAVELING SHOT — HENRY

Not at all concerned about Ben's early lead, apparently.

FULL TRAVELING SHOT

Ben spurts, and Henry does likewise, keeps the distance unchanged.

TRAVEL SHOTS

As they speed down the road and around the turn, neck and neck now.

> Henry (shouts)
> Turn on the speed! There's the fork!

And he does, momentarily gaining on Ben. In a dozen strides Ben is up to him, and they now give every ounce of energy to the last fifty yards.

FULL SHOT — ROAD — AT THE FORK

Henry and Ben race toward the CAMERA, and pass in a dead heat. But Henry passes to the *right of camera* and Ben *to the left*. As soon as they pass out of view —

FULL SHOT REVERSE — THE FORK IN THE ROAD

In the foreground is an old weatherbeaten sign. It reads:

LIBERTY ROAD

NORTH FORK   SOUTH FORK

Henry stops, laughing and puffing, then paces down the North Fork, and Ben does likewise on the South Fork.

                        Henry (laughing)
Nobody won that time.

                        Ben
Reckon not!

CLOSE SHOT — HENRY

Catching his breath, turns slightly to the direction they
will be taking, and waits.

CLOSE SHOT — BEN

He too waits casually for Henry to join him. But as he
waits, a sudden fear seizes him; his eyes go wide in
horror as the inevitable thought occurs to him. Very
slowly, his every muscle straining against the movement, he turns to look at the North Fork.

CLOSE SHOT — HENRY

Already the same fear has possessed him, and now, as
he sees Ben standing rigidly on the other road, his
heart chills.

FULL SHOT — BOTH ROADS, SIGN IN
FOREGROUND

The men stand looking at each other, neither making
a move.

CLOSE SHOT — HENRY

He feels finally that he must break the silence.

                        Henry (his voice strained)
We're goin' the same way, Ben, ain't we?

CLOSE SHOT — BEN

Fighting against the hot angry tears that are rising
in his eyes.

                        Ben
Dunno.

FULL SHOT — CROSS ROADS

Henry starts walking back and stops when he reaches
the sign. He stands there.

Henry

You c'n come this far, Ben.

Ben doesn't move. Henry pleads now.

Henry

Just to here. Reckon we c'n talk about it for five minutes.

Ben (deliberately)

I've got five minutes.

He walks back and the two stand looking at each other
for a long moment. Henry doesn't know how to begin.
Almost wearily, he drops to the large rock near the sign,
and slowly Ben pulls a long stem of grass, starts to chew
it, and sits beside Henry.

SLOWLY DISSOLVE TO:

INTERIOR — MACBEAN CABIN —
CLOSE ON GROUP

Tears are rolling down Lissy Ann's cheeks, and Sairy
is fighting to keep hers back. Gil stands rigid and
Andrew is wide-eyed, fascinated.

Henry (cont'd)

— and from that day on we were — closer than any brothers.
Ate out of the same tins, and shared dry clothes, and
blankets when it was cold. . . It was just two days before the
end that it — Trees were greening up, and the earth was
warm. We knew it was just a question of hours, and Ben
could think only of getting home, and ploughing the earth for
the corn and oats. And seeing you — that's when it
happened. He never thought of himself for one minute
right up to the end; it was all you. . . worrying about the two
years without plantin' and how you'd be needin' his help.
That's when he asked me, and when I promised him — to
come back and help with the work through the first harvest.

No one fights back the tears any longer; they run
unashamed down Gil's lined face, and Lissy Anne sobs
softly.

                         Henry (in final explanation)
We both wanted the same thing; to get the war over with —
to put a stop to killin' — to make this country a free place
for folks — *all* folks — to live in.

                         Sairy
              (after a long pause — in a small voice)
Did he larn writin'?

                         Henry
              (reaches in his pocket and extracts a wrinkled, worn
              envelope, which he hands to her)
He wrote you this letter.

Sairy doesn't even look at it. She just folds it into her
bosom.

All eyes go to Gil — he feels it is up to him now.

                         Gil (slowly)
Was he a good soldier?

                         Henry
Best in the regiment.

Unconsciously old Gil's back straightens, and his
shoulders square. There is another pause. Then:

                         Henry
Reckon I'd better get on down to the school.

No one answers, and he turns slowly to the door
when —

                         Gil (quietly, his voice strained)
Better freshen up, Lissy. You can't go lookin' that away.

The girl's heart leaps, and Sairy almost cries for joy,
and Henry turns to somehow register his thanks; not

with words, because the lump in his throat is too ob-
structive.

Gil

Mought as well drive the team; I'll hitch 'em fer yuh.

Henry (gulping; just *having* to get
out, or they'll see his tears of gratitude)

I'll do that.

And before anyone can stop him he's out the door.
Lissy Anne turns happily from the scene and exits.

THE BARNYARD — DUSK

The wagon pulls out with Henry at the reins. He drives
it to the cabin door. Lissy Anne almost flies upward
into the seat beside him. And the wagon starts off.

EXT. CABIN — MED. CLOSE — SAIRY AND GILL

Side by side. Tenderly she reaches out and takes Gil's
gnarled hand. He doesn't look at her, but the muscles
in his face tighten.

CLOSE SHOT — SIDE OF CABIN

Andrew is combing his hair when he hears Henry call
to the mules to start moving. Startled, he throws away
the comb, and dashes off.

FULL SHOT — LANE — TWILIGHT

The wagon is moving slowly and it is no trick for the
scampering Andrew to catch up with it and scramble
up over the backboard.

CLOSE SHOT — GIL AND SAIRY

Watching the departing wagon.

CLOSE SHOT — A GOPHER HOLE

Paul and Agrippa (the farm hounds) are pawing the
ground away, when suddenly they stop, alert. Through
the evening air comes the sound of music on a harmonica, playing a haunting melody they've heard many
times. With a succession of happy barks, they scoot
away through the underbrush.

LONG SHOT — COUNTRY ROAD

The wagon is moving slowly away from CAMERA some
distance down the road when the two dogs emerge from
the field and start after it. In no time they overtake it
but the two people, with their heads so close together,
don't seem aware of them. Andrew, however, lets down
the backboard for them. They leap on. The board is
brought back into place. Then the wagon is enveloped
in the deepening evening, and only the song remains
as we

FADE OUT.

THE END

The completed script was enthusiastically endorsed by all
concerned, and Jack didn't hold back his feelings of appreciation. Van Johnson, now a recognized star, was hardly
my choice for Henry. Robust, healthy and hefty, he didn't
look like a man who had spent four rough years on the front
lines of the Civil War. But he was under contract and there
had to be a way to eat his salary. We ate it. To our relief,
under the skilled direction of Roy Rowland, he turned in an
excellent performance. And the leading lady, in her first film,
a sweet and simple, lovely young smalltown girl named Janet
Leigh, was a masterful bit of casting on Jack's part. Rowland
brought from her a stunning performance. Thomas Mitchell
was outstanding as Gil McBean, but the great performance

of the film, in my opinion (and of many critics), was that of Selena Royle as Sairy, the mother, whose part I had developed into one of pivotal importance. Dean Stockwell as the young brother was very appealing.

We needed music, of course, both old folktunes of the period and original songs. I pushed for Earl Robinson, who had written "Ballad for Americans" (recorded by Paul Robeson), and Lewis Allan for the lyrics. Allan had written the lyrics to the then famous Black protest song, "Strange Fruit," nationally acclaimed after singer Billie Holiday's recording. Both were known leftists, and there were executive frowns, but Jack couldn't be stopped. His faith proved justified; the music was beautiful and was lauded in the reviews. A few years later, Allan (under his real name, Louis Meeropol) and his wife adopted the sons of the framed and executed Julius and Ethel Rosenberg.

I was hoping for another assignment on the basis of this script, but Jack wouldn't hear of it. Not then. He insisted that I be on the set, in the studio and on location, for the duration of the film. There might be changes needed on location, and he didn't want anyone to monkey with the script. If changes were needed, I would be on hand to make them.

This was film-making for me! Not since working with Burt Kelly had I felt myself part of the process. I will always be grateful to both Burt and Jack for the opportunities they gave me to feel that I was truly sharing in the creative work.

Location was marvelous, a stretch of farmland near Chico, of all places, where Jonnie had lived as a child. When I wasn't needed during filming, I went up a lovely creek that I had fished years before and twice brought back limits of beautiful trout, broiled in the hotel kitchen.

As is customary, the executives saw the final cut of the film before it was ready for preview. They told me that L.B. Mayer cried. Selena Royle as the mother got to him, particularly at the end. When she finally asks, "Did he learn to write?" and Henry handed her the letter, L.B. broke down. He was heard to say it was the finest film he'd seen since *Over the Hill to the Poorhouse*, made in 1920. He cried over Mary Carr, the mother, in that one, too.

I confidently expected good reviews, but the *Hollywood Reporter* astonished me. After their years demanding that this "foreign communist be run out of the industry," their reviewer published the following:

> Van Johnson takes full advantage of the best acting role that has fallen his way since he won outstanding prominence in pictures. In this slice of pure Americana, he plays a back-woods teacher in the Ozark mountains of Missouri during those rugged years that immediately followed the Civil War. Neighbors still fought with each other over issues which made them a divided people in the cause of the North or South. The old help-each-other harvesting days were slow in returning, and some unscrupulous fellows capitalized upon the hatreds. Bands of Ku Klux Klan-like night raiders burned barns and added fresh fires to neighborly feuds.
>
> The excellent Jack Cummings production is based on a novel. The screenplay is fundamentally a love story of simple folk, written with a keen ear and appreciation for the idiom of the Ozarks. Vivid life is brought to the characters by the careful direction of Roy Rowland. It is a splendid job, by turns tender and driving. There are high artistic values to this extraordinarily interesting attraction.

After reading that review, Jonnie and I tried to imagine the confusion in the mind of Wilkerson, the publisher. Did he wonder how a "subversive red," determined to undermine and destroy the nation for which his paper so valiantly (read: profitably) fought, could write something his own reviewer was forced to label "pure Americana"? Could it only have convinced him of how diabolically clever and dangerous we reds were, and how they would henceforth have to increase their vigilance? It seemed so in the coming months.

Variety was more perceptive of the political aspects of the story and the screenwriter's contribution. Its review starts: "Metro is right in there pitching on the anti-intolerance line . . . with Van Johnson, rousing music and an all-around handsome production by Jack Cummings. It looks like a money-maker." And the reviewer continues: "Lester Cole's screenplay, based upon McKinlay Kantor's story, spins an inspiring yarn of life in the border states in 1865 where they were still fighting the Civil War." It goes on to praise actors, director and the songs of Earl Robinson and Lewis Allan.

When the film was released, the reviews nationally were extremely laudatory, and the film became a big money-maker. But of all the reviews that were brought to my attention, the most heartwarming and understanding was the following, in the *San Francisco Evening News.*

Friday, August 15, 1947

'Rosy Ridge' is Inspired Film of Earthy Folk

Post Civil War Problems Told in Dramatic Picture at Fox

By Emilia Hodel

About the time we get to the point where we snarl everytime anyone says "movies" there comes along a picture so fine we renew all our faith in Hollywood and actually turn our prayer rug south.

This happened at the Fox Theater this week in "The Romance of Rosy Ridge."

We admit we raised eyebrows a little when we saw the homespun and whiskers on the advance stills,

and when we heard whispers of "a new Van Johnson." And our air was definitely a "show me" attitude.

But "Rosy Ridge" is one of those pictures that sings along, it is so perfectly conceived.

POETIC

You have the feeling the writers enjoyed working on the dialog. It has a lilt like poetry. The music, some old ballads of Civil War days and some new ones written for the vehicle, are beautiful. There are no trained choruses joining in on the chorus. The singing is down-to-earth and genuine.

The costumes and settings, although about an impoverished period in Southern history, do not scream "theatrical" at you. And the story itself is as honest as the bitter people who fought for what they believed in in the 1860s.

AND there is a new Van Johnson. Poor Mr. Johnson was almost damned by the screams of the bobby soxers and the frothy films he has suffered these past few years.

A REAL PART

"Rosy Ridge" gives him a real part, and he does a sincere job as the school teacher come to teach tolerance to the "blues" and "greys" of a rural community in Missouri.

There are any number of dramatic moments in this picture. It is a credit to Director Roy Rowland that they speak so clearly. And there is a sustained suspense throughout the film concerning the war loyalties of the school teacher.

There inn't any trickery in "Rosy Ridge." It is as if every member of the set knew this film had chances at something more than entertainment. There never seems to be a false moment. Even the colloquialisms, strange as they may sound, rightly belong to the dialog.

"Rosy Ridge" introduces a charming discovery in Janet Leigh, an attractive young woman said to be Stockton born. She has a sympathetic understanding of the role of the young girl with divided love.

Thomas Mitchell develops a strong role as the Southern father. Marshall Thompson as the boy killed in the war. Guy Kibbee, Elizabeth Risdon, Russell Simpson, O. Z. Whitehead and Charles Dingle are some who turn in beautifully etched performances.

But it is Selena Royle as the mother we must give credit as the outstanding member of this fine cast.

The story of reconversion and revenge and the plea for tolerance is as important today as it was nearly a hundred years ago. There are very ugly scenes of Ku Klux night riders, and the message against this viciousness could be read as well by Van Johnson in 1947 California as well as by Van Johnson in the patched pants of a Civil War veteran.

Wednesday, July 2, 1947   THE ╫ Hollywood ╫ REPORTER

'ROMANCE OF ROSY RIDGE' FINE AMERICANA OF EARLY DAYS

Johnson At Best, Janet Leigh Lovely

"THE ROMANCE OF ROSY RIDGE"
[MGM]

Producer . . . . Jack Cummings
Director . . . . Roy Rowland
Screenplay . . . . Lester Cole
Original novel . . . . MacKinlay Kantor
Photography . . . . Sidney Wagner
Art direction . . . . Cedric Gibbons,
   Eddie Imazu and Richard Duce
Songs . . . . Earl Robinson, Lewis Allan
Music score . . . . George Bassman
Edited by . . . . Ralph E. Winters

Cast: Van Johnson, Thomas Mitchell, Janet Leigh, Marshall Thompson, Selena Royle, Charles Dingle, Dean Stockwell, Guy Kibbee, Elisabeth Risdon, Jim Davis, Russell Simpson, O. Z. Whitehead, James Bell, Joyce Arling, William Bishop, Paul Langton.

(Running time — 105 minutes)

Van Johnson takes full advantage of the best acting role that has fallen his way since he won outstanding prominence in pictures. In this slice of pure Americana, he plays a backwoods teacher in the Ozark mountains of Missouri during those rugged years that immediately followed the Civil War. Neighbors still fought with each other over issues which made them a divided people in the cause of the North or South. The old help-each-other harvesting days were slow in returning, and some unscrupulous fellows capitalized upon the hatreds. Bands of Ku Klux Klan-like night raiders burned barns and added fresh fires to neighborly feuds.

The excellent Jack Cummings production is based on a novel. The screenplay is fundamentally a love story of simple folk, written with a keen ear and appreciation for the idiom of the Ozarks. Vivid life is brought to the characters by the careful direction of Roy Rowland. It is a splendid job, by turns tender and driving. There are high artistic values to this extraordinarily interesting attraction.

The MacBean family, father, mother, daughter and small son, are awaiting the return of Ben, the older son, from war, when down the road to their farmhouse swings Henry Carson (Van Johnson) playing a harmonica. He is barefoot, for the shoes he carries suspended from a stick over his shoulder are for work. He promptly pitches in to help the MacBeans with their farm chores. The daughter, mother and kid brother take to him at once, but the father withholds his approval until he can learn if Henry is a fellow Johnny Reb or a despised Yankee. It is not until Henry has won over others in the community, had a hand in organizing some ''play-parties'' and built a schoolhouse, that the MacBean parent learns the truth and gets his comeuppance.

Johnson is great in his characterization, has never been better. Thomas Mitchell is his accomplished self in the difficult role of the MacBean father. Selena Royle is a strong mother, and Dean Stockwell an amazingly talented small brother. A debut of unusual merit is staged by Janet Leigh, a fresh and lovely personality in the first acting she has ever attempted anywhere. It may be remembered that she was a discovery of Norma Shearer.

Charles Dingle has a crotchety backwoodsman to portray, Jim Davis his strapping son, and Guy Kibbee a kindly storekeeper. All do justice to their assignments, as do Elisabeth Risdon as the storekeeper's wife, Russell Simpson as a dancing neighbor, and O. Z. Whitehead as the traveling fiddler. Marshall Thompson has just a bit as Ben MacBean in a reenactment passage, but he makes it memorable. Performances like these are a fine tribute to Rowland's direction.

Sidney Wagner wins an outstanding credit for the photography, and Cedric Gibbons, Eddie Imazu and Richard Duce do right by the art direction. There are a number of new songs by Earl Robinson and Lewis Allan in the show. George Bassman did the excellent music score, and Jack Donohue the staging of folk dances.

— Jack D. Grant.

There was much talk at the time that the film would be sure of an Academy Nomination in 1948, if not an Oscar. But circumstances which followed made it impossible. By nomination time, I had been cited for contempt and blacklisted.

Around that time an urgent matter came before the Guild: I was again first vice-president. With the conclusion of the war two years behind us, the exportation of films started again, and our Guild was called upon to assist in correcting an injustice being done by our industry to French film writers. It appeared that the French producers and exhibitors paid the writers a small sum, equivalent in a way to a royalty, every time a ticket was sold at a movie house. The French writers wanted the U.S. film distributors to take on that obligation when their films were shown here. Our industry balked and brought it to the attention of the State Department for appropriate action.

Harold Salemson, the Guild's director of publicity, had received the French writers' appeal, our executive board had discussed it and approved an action, and I read our proposed resolution to the membership at the meeting, pointing out that in our own fight for royalties, we could do no less than lend assistance in every possible appropriate manner to our French brother writers. The resolution passed. As usual, among the membership were the minority conservatives, and whether Wilkerson acted on his own or after consultation with Eric Johnston, head of the Motion Picture Producers Association, is not known, but the results of the meeting were fed to him in time for an immediate appearance of the following front page:

TRADEVIEWS *by* W.R. WILKERSON

• FOR THE PURPOSE of trying to tag the activity of the Screen Writers Guild generally, and particularly its action proposing to our State Department that the U.S.-French film agreement be renegotiated to give "greater benefit" to the French film writers, we would like to ask Mr. Lester Cole, who authored the motion for SWG passage: "Are you a Communist? Do you hold card number 46805 in what is known as the Northwest Section of the Communist party, a division of the party made up mostly of West Coast Commies?"

The great majority of our people in the studios and throughout the whole industry are annoyed at this writer activity, first, in its attempt to meddle in the PROGRESS of our pictures—to insert itself as a spokesman for our business before our government —second, in its efforts to "party-line" our activities to further Communism throughout the world. All of those people see in the SWG meddling an effort to restrict the distribution of our pictures and their great influence, so that the Stalin gang might feed nations

their brand of dictatorship. They reason that if the SWG was really interested in the welfare of writers, they would move everything within their power to get some relief for the poor writers in Russia and all Russian-dominated countries which punish, with prison and death penalties, all those who refuse their dictation or dare to express their own thoughts in writing; and which cause their writers to work for a yearly pay comparable to the salary that's given our "creators" here for their work for a single day.

Lester Cole proposed the resolution at the last SWG meeting after Harold Salemson, the guild's director of publications, had harangued the meeting for a half hour on the merits of the proposal. Accordingly, a determination of whether he is or is not a member of the Communist party, preaching its doctrines and supporting its cause, would settle a lot of things which good Americans, within and without our industry, now believe of SWG activities.

Cole is a member of the League of American Writers, the American Peace Mobilization, the Hollywood Anti-Nazi League, the Hollywood Peace Forum and Fourth Writers Congress, and many other organizations labeled as Communistic fronts. He, with John Howard Lawson and many other reported Communists and fellow travelers, attempted to defeat Jack B. Tenny, chairman of the Fact-Finding Committee on Un-American Activities in California back in 1942. He has been a contributor to a Communist publication. He was reported to have been one of the chief "yellers" at President Roosevelt to stop the deportation of Harry Bridges, Communist West Coast labor leader. During the period when Hitler and Stalin were pals and loved each other with a non-aggression pact, Cole chairmaned a meeting held at the Hollywood Chamber of Commerce, at which Theodore Dreiser answered Howard Emmett Rogers, who criticized Hitler's ruthless bombing of women and children on the British Isles, with: "If they (the Germans) did away with every man, woman and child in England tonight, this would be a better world."

So again we ask the question of Lester Cole, first vice president of the Screen Writers Guild: "Are you a Communist? Are you a member of its Northwest Division, assigned to that special group known as Branch A of the writers' section and do you hold card number 46805 in the Communist party?" If so, you are in no position to guide the activities of U.S. Screen Writers, as you are attempting to do, and you should be expelled from the Screen Writers Guild, if that guild is to represent writer activities. If you are not, we would be glad to report here that these rumors are false and would like to report, if you will furnish us the information, the real reason, if you are not a Communist, why you attempted to throttle our industry progress and meddle in our industry workings with our government and the governments of other nations.

Needless to say, I didn't reply. The remarks attributed to Theodore Dreiser are a slander. As chairman, I never heard him say anything like that. The Cold War winds were stiffening and the blasts becoming frigid. It was then about six months since Winston Churchill, with Harry Truman at his side, made his "Iron Curtain" speech in Fulton, Missouri, which had officially inaugurated the Cold War. (What was said privately between them was only recently revealed, early in 1979. Churchill had then urged Truman and British Prime Minister Clement Attlee to agree to drop the atomic bomb on the USSR. History shows, of course, that this insane proposal was rejected. But at the time, with that speech, he did fan the flames of hatred and suspicion of a deeply admired and respected wartime ally.)

In May of 1947, before the *Reporter* blast at me and others, a few members of the House Un-American Activities Committee were in Hollywood secretly (Richard Nixon among them) getting interviews with Jack Warner and other studio heads, as well as with the members of the Alliance, who saw victory in the offing.

The appearance of this malicious smear against me turned

all eyes toward MGM. What would they do with their "Commie" employee, "Party Cardholder 46805"? (That was one surprise to me in the *Tradeview*; if that was my "number," no one had ever bothered to tell me. Certainly I never knew it.)

MGM gave its answer in its own way. It called in George and resumed talking contract. We were astonished and could only figure it out this way: not only had MGM valued my work on *Fiesta* and *Rosy Ridge*, but on the completion of the latter I was assigned to work in great haste, turning a radio play into a film for Robert Taylor, a staunch Alliance member who had no assignment and was drawing his thousands a week lolling on the Malibu sands.

To help me complete it quickly, Robert Lord, the producer, assigned a newspaper man, Sidney Boehm, who had never before worked in films, as a collaborator, someone I could help "break in." He turned out to be a writer with a good dramatic sense, and the technicalities came easily. Within a short time we had a script, called *High Wall*. When Taylor read it, he went to L.B. and demanded that henceforth I write all his films. He wanted me put under contract for the length of *his* contract.

Jack had something far more to my liking waiting for me the moment I finished the script for Taylor — a story about an amazing incident that occurred in Seattle, in the new state of Washington, around 1865-70, at the close of the Civil War. The story was recorded in a book written in the 1930s during the brief life of Roosevelt's Federal Writers' Project. It told of one Asa Mercer, an ambitious schoolteacher in a one-room Seattle schoolhouse who wanted to see his state grow. At the time there were only three hundred fifteen "Americans" in Seattle, only twelve of them "American" women. Native Americans didn't count. He offered to bring wives from the East for the three hundred three unmarried men — at a fee of three hundred dollars per man. They all put up their money. Mercer left and brought back women on a ship provided by President Lincoln. I was to take it from there.

One aspect of the assignment worried me. I didn't know what the system was at the studio for selecting the executives. But somehow Sam Katz was made executive producer of this film. You will recall my earlier report on him and Barney Balaban, the two theater-chain owners working out of Chicago in 1932 who introduced Browne and Bioff to the film industry and attempted to bring Mafia control over the trade unions through IATSE sweetheart contracts. This would hardly be the man to look kindly at the story I was about to write. But Jack urged me on; he would stand by.

The feminist theme developed a wonderful role for MGM star Katharine Hepburn as the Civil War nurse, daughter of a physician, herself medically knowledgeable, who through the war worked as a doctor in the Army because of the shortage of medical men (an historical fact). But upon her return after the war, as a woman, she was forbidden to practice as a doctor. So when Asa Mercer was having difficulty persuading genteel women to sign up, (and in my version was forced to take chorus girls from burlesque shows, prostitutes, widows who'd lost their husbands in the war — a very disparate assortment — not quite the "genteel" ladies he promised) the nurse-doctor signs up with the promise she will be permitted to practice medicine there. Asa assures her of an enthusiastic welcome; in all of Seattle there was not one physician. Aboard ship, as they pass around the Horn, she discovers the women have been bought like cattle, that men have paid three hundred dollars for them. She organizes a revolt; they will not be made into merchandise to be purchased. Some prostitutes accept it as nothing new to them; but others argue *they* were making three hundred a *month* in New York, but in this deal only Mercer is getting paid. So when the ship reaches Seattle, and the men on shore sight it, there is a frenzied race to reach the ship and make the best selections.

To their amazement, the women refuse to cooperate. The women win. They come ashore, find work, and make their own choices. Asa Mercer is almost hanged by the men who demand their money back. All ends happily enough, but with a sweet victory for the women. Incidentally, I learned in my research that these women in Seattle and those who followed in the next few years made such a contribution to the good and welfare of the State of Washington that when twenty-one thousand male voters went to the polls in 1870 to elect a President and Governor, on the ballot was a resolution to give women the vote. Only once before in American history had such a vote even been on a ballot; then it was in Kansas, and it lost by something like fifteen hundred to one. But in Washington, in 1870, the resolution lost eleven thousand to ten thousand. It was that historical note which inspired the story.

Well, I'd written a forty- or fifty-page treatment on which I would fashion the screenplay, and Jack sent it to Katz. Two days later we were called into his office.

Katz's expression told everything before he even spoke, but I didn't expect that kind of explosion. He took the manuscript, tore it into shreds, in almost hysterical outrage, threw it into the air and all over the floor while yelling, "Crap! Communist crap! All this goddam *dreck* about women, women's rights! In the kitchen, in bed, that's their place!" And he turned to Jack and said, "Are you nuts? Didn't you read what Wilkerson said about this bastard a couple of weeks ago? What the hell are you keepin' him on for, anyway?"

I was so enraged by this arrogant, corrupt bastard, I started for him. Jack grabbed me and pulled me back. "Come on. Outa here." To Katz he simply said, "You're sick, Sam, sick."

Outside, to my astonishment, he began to laugh. "You know why it hit him so hard. He can't get his up any more. Three weeks ago he went to San Francisco to a hospital and had a transplant. Monkey glands. But they don't work."

"What about L.B.? Can't you go to him?"

He shook his head. "Not now." But when I pressed him he just repeated more firmly, "Not now! I'll know the right time. Don't worry. We'll make it."

Later I found out why. Katz had talked L.B. into going with him to San Francisco for the same surgery, since age had deprived him of that ability also. It can be difficult enough for an ordinary male to come to the realization that he has become impotent, but when a man has the power to bring to his office couch the most beautiful young girls eager for work in films and he no longer can take advantage of the situation, the frustration must be great. Well, L.B.'s transplants were no more successful than Katz's, and though he hated Katz for talking him into it, he still feared Katz would publicize his mortification. Katz had him by his proverbial — and impotent — balls.

Contract negotiations were proceeding. George was asking for more money, a two-year straight contract before the studio would have options, and they were balking. It was at a standstill then, and I saw myself leaving. But not Jack. He had found our next assignment and, before telling me what it was, assured me it would be a welcome substitute until the time we could put *The Mercer Girls* back on the agenda. For ten or more years, he told me, the studio owned a book on the life of Emiliano Zapata, and he wanted to make it.

"The Mexican revolutionary?" I shook my head in disbelief. Along with Juarez, who liberated Mexico in the middle of the nineteenth century, Zapata was a revered national hero. A peasant, a born leader, brilliant and principled, loved by his people as a result of his overflowing love for them and his fight for their rights in the 1910 revolution, his life was one of conflict, learning and an indestructible sense of honor that led him to his ironic and tragic death.

Again I sought to understand this man Cummings, who had become a good friend. We never spoke politics, but his choice of material and his conception of what his films should say to the audience were very close to my own.

Now he handed me the book. I knew of it, a sympathetic biographical novel, by Edgecumb Pinchon. "We bought it along with *Viva Villa* a dozen years ago," Jack said. "You remember, Wallace Beery? Big hit."

"But Jack, Zapata was more than Pancho Villa!"

"That's why it's been on the shelf. I'm taking it off.

"It'll be a great movie," he went on, enthusiastically. "I see Ricardo Montalban as Zapata. Perfect." When I didn't respond, he seemed to sense what was on my mind. "Oh, I forgot to tell you. I told them up front I won't work with Sam Katz any more." He grinned. "I'm free. From now on, no more executive producer. Just Eddie Mannix, general manager, on budget. Nobody else." He smiled again, a little pride and self-esteem spreading with it. "You know, with the last two pictures we made, they can take their contracts and shove 'em. We can go anywhere, pal. We're not such a bad team. Or didn't you know that?"

I nodded, choked up a little. In the fifteen years I'd been in the business, with thirty-odd stories and screenplays produced, there were just these two men, Burt Kelly and Jack Cummings, among the dozen or more producers I worked for who commanded my respect and deep affection.

13

And On To Washington

It wasn't until we were on the plane to Mexico City that Jack told me of his plan and how he had prepared it. My treatment of *Zapata, the Unconquerable* was only schematic. It was about seventy pages in length and relied for character relationships, as well as historical and battle-action details, upon Pinchon's book, referring in the treatment to page numbers in the book. It was written for Jack's eyes only, but to my astonishment he said we needed no more. He felt it had what he wanted in it, so he had put a copy on Eddie Mannix's desk (under three other scripts, he emphasized, so that it would be at least two weeks before he'd get to it). Whereupon he had informed Mannix that he and I were off the next day to Mexico City on a research project.

Fifteen years at the studio had taught Jack just about every angle. When it came to shrewd planning, he astonished me. "While you were working, I got in touch with Indio Fernandez and Gabriel Figueroa. Remember them?"

Of course I did. Fernandez was a top Mexican film director, who in the past had made such outstanding films as *The Pearl* (from the short story by John Steinbeck). Figueroa was acknowledged as the best cinematographer in their country. Jack had engaged them both to help on *Fiesta* a year before. We all became good friends.

"I've got six copies of the treatment in my suitcase. They've promised to read them and give copies to President Aleman, to the Minister of the Interior, and other top government officials. They'll go for this, Lester. And when they do, we're in. This picture is one I can believe in."

"What's the plan?"

"It takes money to make movies, right?"

"So?"

"My hunch is Mexico is going to want this picture so much they'll reach down for some. We'll use both Figueroa and Fernandez — associates on camera and director. A kind of Mexican-American production." In later years "co-productions" between nations would be frequent occurrences, but until then they had rarely if ever been done.

In a week we had our answer from the Minister of the Interior and the President, into whose presence we were ushered to be congratulated. Jack spoke some Spanish, but they used English. Jack was asked what he estimated it would cost to make the film. He said about three million dollars. President Miguel Aleman replied that if Senor Cummings guaranteed to make the film true to the outline he had read, and if the film were shot in Mexico in the historic locations, he was prepared to give MGM one-and-a-half million dollars in services. Troops, uniforms, people, costumes of the period — everything that the company would customarily have had to pay for.

It was, of course, exactly what Jack wanted. He said he would have the head of our studio call for confirmation; after appropriate *abrazos* and handshakes we left. I looked at the smiling Cummings in astonished admiration. "Man, could they use you in our State Department." He enjoyed that.

Back home, Jonnie and I took the boys for a celebration — to Musso's of course — for a dinner, and I tried to explain the magnitude of this film and its clear, unequivocal revolutionary content. I told them excitedly how Jack and I visited Soto y Gama, an elderly retired professor of law from the University of Mexico who, in 1912, a young radical, had helped Zapata write the famed manifesto, *El Plan de Ayala* — a proclamation to free Mexico's peasants from serfdom. This was truly, I felt, the climax of my writing career of almost forty films. How could such things happen? And at MGM! Talk about capitalist contradictions!

Jonnie was thrilled; the boys, not really understanding anything other than that their daddy had achieved some kind of remarkable victory, shared in the elation.

The next morning, Jack announced to Eddie Mannix that we were back and asked if he had read the treatment. Mannix said he had and asked us to come right up to his office.

When we entered, his opinion was all too clear from the expression on his face. And in case we didn't get it from that, his first words made it unmistakable. They were directed at me. "Look, I've been warned. Ever since this communist sonuvabitch came on this lot —"

"Now, wait a minute, Eddie! I'm the one who —" Jack got no further.

"Yeah, I know, I know. He wrote us a couple good pitchers. So what? He's been playin' fer time. How the hell did he ever suck us into talkin' contract with him? He's got you conned, Jack, conned! Set up!"

Jack didn't cave in. Far from it. "Now, look, Eddie! It was my idea. He never knew we owned this book. Yeah, it's about a revolution. So what? How did this country start? Wasn't it with a revolution?"

Mannix exploded. "Goddamit, ours was American! With great Americans. Washington, Hamilton! You comparin' them to the goddam bolsheviks and them lousy spics in Mexico?" He drew in a deep breath; I thought he was going to have a stroke. "Throw it out! None of this revolutionary communist shit is gonna be made here as long as I'm running this joint."

Mannix started his career as a private cop and bouncer, rose to captain in charge of police at the Palisades Amusement Park across the Hudson River from New York City, owned or run by Nick Schenck and his brother. L.B. Mayer met him in the early days when they were making pictures on location there. Mayer brought him out, and put him in charge of security. Over the years Mannix had risen to General Manager of the studio.

Jack never lost his cool. "Will you just wait a minute and listen to what's involved. I figured the picture would budget out at about three million. This treatment has been read by the President of Mexico and most of his cabinet. . . Now wait a minute!" He picked up the phone and said to the operator, "Long distance. Urgent. Mexico City. The office of the President, Senor Miguel Aleman." He turned to Mannix. "I'll let him tell you himself." He held the phone.

"What's there to tell! Anyway, I don't speak Spic."

"He speaks Gringo. Now listen! The Mexican government officially offered us one-and-a-half-million dollars in services down there if we make this *revolutionary* picture. They — *allo? Presidente Miguel Aleman? Buenos dias, mi Presidente.*" And he continued in English. "This is Jack Cummings. MGM Studio. I have here our studio *jefe*, Senor Eddie Mannix. Please tell him what you are offering us if we make this picture in your country. *Aqui es Senor Mannix.*"

Stunned, unbelieving, Mannix took the phone. "Uh, ah, Mister President, yeah, this is Eddie Mannix." He waited, nodded once, then again. "And you'll put that in writing, signed by you?" He quickly covered the mouthpiece. "How the hell do you say thanks?"

"*Muchas gracias, muchas gracias,*" Jack instructed.

"Okay, fine, okay." Mannix wasn't taking any chances with "Spic" lingo. "Look forward to getting it."

He hung up, stunned, shaking his head. After a long suspenseful moment, he mumbled, "A million-and-a-half, a million-and-a-half." Finally he solved the moral problem for himself. He slowly grinned. "Okay, so this sonuvabitch Zapata was a revolutionary. So what? Lotsa people say Jesus Christ was a revolutionary, don't they?" He half-shamefacedly shook hands with Jack. But not with me. "Let's go, Jack. I see Ricardo Montalban as Zapata. Whaddya say?"

"Great idea, Eddie!" Jack said, as if with wondering admiration. "Why the hell couldn't I have thought of that?" Mannix was pleased.

This was September 20, 1947. I started work on the screenplay overwhelmed with a sense of accomplishment, but coupled with visions of doubt and disbelief. Could Jack really pull this off?

The day after the conference with Mannix, George was called in to conclude negotiations on my contract. He stated the minimum terms we would accept, and they listened. I was to receive a straight two-year contract with $1250 a week for the first year, $1500 for the second, with six weeks vacation with pay and, if I wished, another six weeks without pay. Then after two years, they had their first option for another straight two years, the salary being $2000 the first year of the two, and $2500 the second. Same vacations and optional extended time on my own.

Two days later, September 23, I was in the studio barber shop, getting a haircut, when the phone rang. It was for me. Eddie Mannix was on the other end. He was enjoying something.

"Lester? In my outside office there's a U.S. Marshal with a subpoena for you." He chuckled, "You wanna duck while I hold him?"

Despite years of anticipation that the Un-American Activities Committee would finally get around to it, I was unprepared. "Duck? Where to?" I couldn't help laughing — a little hysterically. "Tell him I'm in the third seat in the barbershop. Bring it here."

"Are you nuts? We gotta keep this quiet. I'll hold him here until you come up."

Outwardly it was all very businesslike. I identified myself;

the marshal handed me the subpoena. I went to my office and called Jack Lawson. He'd gotten his at home an hour before.

"Who else?" I asked.

"I don't know."

By afternoon everybody knew. There wasn't a newspaper in the country that failed to carry headlines — smears from "Reds Nipped in Bud: Stopped from Taking Over Hollywood," to more sober headlines announcing the hearings and naming the nineteen "unfriendly" subpoenaed witnesses.

The fear, chaos, and uncertainty are not easy to describe. The reaction among the families of others subpoenaed could not have been much different from that of mine. Jonnie was shocked and fearful. The radio reports frightened Michael and Jeffry. I tried desperately to make light of it. I tried to reassure them it was all newspaper talk, but it was no easy task; my voice could not help but betray my own deep concern. Ugly it was, but not unexpected. For at least ten years I had sensed the possibility of this; now it was here. The ferocity of the radio commentators, the lurid and sensational hints of crime and prison terms were merciless. I dreaded to think what the children would have to face in school the following day.

I don't think we could have ever organized so swiftly out of that chaos had it not been for the ability and energy of Herbert Biberman. He had sometimes been criticized as being domineering and pompous, but it was he who organized it all. In a few hours he phoned the nineteen, received permission to use subpoenaed Academy Award winning Director Lewis Milestone's house for a meeting that night, and arranged to have there the lawyers who had offered to represent us.

We met at eight o'clock. Some of us were confused; we tried to understand what our strategy could be. Was it not just another link with the Smith Act, which was passed in 1940, outlawing the Communist Party as an agent of a foreign power? Browder, then leader of the Party, had been imprisoned; the Party went underground, and not until the U.S. became allies of the Soviets in 1941 was Browder amnestied. Now the cabal of right-wingers, from the Klan to Bundists and right-wingers in both parties saw their chance to take over in the 1948 election and were going to make this the issue.

Three extremely able, experienced attorneys were at the meeting that evening: Robert W. Kenny, civil libertarian, former Attorney General of California under Governor Earl Warren; Charles J. Katz and Ben Margolis, of the labor law firm which included Leo Gallagher;* and Frank McTernan. We had a secretary present, and the nineteen of us: Alvah Bessie, Herbert Biberman, Bertolt Brecht, myself, Richard Collins, Edward Dmytryk, Gordon Kahn, Howard Koch, Ring Lardner Jr., John Howard Lawson, Albert Maltz, Lewis Milestone, Samuel Ornitz, Irving Pichel, Larry Parks, Robert Rossen, Adrian Scott, Waldo Salt, and Dalton Trumbo.

The attorneys were introduced by Herbert. I knew them all. Charles Katz was a particularly close and dear friend for some years, and the others were no strangers. As Bob Kenny began to outline the procedures the committee would employ, I looked over the other eighteen warily. Many of them were Party members I had known for years, others were just acquaintances encountered on various studio lots or met at "cause" affairs. At least three, I was certain, were not Party members.

There wasn't time to speculate how they got swept into the net; Kenny's suggestion, agreed to by the other attorneys, was that we refuse to answer any questions on Constitutional grounds, specifically citing the First Amendment. Free speech included, they insisted, the right to speak or not to speak at all. And we were told of a trick rule invented by the Committee: if after identifying yourself, which you must do, you replied "yes" or "no" to any *further* question, you became obligated to reply to *all* questions on pain of a contempt of

---

*Gallagher was part of the legal defense team for Dimitrov, framed by Hitler in the notorious Reichstag Fire Trial in 1934-35.

Congress charge. But there was an even worse possibility. One of the Committee members might ask, "Are you now or have you ever been a member of the Communist Party?" and you might honestly reply, "no." They then might ask if you knew any members and again you might say "no." If they then could produce a witness who said you *did* know Communists, you faced a certain perjury charge. No cross-examination of their witnesses by your attorney would be permitted. Star chamber stuff!

When someone suggested that we refuse also on the basis of the Fifth Amendment, which permits a witness to refuse on the grounds of possible self-incrimination, this Constitutional ground was rejected, since it would be interpreted as concealment of a crime, and no one there believed he had committed one. In the end, the vote for standing on the First alone was unanimous. We were all heartened. "We'll make a good fight," Herbert said, "and we'll win." We left feeling optimistic.

The next morning I was in a quandary. Should I report to work? Would I be met at the studio gate by an armed guard who would turn me away? Would I be called into Mannix's office and informed that I was dismissed? I decided then I'd go and say goodbye to Jack Cummings and tell him I hoped none of this would hurt him in any way. . . .

The drive out there seemed endless. At the door to the writers' building I found no armed guards, but I did find George. He'd received a call half an hour before saying Mannix wanted us in his office at 9:30. He had phoned me but I'd already left.

George also expected the worst, and we braced for it. Upon entering Mannix's office we were ushered into his inner sanctum by his secretary. He greeted us, introduced us to a man he said was the studio's chief attorney, then handed us a document.

"Read it and see if it's okay."

Whatever their switch was, we weren't ready for it, but when we read the first sentence or two, I asked weakly if I could sit down. It was the contract! Our terms! George and I looked at each other in amazement and then at Mannix.

"Well, it's what you wanted, isn't it?" he growled. "Now, goddammit, go ahead and sign."

We read it through. I signed, George signed, they signed. Only then did Mannix grin. "No half-ass Congressman is gonna tell MGM how to run its business. Okay, Cole. Get to work,"

We left in a daze.

It was incomprehensible; we could only speculate. Were the producers really going to refuse, as Mannix claimed, to allow any small-time Congressman to tell them whom to hire, how to run their business, maybe even what pictures to make? In signing me to a contract the day after the subpoena arrived, were they making their position clear, perhaps as a lead for other studios? Whatever the reason, it was an ecstatic moment in my family, and it heartened the other eighteen when I spread the word, and for hundreds who feared they might be among the next called were the Committee successful.

Then suddenly the confrontation was no longer between the Committee and the Nineteen. We found supporters in a quickly formed group of some of the most famous actors, writers and directors, calling themselves The Committee for the First Amendment. Our supporters included Judy Garland, George S. Kaufman, Bennett Cerf, Lucille Ball, Burt Lancaster, Robert Ryan, John Garfield, Myrna Loy, Frank Sinatra, Edward G. Robinson, Robert Young, Helen Gahagan Douglas, William Wyler, Archibald MacLeish, Humphrey Bogart, Lauren Bacall, Joseph Cotten, Gene Kelly, Margaret Sullivan, Paulette Goddard, Van Heflin, and scores of others, including senators, editors, various branches of the Newspaper Guild as well as the Writers' Guild and the Directors' Guild. They made statements of strong protest and contributed enough money themselves for two national radio broadcasts. It is not difficult to imagine how we were heartened to feel that they saw the fight against the Committee as we did. In our exhilaration I failed then to notice the conspicuous absence among our supporters of the names of such self-proclaimed liberals of the time as Producer Dore Schary and his long-time hench-person, writer Leonard Spiegelgass, — and Ronald Reagan.

I can't recall how it came about that the Committee on the Arts, Sciences and Professions (A.S.P.) sent me to Ronnie Reagan's (then pronounced R*ee*gan) house, to ask him to a a meeting of the First Amendment group. It was early evening when I arrived and Jane Wyman, then his wife, came to the door. I introduced myself, asked to see him, and she became uneasy. Wyman told me Reagan was lying down, not feeling well, but she'd talk to him. She was back in moments, I thought seemingly embarrassed, asked me to tell Humphrey Bogart and Willie Wyler that he was not well, but was thinking seriously about joining them. He would let them know the next day.

He didn't. His career from then on swung more and more to the right. Soon Reagan divorced Wyman, married the wealthy Nancy Davis, and became a pitchman on TV (MC on General Electric Hour). The rest is history in the making. But who would have expected, with his marriage to the very wealthy Nancy Davis, that he would embark on a political career? Probably the success of his close friend, right-wing hoofer George Murphy, who became a U.S. Senator, did it. Reagan became president of the Screen Actors Guild, and joined the Motion Picture Industrial Council. The Council assisted people accused by HUAC, who wanted to keep from being blacklisted by cooperating with the Committee — by informing and perhaps more ingenious devices. Reagan also worked with John Wayne and the Hollywood Alliance, becoming one of the slickest red-baiters in town. Soon he was on his way up the Republican political ladder. His past as a liberal, a contributor to the left-liberal ADA — Americans for Demo-cratic Action — was buried.

At this time, in 1981, he has been in office as President a few short months, and already Hollywood is laughing (jeering?) at such things as his recent statement that there never was such a thing in Hollywood as the blacklist. Numerous articles have been written exposing this attempted fabrication by many "who were there," enumerating incidents in which he participated. One, written in the *Los Angeles Times* (February 12, 1981) by Phil Kerby, a senior member of the Editorial Staff of the paper, tells how, when Reagan was president of the Guild a young actress named Nancy Davis came to him and asked for help: she was being blacklisted because her name was on a list of "Reds." But there was *another* Nancy Davis, who was the Red. Wouldn't Ronnie please help? He did. He cleared her name, a romance began, and they soon were married. Now almost thirty years later, Kerby asks, where is the "red" Nancy Davis? No records can be found. *Was* there another one? And if there was not, and the wife of President Ronnie is one and the same, Kerby is alarmed: with that Nancy Davis as his wife, is not the internal security of our nation in greater jeopardy than ever before?

A week before our departure for Washington I received a phone call from L.B. Mayer's office, saying he wanted to see me at once. What now? I'd been introduced to him by Jack Cummings in the producers' dining room some months ago; Mayer told me he admired my work and was pleased to have me at *the* studio. I thanked him and returned to the writers' table.

Now his secretary ushered me in. He sat behind his desk, his face grim. His office was large and luxuriously furnished, with, of course, the proverbial couch. As I approached, he stretched out his hand, which I accepted; he shook mine warmly.

"I been meanin' to get around to this for days. Look, Lester, to the point. You and Trumbo are a coupla the best writers we got. Your kind don't grow on trees. I don't want to lose you."

"Maybe you won't," I said. "It really looks like we have the law on our side."

"That's it," he said, suddenly agitated. "I don't give a shit about the law. It's them goddam commies that you're tied up with. Break with them. Stick with us. With me. With Jack you'll do what you want. Direct your own pictures? Say so. I believe you'd do great. Dough means nothing. We'll tear up the contract, double your salary. You name it, you can have it. Just make the break."

I couldn't believe the man, yet his eyes were blurred with unshed tears. What could I tell him? How could I make him understand? Would the word "principle" mean anything to him? I suddenly realized all I was doing was shaking my head, and he then roared: "I know about Communism. I know what happens to men like that. Take that Communist Roosevelt! A hero, the man of the people! And what happened five minutes after they shoveled the dirt on his grave? The people pissed on it! That's what you want, Lester? Be with *us*, be smart. You got kids, think of them."

Was he talking out of his heart, or was he now the great con man who'd run this giant organization by hook *and* crook for so many years? Even though I thought that, I was moved.

"All I can say, Mr. Mayer, is thanks. You're a very generous man. I wish I could go along with you, but I can't."

He was on his feet, trembling, pointing to the door. "You're nuts!" he shouted. "Goddam crazy Commie! Get out! Goddam it, GET OUT!"

I got out.

The hearings were scheduled to start on October 20. They would start with the "friendly" witnesses, hand-picked by the Committee, "volunteers," but we had no intention of permitting their prejudice, if not their venality, to go unchallenged if we could prevent it.

Gordon Kahn, one of the nineteen, wrote *Hollywood on Trial,* published a year later, the only accurate book of the hearings, of our supporters and of the reporting in the press. Kahn learned that physical preparations were being made in the hearing room and went to visit it while we, two days before the opening guns, registered at the Shoreham Hotel.

That first evening Gordon told of his experience at the hearing chamber. Cameras were rehearsing J. Parnell Thomas for his entrance. Thomas, Gordon reported, was no more than five feet tall and about as wide. When he approached the rostrum where the Committee would sit and took his chair in the center, he all but disappeared from view. The problem was solved with two telephone books and a cushion so that his bald, round, red-faced head and scalp would dominate. Funny scene, but none of us seemed able to laugh.

A short time later our attorneys returned from their first conference with Eric Johnston and Paul V. McNutt. We were immensely cheered. Bob Kenny had told them that our position was that the Committee was aiming at censorship of the screen by intimidation. They agreed and said they supported our position. Kenny went on to say that Thomas had given press interviews implying that the producers had agreed to establish a blacklist throughout the industry. Kenny then told us Johnston was indignant and quoted him: "That report is nonsense! As long as I live I will never be a party to anything as un-American as a blacklist, and any statement purporting to quote me as agreeing to a blacklist is a libel upon me as a good American."

Our attorneys had shaken hands, congratulated him, and said we'd be delighted to get his message. "Tell the boys not to worry," Johnston then assured Kenny. "We're not going totalitarian to please this committee."

We cheered. We were ready to celebrate and some of us did. But something didn't fit. Johnston was president of the Motion Picture Producers' Association, but did he really speak for all of them? And did the Producers' Association have the final word? If not, who did?

We'd find out soon enough.

The hearings were to start the next morning, October 20, at 10:00 A.M., but Gordon Kahn, determined to miss nothing and write everything, was there at nine. He later reported that hundreds were already waiting, lined up for seats outside the Caucus Room of the House Office Building.

As "invited guests," we and our attorneys had seats reserved for us in the front rows, not far from the other invited guests, the "friendly witnesses." Soon the room was overflowing.

Most of the faces up front were familiar: Jack Warner, Robert Taylor, Ayn Rand (self-acknowledged expert on Soviet Communism), a middle-aged woman we learned was Ginger Rogers' mother, Gary Cooper, that other self-proclaimed expert on Communism, Adolph Menjou — and a dozen others.

The Committee decided to "Fade In," as one writes at the start of a screenplay, on Jack Warner. They'd seen him in private session in Hollywood the previous May and apparently he said some things they considered lively enough for an opening. Having since been coached by shrewder minds, Warner sought to backtrack somewhat, but they wouldn't let him. So he repeated the lie that Howard Koch — one of the "Unfriendly Nineteen" — had attempted to slip subversive material into the screenplay of *Mission to Moscow*, omitting what would have been all too clear were cross-examination permitted. Not only did Warner make the book into a film at the request of Franklin D. Roosevelt, but its author, former Ambassador to the USSR John Paton Davies, was at Warner Brothers studio *supervising every line that was written in the script*! Now Jack warmed up, and after naming four or five alleged Communists he'd fired, he rambled on to Broadway, where he'd seen Arthur Miller's play, *All My Sons*. In his opinion, Miller certainly was a Communist writer, and as for the director, Elia Kazan, no doubt of it! On and on — once in the spotlight, the committee had a difficult job getting Warner out of it.

As the parade of friendly witnesses went on Eric Johnston made it a point to inform our attorneys that despite this circus there would never be a blacklist. McNutt backed him up. We were heartened by this news, but at the same time were outraged at the smears, the open falsehoods, our inability to cross-examine and expose the lies. Somehow, in all that anxiety we still found it possible at times to be amused by some of the outrageous nonsense.

Ayn Rand, self-styled expert on the Soviets, testified that the MGM film, *Song of Russia,* was clearly Communist propaganda because in it the performers playing Russians often smiled. "In Russia," she testified, smiling, "nobody smiles." Nobody smiled at her joke either.

And Ginger Rogers' mama: "I know Dalton Trumbo is a Communist because in a picture he wrote my daughter was forced to say, 'Share and share alike, that's democracy.'" What more proof did they need?

L.B. Mayer took the stand and defended his studio. True, they made *Song of Russia*, but Russia was an ally during wartime, and he pointed in defense to the anti-Soviet films made before the war: Greta Garbo in *Ninotchka* and *Comrade X*. He acknowledged that he believed that two contract writers working for him, Lester Cole and Dalton Trumbo, were Communists, and perhaps Donald Ogden Stewart as well.

Adolph Menjou, trimmed and tailored meticulously like the "maitre d'" at the Waldorf, offered himself as the industry's most knowledgeable expert on Communism. He had read thirty-odd books on Marxism and Leninism, and accused John Cromwell, one of the industry's leading directors, of being a Communist because he saw some books on Communism on Cromwell's library shelves. (Where did Menjou keep *his* books on Marxism — hidden in the cellar?) But of all the books he read on Communism, the most important to him was *Pattern for World Revolution,* written he acknowledged *anonymously.* This book told that Stalin had first killed Lenin by poisoning him, then Gorky, and then the pharmacist who supplied the poison. Mr. Menjou was praised by the Committee as both a great American and a great scholar of Communism.

Robert Taylor was next. He was reluctant to talk about

Song of Russia, in which he starred. Apparently in the secret session in the previous spring, he said he was forced to play in the film; now he softened that considerably, saying merely that he objected until he was told it was "for the war effort." Asked whether he would ever work with a Communist, (he knew Sid Boehm and I had just written what he had told Mayer was "the best script he'd had in ten years"), he vehemently replied, "Never!" But when Thomas persisted and demanded to know if he knew any Communists, he hedged — and finally admitted he'd heard that a writer, Dalton Trumbo, was one, and that another writer, "a gentleman named Lester Cole, also was."

There was laughter. This was perhaps the first time in modern history, and certainly one for the Guinness book of records, that a Communist was classified a "gentleman."

The film Boehm and I wrote for Taylor was released in December 1947 and received excellent notices nationally. But it was the New York City daily, *PM* which made the point:

A Good Movie — Look Who Wrote It

P M Review

High Wall is the best picture Robert Taylor's had the great good fortune to work in, as well as the best written, best directed, best produced and most interesting picture, to come out of Metro in years.

Unlike the usual gilded run off that gilding assembly line, *High Wall* is arresting, has vitality, has actually something to do with life. It is a suspense story, it pretends to be no more. Yet within the rigid traditions of that category, it achieves a rare credibility because its asides and incidentals are made up out of real people, both as individuals and groups, reacting to the conventions, problems, and ethics of their work and environment, as real people do.

Much of *High Wall* takes place in a state mental hospital and a

HIGH WALL, an MGM picture; screenplay by Sydney Boehm and Lester Cole, suggested by a story and play by Alan R. Clark and Bradbury Foote; produced by Robert Lord; Directed by Curtis Bernhardt. At the Capitol.

Steven Kenet	Robert Taylor
Dr. Ann Lorrison	Audrey Totter
Williard I. Whitcombe	Herbert Marshall
Helen Kenet	Dorothy Patrick
Mr. Slocum	H. B. Warner
Dr. George Poward	Warner Anderson
Dr. Phillip Dunlop	Moroni Olsen
David Wallace	John Ridgley
Dr. Stanley Griffin	Morris Ankrum
Mrs. Kenet	Elizabeth Risdon
Henry Cronner	Vince Barnett
Emory Garrison	Jonathan Hale
Sidney S. Hackle	Charle Arnt
Tom Delaney	Ray Mayer

police station. The tired impersonality of such institutions, here portrayed but never insisted on, their staff's self-preserving acceptance of their stultifying routines, the fundamental decency and humanity of their over-worked psychiatric corps, are not exacted by the plot, but by the sincerity, intelligence, and high standards of craftsmanship of the men who made this picture. The story is complicated yet beautifully joined; it is full of the gleam of skill, sensitivity, and creative enthusiam. It has pace and urgency, and yet clarity too. Once or twice the exigencies of the plot show up its suspense story's bare bones, but for the tender way it handles Taylor—converting his sulkiness into the look of characterization and his habitual disgruntled expression into the semblance of determination—it must be forgiven. Besides, the rest of the characterizations, particularly Audrey Toter's, Herbert Marshall's, Ray Mayer's, Vince Barnett's—are so genuine, so vivid, and so good.

It so happens that the script of *High Wall*, outstanding of its kind, was written by Sydney Boehm and Lester Cole. Out of profound loyalty to the House UnAmerican Activities Committee, Metro has recently decided to forget its contractual obligations to Mr. Cole and arbitrarily dispense with his services. — C. A.

With such ironies, it was difficult for those outside not to find amusement lurking somewhere. What the reviewers didn't know was that Taylor not only agreed with them about the script, but that he had told L.B. Mayer that I must write all his future pictures!

It took four days for the patriots to set us up for the kill. Now we would attempt to defend ourselves. Not one word was offered to substantiate the original charge that something subversive had appeared on the screen. Because nothing had! The charge was forgotten: obviously it had little to do with the intent of the hearings.

After each of the "friendly" witnesses had named "unfriendly" witnesses as Communists, our attorneys sought to cross-examine. Each time permission was refused.

Eric Johnston was called to the stand. After his assurances to us, we were optimistic. Moreover, a day or two before, he was quoted in the nation's press as saying, "One of the most precious heritages of our civilization is the concept that a man is innocent until proven guilty." We were heartened.

His opening statement on the witness stand started with this: "Most of us in America are just little people, and loose charges can hurt little people. They can take everything away a man has — his livelihood and his personal dignity." Here was our hero, our advocate! A splendid statement.

J. Parnell Thomas wasn't happy with the statement. Oh, not because of the splendid words; he'd used similar language himself. Something quite different, to our amazement and shock, was quickly revealed. This defender of the little man, who had told us he would never be a party to anything so un-American as a blacklist, was forced by Thomas's reading of the record to admit that the previous spring, in Hollywood, in secret testimony, he had privately agreed with Thomas that a blacklist *should* exist. He had further agreed to *advocate* a blacklist to the producers as part of Thomas's three-point program for the industry (never spelled out in the hearings).

That was Thomas's bitter complaint; Mr. Johnston had betrayed *him*; if he had kept his promise, these hearings would never have had to take place, and the industry would not have been subject to the criticism it was receiving in the media.

Was Mr. Johnston crushed, humiliated? Not at all. He was *indignant*! He had *not* lied to Thomas, nor had he betrayed him. He *had* gone to the producers, as he agreed to, and advocated the blacklist as he promised. But *they* turned it down as too risky legally; a conspiracy charge might be brought.

Mr. Thomas could not doubt Mr. Johnston's perspiring earnestness. Thomas nodded, pleased, as if rewarding a pupil before him with an "A" for effort.

We, of course, were dumfounded. From then on we could make no contact with Johnston.

While little was made of this point in the press, generally the country's leading newspapers had already demonstrated that they saw through the shoddy game Thomas and his hand-picked crew were attempting to play. The following are just some examples of the editorials which appeared within the first few days of testimony from the Hollywood Alliance stooges.

Washington Post
October 21, 1947

Chairman Thomas of the House Committee on Un-American Activities may pretend that his super collosal Hollywood investigation is aimed not at interference but merely at exposure. It's effect, nevertheless, is to intimidate and coerce the industry into an even more rigid acceptance of Mr. Thomas' concepts of Americanism. . . . Those who labor in Hollywood are not accustomed to much privacy; but they should be free, at least, to think as they please.

Chicago Times
October 22, 1947

Of course the real object of Chairman Thomas and the reactionary Republican majority of the House Un-American Activities Committee is not primarily to uncover subversive influences in Hollywood. It is to smear New Dealers and whatever their progressive succesors may be called. So rather than looking at the records, the old familiar Dies Committee smear technique is being used.

New York Times
October 23, 1947

. . . it is clear that the Committee on Un-American Activities is actually trying certain individuals for alleged subversive and un-American acts without affording them the ordinary rights accorded to the most degraded criminal; namely, the right to cross-examine their accusers and the right to call witnesses on their own behalf . . . We do not believe that the committee is conducting a fair investigation. We think the course on which it has embarked threatens to lead to greater dangers than those with which it is presently concerned!

New York Herald-Tribune
October 22, 1947

. . . the beliefs of men and women who write for the screen are, like the beliefs of any ordinary men and women, nobody's business but their own, as the Bill of Rights mentions. Neither Mr. Thomas nor the Congress in which he sits is empowered to dictate what Americans shall think . . . Not Hollywood but Congress is being investigated here.

The next morning the gavel banged hard, high on the rostrum where J. Parnell Thomas was perched. It was our turn. First John Howard Lawson. Before Robert Stripling, the prosecutor, could ask him the first question, our attorneys again requested the right to cross-examine the previous witnesses. Of course, the request was denied. "This is not a courtroom," Thomas said. "Of course not," someone in the audience yelled, "it's an old-fashioned Inquisition." Whoever he was, he was led out.

Lawson asked permission to read a statement. It was handed to Thomas, who said, "I read the first sentence. Request denied." Lawson was furious, although it was not surprising; the statement was an eloquent and precise indictment of the committee and its aims.* It soon became a shouting match, and Lawson said, at that point: "It's a pity I had to come all this way to teach you the meaning of Americanism." Whereupon with a bang of Thomas's gavel, Lawson was ordered from the stand. The Committee members merely glanced to each other, all nodded, and Lawson was cited for contempt.

To break the pattern, Thomas permitted Albert Maltz, the fifth witness, to read his statement, but most of the Committee paid little or no attention. When he was through, they asked the same question as of the others: "Are you now or have you ever been a member of the Communist Party?", and when he tried to answer in his own way, saying the

---

*Gordon Kahn, *Hollywood on Trial*, (New York: Boni and Gaer, 1950).

Plotting strategy. Chairman J. Parnell Thomas (r.) with chief "investigator" Robert Stripling and committee member Richard Nixon prepare for next day's witch-hunt.

question was both improper and illegal, he was asked, like the others, to step down. Contempt.

Lawson, Bessie, Ornitz, Dmytryk, Scott, Trumbo, Biberman, Maltz, Lardner and the tenth, myself. It was pretty much the same with most of us — we were not permitted to read our statements: the "sixty-four-dollar" question, as it came to be known, was asked; we refused on First Amendment grounds to respond with a "yes or no"; then promptly — contempt.

At this point the press did not let us down. Here is a typical example two days before my appearance.

𝕯𝖊𝖙𝖗𝖔𝖎𝖙 𝕱𝖗𝖊𝖊 𝕻𝖗𝖊𝖘𝖘

TUESDAY, OCTOBER 23, 1947

Most Un-American of All

The Committee

THE most un-American activity in the United States today is the conduct of the Congressional Committee on Un-American Activities.

It is so viciously flagrant a violation of every element of common decency usually associated with human liberty that it is foul mockery on all that Jefferson and Lincoln made articulate in their dreams of a cleaner and finer order on earth.

The hypocritically named "Committee on Un-American Activities" should be abolished at the earliest possible moment by the United States Congress and so deeply buried that no other group of publicity-mad zealots could ever again be allowed to tarnish with their stench the greatest institution of our democracy, our halls of legislation.

This Committee is possessed by a denial of human freedom generally associated with the Directorate in the French Reign of Terror, with the Soviet mass slaughter trials, and the Hitlerian blood purges.

No wonder that Stalin, Molotov, Vishinsky and others of that breed refuse to believe us in our protestations that we stand for and fight only for the majestic principle of individual liberty!

THIS Committee makes its own rules as it goes along, with utter disregard of the law of the land, the common law of decency and the constitution of the United States.

That is to say, it does as it pleases.

It has the power to subpena witnesses and send them to the penitentiary if its victims do not obey their orders—with no chance to appeal for protection.

Anything said on the witness stand is "privileged." This means that a witness can slander and libel anybody he pleases and the victim has no redress in court. He cannot sue.

He can be robbed of his reputation with no chance whatever to defend himself against these character assassins.

The committee was spawned under the

wicked aegis of the notorious pop-off pub- **No Congressional Committee**
licity bigot, Martin Dies. His departure in **that robs men and women of their**
defeat has not improved the caliber of the **good names for the sheer sadistic**
Committee under Congressman Parnell **glee of getting headlines should be**
Thomas. **allowed to exist.**

But despite the media criticism of Thomas there was a division among those who had flown from Hollywood to support us. Our fight-back mood was viewed by some as "ungentlemanly," and some expressed uneasiness.

I am delighted to recall, however, that one of the great writers of the twentieth century never flinched in supporting our principles. This was his unforgettable statement, heard by millions in a national broadcast:

I have the honor to expose myself as a hostile witness.

I testify that I am very much interested in the moving picture industry and that, since my arrival in the United States nine years ago, I've seen a great many Hollywood films. If Communist propaganda was smuggled into any of them, it must have been most thoroughly hidden. I, for one, never noticed anything of the sort.

I testify, moreover, that to my mind the ignorant and superstitious persecution of the believers in a political and economic doctrine which is, after all, the creation of great minds and great thinkers — I testify that this persecution is not only degrading for the persecutors themselves but very harmful to the cultural reputation of this country. As an American citizen of German birth, I finally testify that I am painfully familiar with certain political trends. Spiritual intolerance, political inquisitions, and declining legal security, and all this in the name of an alleged "state of emergency" . . . that is how it started in Germany. What followed was Fascism and what followed Fascism was war.

— Thomas Mann

The broadcast, along with the courageous critical statements of a dozen more, from Judy Garland to Frederic March, George S. Kaufman, Gregory Peck, Lucille Ball, Burt Lancaster

and other equally famous and respected figures hit the Committee hard. There were rumors they were going to close
down the show, but they couldn't. They needed at least one
winner. They tried Ring Lardner, a poor choice. He all but
mocked them and was ordered from the stand after they
asked him, "Why won't you answer the question?" He replied,
"I could." "Then why don't you?" To which he responded,
"If I did, I couldn't look at myself in the mirror in the
morning!"

"Contempt! Witness excused."

My turn came, Unfriendly Witness number ten. Having
seen all but one of the statements offered rejected after the
first two sentences were read, as "Vilifying, subversive," the
previous night I revised my opening paragraph to make it
milder, but equally truthful. It read: "I want to say at the
outset that I am a loyal American, who upholds the Constitution and Bill of Rights of my country, who does not
advocate force and violence or subversion, and who is not an
agent of a foreign power." Thomas hardly glanced at it,
certainly not for enough time to read it. He tossed it aside
and said, "Like the others. Vilification, subversive. Request
denied. Start, Mr. Stripling."

When I insisted upon my right to read it, or state the
content of the first paragraph, the little fat man got red in
the face, banged his gavel fourteen times, shouting, "No!"
with each bang, then ordered his inquisitor to question me.

The same routine: first, name, where born. These could
be answered. Then, first question: "Are you now or have you
ever been a member of the Screen Writers' Guild?" That was
always first; remember, if you answer one question, you must
answer all. I refused to answer. Then routinely, "Are you
now or have you ever been a member of the Communist
Party?" I asked permission to answer the question in my own
way. A "yes" or "no" was demanded. I refused: I said I
could speak or remain silent under my First Amendment

right. The same routine: removal from stand and an instant citation by the Committee for contempt.

Ring left for the hotel after his appearance, but following me, number eleven, was Bertolt Brecht, from whom Thomas expected a victory. They failed, but they tried to turn it into one. Brecht wanted no attorney, but he asked me to wait, to listen. He gave his name, birthplace (Germany), and proceeded to answer the questions. He said he was not, and never had been a Communist Party member. They tried to trick him, by reading some of his revolutionary works, poems, etc.; but he dismissed those as translations only. The Committee had had enough. They thanked him, the first cooperative witness. He was excused.

In the cab, returning to the hotel, Brecht grieved; he wondered whether any of us would ever understand and forgive him. Alone in this country, a foreigner, they could hold him, as they did Gerhardt Eisler, under one of the Alien Registration Acts in prison for how long —? He wanted to go home, to the new German Democratic Republic, where there was work for him to do. I put an arm around him. Little comfort. At the hotel he explained. The others did understand. And the next morning, early, he bid us farewell. Within a day he was on a ship for Europe.

Thomas was getting nowhere except deeper into the pit he was digging. He needed a Cold War bombshell to close out his hearings and that afternoon, after we left, he produced it. His final witness testified, and his allegations sent reporters from the Hearst and tabloid press scurrying to the telephones.

That evening on the radio networks, and the next morning in the tabloids, his much-needed face-saver appeared.

Daily Mirror

Vol. 24. No. 112.   NEW YORK 17, N. Y., FRIDAY, OCTOBER 31. 1947   C   COMPLETE SPORTS

FILM REDS AIDED
A-BOMB SPIES
10 Held in Contempt as Probe Ends

The story that followed was by one Louis Russell, former
FBI agent, and was directed against J. Robert Oppenheimer,
wartime director of the Los Alamos Atomic Plant. But the
way they tied it to us was by printing the headline of "A-Bomb
Spies" and the Ten together. As did the *New York Daily
News* in the following:

Film Red Quiz Bares
Atom Bomb Spy Plot

By RUTH MONTGOMERY
Of THE NEWS Bureau

Washington, D. C., Oct. 30.—A former FBI agent today linked Hollywood
film Reds with a Soviet espionage attempt to worm atom bomb secrets out of
J. Robert Oppenheimer, wartime director of the Los Alamos atom bomb plant.

Electrifying a House Committee on Un-American Activities hearing into Communist

Bares Red Plot To Get Atom Secrets

By ROSE McKEE

WASHINGTON, Oct. 30 (INS).—The House Un-American Activities Committee was told today that Russia knew of American attempts to produce an atomic bomb as early as 1942 and attempted then to get details through espionage. Hollywood figures were linked with the charges. Louis J. Russell, committee investigator, testified J. Robert Oppenheimer, top U. S. atomic scientist, was approached by an emissary for information for the Soviet in 1942.

It was not until three years later—August, 1945—that the world learned of the bomb, when it was dropped on Hiroshi-

With this triumphant "revelation," Thomas announced the hearings were temporarily suspended, his duty to the American people fulfilled. He said he proved we not only sneaked propaganda into films, we aided atomic spies as well.

That night before leaving for home we ate dinner at Harvey's Restaurant. The columnist Drew Pearson dropped by. He'd been very supportive, even though he admitted there was little he could do. But now he told us that while he might not be able to help us, there was something he could do about J. Parnell Thomas. We were curious, but he'd say no more than, "You'll read about it." Wishing us luck, he left.

How closely we were kept under surveillance will be seen by this incident: during dinner, Herbert Biberman made a sarcastic remark about J. Edgar Hoover. A few weeks after he returned home, he was visited by two FBI men who warned him that another crack like the one he made in Harvey's about Hoover would mean, in addition to a year for contempt, another ten for slander.

Early the next morning most of us took the train for home, anxious to see wives and children and attempt to assure them that despite the contempt citations, all would end well.

Before I returned to Hollywood, I found this piece of

good news in Sidney Skolsky's gossip column in the *New York Post:*

> While in Washington for the hearings, Lester Cole, classified as an "unfriendly witness," was kept on the Metro payroll because James K. McGuinness, classified as a friendly witness, was also on the payroll and the studio wanted to display fairness.

With the problem of "fairness" solved by the MGM Press Department, I reported back to work at MGM, and Jack Cummings greeted me cordially, almost as if nothing had happened. I resumed work on the script of *Zapata.* Such newspapers as the *New York Times* and the *Herald-Tribune* stated that the failure of the Thomas attack on the motion picture industry was a victory for the American people. But a few days later we were cited for contempt by the Congress.

The industry had its own ideas of what constituted victory. First in line with a knife for our backs was Eric Johnston, with a major speech radioed across the nation. He said, "Freedom of speech is not a selective phrase. We can't shut free speech into compartments. It's freedom of speech for all American institutions and individuals, or it's freedom of speech for none . . . and nobody." We were back in the splendid statement department. Instantly he made his typical switch: "We do not defend them (the Ten). We did not defend them then, we do not defend them now. On the contrary, we believe they have done a tremendous disservice to the industry which has given them much in material rewards and an opportunity to develop their talents." Nothing was said, naturally, of the fact that the industry had taken advantage of *all* talent to reap profits many times more substantial than our "material rewards."

This was the opening gun. We sought to reply with advertisements and press releases, which reached few of the papers.

We were outgunned, outmanned, and, of course, outfinanced. Humphrey Bogart, frightened, led an exodus from the Committee for the First Amendment, and many followed.

A week later the producers met in New York with their financiers, the bankers. Present were all heads of studios, including, of course, executives Barney Balaban and Sam Katz, of Browne, Bioff and Mafia renown; Nicholas Schenk, their go-between, all out of prison, alive and well; Eric Johnston, who had but a month before assured us there would never be a blacklist as long as he lived; there he was, alive and well. Also, to the surprise of few, among the high and mighty was none other than Dore Schary, the former writer who, you will recall, in 1941 came to my office at Paramount and pleaded with me to use my influence against the strike which was planned to gain recognition for the Guild.

Then, in 1947, as executive producer at RKO, Schary had appeared as a witness at the Thomas Committee hearings and bravely stated that he would *not* have discharged Dmytryk and Scott as director and writer-producer of *Crossfire*, the powerful film against anti-Semitism, unless it was proved to him that they had broken some law and were convicted of a crime. He concluded by saying that he would employ them again, and "I would still maintain his [the writer's] right to think politically as he chooses."

Apparently it didn't take him long to change horses again when his mount seemed to weaken. Here he was helping turn defeat for Thomas and Rankin into victory by becoming a co-signer of the following statement:

THE WALDORF-ASTORIA STATEMENT

Members of the Association of Motion Picture Producers deplore the action of the ten Hollywood men who have been cited for contempt by the House of Representatives. We do not desire to prejudice their legal rights, but their actions have been a disservice to their employers and have impaired their usefulness to the industry.

We will forthwith discharge or suspend without compensation those in our employ, and we will not re-employ any of the ten until such time as he is acquitted, or has purged himself of contempt and declared under oath he is not a Communist.

On the broader issue of alleged subversive and disloyal elements in Hollywood, our members are likewise prepared to take positive action.

We will not knowingly employ a Communist or member of any party or group which advocates the overthrow of the Government of the United States by force or violence, or by any illegal or unconstitutional method.

We are frank to recognize that such a policy involves dangers and risks. There is danger of hurting innocent people, there is the risk of creating an atmosphere of fear. Creative work at its best cannot be carried on in an atmosphere of fear. To this end we will invite the Hollywood Guilds to work with us to eliminate any subversives; to protect the innocent, to safeguard free speech and a free screen wherever threatened.

The absence of a national policy, established by Congress with respect to the employment of Communists in private industry, makes our task difficult. Ours is a nation of laws. We request Congress to enact legislation to assist American industry to rid itself of subversive, disloyal elements.

Nothing subversive or un-American has appeared on the screen. Nor can any number of Hollywood investigations obscure the patriotic service of thirty thousand Americans employed in Hollywood who have given our Government their valuable aid in war and peace.

This statement, broadcast and printed in the media throughout the nation, included the names of all the heads of studios, but not of *their* bosses, the bankers and financiers in New York and Boston who had forced them into it.

The next day Dalton Trumbo, Donald Ogden Stewart and I were dismissed at MGM, Ring Lardner at Twentieth Century; we were the only ones employed — and under contract — at the time.

The Truman Congress and the big business in the East that ran Hollywood had their way. But the American people weren't so sure they were right. Five days after the Waldorf-Astoria Statement, this Gallup Poll column appeared:

Gallup Poll Finds Sentiment Divided on Methods Used

BY GEORGE GALLUP

PRINCETON (N.J.) Nov. 29. The House contempt citation against the Hollywood inquiry witnesses who refused to say whether they are members of the Communist party is in line with the main sentiment of the voting population.

Voters who had heard or read about the Congressional investigation of Hollywood showed a pronounced sentiment in favor of punishment for those now held in contempt of Congress for failing to answer questions concerning alleged Communist connections.

However, opinion is closely divided on the question of whether the investigation of Hollywood was properly handled by the House committee.

To probe public attitudes the American Institute of Public Opinion used a series of questions designed to cover various aspects of the situation. The survey was completed before the House took action on the contempt citations.

The first question sought to find how many people are familiar with the Hollywood investigation. It was found that approximately 8 out of every 10 had heard or read about it.

These people were then asked:
What is your opinion of this investigation — do you approve or disapprove of the way it was handled?

Approve	37%
Disapprove	36
No opinion	27

Do you think the Hollywood writers who refused to say whether they were members of the Communist party should be punished or not?

Should be	47%
Should not	39
No opinion	14

Further analysis of the poll returns shows noticable differences in attitudes on these questions among educational and occupational groupings.

Here is the way, for example, the various classifications vote on whether the witnesses should be punished who refused to say whether or not they are Communists:

	Should be pun-ished	Should not be pun-ished	No opin.
By education:			
College	34%	54%	12%
High school	44	43	13
Grammar	53	31	13
By occupation:			
Prof. and Bus.	41	47	12
White collar	36	47	13
Farmers	62	23	15
Others	48	36	16

The analysis was simple enough: it was the uneducated that the miseducators most easily influenced: those who never got beyond grammar school; farmers in the hinterlands; workers divided and conquered. They were the ones who needed educating about the Bill of Rights — their Bill, their Rights.

Two days later, upon the request of the producers, a meeting was called of the members of the Writers' Guild. There was fear and some uncertainty in our ranks, and only about four hundred members appeared in the large hall of the Hollywood Roosevelt Hotel. When the producers appeared, we were astonished: along with Eddie Mannix were the liberals Walter Wanger and Dore Schary.

There was an audible gasp through the audience as Mannix and Wanger faded into the background and Schary became the spokesman for the producers. He told how the producers hated to do what they did; that at the Waldorf, despite the unanimous signing of the Blacklist Statement, many disagreed with it, himself included.

"And," he went on, "we do not ask you to condone this [what we have done]. . . ." But what was wanted was the Guild's cooperation with a big, all-industry public relations campaign to restore the good name of Hollywood by convincing the American people that the action taken by the industry against Communism and Communists was justified.

The membership present was somewhat less than impressed. With Schary, Wanger and Mannix still present, the four-hundred-odd men and women present cast only eight votes to support their resolution, and over four hundred to demand an end to the blacklist.

It's almost impossible to believe, yet just eight days after Johnston, Schary and associates pronounced the blacklist, an organization in Philadelphia, called the Golden Slipper Square Dance Club, selected a film it considered the best of the year, to which it gave the club's annual humanitarian award. Who else but the nimble, sleight-of-mind Eric Johnston ac-

cepted the invitation to be guest of honor? At the proper
time he rose to accept the award and said:

> Intolerance is a species of boycott, and in any business or
> job, boycott is a cancer on the economic body of the nation.
> Hollywood has held the door of opportunity open to every
> man and woman who could meet its technical and artistic
> standards . . . what [our industry] is interested in is his or
> her skill or talent, ability to produce pictures for the joy and
> progress of mankind.

This spokesman against "intolerance . . . . and for . . . . the
joy and progress of mankind" was accepting the award from
a group whose selection of the best film expressing humani-
tarianism that year was none other than *Crossfire*, written
and directed by Adrian Scott and Edward Dmytryk, two of
the Hollywood Ten he had just decreed blacklisted.

Daily World Photo

Seven of the Hollywood Ten in Washington, D.C. before sentencing by the District Court. (l. to r.) Alvah Bessie, Albert Maltz, Samuel Ornitz, Herbert Biberman, Ring Lardner, Jr., Lester Cole and Edward Dmytryk.

14

Victory—and Defeat

Early in 1948 we went to Washington to appear in the District Court and were all speedily, automatically convicted. While most of us received fines of $1,000 and sentences of one year in jail — the maximum for a misdemeanor — Biberman and Dmytryk, appearing before a different judge, were given only six months and a $500 fine. They had the same lawyers, offered the same defense, and were as quickly sentenced. The only conclusion we could come to was that the judge was showing his disagreement with the belief that it was indeed a misdemeanor. Wryly, we congratulated them on their good luck. With those convictions, we now faced the costs of our appeals and, those failing, the final defense in the Supreme Court. It would take two years before we knew our fate; but we were optimistic. On that nine-member bench, we felt confident we could count on six Justices: William O. Douglas, Harlan E. Stone, Robert Jackson, Frank Murphy, Wiley Rutledge and Hugo Black.

But we couldn't be idle in that period. We would take to the road and gain support in every city and town our finances would permit us to visit. We would speak to trade union groups, civic clubs and every and any gathering that would have us. We already had opened a small office a block from Hollywood Boulevard, with a sign outside indicating it was the office of "The Hollywood Ten," a substitute of our choice for "The Unfriendly Ten," the hostile label with which the press sought to tag us. It was from that office, under Herbert Biberman's organizing talents and boundless energy, that speaking dates were set up nationwide for those of us who could travel; we concentrated in our speeches on our concept of the Bill of Rights. Those were the most tumultuous years; never had I worked so hard, under such pressure.

Shortly after Dore Schary's attempt to get the Guild into the Producers' embrace, the opposite occurred; the executive board received a vote of confidence from the membership to start legal action against the Producers' Association to demand damages for the blacklist and a court order demanding its formal retraction. Thurman Arnold, former Attorney General, was engaged as counsel.

At about the same time, Charles Katz, Robert W. Kenney and Ben Margolis, our attorneys, started preparing my suit against MGM for breach of contract. On top of the speaking engagements and all the Guild activities was the greatest pressure of all — the need to earn a living, to write and somehow sell what we wrote. I had to cover living expenses then and, if possible, put away something for Jonnie and the children. At best there appeared to be a very uncertain future for my family.

Like the others, I made time in the early morning and late at night and managed to write a story. It was submitted by George Willner under what was to be the first of many pseudonyms; this one was Jonnie's maiden name, "J. Redmond Prior." To our delight, George sold it to Warner Brothers as a vehicle for Humphrey Bogart for $20,000.

Complications quickly set in. Jack Warner wanted George to bring the author to the studio; he wrote like a screenwriter,

Warner said, and perhaps he could be induced to do the script. George stalled and lied; the author was a novelist, lived in the East, and couldn't be induced to come to Hollywood. For Warner that was preposterous, and a challenge. He demanded the writer's address. When George insisted the writer wanted anonymity, the studio became suspicious and demanded to know whether the writer was one of the Ten. George refused to answer. When an informer and an FBI investigation pointed to me a year or two later, George was himself blacklisted. Of course, at the time I knew nothing of the FBI's agents and informers, but it now seems they wanted me very badly. If they couldn't prosecute for subversion, they might at least charge me with fraud. Hopefully they searched the Internal Revenue records to see whether I had evaded paying income tax. Apparently they were somewhat disappointed when their investigation showed that I had not.*

Warners did what they could to disguise my connection with the film once the story leaked to the press. Anthony Vellier, Jr., the writer-producer assigned to it, was ordered to alter it to the degree that my pseudonym could legitimately be eliminated by keeping less than one-third of my original story (a Writers' Guild arbitration rule). He tried. They changed the title to *Chained Lightning*, rewrote and rewrote, but enough remained that the credit on the screen remained: "Based on a story by J. Redmond Prior."

All this was going on while we prepared for my civil suit against MGM's breach of contract. In previous years the producers had no difficulty in diverting the public from their shady union-busting dealings with the Al Capone mob: they simply filled the media with sobs and wailings of Mafia blackmail. This time they hoped to delay court proceedings, if not squelch them, by publicly accusing the presiding Judge, Leon Yankwich, of prejudice. For the best description of this sordid smear attempt, I am indebted to the FBI. The

---

*FBI report, December 1979.

following is a verbatim report by Special Agent (name blacked out), dated March 25, 1948:

> The *Los Angeles Daily News* in its edition of March 22, 1948 contained a story to the effect that LESTER COLE was suing MGM for recovery of his "$1800 a week screenwriting job" and that the studio has asked Federal Judge LEON YANK-WICH to disqualify himself and transfer the case to another judge because of prejudice on his part." The affidavit further alleges that in a conversation at the home of a friend, YANK-WICH said "that none of the cases arising out of such suspensions and discharges came before him; but if they did he would have no alternative but to render judgment for the plaintiff." . . . and that YANKWICH said if he were attorney for COLE and his colleagues, that he could recover judgments in their favor for "millions of dollars." Allegedly the affidavit was signed by E.J. MANNIX, Vice-president of LOEW's Inc. This statement was denied in a story carried by the *Los Angeles Examiner,* March 23 last, when that paper quoted Mrs. HELEN MELLINKOFF at whose home the party was held where YANKWICH allegedly made the statement. She said, "Having checked on my own recollection with that of other guests present on the occasion mentioned, I am able to state unequivocally that the remarks Mr. RUTTMAN has attributed to Judge YANKWICH were not uttered either in full, in part or in substance by Judge YANKWICH or anyone else present.*

When that attempt failed, the producers evidently resigned themselves to the situation and the trial was set by Judge Yankwich for November 16.

It was a busy period for the informers. On March 15, one was present at a Beverly Hills Hotel dinner held under the auspices of the Committee on Arts, Sciences and Professions, honoring the eminent Harvard professor, astronomer Harlow Shapley. According to the informer, Shapley ended his talk by saying that if J. Parnell Thomas asked him questions which amounted to a violation of civil liberties, he would

---

*FBI report.

answer, "None of your damned business." The informer went on to say that Shapley received a standing ovation, and the Hollywood Ten "stood to receive the applause" with him.*

No doubt this was advice for the FBI to keep their eye on Shapley from then on. According to later accounts, they did.

Two years before this hectic period, in 1946, my father retired, sold his business in Baltimore and moved with his wife to Los Angeles. They bought an eight-unit apartment house, occupying one and renting the others. He was then seventy-four and suffering from extremely high blood pressure. Whether it was the excitement of the forthcoming trial or additional stress of a personal nature, he died the night before the trial began. I was not in the best condition to face the court that morning.

Picking the jury, with the current anticommunist hysteria mounting, was not an easy job, but somehow Charles Katz and his colleagues got through it. There was one woman on the jury they were afraid of; an elderly mid-westerner, her face heavily lined, with thin stern mouth and cold, piercing eyes. But they couldn't get rid of her. We could only hope for the best.

We started our attack by showing newsreel films of me in the Washington hearings. Some reviews of my films were quoted, as was the First Amendment. Then it was MGM's turn. They were confident: there was the morals clause; had I not disgraced the company in the eyes of the public by my actions in Washington? And, as their prize witness, their attorney Selwyn brought L.B. Mayer to the stand.

When he was sworn in and took the stand, he glanced at me for the first time. It was an enigmatic, strange look, but I was soon to understand. As Selwyn began asking him about my "immoral" acts, L.B. seemed surprised, and his answers dismayed his attorney. He had known me more than two years, he said. I had written three fine films for

---

*FBI report.

his company and was on good terms with everyone at the studio. As far as he was concerned, my morals were just fine. Selwyn hastily muttered, "Thank you, that is all."

But it was far from all. To clinch it, my attorneys read from the depositions given some days before by Eddie Mannix and L.B. Mayer. In his deposition Mannix said:

> My stand on this was that I was not in a witch hunt and that I was not out to find Communists or hurt Communists as long as I was able to protect material on the screen and as long as the screen was free from any Communistic propaganda.

L.B. Mayer's deposition was read, and it said, in part, referring to the Hearings of the Committee in Washington:

> I didn't think the industry was wrong and I thought this was just a shoddy way of getting publicity. They asked about LESTER COLE and DALTON TRUMBO and I said I didn't give a damn whether they were Communists or not. All I'm interested in is getting people to write scripts for me and my responsibility if he is a Communist, a Democrat or Republican is that the ideology is not put on the screen.*

Following the judge's instructions to the jury, its members left to deliberate. A few hours later they came back with their verdict in favor of the plaintiff. Judge Yankwich then thanked them for the decision and delivered, in the words of *Variety*,

> . . . one of the most scathing attacks ever heard from a Federal bench on ERIC JOHNSTON and went on to say: "LESTER COLE was made to suffer a penalty not for what his employers thought of him, but for a dogmatic attitude on the part of JOHNSTON, who insisted his doxy was orthodoxy and everybody else's was heterodoxy. COLE had a debt of gratitude to Louis B. Mayer. MAYER won the case for COLE even before COLE took the witness stand."*

----

*FBI report.

Through our jubilation and embraces, Judge Yankwich again thanked the jury. Charley whispered that I should go over to the jury box and do the same. I did with pleasure. In the back row was the elderly, grim-faced woman we had so feared; now her face was wreathed in smiles. When I thanked her, she said, "The worst that could have happened would have been a hung jury, eleven to one. I never would have voted against you." "Why?" my eyes must have inquired. She went on: "Twenty years ago I used to be a school teacher in Nebraska. I was blacklisted for trying to form a teachers' union. I've been through it all." And she squeezed my hand. "Good luck," she said softly, firmly.

I told Charley. He shook his head in wonderment. "So much for reading faces," he muttered, and went over to thank the jurors.

That wasn't the end of the case by far. The producers immediately announced their intention to appeal and take it to the Supreme Court, if necessary. That was not going to be easy for us. The obvious fact was that the producers had the money to carry on forever, while we still had ten contempt convictions to fight in the Court of Appeals and, if lost there, in the Supreme Court. The producers knew it and offered us a deal. The total sum owed Trumbo and me under our contracts was well over $300,000; they offered us $125,000 to close the case then and there.

We talked it over. We had little choice. Much of that money would be needed not only for lawyers' costs, but for living expenses, for food and shelter. At least five of the Ten were broke. Trumbo and I decided on the way to go. Votes were taken on how much to put aside for legal expenses, how much to give the others for living expenses. Five of them were without a dime. We shared with them. I think Trumbo and I each ended up with $9,000 out of the $62,500 each had won in the settlement. In a way it was still a victory, perhaps something Thurman Arnold could use when the Guild got around to starting its anti-blacklist suit against the producers. For the time being the blacklist remained.

Here are but two samples of the kind of stories that appeared in practically every newspaper in the country and on the radio networks:

$74,250 due contempt case figure

Screenwriter Lester Cole last night won an unqualified verdict against Metro-Goldwin Mayer Studio in his suit for reinstatement and the payment of back salary.

The verdict was returned after only four hours' deliberation in the courtroom of Federal Judge Leon J. Yankwich.

Its effect, short of possible appeal and reversal, is to restore Cole to the MGM payroll at $1350 a week, and compel the studio to pay him an accumulated salary of $74,250.

Council for MGM indicated the case would be appealed.

Cole was seated between attorneys Ben Margolis and Robert W. Kenny when the jurors came back to the nearly emptied courtroom.

He wept quietly as the court clerk finished reading the Jury's decisions on four questions which they had been instructed to answer by Judge Yankwich.

Cole, who made headlines and lost his job when he defied attempts by the House Committee on Un-American Activities to force him to give a yes-or-no an-

(Continued on Page 9, Col. 2)

There was little alarm in the opposition. The Un-American Activities Committee, along with its allies in Hollywood, John Wayne and his Motion Picture Alliance for the Preservation of American Ideals, patiently awaited the outcome of our trials in the higher courts. They were confident.

The MGM money helped pay expenses for road tours for those who could travel and speak. Herbert made arrangements for me to go to Cleveland, Philadelphia and New York, where we would appeal to groups of trade unionists and others for support.

In Cleveland, my first stop, I was met by Hugh DeLacy, a leading trade union organizer, who would soon become a Congressman from his home state, Washington. I was set to speak to a trade union rally, which I did, and we received

Cole Wins Suit to Regain MGM Job;
Case a Test of Anti-Red Sanctions

Special to The New York Times.

LOS ANGELES, Dec. 17—A Federal District Court jury tonight returned a finding favorable to Lester Cole in his suit against Metro-Goldwyn-Mayer Studios for reinstatement in the $1,350-a-week screen writing job from which he was removed for his defiance of the House Un-American Committee a year ago.

The jury of eight women and four men, after three and a half hours of deliberations, found, in answer to four key questions of fact, that Mr. Cole in his conduct at the committee's Washington hearings had not jeopardized the studio's public relations to a degree warranting his suspension. On the contrary, the jury held, the studio had given tacit sanction to his conduct by leaving him in his position for a month after the hearings.

(Mr. Cole, along with nine other Hollywood figures, declined to give categorical answers to certain committee questions, including whether he was a member of the Communist party.)

The case was the first legal test of the film industry's sanctions against the ten men. The final judgment in the trial remains to be promulgated by United States District Court Judge Leon Yankwich. There was no indication that he would not likewise rule in favor of Mr. Cole.

The plaintiff, a 44-year-old native of New York City and a screen writer for twenty years, wept with relief on hearing the jury's verdict.

The eleven-day trial of the writer's action closed with two hours of instructions to the jurors by Judge Yankich which the defense protested amounted virtually to a directed finding for Mr. Cole.

Judge Yankwich denied that his instructions, to which Mr. Cole's counsel also took some exceptions, were in favor of either side, but

Continued on Page 13, Column 2

strong support. Among the members of DeLacy's committee which had welcomed me were Irma and Mordecai Bauman, who generously put me up at their house. I had met Mordy some years before in Los Angeles when he toured the country with Hans Eisler, the anti-Nazi refugee, a famed composer and collaborator of Bertolt Brecht. Mordy was an accomplished musician; he played and sang Eisler's songs at benefits for the anti-Nazi cause.

Now a marvelous opportunity quite unexpectedly opened up for us. The prestigious City Club offered a luncheon speaker of national renown once a month. Its guest for that Saturday — the very next day after my speech at the trade union rally — U.S. Admiral Halsey, had been forced suddenly to cancel. Quickly, Mordy offered me as a substitute. Desperate, no doubt, because of the cancellation, the City Club director agreed, with one stipulation; following my speech, during the period of questions and answers, I would reply if asked to "the sixty-four-dollar question." I agreed, with the proviso I could do so in my own way; no "yes" or "no." They agreed. That night my appearance was announced on all the radios, and the next morning on the front pages in the Cleveland press. (My appearance before the trade union rally didn't get a line.)

Assisted by DeLacy's and Mordy's intimacy with local folklore, I worked half the night rewriting my speech, which was limited to a half hour. And I worked carefully on the sixty-four-dollar question right up to the time of the luncheon.

The large hall at the City Club was packed. Stories prominently announced that I would answer the sixty-four-dollar question, and that the address would be on statewide radio.

An elegant luncheon was served. I ate little. Finally my time had come and promptly at 1:30 I was introduced. The chairman said, in a warning undertone, that I had to conclude by two o'clock; the Ohio-Michigan football game started then, promptly. I nodded; it would not be difficult. The speech was twenty-two pages long, including my reply to the big question. Hundreds of additional people had come to hear that, I had been told.

The title of my address was "On Trial: Our Traditional Freedoms." I still have a copy of it. Far too long to include here, I will briefly summarize: I spoke of the events in Hollywood (now well-known to the reader) that led up to the hearings. I was surprised by the warm reception and repeated applause which followed some strong statements about democracy, and a seeming understanding that I, indeed the Ten of us, were defending precisely that.

I spoke about the civil suit I had just won, how we were forced to settle, and then of the hypocritical, double use of the morals clause. At that time Robert Mitchum, the film star, had been caught using marijuana, then a felony, and I spoke of it in this way:

> Now about Mister Mitchum. He had an identical morals clause in *his* contract. As in my case, when the news broke of his arrest, the producers rushed into print. But what did they say? No, they didn't plan to invoke the morals clause, to break his contract; on the contrary, they said, "Well, Mitchum really wasn't very well, he wasn't quite, really, you know, aware of what he was doing." They believed in Bob, good old Bob, and believed when he came out of jail — and they pleaded for his immediate parole — he'd come out a fine man, as a result of his experience. Pictures were taken of his wife, of course — you probably saw the captions. Right out of silent film days' titles: she had faith in Bob, she'd always be loyal and wait for him.
>
> I'm glad Mitchum came through and made it. I'm glad he went right back to work, and I hope he's a wiser man for his experience. But I couldn't help wonder — why the silk glove for him, the torture chamber for me? What was the great difference? Both Americans, both had gone to school here, and, as each matured, each found something in this society which dissatisfied him. And then, a further similarity, each sought some way of expressing our dissatisfaction. So far, we're two peas out of the same pod: Mister Mitchum sought tranquility through an avenue of escape; I sought peace of mind through study of what I believed were the realities of our times and a vocal expression of them. There it was, the only difference between us: Mr. Mitchum inhaled, and I exhaled.

That brought considerable laughter and, I felt, a point had been made. The speech took longer than I thought, but I was coming to the end where I was to answer the sixty-four-dollar question. I said, "As I promised, the answer will be a responsive one, and will take little more than one minute or so."

Just then there was commotion behind me, and I was asked to hold up. Someone at the rear of the platform was talking agitatedly over the phone and finally came up with an explanation.

"As you know," this man said to the people at the luncheon, "we have been on radio all over the state of Ohio. It is now two o'clock, and we are being switched off as it's time for Ohio State and Michigan to start their football game. We are being cut off the air. So if you will bear with us, we will tape Mr. Cole's speech now and give it to the radio station for later broadcast, as they feel so many in their listening audience have been waiting for just this portion of what he had to say."

There was laughter. A tape recorder was hooked up to the microphone. Things quieted down, and I began again:

Here is my answer: Following the presidential election in the year 1856, it became known to the community in which he lived that one Professor Hendricks, who held the chair in Agricultural Chemistry at the University of North Carolina, had voted for the Republican presidential candidate Fremont. To vote for a Northern Republican then can be compared only with voting for a Communist now. So outraged was the slave-owner community that Hendricks was hung in effigy on campus. His wife and children fled to the North, and when an attempt was made to tar and feather him, he but narrowly escaped death. He reached his wife, who was safely hidden by abolitionists, *Southern White Abolitionists*, who succeeded in getting them across the Mason Dixon Line by secret trails taken at night, from one underground depot to the next. Of course, the danger to the white abolitionists was great; they weren't hung in effigy — they were hung.

Today, there is no Mason-Dixon Line as a barrier for safety. For those who hold unorthodox views, this entire nation has become that 1856 Dixie — for the recently convicted thief, ex-Congressman Thomas, the Jew and Black hater Congressman John Rankin and this new upstart trying to get into the act, Senator Joe McCarthy. Today, men's homes, shops and offices are spied upon, their phones tapped. At school their children are scorned and ganged up on — all this I know from personal experience. Windows become targets for rocks at night, and little patches of lawn the settings for burning crosses.

This is not an atmosphere in which free speech can survive, let alone prosper. The man who admits he is a Communist or is interested in Marxism under such conditions of whipped-up hatred is free only to reap the whirlwind of a savage, hysteria-driven mob. Such a man is either a fool or a martyr.

And the man who, in such an atmosphere of diseased morality, under pressure of inquisition, seeks to save himself by admitting he was a Communist and accommodates his inquisitors with the names of others, vainly hoping to divert the violence from himself, is both a fool and a coward. I trust I am not a fool, I have no intention of being a martyr. And I pray I'll never be a coward.

And I concluded, after strong, heartwarming applause, with this: "Today the Bill of Rights is at stake. I believe our pride in this nation's great achievements, and our love for its finest traditions, demands that we spare no effort, in these critical times, to do all we can to preserve them. Thank you."

Well, that answer went on the air after the football game and much of Ohio heard it. It was reported in all the Cleveland papers at length. Mordy, Irma, and DeLacy were delighted, as I was.

New York. Family, friends, but more speeches. I was getting weary and terribly homesick. I spoke to the boys and Jonnie every other night or so, but all the kids would ask is, "When're you comin' home?"

At last I could tell them. One more meeting the following night in New York and I'd be on my way. I mention that meeting here only because of an irony; at this meeting would be the famous writer, revered darling, star novelist of the Party literati, Howard Fast. His novels about great figures in American history had been in school libraries throughout the country; in that Cold War time they were beginning to disappear from the shelves — he, too, was being blacklisted. He had been a proscribed member of the Anti-Fascist Refugee Committee, and, I believe, already had spent a few months in jail for contempt. I was expecting his strong support.

Perhaps forty or fifty men and women — playwrights, novelists, actors and actresses, directors, many Party people like Fast, as well as other progressives and members of guilds and unions and politically oriented organizations like the League of American Writers — were there to hear me. I tried hard to make clear the difficulties we faced, the kind of people-power it would take to make sufficient impression upon the Supreme Court when we arrived at that point for the final decision. And I gave some idea of what this was costing us individually and how our friends' contributions helped. Then I concluded by asking who in the room could make a contribution, and who had any ideas on how to raise money.

The first hand up was Howard Fast's, the Party's stalwart, white-haired boy. "Yes, Mr. Fast?" I asked.

"If you are in such need of funds, why don't you sell your fancy houses in the hills and your swimming pools?" He looked around for applause, got a few giggles, then a shocked silence. Some of the people there, I felt, when the collection was over, gave more than they might have to offset that extraordinary remark. Needless to say, Fast's resignation came shortly thereafter; it was apparent with that remark that he was already planning it.

I devote space to this incident because of an article which appeared thirty years later in *TV Guide*, entitled "Why Endure the Humiliation?" written by Fast. In it he tells how he is having lunch in Jerusalem with author Irwin Shaw. Speaking of TV, Shaw said, "You don't need the money, and doing anything decent for the idiot box is highly unlikely. Why endure the humiliation that goes with it?" Fast defended himself and said the writer had to "accept the facts of life." Unfortunately, he went on, when young writers' best efforts are rejected or mutilated "the swimming pool and the house in the hills become a salve for his bruised ego." He had it all worked out that way thirty years ago — for us. And then when he saw the way we were forced to go, he found his goals. The swimming pool and house on the hill in Hollywood, I have recently been told, are now his at last.

November 1948 showed a remarkable shift in the Guild. A year before, the *Screen Writer*, our monthly magazine, had achieved such prestige that George Bernard Shaw wrote an article for us, "Authors and Their Rights," published in August 1947. Oscar Hammerstein II wrote in reply, and a special section was devoted to the critical economic condition of the film writers. Under the heading, "1 percent of the Gross," five writers wrote on the future economic outlook for writers. My article was on royalties, on a percentage of the gross; Ring Lardner and Philip Stevenson added to this; and other aspects on the deteriorating situation were described by Paul Gangelin and Martin Field. They were strong, militant. Every article urged writers to be prepared to fight when the new contract was due for renegotiation the following year.

The famed Southern California weather couldn't prevent these years from being the winter of discontent for many and the time of fear for many more. A long-time left-wing writer, Milton Krims, who in 1939 had collaborated with John Wexley on the screenplay of *Confessions of a Nazi Spy*, didn't wait for the whistle to blow, perhaps sounding his name. He quickly built his defense with an anti-Soviet screenplay called *The Iron Curtain*; who could offer better testimony if and when "they" called him to the stand?

Despite setbacks, the anti-blacklist suit was being continued with Thurman Arnold as counsel, and we remained confident in our fight against the contempt citations. Then, to our shock and dismay, one after the other, Supreme Court Justices Murphy and Rutledge, two of the most liberal, died in late 1949 and early 1950. They were among the six upon whom we counted; now, with former Attorney General Tom Clark elevated to the high bench with another conservative whose name is forgotten, President Truman shockingly lowered the curtain on us.

There was some celebrating in Hollywood. The Alliance, Roy Brewer and their right-wing followers, had triumphed. But there were others who felt differently. The decision, if I recall, was handed down in April, and we were ordered to appear before the judges in Washington for sentencing in June. The day after the decision I received a phone call from Jack Cummings. Would I — alone — come to his house that night; he wanted to talk to me.

When I arrived he shook my hand warmly, poured a couple of drinks, and then said, "How are you fixed? You know, financially?"

I explained how the years of trials and travels had taken their toll, but we'd retrenched and I thought my wife and sons would make it until I got out. In three years we had sold three houses, each time buying a cheaper one, now ending in a little bungalow on Orange Grove Avenue between Sunset Boulevard and Fountain Avenue that I bought for eleven thousand dollars. It was in the clear. The taxes were low.

He nodded. "I want to make you a proposition. Have you any idea how many weeks before you go in?"

"Looks like about eight or ten. We're not sure yet."

"Okay. Have you got a friend, a writer you can trust? Someone not in any way involved?"

I wasn't sure what he was getting at, but I said I knew I could find one.

"Okay, get him. Someone, if possible, who earns at least as much as you. I've got a book by Frank Harris, some episodes of his life in Spain. Make a deal with the guy —

trustworthy, mind you, who can keep a secret — he'll be hired, come to the studio part of each day, go back and work with you the rest of the day, and you two decide how to split the salary." He grinned, he felt good about it. I know tears rose in my eyes. I hugged him. We drank to it. Then he added: "Look, make it clear. After you go, if I can keep him on, he still sends your wife your split every week."

I nodded, gulped my drink. "You'll hear from me soon, Jack."

There was some thinking to do. A good writer, a trusted friend. And my mind went to those I knew who were in need. Mel Levy, with wife and two daughters, not black-listed but hadn't worked in almost two years. How marvelous! As soon as I got home, I called him, told him I had a job for him, to come to the house first thing in the morning. Of course, he wanted details right then; how could I have a job for him when I couldn't get one for myself? He'd have to wait for morning, I told him.*

When I explained it to him, we discovered a problem. His last salary was only six hundred a week; how could he get enough to share so that Jonnie and the kids would get something worthwhile out of it.

Jack solved it. How he got Levy my former salary, twelve hundred fifty a week, I don't know, but he did. I decided to split it evenly with him, on the condition that should the job last beyond my departure for jail, he would continue to give Jonnie my share to the end. He happily agreed, and we started to work.

Finally the Court notices came. First Jack Lawson and Dalton Trumbo in early June, and we eight to follow in a couple of weeks. Jonnie came east with me for that last day, to be there at the sentencing. Whether we could afford it or not, she had to be at the prison gate to kiss me goodbye.

---

*This is one of the few events the FBI never learned about. It's theirs now; no charge. I name the name — Levy — for reasons soon to be explained.

The boys were with my mother, at our house. I tried to cheer them up. Mel Levy assured me he'd hang on to the job by hook or crook for as long as he could. Friends and comrades, we embraced.

At the airport newspapers estimated a thousand loyal supporters were there to wish us well. Large posters demanded that the government "Free the Hollywood Ten." Tearfully we said goodbye and boarded the plane.

From then on it was routine. Back in Washington, each stood before his convicting District judge to be sentenced. One year in a federal prison, $1,000 fine. Each of us was permitted to make a statement before being sentenced. We were advised of this ritual the night before by our attorneys, and each of us spoke briefly. I said:

> Your Honor: Aside from varying degrees of skill, all writers, including lesser ones such as I, possess but two fundamental tools with which to work — our minds and our hearts. The writer who sells either does not add to his wealth. He squanders it. A few short years ago the Supreme Court handed down a decision which made an indelible impression on my mind. In part, it said: "If there is a fixed star in our constitutional constellation, it is that no official, high or petty, shall prescribe what shall be orthodox in politics, religion, nationalism, or in matters of opinion, or force citizens to confess by word or act their faith therein."*

I went on:

> I am guided by that star today, as I was when I appeared before the Committee on Un-American Activities two and a half years ago. For I believe it is in the light of that fundamental concept that there can exist the freedom of thought and conscience necessary to guide our nation to the path of democracy and the world to the road of peace and fraternity.

Was this honestly spoken? Can a Communist believe, as

---

*Supreme Court Justice Jackson for the Majority, *Hartnett vs US*, 1955.

I said, in the Constitution? Emphatically yes, but with the Constitutional right to amend it. With freedom of thought, with peaceful coexistence of nations, it is my deepest conviction that the contradictions in the present system will bring about its eventual downfall, that man's exploitation of man's labor for profit cannot last forever.

That last night in Washington with Jonnie was beautiful. Love, vows of loyalty, talking of what she could do to make it easy for the children. She told again with laughter and pride something Michael, now eleven, had said a few months before when the Supreme Court turned us down. The news had been in the papers that morning, and in Michael's civics class the teacher had been jubilant and spoke of how splendidly our democratic system worked and that the Hollywood Ten would now surely go to jail. All eyes, as Mike told us later, were on him. It seems just about everyone in that class except his teacher knew his father was one of the Ten. Finally, he raised his hand and said, "Miss (So-and-So), you couldn't say that if you'd ever read the Constitution. Why don't you just read the First Amendment?" More than half the kids in the class applauded as Mike, tears in his eyes, walked out of the class and came home. We induced him to return that afternoon, and the next day his teacher made some sort of apology.

Now it was time. We remaining eight appeared at the proper time at the entrance to the Washington, D.C., jail, tears in the eyes of wives and husbands. Desperately, we broke from embraces and hurried in. Washington was only temporary, two to three weeks, after which we were to be separated to the prisons nearest our relatives. There were eight such minimum security prisons spread throughout the country at the time, but the closest to California was in Oklahoma, and I chose Danbury, Connecticut. With mother and sister in New York, I planned to move Jonnie and the kids there as soon as it could be arranged.

There, in Washington, during the daily exercise period,

we'd meet and march around the inside perimeter, discussing news, plans to pick our prisons. Ring's mother had a home not twenty-five miles from Danbury. We both requested transfer there. During those ten days, the Korean War broke out and convicts began looking at us with hatred, as if we were killing American boys. However, I did accomplish something during the two-week stay there. A traveling library came to the cells each day with books, and I found something that all my life I had wanted to read and never had found time for: Tolstoy's eleven-hundred-odd pages of *War and Peace*. I finished it the night before Ring and I were transported to Danbury Federal Correctional Institution.

In Washington that morning we were handcuffed to each other. The guard who was in charge of us — only one; we were not violent criminals — suggested we throw one of our jackets over the cuffs to conceal them. It did make us look as if we were walking hand-in-hand, but we must have concluded that would be less conspicuous and embarrassing than the visible cuffs.

By train from Washington to New York. Transfer to the New York, New Haven and Hartford out of Grand Central Station, off at South Norwalk, Connecticut, and from there to Danbury by bus, up Highway 7.

We didn't speak much, except about the friends we'd meet there. The late Dr. Jacob Auslander was finishing a three-month sentence for refusing to talk to the Committee about his participation in the Anti-Fascist Refugee Committee. It had aided Spanish Republicans who had escaped to France after Franco, Hitler and Mussolini had crushed Spain's democratically elected government, as well as supporting the International Brigades which volunteered their aid to the Spanish Republic.

Another friend was Carl Marzani, a brilliant Rhodes scholar, formerly in the State Department, a Marxist, who was framed on a perjury charge. It would be helpful, comforting to have friends there who were already experienced.

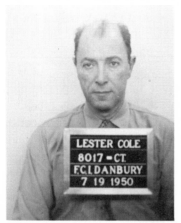 

Mug shots, courtesy the Danbury Federal Correction Institution.

There would be much for us to learn. They would make it easier.

In the town of Danbury we were picked up by a prison car, and in fifteen minutes were atop the broad flattened hill where the "institution" was located. It was a quadrangle, perhaps two hundred or so yards on each of its four sides, two stories high. The outer grounds were well kept, lawns and shrubs everywhere, and, as we were to learn, the large interior garden was a lawn with a baseball field and a four-tiered "grandstand" of benches for those who weren't playing on the teams to watch the games.

We arrived in mid-afternoon, were admitted, and at once the handcuffs were removed. Led to a room where we un-dressed, showered, went through the unvarying delousing procedure, we checked our wallets and whatever valuables we had in sealed and signed envelopes. We were permitted to keep our wristwatches. Issued prison garb of underwear and grey jacket and pants, we were then led to a room where a prisoner, obviously a trusty, fingerprinted us, placed a number on our chests and photographed us. Ring became 8016 and

I 8017. Ring was then taken away, and soon I was in the office of a parole officer; Ring was in the next room being interviewed by another.

A weary-seeming, impersonal man, he first explained routinely about Danbury: "This is not a prison, Cole, it is a correctional institution. No special privileges for anyone; you're all numbered and treated as numbers. By keeping your nose clean you get, by statute, five days off each month for good time. That is called Statutory Good Time, or SGT. If you have one year, SGT cuts it to ten months. Beyond that, for any innovative service you might introduce to institution life, there is MGT, or Meritorious Good Time. For this it is possible to gain as much as a month more in the year. That is decided by the officials at regular meetings. Another thing, very important. This is a minimum security institution. There are no violent prisoners here; business fraud, income tax evasion cases, auto theft across state boundaries and the like. No violence." Then he paused for emphasis. "The punishment for violence is severe. Solitary confinement, and then transfer to a maximum security prison. Am I making myself clear?"

I was puzzled why he placed such emphasis on this. "Of course!"

"I would like more than that," he said. "I want you to know you will be watched, and at the first sign of intended violence —"

"Wait a minute! I'm here on a misdemeanor, which has nothing to do with violence. My feeling toward Congress — I was convicted for contempt, not violence."

He didn't seem satisfied. "There are rumors already here in advance of your arrival that both you and Lardner are prepared for violent revenge if you can get away with it."

I was astonished, to say the least. "Who the hell could have said that? I only know a couple of people in here, but they're my friends."

He nodded. "Auslander and Marzani. I'm not talking about them. No one else?"

"Not to my knowledge."

"Will you swear you are not planning some sort of revenge against J. Parnell Thomas, who is in this institution?"

For a few seconds dumfounded, I suppose I must have laughed long and loud. What a delightful coincidence! We had read, of course, of how Drew Pearson had remained true to his vow. He gathered evidence that proved Thomas was taking kickbacks of a few dollars a week — chicken feed — from the friends and relatives he had put on his staff. Thrown out of Congress, then pleading *nole contendre* in Federal Court, Thomas was sentenced to a term of six to eighteen months and hauled off — where to, we had no idea.

"This is no joke," the officer said severely. "The rumor is persistent."

I shook my head. "He must have started it himself. Kill him? My greatest pleasure will be seeing him here with his own kind, petty thieves."

The officer looked a little uncomfortable. "It's true; it was Thomas who suggested it when he learned you were coming here."

"Sorry," he added, "but it was my duty to look into the matter. Consider it closed." He then told me I would be permitted to spend ten dollars a month in the commissary, I would work in a job for which they considered me suitable; and my salary would be twelve cents an hour for an eight-hour day. The interview was over.

He then walked me down the hall to the large quarantine room, where new prisoners are held for three weeks to see if they have any communicable diseases or emotional disorders, and where they take IQ tests and are evaluated for job placement.

The officer left me inside the door, and waiting there was Ring. Our eyes met, filled with mirth, and instantly we knew we had been asked the same question.

"What luck!" he said, and we both laughed. "There's got to be a way, a dozen ways, to make the bastard miserable."

"We'll find at least one." I laughed. "Kill him? Christ,

that would just be putting him out of his misery! We can do better than that." And our chance came, as devilish a diversion as any men ever found in a prison — or even a correctional institution.

During those first three weeks, we went through physical tests and went to eat in the main mess hall after the general population had finished their meals. On the very first day, Carl Marzani and Jake Auslander were waiting outside to greet us. We weren't permitted then to talk or shake hands, but what a wonderful feeling to see their smiles; there was such reassurance in their calm and seemingly sprightly manner that I know I for one felt bolstered, strengthened.

And in three weeks we were out in the "population," as it is called, assigned to dormitories which housed forty-eight inmates. Privacy was provided by steel enclosures around each bed, leaving an area of perhaps six by nine feet, four feet six inches high, and an opening without a door for entering and leaving.

The place was clean; ample showers, clean bedding. Built as one of Roosevelt's Federal Projects, it was something of a model, and it was well maintained. Quickly we noticed, however, that when it came to housing and the mess hall, Jim Crow ruled. The population was about four hundred fifty, and the Blacks were a distinct minority, somewhere between one hundred fifty and one hundred seventy five. They were housed on the second floors of the dormitories, we on the first. And in the mess hall, which served cafeteria style, there were two lines, one for Black, one for white. The meals were the same, but at the serving table they received the food on the left side of the steam table, we on the right.

I soon became familiar with the layout: the "campus" was the well-kept lawn, and the softball field, and at the rear was the gate leading to the farmland, where assigned prisoners went out each day to work. There was a library with perhaps eighteen thousand books, and prisoners were permitted to have books sent in if they came from bookstores. If fiction, they became the property of the prison; if non-fiction, for study or educational purposes of any sort, the books remained your private property, to be released with you. There was an education department, where night classes were held under the tutelage of educated convicts who taught illiterates to read and write, and semi-literates to improve themselves. As one of the latter, I enrolled in a correspondence course of the University of Chicago. Immediately I wrote to my mother, to tell her how wonderful it all was. At last I was going to college and at government expense. Free college education, just like in the Socialist countries. She didn't think that was funny. (Maybe it wasn't.) I took courses in English, in writing prose and fiction; I read some fascinating books recommended by a professor named Rappaport (his first name escapes me) and a book, *Language in Thought and Action*, by Professor S.I. Hayakawa. Written in his youthful, liberal days, it was a revelation of how those who manage our economy also manage the manipulation of language to convey and create impressions by distorting phraseology. (Who would have thought he would become an expert practitioner of such misuses himself, first in the late sixties as strike-breaker of the Black Students Union at San Francisco State College, and then in the U.S. Senate?)

Ring got a job in the parole office as a typist-clerk; I was put to work in the warehouse, where the food came in. Cases of canned food, sides of beef and pork arrived daily, and I would arrange the various items in orderly fashion for inventory and future ordering, as well as easy accessibility.

Our first day out of quarantine, we saw J. Parnell. In the large grass quadrangle, you could always spot him, five-by-five, scurrying at least fifty feet away when he saw us coming.

Thomas was in charge of the chicken coops where hundreds of hens laid eggs daily, supplying the institution. His job was to gather the eggs and scrape up the droppings. These coops were on the prison farm a short distance outside the back gate, in a hay field. At night, a few guards, or "screws," as they were called by the cons, often would stop on their way home and pick up a couple of fresh eggs for their kids. Thomas's patriotism was outraged, and he reported the screws by name to the warden.

A snitcher, stoolie, canary. Cons and screws not only hated him, but spread the word to see that Thomas had a bad time.

My own personal confrontation with Thomas came a month or more later. The hay was ready to be cut, and it was done by hand. I was taken from the warehouse for a few days, along with others, handed a scythe and put to work cutting. My work area took me to the enclosing wire of the chicken yards, and there, atop one of the coops was Thomas, a hoe in hand, scraping chicken droppings from the roof to which the hens would fly when released for exercise.

He saw me, and no doubt feeling secure with an eight-foot barbed wire fence between us, called down, "Hey, Bolshie, I see you still got your sickle. Where's your hammer?"

And I yelled back, and the cons heard me, "And I see just like in Congress, you're still picking up chickenshit." The cons knew about his petty thievery. They got the point. From then on he was politely addressed as Congressman Chickenshit.

Letters came from Jonnie and the boys, and the second one bothered me. Mel Levy, now working alone, had paid her my share the first week, then stopped. She called him, he had said, yes, he was still on the job, but he needed it for his mortgage, was sorry he didn't call, but would make it up the following week by sending her the whole amount. The following week nothing came. It was incredible; was this my Comrade, the man out of work for two years, welshing, stealing from my wife and kids? I couldn't believe it. I wrote to her at once, told her to demand it. She did. He said he was sorry, or words to that effect, but nothing came. I told her to call Jack and explain. The day she called Jack, Levy was fired. I told her to inform the Party. I heard more about Levy later.

Jake Auslander finished his time and left. Marzani still had a year and a half to go. He worked in the boiler or engineering room from midnight to eight in the morning. As a result, he lived in a building with single cells for night workers. Thomas, when he heard we were arriving, pleaded with the warden to give him a single cell which would be locked at night — for protection against bodily harm. Coincidentally, their cells were adjacent. But they had never spoken.

At this time Ring, Carl, and I were planning something a bit chancy. There was no way we could end Jim Crow in the sleeping quarters, but we thought of a simple way to end it in the mess hall; we decided to try.

Lines formed along walls to the right and left. Since the Blacks were such a minority, their line was always half the length of ours; they'd get their stomachs filled twice as soon. Can an empty stomach change a mind? We could try. One lunch time there were at least two hundred fifty on the white line, and maybe one hundred on the Black line. Carl, Ring and I calmly walked over and got on the shorter line. The whites looked over in astonishment; the Blacks were both curious and wise; the wise ones grinned their appreciation.

Two days later, a similar disparity existed, and three other whites joined us. In a week the Black line became longer than the white, and the Blacks were going over to the shorter white line. It was over.

Through the grapevine we heard the Associate Warden, a Georgian, was so outraged that he complained that the Reds had upset the whole routine in the dining room. But the Warden, a New Englander, listened with astonishment. According to the gossip, he said he'd been trying for years to end that goddam stupid Jim Crow practice. Thank God it was over. When the grapevine brought us this news, we were overjoyed and, frankly, not a little relieved. Who knew what punishment we might have received had the Associate Warden been in charge?

The time was passing quickly when one of us hit upon the idea we were long awaiting — how to torment Parnell Thomas. He had maintained that not only were we atomic spy agents, but that Marzani's Red comrades ran the State Department. "Ask McCarthy," he would say. This is what we devised:

Thomas's consideration for parole was due after the first six of his eighteen months. That was two months away. By this time we had plenty of friends among the prisoners, men we felt we could trust. We got two of them to go to Thomas and tell him they knew how right he was about Marzani's power in the State Department, but he had drag in Justice, too. They let on that they had overheard Carl talking to us about getting his important friends in that department to stop Thomas's parole from going through. The best thing Thomas could do was be nice to Marzani; they advised Thomas to butter Marzani up, and make sure he wouldn't use his influence against Congressman Chickenshit.

The next morning, as Carl was coming in from the boiler room, he was "astonished" by Thomas bidding him a cheerful good morning and offering daily to exchange his *New York News* for Carl's *New York Times*. Carl was not going to be that easily had. So he looked with contempt at Thomas and said, "Suckin' up for something?" and walked away. But Thomas didn't, couldn't, give up; he offered, if he got parole, to use his influence to get Ring and myself paroled — he did everything but kiss Carl's hand — and more. Carl played tough.

Thomas's parole date came, and he was refused. The cons were overjoyed, and gleefully our prisoner co-conspirators told Thomas it was his own fault; he simply wasn't nice enough to Carl. Thomas swore there was nothing more he could do and promptly fell into a slump that put him in bed for a week.

At this point Carl felt we'd gone far enough. He gave nothing away, but went to Thomas's cell and told him, "Look, I just want to say, whatever power I have, or you think I have, I will not use it against you. Okay?" Thomas was tearfully grateful. When, three months later, after nine months, President Truman pardoned him, Thomas tearfully thanked Carl, went to the wardrobe for his clothing. Later the trusty in charge reported him snarling, "Those Reds! They're running the country. They got so much clout they even got Truman to pardon me. If it's the last thing I do, I'll see everyone of them in for life." After delivering that righteous vow, he left, and within months drank himself to death.

Suddenly Carl was no longer at Danbury. He was gone! Where? We soon learned what had happened: in that boiler room where he watched gauges on the wall, Carl was working hours each night on a book calling for peaceful coexistence between the U.S. and the USSR., which he titled: *We Can Be Friends.** Although the prison rules strictly state that an inmate can keep whatever he writes so long as it does not speak of prison conditions, Carl was afraid they would confiscate his manuscript. He was determined to outfox them. We tried to think of ways: Blanche, my sister, visited every two weeks, as did Ring's mother. But obviously to risk their sneaking out pages could criminally implicate them, and we discarded all such ideas.

Since Ring's mother lived not more than twenty or thirty miles away, and she drove her car to visit him, Marzani's final plan was this: a young farm lad, in for some minor crime, had taken a liking to Carl, and since the youngster went out the gate to the farm to work each day, Carl asked him whether periodically he would tie six or eight pages of his manuscript to his thigh, to avoid its detection, hide it in the floor of a well-known deserted farmhouse on the edge of

---

*Carl Marzani, *We Can Be Friends*. (New York: Marzani & Munsell, 1953.).

the dirt road where the prison farm ends. There Mrs. Lardner would pick it up on her visits to Ring.

Everything went smoothly. Carl had perhaps two hundred pages written and stashed away, soon ready for Mrs. Lardner to pick up. It was then the screws discovered what the kid was doing. Into solitary went Carl. The manuscript was confiscated. At dawn the next morning he was shipped to the Lewisburg, Pennsylvania, Reformatory, a medium-security prison. He was, of course, stripped of parole possibility and of SGT. He served his full three years to the day, and it was more than two years before we saw him and heard the ironic climax: upon leaving prison, he was told what he had already known: the only writing not permitted to be taken out was that which described prison living conditions. All he had written belonged to him. His punishment was not for what he had written, but for the method of attempting to get it out.

We were not idle. There was always something to do. Ring and I organized a bridge tournament, which helped pass the time. But more varied events kept time moving. One day a young con, about twenty-eight, came to work with me in the warehouse. He was a four-time loser, a thief, sent up from Atlanta Penitentiary to spend his last months in minimum security, to acclimate him to something "closer to the outside." The idea was sensible. Unlike Atlanta Penitentiary, smoking was permitted here in the mess hall, as was conversation; silence was demanded everywhere in maximum security pens.

A muscle man, he worked out in the gym every night, and from then on it was he who would carry the hundred-pound bags of rice and potatoes into the building from the loading platform.

The first day he came up to me and said, "Look, I know about you."

"How come?"

"Gene Dennis told me to look you up. Great guy." Dennis, former head of the Party, was serving time in the Atlanta

Pen under the Smith Act. "We got a lot in common."

Had Dennis converted this youngster? He answered the question for me. "It's this way. I steal for a living. Cars. Stealing is no crime. Everyone from Truman on down is crooks. A crime ain't stealing, the crime is getting caught. You don't like this government, and I don't. That puts us on the same side."

And it did. In two days Smitty was criticizing my waistline, which had grown to thirty-nine inches and my weight to one hundred eighty, up twenty pounds. He insisted that I come to gym with him and he'd put me into training. He did. When I left Danbury I weighed one hundred fifty-eight on the warehouse scale. 8017's waistline was down to thirty-two.

Ronald Reagan (r.) with Bonzo, star of his most memorable films. When Reagan became president of the Screen Actors' Guild he became the industry's watch-dog, making sure that blacklisted actors could not work.

15

The Great Debate:
Resolved: That Prisons Serve A Useful Social Function

One day a break came in the routine of reading, working and going to the gym. A young Canadian of about twenty-two had been drafted and deserted because he was opposed to the Korean War. He slipped to this country without a passport, was caught, got a year and a day, and ended up in the Educational Department teaching the illiterate among us. But he was a — no other word will describe it — fanatical Marxist, which of course, he concealed from the head of the department. He asked if he could hold lectures on "current events" one evening a week. Permission was granted, and he immediately began a course in Marxist interpretation of current events. The inmates didn't complain, but he did — to Ring and me. He couldn't understand why so few men attended, how so many could miss matters of such importance.

We tried to explain. We told him of some of our experiences. One Saturday night at the prison movie the cons' resentment against the government was so great that when the newsreel film pictured Stalin as the greatest enemy of the U.S., perversely they cheered. Were they Communists? When they next saw a picture of Hitler, they *also* cheered. They knew nothing of politics and history, and few gave a damn. They were doing time and hated those who were forcing it on them.

The Canadian was so downcast that Ring made a suggestion. How about enlivening his meetings by holding a debate — but on a subject that would directly interest the inmates? And what was that, the miserable young man wanted to know, "Sodomy?"

Ring thought for a moment, looked slyly toward me, and said, as if the idea just came to him, "I've got it! The debate should be: 'Resolved, that prisons serve a useful social function'."

The kid stared at him as if he were crazy. "We could get a hundred guys to take the negative in here," he said, "but who's the goddam fool'd risk taking the affirmative?"

Whereupon Ring, prepared for that, grinned and calmly jerked a thumb toward me. "Lester will."

He was right; I would. A year or so before coming to prison, I had read in *Political Affairs*, the Marxist monthly, a fascinating translation of a section of a chapter from Marx's little-known fourth volume of *Das Kapital*. Only this section and a few other excerpts had thus far been translated into English. Marx, in his polemics, often showed a keen sense of humor, and this piece had given me an idea for a play which I was working on. I nodded, "Yes." We both laughed, and agreed that neither would show what he was going to say to the other.

The debate was announced in the little weekly four-page *The Nutmeg*, put out by inmates. The paper reported who got parole, new arrivals, coming movies, etc. But the item which now excited the greatest interest was the one which read: "DEBATE, February 10, in Education Room 212 at 7:30. Subject: Resolved, that prisons serve a useful social function. For the Negative, 8016, for the Affirmative, 8017."

I was transformed in less than an hour from one of the

more likeable and respected cons to a "fink," "stoolie," an "ass-kisser for parole." Smiles became scowls. My friend Smitty, loyal as he wanted to be, was worried; what the hell was I up to? I assured him there was a catch to it, a funny one, and for him to take my word for it; I didn't want to spoil the evening by telling him in advance. Skeptically, he let it go at that.

The rooms in the Education Department seated about twenty people, but on occasion the sliding doors, room-wide, could be opened if two rooms were needed. That night, four room doors were opened. By 7:30 over sixty-five men had gathered. Our young friend was astonished, but so were the screws. Usually one guard sufficed; they now called for reenforcements.

The debate, usually with two on a side, was limited to Ring and myself. While Ring could get plenty of associates for his side, no one wanted to join me in the Affirmative.

A chairman had been selected; a businessman who ran afoul of the IRS and knew the rules of order. He took his seat. Ring stood up to wild cheers, and when I followed it was boos and hisses. The Chairman rapped for order. Silence at last, he said:

"Our subject tonight is, alas, all too well known. We have for the Negative, 8016." Lardner rose, his papers in hand, to tremendous applause. When it finally quieted down, he began. What follows is an abridged but accurate report of the debate. It was written by us during the preceding week and confiscated by one of the guards immediately after we concluded. But a friendly guard surreptitiously slipped it to me months later as I left Danbury. I still have the worn, yellowed pages.

Ring started by apologizing to the assembled cons for any possible academic language he might use instead of resorting to the more colorful lingo of his prison mates and went on to state the three historic and one modern socially useful purpose *claimed* for prisons: to protect society by keeping the dishonest in jail; to punish criminals as a warning against repeating their crimes in the future; to prevent potential criminals by threat of punishment; and, finally, to rehabilitate the wrongdoer.

"These four propositions, I shall prove," he said, "are unsound, fallacious, preposterous, and totally lacking in reality . . . prisons will be seen as institutions serving no social purpose whatever."

He proceeded cleverly and amusingly to develop his argument pointing out that after serving time a prisoner is paroled or released and that he then has to make up for lost time by practicing his "profession more intensively, proven to everyone by the high rate of recidivism. No punishment in history ever stopped crime." He showed that despite jails and "other forms of torture" throughout history, such as the rack and wheel and the Iron Maiden, and the modern form of torture — keeping human beings locked up — crime increased century after century. ". . . our courts still use torture to get confessions and concessions," he went on. "Torture a man by promising him a lighter sentence or even immunity if he'll snitch against one of his co-workers." He called that procedure ". . . no less barbaric morally than the physical method of pulling fingernails or squeezing a man's balls in a vise." At this point some of the cons yelled, cheering him on. They were with him, lapping it up.

"Previous societies," Ring continued, "had more common sense than the hypocrisies of today. Then, if a man committed perjury, you'd stop repetition more effectively by cutting out his tongue than giving him three years in a pen filled with other liars who will only help him improve his technique.

"As for rape, which is more effective — cutting his cock off or putting him in a compulsory monastery from which he comes outside so horny he knocks over the first woman he sees?"

At this point someone yelled: "If he don't find himself a young punk *in*side." They laughed so hard some nearly fell out of their seats.

Ring then declared that "to the typical police mind," the importance of jails is their supposed inhibiting factor to the "potential offender." Hitler, he said, was the most devoted practitioner of this theory in modern times; to him it was just as logical to punish the innocent as the guilty. Ring quoted a character in a Dickens novel who was angry because they couldn't find the murderer of his cousin to punish and declared, "Better hang the wrong fellow than no fellow." "If, however, you don't believe that, if you don't believe that fear generates deterrence . . . then the whole question of deterrence makes no sense.

"Scaring people into being lawful has never worked. Three hundred years ago in England they handed out the death sentence for stealing a loaf of bread. This killed a lot of hungry people, but it didn't lessen the number of loaves stolen. What does a hungry, out-of-work man do to feed his family?"

"Steal!" the sixty-odd men roared in unison.

Ring nodded. Then he told how "penology" was developed into a new profession, which advocated, instead of punishment, ". . . the teaching of the virtues of honesty, decency, and the faithful serving of society." He had the audience waiting on his words now. "Okay, so here we are in a modern, enlightened type jail. It's clean, and I like that. I'm grateful that it's not one of those filthy, rat-infested slammers where many of you have spent years of your lives. Well, how are they rehabilitating us? We've got an educational department here, but less than 10 percent use it. What are you going to do with the education when you get out? Have they got a good-paying job for you, or are you learning in here so that you will have the honor of getting killed in Korea when they open the gate?"

He argued that the authorities are aware that what they are doing isn't any good, but they don't know how to change the society so that those who rebel against it no longer commit crimes. The rate keeps growing.* And he quoted Christ "Judge

---

*The prison debate was in early 1951. Thirty years later the crime rate is growing faster than ever. As this book goes to press, a recent headline somberly announced: "U.S. STARTS PLANS FOR ATTACKING CRIME."

not, lest you be judged. Resist not evil. He that is without sin, let him cast the first stone." Then he contended that the death sentence by the government is as great a sin as when a mentally deranged person kills with a knife, a concept so clear that "only a man of the church could find the ability to misinterpret it." And then he concluded with a sly twinkle, looking at me, "I cannot see how my opponent, in arguing that this pernicious prison system serves a useful social purpose, is not engaging in a very *un*-American activity." They knew my "crime" and they roared. Ring concluded by challenging me to prove that prisons are "ethical, Christian and American."

There was much applause and then the chairman said, "And now, 8017 for the affirmative." They booed and hooted and made farting noises, and one con clowned as though he were my second, fanned me with a piece of paper, pushed me out as if I was a fighter in a ring who had been punched silly for ten rounds.

Finally it quieted down and I started. "For the last week, since it became known that I consented, for the sake of what I hope will be for you an evening of amusement and enlightenment, to prove that prisons serve a useful social function. . . ."

From all parts of the room came yells of scorn and disapproval. "You're suckin' up for parole, you fuckin' fink."

"Let him go on," a few yelled, and the audience finally quieted down. I began boldly by calling the prison the cornerstone of the social structure in our society today. I emphasized *today* because, I said, "our society, like all others, will change . . . The prison today is as indispensable as marble pillars are to the temple, as the keystone is to the arch. Without the pillars the temple would topple, without the keystone the arch would collapse into the swirling waters of anarchy."

They weren't buying it so far. "Fink! Stoolie!" they yelled.

"Hear — me — out!" I yelled, and when they quieted down I went on. "To solve the problem, there are just three avenues open to our wise law-makers today, to our great self-less statesmen and professors who give their time and effort for our nation's welfare — and for a fat fee, of course. These three avenues are to eliminate punishment for crime, letting everyone steal and the devil take the hindmost; eliminate the criminals themselves by invoking the death penalty for every crime, no matter how trifling; and third, to eliminate crime itself. Which of these three can be done?"

There were still a few hoots and howls, but some were beginning to show interest. I proceeded to analyze the pos-sibilities of each. By the elimination of punishment, no one would suffer more than the thief himself. Instead of having two million crooks, because more people would be out of work by eliminating punishment, we'd have fifty, sixty, a hundred million thieves. "The competition would be cutthroat, and you'd be fighting each other instead of the cops," I argued.

I told them how a few years ago two professors conducted a sociological survey out of a southwestern university. "They wanted to find out how many so-called respectable people, like themselves, had committed undetected but indictable crimes during the past year. They confined their questions to such normal occupations as larceny, tax evasion, fraud, robbery — in fact, all the practices in society common to all of us seeking life, liberty and the pursuit of happiness. That's what the Declaration of Independence says we're entitled to, and if it's true, that would give us all immunity. . . . well, the con-fidential anonymous replies of eighteen hundred people in all walks of life, from all parts of the country, revealed that 91 percent had committed at least one crime which, had they been caught and indicted, would have meant imprisonment. I refer to this phenomenon for one reason: it shows the needs and wants of people finally dictate the laws, the laws do not dictate the needs and wants. It is why the maxim, 'God helps those who help themselves,' had been revised without our permission, by those who make the laws, to read, 'By all means help yourself, but God help you if you get caught doing so!'"

There was laughter for the first time, and Smitty was on his feet, yelling excitedly, "I been sayin' that fer years! The penalty ain't for stealin', it's for gettin' caught!"

"Thank you, Mr. Smith," I said with warm gratitude, "that is precisely my point." I had their attention now. "So to conclude Point One, which is what would happen if we eliminated punishment for crimes committed, instead of two or three million thieves, 90-odd percent of our population would be engaged openly in crime. We'd be stealing from each other. In no time, there'd be nothing left to steal but what had already been stolen."

I went on to Point Two, the elimination of criminals. "This idea has recurred throughout history. In primitive societies the devices were crude. In the Stone Age, the unworthy fellow was placed at the bottom of a cliff in the path of a boulder which they'd roll onto his head. As technological skills developed, we passed through such picturesque devices as nailing a culprit to a cross, there to let him bleed and starve to death, to hacking off his head with beautifully sharpened scimitars . . . the rack, the wheel, the comical idea of drawing and quartering him by tying him to four horses by his four limbs and having the horses separate, tearing him apart, giving gentlemen spectators the opportunity to wager on which limb would be the first pulled from his body. Then the very civilized and cultured French introduced the guillotine, the sports-loving British the hangman's noose, and, finally, thanks to American superior technical knowhow we have electrical devices which speed the departure of the miscreant in but a moment or two, as well as the ultra-modern gas chamber in which the fortunate fellow need only draw a few breaths. As ingenious methods of elimination multiply, and the threat of their use is ever more highly publicized, something seemed wrong; unemployment increased, more people need and want more than ever before because advertising whets their appetites, and along with it the rate of crime increases.

"You've heard it said, and we know it to be the truth, that an artist lives to paint his pictures, a composer lives to write his music, a writer lives to create his novels and plays and poetry. But a thief is different. He doesn't live to steal. He steals to *live!*"

Some cons got to their feet and cheered at that!

"Perhaps the most vivid and illustrous failure of applying the severity of punishment as a deterrent to crime occurred during the reign of Queen Elizabeth in England, during the seventeenth century, when, as you heard, the death decree was issued for stealing a loaf of bread worth less than one shilling. From this my worthy opponent drew the wrong conclusion. It was *not*, as he said, that despite the death threat for stealing bread they continued to steal. The punishment failed for quite another reason, which is at the heart of my argument.

"In those days, among the common people, crime was so widespread because of poverty and hunger, so pervasive in town and country, that the authorities passed this most stringent law — death for stealing a loaf of bread. Yet despite this severity, in defiance of Her Majesty, an entire country openly and publicly went out and looted everything in sight. It was insurrection. No queen could tolerate such defiance. Her wrath at the boiling point, she ordered thousands executed, according to law. But before that could be carried out, the wise Earl of Warwick, one of her principal advisers, asked to speak to her in private chambers. There it is reported he said, 'Stay thy hand, good Queen. Hasten not with this law. Would you, to eliminate thieves, eliminate *all* the working folk? Would not the land then have to be plowed by your noblemen, and your ladies labor at the weaver's trade?' *That* horror ended the idea of killing them off, the fear of having the nobility themselves go to work. During Queen Elizabeth's time, the people were needed for the plow and the harrow in the fields, for the tending of sheep and cows, for the spinning of wool, and the making of cloth, for armor and swords and the building of palaces.

"Today, in our land, the people are needed not only on the farms, but in factories, industry and offices, in social services of all kinds. And people are *needed in crime,* which is why no attempt is made to eliminate it. Those in power know it is not practical, because *crime is a key industry in our society.* Life as we know it would disappear from this land without the criminals. The criminal population of our land must be preserved, as any other commodity we develop. Look at this modern, well-equipped jail we are in. Why was it provided, built during the depression fifteen years ago? It put hundreds, perhaps thousands of honest skilled men to work, and why? To help the faltering concrete and steel industries, for one thing. And because we are valued, as any other surplus. Think of this as a warehouse, a human granary, where we are stored until we are once again ready for their market.

"Yes, prisons are human warehouses. We are kept alive and healthy so that when needed we can again perform that indispensable social service known as crime.

"Yes, they need us. Do you know how much they invest every year to maintain the police and courts and prison systems, money put out by the people in their taxes? More than thirty billion a year!* And for that amount, thirty billion, what are they getting in return? The thieves in this country, the ones that get into joints like this, I don't mean the big shots — the thieves steal around five hundred million to a billion annually. Of that amount, about half, or about five hundred million, is recovered. So they're spending thirty billion to get back half a billion. Does that sound like the financial wizards, the highly touted geniuses of our industrial and financial world? Is that American know-how? In this wonderful nation of

---

*In 1980, it is of course double that.

ours, where everyone goes on the principle that five'll get you ten, are those most successful men going to put up a hundred to get back one? Of course not. What really happens?

"First, they do it because they don't put up the hundred; the taxpayer does. The working people. So for them it's good business. Criminals keep so-called honest people working. We're socially useful. Look!" I pointed to the door where the screws were standing, a little stunned. "Those gentlemen, honest, decent, hardworking, with families they love. Would you stop stealing and throw them out of work?"

The audience whooped and laughed like they'd shake the goddam building. Then I shook my head as in sorrow and pity.

"Would you be so unkind? So inhuman? What would these hard-working, honest men have to do if their children were hungry and they were out of work?"

With one voice, they yelled, "Steal!"

Afterward Smitty said from then on I had them like the conductor of a symphony. I waved my baton, and like a whole orchestra they played the same note.

I went on: "Right. But just think, it's not just the screws; all over the country, with no work, all the cops, judges, the D.A.'s. We're their means of livelihood. We're holding down unemployment. We're doing a great social service. We're the true patriots!

"So, remember, don't feel guilt — take pride. We are responsible for the economic welfare of countless numbers of our citizens. You know what would happen if all the crooks stopped stealing? In no time you'd hear those bleating, self-righteous bastards who now defame us, beg us to go back to work, that is, to steal.

"That is why all honest, understanding thieves have a legitimate beef. They are the most exploited workers in this country, and the poorest paid for their services. Thieves average less than $800.00 a year. And they get no social security when they get old, and no unemployment insurance when they haven't pulled a paying job.

"So I say in return for such social services as thieves perform, the least the rulers can do is treat us like first-class citizens. See that we are all well-fed, well-clad, well-housed. Allow us while in here what is politely called connubial privileges with our wives and girlfriends over the weekends. Treat us like human beings until we are once again out on the bricks performing our patriotic duties like the others. We are workers, and we want to be treated like workers!"

They were cheering now, and I couldn't believe it. Smitty, along with the others, got to his feet; to finish I had to shout over them.

"No social gains have ever been won without a fight. I say we have a right to organize for our rights in here just like workers do outside in the industries, the factories. Form a union. Great gains have been made in this country through organization, and we can start it here. So I end my part of this debate with a pardonable paraphrase of a world-famous philosopher's call to action: He called on the workers of the world. I now call on prisoners of Danbury to unite, you have a world to gain and nothing to lose — but your S.G.T. Thank you for your kind attention." That was it.

They cheered us both, surrounded us and thanked us for a great evening. The three guards — they had to add two as the crowd increased — were dumfounded, and we heard via the grapevine that word came up from the Warden's house demanding to know what all the uproar was about. Some of the cons suggested to the Education Director that we repeat the debate before the entire population Saturday night after the movie; he looked at them as if they were crazy. I suppose at that point he was wondering whether the Warden would tear his shirt off for letting the debate between Ring and me occur in the first place.

Now for us the time was growing short, and as it did we learned a harsh fact of prison life. As the prison time grows shorter, the days grow longer, harder to live with. A month before our S.G.T., the ten-month period, we were moved to a house that had no cells or dormitories, but single bedrooms neatly furnished. A transition physically, preparation for home. Somehow this made it worse. And the tension increased; word came that the Warden and his staff were to meet and discuss M.G.T. — which prisoners soon to leave would get meritorious extra time for contributions made to prison life.

My screw in the warehouse hinted he was putting me up for two weeks M.G.T. Ring's boss gave him a similar hint. That morning of the M.G.T. meeting, as always, some con had an ear to the door, and half an hour before the meeting was over the grapevine had spread the word: Ring had received two weeks, I not a day.

Not only was it a severe blow; those two weeks loomed ahead longer and gloomier than the preceding nine months. But why not I? That soon was made clear. The Catholic priest had been told by one of his prison parishioners that in the dormitory I was actively preaching anti-religious propaganda, spouting Communistic atheism all over the place. And the priest was supported in his negative vote by the Protestant minister, the Reverend Dominic. That was enough.

I was outraged. I went to Dominic and asked him what proof he had. One man said it. Did Dominic seek witnesses? Would the informer confront me? Let me bring witnesses? Could not the man be a Judas, seeking something for himself? The minister refused to discuss it with me and asked me to leave. I didn't know what to do.

But when my friend, twenty-eight-year-old four-time-loser Smitty heard about it, he knew exactly what to do. He knew that the con who reported me had constantly baited me as a red and an atheist and knew I had ignored him. He also knew that I refused to get into any arguments with him. That evening Smitty got the man into the shower and demanded that he go to the priest and admit he lied. When the man refused, my muscled friend went to work on him. He literally beat him senseless, knocked him unconscious, then turned the cold shower on. And when the con revived, Smitty promised further action.

That did it. The bruised and battered liar confessed to the priest that he had invented the story in the hope that it would increase his chances for parole. Embarrassed, the priest called for a meeting of the Board, but, according to the rules, it could not be held for a week.

That week was torture, not because of the interminably long days and nights that is the lot of the "short timer," but because the House Un-American Activities Committee, by then simply called HUAC, had started new hearings in Hollywood. Each afternoon came the radio reports. One of the first witnesses was Richard Collins, one of the original nineteen who, with Paul Jarrico, friend and collaborator for some years, had written *Song of Russia.* The shock was great. Collins became the first snitch, stoolie, squealer, call it what you will. He named a dozen or more of his former Comrades including, of course, his close friend, Jarrico.

The Committee had done its work well. Meta Reis Rosenberg, writers' agent, admitted former membership, then proceeded to smear the stage with Reds she had known. More followed, every day.

So, every afternoon when work was done, the cons would gather around the radio and listen to the news. My name was mentioned almost daily. They looked at me and shook their heads, some with pity, most with contempt. Smitty summed it up for all of them when he said, "What kind of horse's ass are you to get into that lousy mob of stool pigeons?" How to explain why so many of my "mob" had become stoolpigeons? All I could do was shrug uneasily and say something like "Why does anyone become a stoolie? Fear? Payoff? You name it."

The Warden's M.G.T. committee met at the end of the

week. The priest "confessed." I was given my remaining six days as M.G.T. I would leave the next day.

Could it be true? I was allowed to phone my wife. She said she and the boys would be at the gate to meet me. Cedric Belfrage would probably come with them. The remainder of that day and night were the longest in my life.

That day, though, there was one most gratifying diversion. About twenty-five of the Reverend Dominic's parishioners had organized, informed him they were boycotting his service the following Sunday and would picket them because he had accepted the testimony of a Judas without verifying it. So disgraced did he feel that he asked for immediate transfer. He left Danbury that day.

I felt somehow vindicated and thanked the men I knew who had gone to Dominic and given him their ultimatum. But I couldn't sleep that night. I found myself thinking back a couple of months, when Jonnie and the boys had just come East, and she brought them to visit me for the first time. It had then been seven months since I'd seen them. I had sat in the wicker-furnished visiting room where prisoners meet their visitors, and when the boys came in they rushed to me and hugged me. At last I managed to get loose long enough to kiss Jonnie.

When visiting time was up, the unforgettable incident occurred. I was permitted to walk with them down the corridor to the exit. Each boy held a hand. Then Mike said, "Gee, pop, this is really a nice clean place, ain't it?" But his voice was an anguished plea, as if begging me to tell him everything was all right.

And Jeff squeezed my hand hard, and I nodded and tried unsuccessfully to hold back the tears. "Okay, it's okay. . . ."

At that moment I must have fallen asleep. It was 6:30 A.M. before I knew it. I was to be released at eight o'clock.

At last the time came; 7:45 A.M. I was brought to the room I saw when I first arrived and changed into my own clothes, now much too large for me (under Smitty's guidance

I lost about thirty pounds and was down to bone and muscle).
The trusty handed me the envelope with my wallet, the screw
led me down to the small steel door through which convicts
exit. There he handed me the envelope with the debate inside. I
asked him to thank the man who saved it for me. He unlocked
the door, swung it open, and I was out. OUT!

And there they were, waiting. I ran to them, they to me,
and as we all four embraced we heard a cheer. Looking up
behind me, I saw the open but barred windows of the in-
firmary on the second floor. There was Smitty with a dozen
or more cons, waving and cheering: "You're out! You're free!"
some of them shouted.

I waved back, Michael, Jeffry, Cedric and Jonnie all waved
to them. It was too much; I broke down. From some friend,
Cedric had borrowed a car, and he hurried us to it.

The three-and-a-half hour drive to the city was vibrant.
Both boys talked at once — shouted — all about their school,
and more about the flat at 115th Street and Riverside Drive
which they had exchanged for a few months with New York
friends, the Fishers, for our house in Hollywood. Finally,
Cedric had a chance to show me a picture of his new wife, a
beautiful young Puerto Rican who had graduated from medical
school and was already an intern in a Manhattan hospital.
News, news, the outside world that was inside my family and
friends was pouring like warm soothing water over me. Until
then I hadn't fully realized how much I'd missed it all — or
had I kept myself from thinking of it?

Then suddenly the shouts from the prison window echoed
in my mind. "Out, you're out." But not free, I thought. The
thoughts of the Inquisition in Hollywood filled my mind,
plagued me with indecision: should we stay in New York,
find any kind of work, and should I write my play, and other
plays, or should I return to Hollywood and try to stem the
tide of the informers? Then I noticed. Jonnie, for some time,
had been strangely quiet.

16

The Hard Years

If, along with his sterling qualities as patriot, self-appointed film censor, and petty thief of kickbacks from his staff's wages, J. Parnell Thomas had any room left to enjoy a victim's pain, he would have been immensely pleased to learn that the first severe blow to the gut was soon to hit me. All of the Ten had difficulties and hardships to face, but this was a blow for which I was unprepared.

We had been in New York about a month, and even though we were far from short of funds, I couldn't be idle and unearning. Jonnie seemed strangely upset and didn't want to talk about it. She was trying to think it through, she said.

Almost immediately I reestablished my political connections, met a couple of interesting and amusing writers, and an idea was born. How about putting on a satirical revue about the Committee and other Cold War plagues? We could do it under the auspices of the ASP, the Committee for the Arts, Sciences and Professions, which was struggling to keep alive. Perhaps we could even make enough to pay the actors a pittance. Some had returned from Hollywood, having refused to cooperate with the Committee. Blacklisted in films, they hoped they could still work on the stage. They were enthusiastic about the revue idea. And there were eager young people, like the very talented Ruby Dee and Ossie Davis, always ready, willing, and most able. With so much talent — musicians, actors, singers, poets, skit writers — it quickly developed into a sort of vaudeville evening. We called it the A.S. Prevue and we played every Friday night at the Jugoslav Hall on Forty-first Street near Ninth Avenue. A new program every week filled the house to capacity. We made money for the ASP and a dribble for the performers and writers. I quit as a waiter to devote myself to the revue and soon suggested to ASP Director Hannah Weinstein that I tour the Borscht Circuit where most of our talent hoped to be working that summer, look over the acts, and see if we couldn't select the best and put together a show for a steady run. There were enough sympathetic people in New York to keep us going in a modest-sized off-Broadway theater for some time.

The plans were developing, and I was already on my third Prevue, perhaps two months after my release. But Jonnie seemed more and more agitated. I tried to find out why, but could get no answer from her.

Then one evening, just before I was leaving for rehearsal, the phone rang. She answered it. I heard her gasp. I looked up and saw she was ashen. "It's for you," she managed to say, and ran out of the room.

I picked up the phone, wondering and apprehensive.

"Lester, this is Tony Haber in Los Angeles." I knew her as a very rich San Francisco heiress with a slightly less rich husband.

"Yes?" Now I was muddled; why in hell was she calling me? Before I had a chance mentally to relate Jonnie's startled retreat to this phone call, Tony Haber was saying, "I thought it would be better for you to hear about it this way than read it in the papers. I'm divorcing Joe, and naming Jonnie as the what-d'ya call it — co-respondent? — for alienation of affections."

Did I say "Thanks," or just hang up, or bang the receiver down and run to our bedroom, where I found Jonnie stretched out, sobbing? I stood over her, waiting. It certainly was not my turn to speak.

Finally, she got up, went to the mirror, dried her eyes and brushed her hair. Then she was ready. "Yes, it's true."

"Money, of course."

She said, "I knew what you'd have to do. Become a short-order cook, a waiter. There's no work I can do. And the kids! The *kids*! When what there is in the bank is gone, we're through." For the first time her voice rose, trembling and close to hysteria. "Through, through! My children in the streets!" And then she sobbed, "I love you, but I'm in love with him. That's as close as I can put it." She ran out of the room. I followed. She poured herself a big drink. I did, too. Nothing more was said.

But down the drain went eighteen years, most of them very, very close and loving years. Two boys we both loved. Suddenly it was over. Drano. Of course, people fall in love and fall out of love, but how could she — I didn't want to think about it; myself in jail, desperately trying to make plans for *our* future, while she was out there, coolly making plans for *hers*.

The next months are no longer clear. I know that I phoned Tony Haber and convinced her to drop the alienation charge — make it simply irreconcilable incompatibility; this for the sake of my sons, if for no one else. Otherwise, the injury to them would be incalculable. She finally agreed. When and how Jonnie and the boys left, I cannot recall, but I do remember one stipulation—she would have the use of the house (and she did, and her rich, soon-to-be husband moved in—thrifty fellow!), but only up to the time the boys were ready for college, at which time we would sell it (I retained co-ownership) and *all* the proceeds would go to our sons for their education.

I don't remember where I moved after Jonnie and the boys went back. It was all a blur for some time. But I kept putting on the A. S. Previews. I was desperately in need of people. Pity, sympathy? Then forty-seven, lean and full of energy, I searched, warning myself to be careful, not permit myself to rebound into the first inviting arms offered. In our small community of radicals and progressive people, I was something of a special person; I'd been through a lot, in most people's eyes, and did not want for invitations. There were meetings, and I was trying to write the play that I'd started in Danbury. Somewhere about then I went back to work as a waiter. I advanced to short order cook.

What helped jolt me into a reminder of Hollywood was the second appearance of Edward Dmytryk, one of the Ten who had served his term, again on the HUAC witness stand. He was the most calculating witness yet to appear, and the most shocking. So morally degenerate it is almost impossible to comprehend. I say "almost" because actually you can think of it easily when you relate it to jobs and money. Remember Eric Johnston and Dore Schary. But in his vilifications Dmytryk outdid them all. Shamelessly, he accused all he named as guilty of treasonous associations, conspiracy, what not. As examples, he cited Nixon's then-prime target, Alger Hiss (who, thirty-five years later, is still fighting in the courts to prove that he was framed) and Judith Coplon (who shortly thereafter was proven innocent and exonerated by the court).

At the conclusion of his testimony, to rationalize and justify his depraved performance, Dmytryk complacently stated that some people, not only Communists but Liberals, would look upon him as an informer. Aware of this, he had gone to his dictionary and there found that an informer, "roughly speaking," is a man who informs on his colleagues who are engaged in criminal activity. And he concluded, "I never heard of anybody informing on Boy Scouts."

Of course he conveniently forgot the fact that he had gone to prison to protest just what he was engaging in now.

True, he did say he was "roughly speaking," and indeed it was rough on a dozen or more people who had never harmed him and were guilty of nothing. Many people's lives were literally destroyed by his bland "Boy Scout tattling."

However, *accurately* speaking, *Webster's Dictionary* defines "informer" thus: "One who informs against another; specifically one who makes a practice *especially for a financial reward* [my emphasis, L.C.] of informing against others for violation of penal laws — also called *common informer* [Webster's emphasis]."

Those against whom he informed had broken no penal laws. It was he, the Judas, who had violated all moral, ethical, human laws.

The Judas "reward": thirty pieces of silver multiplied by varying annual inflationary rates one thousand nine hundred and thirty times —

I got a call from Alan Max, then managing editor of the *Daily Worker*. Max was trying to write a play but dissatisfied with his work. He asked me to read it, and when I offered my suggestions he liked them so much he asked me to collaborate with him. Doctor Cole was back in practice. I knew that this play against racist violence in the South, which he had titled *Potiphar's House*, would never make it except in a Left theater. In 1951, theaters of the Left were but a memory of saner days. Yet I liked the play and went to work.

It was a good play, and after a couple of agents, including Frieda Fishbein, said it was not commercial — a euphemism for being anti-racist — I had an idea. I would sent it to Bertolt Brecht in Berlin and suggest it be translated and done there. And so it happened; he wrote to say he liked it and an associate of his, Margaret Hauptmann-Dessau, wife of Walter Dessau, the composer, would translate it. To our delight, it was produced and very well received in the press and by G.D.R. audiences. The problem for nationwide production was both technical and political. The cast required six whites and six Black performers, and the East Germans, sensitive to all radicals' rejection of blackface, whether in *Othello* or minstrel shows, were reluctant to produce it very often. But we felt we had reached out; those who saw it learned anew in an emotional way about the degradation of racism, which not too long before was a horror in their own land.

Another writer who had left Hollywood before the Committee returned had a job as a story editor for Time-Life TV in New York. He got me a couple of jobs under an assumed name doing half-hour teleplays, mainly adaptations of short stories. He was fingered that year and fired. End of Time-Life TV connection.

A woman friend, concerned about me, introduced me to a woman friend of hers, also on the rebound. The attraction was instant, the need intense, and warnings to be careful when on the rebound dimmed. We soon were living together. A year later we married, and a couple of years after that, we realized what we should have recognized in the beginning regarding rebounds, and we divorced, if not with joy, at least with resignation to the inevitable.

That autumn of 1952 my mother's brother, my Uncle Joe, died and left his few thousand dollars, a lifetime of savings, to my mother, sister and me. Blanche and I turned ours over to my mother, and though approaching seventy she still wanted action. She followed the advertisements and found a place in Brewster on Cape Cod, a small inn with restaurant and bar, which she went to see. The next day she phoned us, and she insisted we come to look at it. She said she would run it, but Blanche and I knew we'd have to do the work. I gave up my job as a short-order cook and became an assistant chef in the Brewster Inn late that spring. Blanche had a woman friend interested in buying into the bar and running it. After we were all set to go, my mother inexplicably dropped out. Per-

haps it was the bar; she never drank. Blanche, her friend
and I had a fair summer, but we both decided it was not for
us; we were there only because my mother had gotten into
the project. Blanche retrieved the money we invested, returned
it to mama.

My most vivid memory of that summer was the 19th of
June, my forty-ninth birthday, the day the Rosenbergs were
to be executed at sunset. I went alone to a solitary stretch of
Cape Cod beach looking across the calm waters of the Bay
toward Sing Sing prison in New York. My heart was pounding
as I tried to estimate how many minutes or seconds it would
be after the sun set on my horizon before it set on theirs and
the switch was pulled. Their courage filled me with grief and
pride. Their refusal to admit to the crime, when any kind of
crawling admission of guilt would have saved either one or
both of their lives, kept cutting into my mind, making me
think how little I had suffered in comparison.

Darkness had fallen, and with it Julius and Ethel Rosenberg were gone. Their courage was as great as their cause
was just, and I vowed I would never betray it.

Now a new friend came to help out. Back in the city,
Jesse Reed, who was manager of a midtown sales office for
an Italian importing firm of marble table tops, had a job for
me in the company's warehouse, just across the river in
Brooklyn. Eighty-five dollars a week, an eight-hour day. I
would be able to write evenings. That helped make everything
more bearable.

Richard Collins and Edward Dmytryk merely started the
flood. Some of the stool pigeons rationalized that once a
person had been named, they could do the individual no
more harm by naming him or her again, and so the leaders
of the parade were followed by other writers and directors:
Frank Tuttle (remember Tuttle, director of *Hostages*?), Roland
Kibbee, Budd Schulberg, Isabel Lennert and, of course,
Melvin P. Levy, who for his sense of guilt in having stolen
weeks of my wife's rightful share of the salary coming to me

couldn't *stop* mentioning me. I believe his testimony shows he repeated my name five times, even after a committee member reminded him twice he had already mentioned me. Perhaps he was trying to drown me and, with me, the return to the surface of his conscience of such guilt as he must have felt.

Before the flood of sewage was over some four years later, there were more than sixty informers.

It was difficult, if not impossible, to hold down the fury and frustration I felt at what was going on in Hollywood. I tried to see a difference between myself and those who were singing like canaries: could it be that as middle-class intellectuals, which most of them were, they couldn't face the prospect of being forced "down" into the working class which as Communists they had until recently so ardently championed? And that I, coming from that class, wasn't being forced down anywhere; it was where I'd begun life and always felt myself to be, even when a financially successful writer. Was that enough to excuse them? Or was I looking for some rationale that might cool the anger raging in me?

Mordecai Bauman, at whose home I stayed when I spoke at the City Club in Cleveland a few years before, had with his wife Irma bought a beautiful old mansion outside Stockbridge, Massachusetts, turned it into a music and art summer camp for teenagers, and it was flourishing.

Some time in the fall, after camp had closed, I received a phone call from Mordy. By now he, Irma and I had become close friends, as we remain to this day. He wanted me to meet him downtown for lunch. "Don't ask who or why, just come. Someone has a message for you."

We met in a small restaurant on Twenty-third Street. I found him and a writer friend, Bill Reuben, sitting with a tall, slender, shy-looking man a few years younger than myself. As I approached, he rose, and Mordy said, "Lester, meet Alger Hiss."

That was startling. I'd read he'd been recently released

from the Lewisburg, Pennsylvania, Reformatory, but what message could he have for me? We sat down, and after a few pleasantries, he said, "About the message. Do you remember a man named Dominic, the Protestant minister at Danbury?"

Did I! Would I ever forget him? "You've got a message from *him*? For *me*?"

He grinned. "He's the Protestant minister at Lewisburg. I worked as his clerk. The night before I left, he said, 'Will you do me a favor?' I was taking no chances and said I would if I could. And he said he was sure I could; on the outside I'd be sure to run into a man named Lester Cole. I didn't know how the hell he could be so sure, since you and I had never met, and I told him so, but he said, 'Well, if you do, please do this for me. Tell him that the Reverend Robert Dominic apologizes for the injustice he did to him. It's weighed on my conscience ever since.' Then he told me what happened, and how you had criticized him for not making the fink produce witnesses and he ended up with what I thought was a note of real bitterness. 'And to think I had to learn about Christian justice from a — a *Communist*!' "

We all laughed, and I said, "Poor guy. He didn't know that at that moment I wasn't a Communist — just a jail house lawyer!"

Hiss spoke of some of his experiences in Lewisburg; I told him of the debate with Ring and the trick we played on J. Parnell. A couple of jailbirds reminiscing; it was a pleasant lunch, with Mordy probably enjoying it most. Hiss was and is a gentle but determined man. Some might think his thirty year fight to prove his innocence is in vain. Not I. He hasn't lost. You can't lose as long as you keep fighting.

Evidently Elia Kazan was prepared when he got his subpoena to appear on April 10, 1952. He became informer number thirty-seven, but showman to the last, he played his part with

a most theatrical flourish. In the Hollywood trade papers —
and, if I recall, the *New York Times* — he took out large advertisements to publish confessions of his "sins" of being a
dupe. Now he was a virulent anti-Communist.

Informing on his friends was hardly enough. With Budd
Schulberg, fellow stoolie, to write it for him, he directed *On
the Waterfront*, a film designed to justify stoolpigeons and
slander trade unionism. Praised by all the right people for
his patriotism, Kazan was still determined to prove he was a
"born again" American, and with John Steinbeck, by now a
converted cold warrior writing the script, he directed *Zapata*,
which MGM had unloaded on Twentieth Century with the
promise, written by President Aleman in Mexico five years
earlier, of $1.5 million in services.

A report came to me from a friend at Fox about what
happened. It provided delightful, if bitter, satisfaction regarding
Kazan and a renewed faith in the Mexican people. Upon
reading Steinbeck's script, the Mexicans officials said not only
would there be no $1.5 million in services for this immoral dis-
tortion of history, but Fox would not even be permitted in the
country to shoot the film. So the U.S. Southwest became the
location of this perversion of the story of that Mexican Revolution. Whatever profit there may have been in the finished
product for the company, Kazan was the final winner; no
one could ever again doubt how much he despised and held
in contempt the common people. In his and Steinbeck's film,
Zapata, one of the Mexican people's greatest heroes is turned
into a "Spic" simpleton. What a contribution to the art of film!

After a few months I was promoted from the warehouse
in Brooklyn to the showroom in midtown Manhattan. Easier
work, shorter hours, a raise in pay. A new rhythm was developing in my life. I finished a draft of a new play in a few
months.

You will recall my telling of an experience in Cleveland at
the City Club when asked the sixty-four dollar question. I
responded with the tale of a professor in Carolina just before

the Civil War who was discovered to have voted for Fremont for president (a vote against slavery), was hanged in effigy and just escaped lynching through the aid of the underground railway. The new play used that incident as its theme. The time became 1856, the locale a plantation in northern Virginia. Hidden on it, under a barn, is an underground railway station, the existence of which is unknown to the man who runs the plantation, the oldest of three owners — brothers. The analogy between the underground railway workers of the 1850s and the Communists going underground in the early McCarthyite 1950s was the point I wished to make. Another message was what economic pressure can do: when the middle brother, who lived in the North and was an openly professed abolitionist, finds himself in dire financial straits in the economic panic of 1857, he threatens to expose his younger brother if he doesn't join in forcing the eldest to sell. The liberal's dilemma kept the play off Broadway. A successful liberal producer told me that the Northern brother represented 80 percent of the people who bought orchestra seats in his theater, and were he to produce the play it — and he — wouldn't last a week.

The success of the Thomas Committee cannot be over-estimated. The panic reached TV quickly enough. When the First Amendment proved no defense and we Ten went to prison, the honest and courageous among progressive people were driven to an unpleasant second line of defense. They took the Fifth Amendment, which protected them from being forced to incriminate themselves. This worked so far as contempt citations and possible jail was concerned but they were labeled by the hostile press as "Fifth Amendment Communists" — and, of course, blacklisted.

It is impossible to measure the damage done to the progressive movement when Martin Berkeley became the Un-American Activities Committee's chief informer. During its inquisition, over three hundred fifty people in the industry were named — accurately and otherwise. It was Berkeley who opened the floodgates; out poured the poison.

Was the Party guilty for not expelling Berkeley in 1939, when he was found trying to plagiarize a comrade's film story? If he had been expelled when he knew perhaps only fifteen or twenty men and women in the Party, would he have been able to spend the next decade — out of spite, hatred, revenge? — secretly collecting the names of the one hundred fifty-one people which he reported to the committee? If he had only those dozen or more names he knew in 1939, could the dozen not have done what we had done in 1947, take the First or Fifth Amendment to protect themselves as best they could against the Committee?

There are two questions about Berkeley: first, where was he prowling inside the Party between 1939 and 1951? How did he get the names not only of writers, but of doctors, teachers and others not known to any of *us*? What were his "inside (informer) connections"?* Second: there is a story, unconfirmed, but believed authentic by some, that when he received his subpoena early in 1951, he wired the Committee that he was not and had never been a Communist. If he thus gave false information, he was as guilty of perjury as if he had sworn falsely before the Committee or in a courtroom. This may have been the price he was forced to pay. Whichever it was, had he been expelled in 1939 he could not have done the incalculable harm he went on to do; the Party must take the blame.

Thus, with almost a complete breakdown in the morale of the progressive movement, from left to liberal, the opposition campaign intensified. Roy Brewer had been put in charge of who would or would not be blacklisted. He was aided by John Wayne, then president of the Motion Picture Alliance (and recipient before his death of a gold medal for his "American ideals, patriotism and integrity"); together they became judges and jury, the chief decision-makers as to who could and could not go back to work. By late 1953, under the tremendous fear of the Blacklist and the terror of McCarthyism,

---

*Is Berkeley one of the blacked-out names in my FBI dossier?[L. C.]

the Guild's executive board was itself so fearful of being labeled that before negotiations for a new contract it called off its legal action against the producers, accepting the producers' verbal assurance that no blacklist existed! As if that weren't a sufficient demonstration of their willingness to collaborate with the most right-wing elements, a new constitution had this incredibly slavish, subservient amendment included:

> Notwithstanding anything herein contained to the contrary, no person shall be eligible to retain membership in the Guild or any of its branches, who refused to testify before the House Un-American Activities Committee or any other duly constituted Congressional Committee that he is a member of the Communist Party, or who is convicted in a court of competent jurisdiction of knowingly or willfully advocating, abetting, advising, or teaching the duty, necessity, desirability or propriety of overthrowing or destroying the Government of the United States by force and violence.

Shades of the Motion Picture Alliance for the Preservation of American Ideals and of the Motion Picture Industry Council, where Dore Schary and Ronald Reagan sat on high!

The executive board, in changing the Guild's name to the Writers' Guild of America, might more appropriately have called it the Un-American Activities Committee's Writers' Guild. Not only had we been blacklisted by the industry, we were now blacklisted by our own Guild, which many of us had helped to found and whose first contract we had fought for.

Morale, integrity, conscience; all had withered or been forced into hiding. These pitiable people now in power obviously were fearful that unless they kissed Joe McCarthy's — well, hand — they would be themselves labeled as communists or fellow travelers who condoned and defended "force and violence."

While the "slaughter of the innocents" was proceeding, on the desert in New Mexico Herbert Biberman, Paul Jarrico and Michael Wilson were writing, producing, and directing

Salt of the Earth, the story of a Mexican-American miners'
strike. It was a militant film and a feminist one — revolutionary
for that time. Rosa Revueltas, a magnificent actress, was
brought from Mexico to star in the picture. The opposition
encountered in making the film, the force and violence of
terrorists and subversive attempts by the Un-American Activities
Committee to halt it — even the federal deportation of Rosa
Revueltas a week before completion — could not stop these
dedicated film makers.* The finished shooting was a triumph
of determination and dedication.

When Howard Hughes, the Un-American Activities Committee and every facility controlled by the Hollywood producers
failed to stop either the production of the film or its editing
and processing, Roy Brewer stepped in. He attempted, through
his control of laboratory technicians, to stop the development
of the negative and the printing of the positive. When that
failed, he played his trump card; he ordered the Projectionists
Union of the IATSE to refuse to run the film. That did it.
Aside from a very brief, all-but-boycotted appearance for a
week in New York City, a one-week run in a small independent theater in Los Angeles twenty-five years later, and then
as brief a run in a small San Francisco theater in 1979, the
film has never been permitted to run commercially in this
country. Despite a fortune spent on legal suits to break Brewer's
power, distribution couldn't be accomplished.

To the chagrin of those seeking to suppress it, the film
became famous throughout the world, not only as one of the
finest examples of film making, but as a clear example of
U.S. political repression — of speech as well as the arts. On
its merits, the film won prizes at many film festivals, broke
all records for commercial runs of American films in Paris,
and has been shown by hundreds of trade unions, universities
and colleges throughout the U.S. Herbert and Michael Wilson

---

*The full account of this extraordinary fight for freedom of artistic expression has
been published in Biberman's meticulous account of the event, *Salt of the Earth*
(Boston: Beacon Press). The volume also contains Michael Wilson's screenplay.

lived to see much of that. Herbert died a short time after the Paris triumph, Mike a few years later.

What I had heard from blacklisted actors who had gone from Hollywood to New Mexico to play in the *Salt of the Earth* made me decide to ask Herbert to read my own new play. I hoped he might even produce and direct it.

I sent it to him in Hollywood, and four days later he phoned me. He thought it was great, but he was so tied up legally trying to get *Salt* in theaters that he didn't know when he could even begin to think of directing it as either a film or a play. But he had a suggestion.

At the First Unitarian Church in Los Angeles, where Stephen H. Fritchman was minister, an arts festival was held annually. The festival committee was chaired by Kay McTernan, and Herbert had taken the liberty to give her the script and recommend it as a feature of the festival, where it would run for a week.

Three or four days later Ms. McTernan phoned. They wanted me out there for the rehearsals; the festival committee wanted to produce the play. They would pay my fare. I left the next day.

For a small number of people, my return after five years had the air of a big event. A welcoming party was given; many "Fifth Amendment Communists" were there. Suddenly I had this strong feeling of being home and of wanting to go around and see the scores of places I had lived in, where my children were born and grew up. I saw my sons almost immediately, and they promptly implored me to return.

I was particularly welcomed by Kay McTernan, who was in charge of the festival. She was extraordinarily attractive, divorced, living in a modest house in West Hollywood with her two children, Kathy, eleven, and Deborah, four years younger.

Casting started almost immediately, then rehearsals, and we had some of the best blacklisted actors in Hollywood in the cast. A young Black director, more skilled than experienced, did very well with it, and *The Echoing Hills* opened to great, if limited, critical acclaim and full houses for its six or eight performances. Many writers, politically neutral or hostile, came out of curiosity to see what I had written.

Herbert Biberman and Gale Sondergaard, his wife, of course were there opening night. I had not been in town a week before old friend Charles Katz told me of two producers of feature-length ninety-minute TV shows — legal clients — who had a quick re-write job for me. It would not take long; I could do it while the rehearsals were going on, and they would pay a thousand dollars.

How could I refuse? The job was done in less than two weeks. They were more than satisfied; I was offered another at much higher pay, and there would be more to come. I phoned my wife, asked her to move out. She refused; the rebound was over and I would soon get a divorce.

I met many old friends, among them Eddie Huebsch and his wife Bea. Eddie was a younger blacklisted writer who was attempting to eke out rent and food for his family as a TV repairman. I suggested he work with me. It was a new start for him too, and the first of three or four projects on which we collaborated.

Soon enough Kay McTernan and I found we had much more in common than art festivals; the attraction was intense and irresistible. No doubt that contributed to making much of the past seem more remote. Hollywood once again became home; my life as a screenwriter was not over, just beginning in a new and even more unpredictable way.

Far more than in these times it was common in the thirties to find men and women of wealth active on the Left. When at Sarah Lawrence College, Kay had as her sociology professor Helen Merrel Lynd, who, with her husband, Professor Robert Staughton Lynd, had achieved fame with their book, *Middletown*. Kay thrived under Helen's influence and later worked as an assistant to the Lynds when they updated their book during the depression to *Middletown in Transition*.

Kay was the daughter of one of Salt Lake City's more prominent non-Mormon families named Hogle. But judging by the way she lived, the simple home, small car, unpretentious clothes, I assumed her income was on that modest level. Even if her income exceeded the eight or ten thousand dollars I now could anticipate earning on the black market, at least I could contribute my share. She and the children were three, I one.

There were misgivings among friends, but so strong was the attraction which developed in this short time that we could not be deterred, and in the spring of 1957, our good friend, Rev. Steve Fritchman, performed the ceremony before a small group of our children and friends. And I moved in.

During this period I was heartened and inspired by Paul Robeson's response as a witness before the Un-American Activities Committee. When we heard his responses to his inquisitors, reported live on radio, many of us felt we could not have found a truer spokesman.

The Chairman that year was Congressman Walter, and Richard Arens was the interrogator. When he asked Robeson about his membership in the Communist Party, Robeson asked *him*:

> What do you mean by the Communist Party? As far as I know, it is a legal party like the Republican and Democratic Party. Do you mean . . . belonging to a Party of people who have sacrificed for my people and for all Americans and workers that they can live in dignity? Do you mean that Party?

It didn't stop there. He accused the chairman of being the author of a bill (the Immigration Act) ". . . to keep all kinds of decent people out of the country." He baited and exasperated him to the point where Arens' only reply to him was, "Proceed." And when that worthy asked Robeson whether it was true that he had said in Paris that American Negroes would never go to war against the USSR, he replied that it was unthinkable his people would take up arms in the name of a man like Senator James Eastland of Mississippi against *anybody*. In his uniquely magnificent voice he was roaring angrily that the Committee was comprised of "un-Americans" and "non-patriots." He had previously stood on the Fifth Amendment so they could not cite him for contempt and now, retreating in exhaustion, they called the hearing to a close with Chairman Walter, humiliated and exhausted, saying, "I have endured all of this that I can."

The question of revoking Paul's passport hardly came up, but it was subsequently revoked. And although the committee felt he certainly was "contemptuous," they decided not to pursue it, lest they give him the courtroom as another stage for his defiance.

Not only was it a great victory, but it must have inspired those who followed; after Paul's appearance, there was never again one "friendly" witness. He had put an end to that.

Now working on the black market under assumed names, I was most shocked by what happened in the Guild. Following the 1954 anti-Communist amendment to the constitution, a surreptitious system was introduced to prevent a writer who was working under an assumed name from becoming a member. A producer who engaged such a writer jeopardized his own career through exposure by Guild watchdogs. Economically, it was disastrous to the blacklisted writer; since his pseudonym could not be officially recognized, he could not receive residuals on such films as played on TV: nor could he claim payments to his Social Security fund. The result was that in my sixty-to-sixty-fifth years, the most important for Social Security, I could not make payments under my name, and my pension later started at the minimum, both in the Guild and the Federal Government. In those years the Guild had indeed become an instrument of the industry; Roy Brewer, Ronald Reagan and John Wayne could have asked for little more.

The Party had been decimated. Just a handful had escaped exposure, and to fight the passive and accommodating role of the majority in the Guild was all but impossible. Those who managed did what they could. But it wasn't much. A coalition of conservatives and right-wing liberals were in control.

For the next four years, most of us on the blacklist worked for what two decades earlier MGM producer Irving Thalberg had described as "plumbers' wages." But we were "plumbers" without a union. Writers who had previously earned thirty-five thousand dollars for a script considered themselves lucky on the black market to get five thousand. The producers claimed they were being generous as well as courageous, and that the writer should be grateful for what he received.

Eddie and I did two more scripts for such producers, one of which, *The Pied Piper*, starred Van Johnson. Written in rhyme, it was a big hit on TV and played in theaters throughout Europe for which, aside from the five thousand we received for the screenplay (twenty-five hundred dollars each for at least four months' work), we did get another ten thousand dollars for theater exhibition, which was in the agreement. The producers, who were also songwriter and lyricist, decided against pseudonyms for us and used their own names as authors.

But better jobs came. Jack Cummings, who had retired from MGM, was seeking to make films independently and had found a story of a sea captain named Adams, who was the first white man to reach Japan early in the eighteenth century. Adams stayed there, fighting off attempts of his countrymen to overthrow the Emperor and colonize the islands. Again I worked with Eddie Huebsch, and we produced quite a good script. Jack was asking a lot of money for it, or a big chunk of the profits if he also produced it. Eddie and I had received what for blacklisted writers was a very decent sum from Jack for the script, and when Harry Cohn at Columbia liked it and agreed that Jack could make it, the latter elatedly told us he was in for a percentage and we'd get a cut of it. The terms were being worked out between Jack and Cohn's lawyers at the studio while Cohn went on a holiday to Mexico. There he died of a heart attack. That ended the deal.

But we'd been paid fairly well, and I had an idea for Sidney Poitier, who was nearing stardom. I wanted to do a modern version of *Othello*, with Poitier a captain in the 99th Squadron, the all-Black pursuit unit in the Air Force in World War II. Stationed in Italy, he meets Desdemona, and the story pretty much paralleled the Shakespeare original, but with exposures of American racism and discrimination which fit in only too well, supplied by Iago, whom I made the public relations officer with the 99th.

I knew Sidney from the A.S. Prevue days in New York. He liked the idea, and we soon got a young producer named Martin Poll interested, and the deal was made. For me, it was the best yet: five thousand upon completion, twenty-five thousand when the film was sold to a studio, and 5 percent of the producer's profits. Eddie and I wrote a lengthy treatment, which everyone liked, the deal was set with United Artists, and I began to feel a little like myself again.

But when it came to the details of the screenplay Eddie and I had our first sharp differences, which became irreconcilable. We didn't want to take them to Martin Poll for arbitration, and we decided upon this: each would write his screenplay independently, turn in both without our names on either, and let Martin decide. The one he accepted, we agreed, would receive 75 percent of the twenty-five thousand dollars, the other 25 percent.

My script was accepted. Eddie was terribly disappointed. Naturally I did the final draft alone. A deal was being set at United Artists. At that point, to our dismay, Poitier backed out. He said he had been advised by friends that even though it followed Shakespeare's classic and would be recognized as such, by modernizing it a Black man was put in the position of murdering a white woman, and it would cause great uneasiness, if not riots, and increase racism.

Now it was my turn for disappointment. Perhaps he was right. But without Poitier United Artists dropped it, I wasn't paid (nor Eddie, of course) and at Poitier's suggestion Martin Poll engaged John Cassevetes to rewrite it.

I read the script; aside from the 99th Pursuit Squadron in World War II, very little of Shakespeare or my work was left. But Paramount bought it. Poll promptly turned over twenty-five thousand to me, from which I as promptly gave Eddie his share. Then pre-production was started: World War II planes were moved to Italy, people were cast. Six days before shooting was to begin, the project was called off. No one ever explained why.

Following the one-week run of my play, *The Echoing Hills*, in Los Angeles, I decided it could be improved, did considerable work on it and felt I found a more suitable title; I renamed it *The Blossom and the Root*.

Bob Kempner, a friend from the early fifties in New York, who had read the play, surprised me with a phone call. His wife had a friend, a visitor from Czechoslovakia, who was here looking for plays suitable for the Czech theater. He suggested I send the play immediately. If this Miraslava Gregorova shared his admiration for the play, she would translate it and see it got a production. A few weeks later I received a letter from her; she liked it and wanted to translate it. I gladly gave permission. A few months later we heard from her. It would be produced that summer in at least two theaters. That was spring, 1959.

Kay and I were invited to attend as guests. And when it was known we were going, someone told us, following the opening, that we should try to go to Moscow where the First International Film Festival was to be held. We didn't have to try. Astonishingly, we received word from the Soviet Consulate in Washington that they would be honored to have us as guests at the Festival. We soon found out how that happened: Paul Jarrico had been invited to the Festival. He told his hosts that I would be in Czechoslovakia at that time and thus the invitation was extended. We went to Moscow first. It was truly an amazing world to us. With over twenty million people killed but fifteen years before, thousands of factories and hundreds of thousands of homes destroyed, these people were calmly, determinedly rebuilding. They were constructing everywhere. Having lived so long in New York, I was overwhelmed by the contrast of the Moscow subway with the one I had known. It was a miracle of cleanliness and beauty. The people could not have been friendlier. I cannot remember any of the films I saw in those two weeks, but one incident remains vivid in my memory.

The final day the Festival was held in the giant Lenin athletic stadium. Kay and I took the Metro out there, where more than sixty thousand people came to listen and applaud their filmmakers, and those from other lands in Europe, Africa and Asia who received awards.

When it was over, and we left the stadium, we were lost in the vast crowd. Where was the Metro? How did we get to the one which would stop close to the Moskva Hotel, where we were staying? We tried talking to people who didn't understand English, used sign language, and were getting desperate. Then some people in what looked more like European attire were seen walking a short distance away. Between Kay's French, my cross between Yiddish and German, we might have some luck. But first I tried English.

To our delight, one of the people replied. No, he wouldn't tell us where the Metro was, he'd drive us to the hotel! Lost and found! He turned out to be the Ambassador to the USSR from Israel, with five people from his staff. All seven got in the car, sitting on laps.

We each competed with questions to the other. He wanted to know about McCarthyism in America, we wanted to know the facts about anti-Semitism in the USSR, as reported in the U.S., and whether it was true that Jews were not being permitted to leave and take residence in Israel.

His answer surprised us. The ones who most wanted to go were the older people. While Russian synagogues were open to them, they wanted Kosher meat, a Hebrew homeland: "Those old people," he said. "The Soviets will let them go; it's that we can't take them all. They'd be a burden. What we want are the young, scientifically trained — doctors, others skilled in different professions. But these they won't let go."

"Why not?" Kay or I asked.

He shrugged. "Perfectly reasonable. They explain that the worker in the mines, in the factories, pays for the education these scientists get, which goes on for years. The workers' understanding is that the knowledge and skills the scientists acquire will then be used to make their own lives better, not to make them rich in a capitalist country. Who's going to argue against them? Not only that, but many of these younger Jews are atheists, non-religious. When I speak to them they say even if they could come they wouldn't. What have we to offer them? Zionism, the Talmud, the Wailing Wall? Can we compare the way they'd live in our country to the research, education, the ballet, the new housing, the theater?" Then he shrugged. "So what we don't need, the old people, we can have. But what we do need we neither can have, or if we could they would reject us."

That was 1959. There have been changes, but basically it is much the same today.

Miraslava Gregorova and the author in Ostrava, Czechoslovakia.

17

At Home Abroad

The Blossom and the Root was in rehearsal in Ostrava, a coal mining city in Eastern Moravia, close to the border of Poland. Blanche had arranged her vacation so she could come to Europe and be with us. With Miraslava, my translator, accompanying us and acting as interpreter with the people we met, it was one of the most gratifying experiences I had ever had. Not because of the success of the play, which was great both there and almost simultaneously in Prague, but for more important reasons.

Before and after the play opened, the artistic director of the theater, a person of great experience and equal prestige, personally called meetings in factories and apartment complexes for the express purpose of telling the people about the play. Miraslava explained that it was not enough for them to come and see it; the policy of the Czechoslovak theater was to send its directors around and explain a play's social and political meaning to the audiences who would see it. The play was to be not merely an entertainment, but a learning experience. Thus we heard him quote from the play; he explained both its political significance and how it paralleled historical events in their own country's recent history.

If I ever thought telling the story and explaining the play's meaning to prospective audiences might discourage them from seeing a play, I learned a lesson in Czechoslovakia. Not only did they applaud him, but they would come to him, Miraslava told us, after seeing the play and express their agreement or differences. They didn't just go to see a "show"; they became involved in theater! For the Czechs it was not "magic", but the art of illuminating reality.

After Ostrava we went to Karlo Vivary, the famous mineral watering place and resort. Following this delight we returned to Prague for the opening of the play in one of the principal theaters, the *Realisticke Divadlo.* There was an ovation for me when I was introduced after the show, and Miraslava translated my thanks and gratitude. I expressed the hope that I had made a contribution to their theater, as they were making to my life.

After the opening, the next day, Miraslava told me excitedly of the marvelous reviews, and that the Arts Committee had decided to put two, and, if possible, three companies on the road, to travel to the smaller towns throughout Silesia, Bohemia, Moravia and Slovakia.

As to our leaving, not a chance for at least a week. I was scheduled to speak of the Hollywood situation, the blacklist, McCarthyism, and the directors of the famous Barrandov Film Studios had invited Miraslava and us to lunch. They were eager to speak to me about the possibility of writing a screenplay for them and perhaps coproducing it. After a dozen years of writing on the black market, as a professional outcast not only in the industry, but in the very union of which I had been both an organizer and founder, this kind of public recognition, warmth, friendship and open admiration was pretty heady stuff, an ego-lifting for which I must have been starving for a long time without realizing it. I suppose shamelessly I made the most of it; luncheons with leading writers, film people at the prestigious restaurant, *The Moscova*, and to climax the trip, the lunch and conference at the Barrandov Studio across the Charles River, high on a cliff.

Hitler's architects and engineers had chosen the site shrewdly when they had taken over the country after the Chamberlain sellout at Munich. They had prepared for all possible contingencies. I was shown the modern sound stages, but most remarkable of all were the factories included in the complex. Perhaps fearing eventual bombardment of his own facilities, Hitler's engineer constructed the most modern machine shops to build cameras and sound equipment. Everything, as I recall, but lenses.

Introduced to actors and actresses, writers and directors, cameramen, we were taken to an elaborate luncheon where we then were introduced to students. As if this Barrandov complex didn't have enough going on there, it also had a school in which acting, writing, directing and cinematography were taught.

After lunch one of the directors suggested these alternatives: I could stay and work on the film, with Miraslava translating, or I could take it home and send it back for translation. I would then return and work through the film on location and in the studio until completion. I said I would read the material.

After luncheon a young official from the studio accompanied us when we left. When we reached the hotel he asked to speak to me alone. Then, for the first time, I learned that all was not as calm and bright as it appeared on the surface.

He told me something of the trials and difficulties of the country since the downfall of Eduard Beneš. Particularly among the intellectuals there was great factionalism, and one of the centers of the turmoil was the Barrandov Studios.

The top officials, studio manager, administrator and a few others with whom we had lunch, he said, were all Party members, but not all were trusted. Some had an unsavory history. When Hitler took over, they did not join the resistance, or even keep neutral; they collaborated. They worked for and with Nazis and learned their skills both technically and intellectually. With the Soviet counter-offensive crushing the Nazis and running the Germans out of the country, there was a rebirth of Communism and of Social Democracy. The latter won, with Beneš returning. The men at Barrandov immediately joined his Social Democratic Party and worked for Beneš. Then, when he turned over power to the Communists under Gottwald in 1948, three of the studio chiefs were the first in line to sign as Party members.

The problem now was the way they were running the studio; the students were mainly children of professional people — practically none from the working class — and the Party's problem was that since taking control in Hitler's time, they had developed an organization with people of their own choice. The result was that without their skills the industry would shut down. The Party had not yet solved this dilemma, and this official hoped I would not cooperate with them and add to their prestige. I agreed. I remember his saying, with a wry smile, "We thought once we have socialism, our problems are over." He shook his head. "Problems are part of life. It's just that under different systems there are different problems."

I came home aglow. And a job was waiting for me. Within a few days I got a call from Sam Bischoff, who had been executive producer over Burt Kelly at Columbia when we made *None Shall Escape*. He now was producing independently at one of the quickie studios, and he had collected some material from the papers for a film he planned to call *Operation Eichmann*, which would be about the search, chase and capture of the Nazi responsible for the transportation of thousands of Jews to Nazi ovens. Eichmann had been brought to Israel where he would stand trial. The picture had to come out by that time — "tomorrow" — and I had to guarantee a script sooner than that. He would pay well, he assured me. I asked him what he meant by "well," and when he told me I said the word he should have used was "ill." We settled for nine or ten thousand dollars. I wrote it in less than three weeks, a

Artistic Director of the theater in Ostrava.

conventional spy-chase "thriller." I hated it. It was shot in less than ten days. I never saw it, but did hear it was something less than sensational. No surprise. At times like that I was grateful a pseudonym was used. But what was I doing with my life?

Not long after that Kay and I reached a decision. We would go to England. Kathy was in boarding school in Stockbridge, Massachusetts, and we'd find a good school for Deborah, and a place for us to live in London. Adrian Scott had found work there; why shouldn't I? And we had many old friends from Hollywood there: Bernie Vorhaus and his wife, Hetty, he once a fairly successful director who left the U.S. about the same time as many others to escape the inquisition. Donald Ogden Stewart and his wife, Ella Winter; Joseph Losey, Jack Berry, and many others, all old friends. We wouldn't be lonely.

We didn't know how long we were going to stay, so we kept the house, installed my mother, packed and soon left. We were warmly welcomed in London, and Kay quickly busied herself in the activities of the Campaign for Nuclear Disarmament, along with Hetty Vorhaus, and there she met the Bernals, J.D., affectionately nicknamed Sage, and his wife, Eileen. He was one of the leading and most respected scientists in Great Britain, a powerful force in the Nuclear Disarmament Campaign; we soon became fast friends.

Kay found schools for the girls, both away from home, and both were happy in their new environment. In little more than six months she decided — and I agreed — that this was a wonderful place to live. We made arrangements for the sale of the house in Hollywood and bought the lease on an eighty-five year-old house at 13 Well Walk in Hampstead, less than a block from the Heath.

I started looking for work and found none. But I was encouraged to write an original screenplay. England still had considerable talent and independent production facilities unlike today when the U.S. companies have about ruined

F. Krasl

With Kay in Ostrava, Czechoslovakia

British production forces by buying practically all outlets for film release. Their films of the previous decade were outstanding, although what helped to bankrupt Britain's studios was the inability to get top distribution in the U.S. They had to content themselves with modest revenues from the small "art" houses here, while the U.S. product all but dominated their theaters as well as our own. Such films as *Tight Little Island, Passport to Pimlico, The Man in the White Suit, The Lavender Hill Mob,* despite their excellence, incomparable wit, the performances of outstanding artists like Alec Guinness and many others, got buried in this country.

They were not afraid of social content. I was not discouraged. Despite the lack of immediate employment, I kept saying to myself that as long as I kept trying, fighting, writing, I hadn't lost. The blacklist had changed my world; now it was up to me realistically to adapt to the one in which I would have to live.

My sons, Michael twenty-four, and Jeff twenty-three, were both doing well. Jeffry was studying for his teaching credential, and Michael had already achieved his Ph.D. in experimental psychology and had learned to speak, read, and write Russian while earning his doctorate. Now exciting news was to come from him. Michael and Sheila — married three years before — were on their way that September to Moscow. He would spend a year doing post-doctoral work at the Institute of Psychology under the direction of the renowned Lenin Award Winner, Professor Alexander Luria.

They settled in at Moscow University, and in the winter of 1962 I went there for a visit.

Those two weeks were tumultuous, from the moment Mike and Sheila met me at the airport — temperature twenty-two degrees below zero — to the tearful departure two weeks later. Moscow was a picture postcard, the trees heavy with snow, thronging with people wearing fur hats and bundled in heavy coats. I was booked at the National Hotel and at dinner that night we were joined by two dear friends whom I'd met on my visit two years before, Alki and George Sevasticoglu.

When Mike and Sheila wrote me of their proposed trip, I told them to look up George and Alki. They immediately became good friends.

The Sevastacoglus were political refugees from Greece. A professor of classic Greek drama, George had become a member of the underground guerrilla forces in World War II. Alki, a daughter of a prominent Greek upper-class family, met him then, married him, and joined the forces fighting the Nazis. When the repressive Greek government was installed after the war, they quickly were forced to flee for their lives. He got to the USSR via Yugoslavia; she was captured and put in prison. But her prominent family got her out after a few months, claiming she had been duped. She accepted that defense to get out and immediately left for Italy, where, through the Italian Communist Party, the search for George started. Hundreds, perhaps thousands of Greek refugees were scattered, working everywhere. They were lost to each other, but never gave up hope. Five years later, George was found, teaching Greek in a university in Uzbekistan. She immediately flew to him. Imagine their reunion!

Try to imagine ours that evening! The Sevasticoglus had a second child; George was teaching at Moscow University, Alki writing children's books.

The National Hotel was alive with travelers from everywhere. One evening a startlingly handsome and equally theatrical looking woman swooped through the dining room, her face familiar, yet I was unable to place her in this foreign land. But the National Hotel was international — nothing and nobody was foreign there. I soon recognized Stella Adler. We had met years ago, and now again; she was here to attend a memorial for Konstantin Stanislavsky, the great theatrical director whose famed acting methods she taught in New York.

Each day overflowed. We visited the art exhibit of new works in sculpture, prohibited by Stalin but now permitted in the Khrushchev "thaw." Literally thousands of people collected in tight little groups before each work — workers, peasants, intellectuals all hotly arguing the pros and cons. And around each arguing group, fifty, sixty people listened. It was incredible; can you imagine arguments that get close to fist fights in America not over football players, but over *artists and their works!*

Through Bella Epstein, whom I knew from the U.S., an executive at the Writers Union, I met again Alexie Kapler, a leading film writer, and Sergei Yutkevitch, one of the top directors of satirical films. With the help of Kapler's and Yutkevitch's fair understanding of English, I visited Mos-Film. It was unlike anything in Hollywood — naturally.

One night, after more than a bit too much vodka and cognac during and after dinner at the Sevasticoglus, I returned soggy and sodden to find a note on my door. "Whatever hour, Lester, please knock. Room 221. Ned."

Ned! How many Neds did I know? In the entire world, only one! Ned Young was a blacklisted actor turned waiter, bartender, writer. Under the name Nathan E. Douglas he wrote, with Hal Smith, not blacklisted, the original screenplay, *The Defiant Ones*, starring Sidney Poitier and Tony Curtis. It won most of the awards that year and made Poitier a star.

I staggered to his door. We embraced happily and wept in each other's arms. Then he opened the double window and brought in a bottle of vodka from the twenty-five-below-zero outdoor window sill. He held up his glass in a toast, and I could see he was trying to smile. I knew something of his misery: Ned and his lovely wife Frances had for years been deeply in love. When he was blacklisted, she was shattered, physically, emotionally, mentally; it was diagnosed as paranoid-schizophrenia. When she became ill, in moments of irrationality she begged, then ordered him away from her — out of the house, out of her life. He wandered in misery, landed in Paris, and finally had just come to Moscow searching for he knew not what. I tried in vain to cheer him up. It was daylight when I left, the bottle empty, but I failed. The next day

Ned and I tried to find Jack Lawson, who we knew was ill and in a sanitorium. Bella Epstein got him on the phone for us — at Yalta on the Black Sea, where Jack was recuperating from a long illness. He had finished his book, *Film: The Creative Process*, soon to be published in the U.S. by Hill and Wang. He'd had wonderful treatment in the Soviet Union, but he and Sue were homesick.

Ned left in a few days. By the time he got back to Hollywood he heard that Frances had committed suicide. He died a few years later, broken-hearted, convinced the blacklist had caused her illness and her death. Hers, and his.

The two weeks were over all too quickly. I became good friends with Mike's mentor, Professor Alexander Luria, and the parting from them all — George and Alki, "Sasha" Luria, Kapler, Yutkevitch, Bella, Mike and Sheila — was overflowing with emotion; laughter and tears fought each other to the take-off of the plane for London.

The reunion with Kay was wonderful. Recounting the experiences, I relived them and soon I again found a rhythm for writing; an idea came, and I once again was energetically back at work.

The idea for the screenplay grew out of the militant marches of tens of thousands of people, then organized in England by the Campaign for Nuclear Disarmament. It seemed to be an idea which could find a commercial producer. The characters being English, I needed an English writer for help with the dialogue, social customs and mannerisms of the people whom I was just vaguely getting to know. Roger Woddis, a writer of witty, pungent, socially oriented articles, was suggested by a friend. And when we met, he liked the idea, and we liked each other. The work started at once.

I had conceived the notion of a modern version of *Lysistrata*, a "play-within-a-play" movie, which would be clearly analogous with the current marches, war protest meetings and other actions of the anti-nuclear bomb advocates. The story takes place in a London suburb's community theater, whose amateur actors are middle-class housewives and their business and professionally engaged husbands; drama is their creative outlet. The women, peace-conscious, decide to put on the Aristophanes play; their husbands, more business-conscious, refuse to play in it. The men see the political and feminist implications clearly enough as a threat. At first frustrated because they need the males for the cast, then furious, the leading woman, the Lysistrata, gets the other women to join her in a pledge: the men may make it impossible to put *Lysistrata* on the stage, but they cannot prevent each one of them from playing Lysistrata in their homes. So the women refuse to sleep with their husbands until they agree to perform in the play. The comic complications develop from that. And the women, as in the Aristophanes' play, win out in the end.

Roger's collaboration was invaluable, and those who read our finished script thought it quite wonderful. But not the British producers. We were, of course, dreamers. Obviously, they didn't like the peace politics and the feminists' final triumph any more than their counterparts in the script.

Now what to do, where to turn, what to write? There were delightful, informal Sunday afternoon gatherings in the lovely old home of Donald Ogden Stewart and Ella Winter in Hampstead, where fascinating people came. The talk was lively, witty, and anti-establishment. Fun, enlightening — but I needed work, desperately.

Then came an opportunity. Eileen Bernal had received a book from a dear friend in the USSR, Ivy Litvinova, an Englishwoman who was the widow of the late Maxim Litvinov, Soviet Foreign Minister. Expert in Russian, she had done the English translation of two of Dostoevesky's novellas; one *The Gambler*, quite famous, and one called *My Uncle's Dream*, the latter his only comedy, never before translated into English.

Accompanying the book to Eileen and Sage Bernal was a letter from Litvinova suggesting that an adaptation of *My Uncle's Dream* would make a marvelous comedy for the theater. Knowing of my need, Eileen handed me the book to read.

When I expressed my delight and more than willingness, she immediately wrote to her friend, told her about me, and I received permission to do the stage adaptation.

My enthusiasm and the energy it created revived me. The book, Dostoevsky's only comedy, required changes to fit physically in to the theater, but no changes in his characters. The project occupied me day and night. Although the story is told by the nephew, the main character in the book is the woman, only secondarily the uncle. I later changed the title to *The Mistress of Mordasov*, the village in which she was First Lady. When completed, my agent, a resourceful and capable woman, Hope Leresche, had a dozen copies made, and it started the rounds, not only in England but in Germany (West), France and Italy.

There was considerable interest almost immediately. A London producer, husband of a well-known leading lady, took an option for an English production, and in Munich an agency called *Drei Masken Verlag* bought the German rights, having the play immediately translated and published in paperback.

For a play that wasn't produced for almost five years, and then for only two weeks in a regional theater in Leicester, ninety miles out of London, it had quite a career. It was optioned at least five times in Europe, first by a famous woman star for the German-Swiss theater who became seriously ill a week before rehearsals were to start. *Drei Masken Verlag* then sold it to German TV, and it was staged on TV exactly as written, as a two-hour play, receiving wide acclaim. Once again I saw the tendency in my writing which has never changed: *Uncle's Dream* was not political, but it was a satirical comedy of the manners of the petty nobility in a small village in Russia in the year 1857, and it truthfully depicts the lives, loves, ambitions, and frustrations of such bourgeois characters in their time. It was Dostoevsky's; I was merely the cabinet maker who, with what skill I had, reshaped his creation for the theater.

All was not going well between Kay and myself. We saw a marriage counsellor a few times, but it didn't seem to help. In the U.S. Kathy had entered college, and Kay began to feel torn. We frequently visited Debby at her school outside Bristol, in West England, but I knew — because she said so — Kay was beginning to think about returning to the states. I was not.

Life was suddenly full — for me. Ivor Montague, distinguished British film historian and scholar, phoned me. In the German Democratic Republic, he said, Annalie and Andrew Thorndike, distinguished documentary film-makers, had just completed a four-hour, two-part film on the USSR and required an English narration. Montague was gathering a group of English actors to direct the English dialogue and wanted to know whether I would come with them and, from a literal translation of the German, adapt it to English. Would I!

All expenses paid plus salary. And while the pay would be in East Marks, not exchangeable for Western currency, I was able to purchase what I wanted there and bring it home. I could buy the best cameras, lenses and other equipment — the only cost to me would be the duty bringing it into the country. A bargain.

The Thorndikes were delightful. Andrew was the son of an Englishman, brother of the famed actress, Dame Sybil Thorndike; his mother German. He spoke some English, his wife Annalie very little, but within four or six weeks we had the job done. When it showed in London some months later, it was not a success; the cold war created an icy atmosphere. (But in 1978, at the San Francisco Film Festival, Annalie Thorndike brought over the first half — two hours — of that film, *The Russian Miracle*, the section which dealt with the Revolution and the devastating Civil War that followed, and it was enthusiastically received. We had a heartwarming reunion, after so many years, and after she was introduced to great applause, she called me to the stage to introduce me as the adapter of the narration. A wonderful moment.)

In 1964, Kathy McTernan, at San Francisco State College, was suddenly afflicted with a serious illness. Kay went half out of her mind with fright and grief and left at once. For weeks she was at Kathy's bedside at the hospital, and finally Kathy recovered sufficiently to be moved to the guest house of Kay's brother, George, in the hills of Palo Alto. I missed Kay terribly.

It was then I got my first commercial offer. Sam Jaffe and Paul Radin, former agents in Hollywood, had come to England to produce Joy Adamson's book about Elsa the Lion, *Born Free*, and wanted me to write the screenplay.

The idea absorbed and fascinated me. It would pay, of course American Blacklist style, which now meant for me about ten thousand dollars. The job was a lucky thing for me then; it partially helped overcome the shock of a letter from Kay in which she wrote that she did not want to come back to me. I guess we both had known it would come to this, and when it did neither of us was too gracious about it. But we settled practical matters as time passed. I sold the house, the Jaguar, bought a VW, and found a small, pleasant little flat in Chelsea. I tried desperately to start life anew. I was under great stress, but still not without hope: *Born Free* would be a big hit (I hoped!), and it could mean a new start in films. In Hollywood, Trumbo, Waldo Salt, one of the original nineteen, and Ring Lardner were back at work; my time might still come.

It was only after I was already signed and at work on *Born Free* that I discovered Paul Radin, the co-producer, had been an informer in Hollywood. I was stunned and stumped. What to do? Luckily, I didn't have to solve the dilemma; Carl Foreman did it for me. Grey, if not blacklisted, in Hollywood, but with such distinguished films to his credit as *High Noon, The Champion*, and others which were also *money-makers*, he, like Adrian Scott who found work with MGM in London, became a writer-producer in England for Columbia. Carl had already made *Guns of Navaronne*, and when Jaffe and Radin ran out of funds Columbia bought them out, he took over as executive producer, and kept them on as associates. Radin was out of contact on the writing and I felt better. Cut to: Hollywood, at Columbia. When the head man heard who was doing the script, he ordered Carl to fire me. Carl laid his own job on the line; he refused. I stayed.

There was a fascinating story behind the book, *Born Free*. While writing the screenplay, I had to dig into the background of Joy Adamson and her husband, who for almost twenty-five years had been a wild game warden in Kenya.

I visited the publisher of the book. In a tiny room I met a gentle little old lady, who, I learned to my astonishment, as "editor" had actually written the book from some notes put together by the Austrian-born Mrs. Adamson, whose English was somewhat fractured. No credit, and a wage of twelve pounds a week. Shades of Hollywood junior writers prior to the Guild! And I learned about Joy Adamson, a dominating, aggressive woman whose exploits with Elsa the Lion outraged the Kenyan officials. The animal caused damage to natives' homes and gardens, and her husband was helpless to stop her. As a result, he was discharged within six months of his retirement date and lost his pension. But the picture's profits made that a pittance.

Yet Mrs. Adamson was hardly like the sweet, tender, lovable lady who appeared in the book and on the screen. I think I tried to get some of that toughness and ambition into her character. But she had script approval in her original contract with Jaffe and Radin, so Carl wrote those parts out and made it, as in the book, all sweetness and light. He should have shared screenplay credit with me, but for reasons of his own refused; I of course used the pseudonym Gerald L.C. Copley.

My work on the film done, now alone, I kept telling myself to keep busy, keep busy. Old friends helped. And then Felix Greene, just returned from China, asked me to help him put together his documentary. But the pressure, the stress of being alone was great. It was while acting as a sort of editorial consultant, editing his commentary to fit the cut film, that I found myself, one afternoon, walking from work to the bus, suddenly struck by severe pains in my upper back. The pain was so intense that I couldn't breathe or take another step and was forced to sit on the curb, hunched over and gasping. A cab stopped, a passerby helped me into it. I managed to get home and to the phone. The person I was able to reach was Eileen O'Casey, with whom I had become friends after many Sunday afternoons at Ella's and Don's; without her, I don't think I'd have made it. She called a doctor, who came over immediately. It was a myocardial infarction. He rushed me to the hospital.

I was in the hospital for six weeks, no charge, on socialized medicine, in a ward with twenty-five other patients. It soon became clear, as I rested (the pain receding) that I would recover. I began to enjoy the other convalescents around me, and the excellent attention given to us all. With that, I had Eileen as an almost daily visitor until she hurried back to the West of England, where Sean was dying, but many of my friends brought books, gifts of fruit, and even an occasional forbidden martini when I felt confident enough. In six weeks I was out, weak, feeling hopeless and despondent. My sons begged me to come home as soon as I was finished with the post-hospital visits. I was concerned; a few inches below my heart a slight bump appeared. When I showed it to the examining intern on my final visit, I was told not to worry; it was probably just a bit of intestine bulging. The hospital dismissed me. Low in spirits, I worried about that bulge. I decided to go back to the U.S. at least for a visit.

I flew to Hollywood, stayed with Charlie and Vesta Katz. Charlie didn't like the way I looked, and the thing below the heart alarmed him. He took me to his doctor, an old friend and a cardiovascular specialist. As soon as that expert examined me, he ordered an arteriogram. It was as he suspected; I had an aneurism of the aorta. He immediately phoned Dr. Howard de Bakey, an old friend and colleague, in Houston, Texas, who was an innovator of the type of surgery required, and that evening I flew South and immediately went to the hospital. Monday the surgery would take place, after the usual preparations.

The hospital had an air of excitement among the nurses and I soon found out why: Edward VIII, ex-Prince of Wales, had been given the entire floor above where my room was. He was there for the same surgery, and the same Monday morning. I found little thrill in that, rather some apprehension; would this distinguished nobleman get my surgeon, de Bakey, and have me handed down to one of his assistants? I finally got up the nerve to ask and was assured there was nothing to worry about. De Bakey would do neither the prince's nor mine; he merely supervised, and his trusted associates would do the actual work.

When it was over and I was out of intensive care the next day and could move enough to see what happened, there were only bandages from my solar plexus to the groin. I learned almost the entire aorta had been replaced with a tube of dacron or some other plastic from just below the heart to the kidneys and on to the bifurcation at the groin where the femoral arteries go down to each leg.

Recovery was surprisingly rapid. Within a week, I was sitting up and able to reach the phone when it rang. That morning it was from San Francisco; Kay. Could she come down to visit me? I told her that would be delightful, but why not wait another ten days until I returned to Los Angeles? She didn't want to, and the next day she was there.

She was tense, affectionate, uncertain, and, it seemed to me, was hinting that she'd like us back together. I could come to San Francisco, take my time recuperating. I was sixty, she reminded me, and what with the recent heart attack and now this surgery, it was time to take it easy. I was touched. I loved her then and despite the fierce conflicts since, I still do. Something inside me agreed; when strong enough I would return to England, get what I wanted of what I had left, and go back.

It wasn't easy. Back in England, saying farewell to friends I felt uncertainty in every muscle and vein. What was I returning to, what was I? An invalid, taken into the care of a generous wife, who until a month ago was in the process of divorce. In some sort of mad despair, I started throwing away dozens of papers and manuscripts, giving away books I'd treasured. Return to Kay? It was wrong.

No, I couldn't do it. I'd return to Hollywood, and with *Born Free* a possible hit, I'd work my way up to the next rung in the black market. Back in Hollywood word got around that I'd written the film and I began to get job offers. For animal pictures. I had suddenly become an expert on pet movies. I did a story about a boy and his elephant. It was too much. And with friends imploring both Kay and me to try again, I realized I had to. In a short while I found myself on the plane, returning to Kay in San Francisco.

With Kay in Leipzig in 1973

18

On To San Francisco

It is close to impossible for me to believe that over fifteen years have passed since I arrived in 1965 in San Francisco. As I sit here and attempt to write about those years, then to now, the first thought that comes to mind is that this city has become, if not my home, certainly my "turf." Although I have traveled during this time back to England, France, the German Democratic Republic, Czechoslovakia and the USSR, in most ways I feel I have truly come into my own here, fulfilled and rewarded in countless ways, saddened in but one. As in childhood, I couldn't heed my father's admonition, "to learn when to speak, and when to keep your mouth shut." This characteristic is now perhaps often cantankerous and acrimonious, as some old men frequently tend to become. But I think the good friends I have made, young men and women, as well as old, feel I balance out that flaw in other ways.

It was wonderful, arriving here, welcomed then by old friends like Harry Bridges, and to meet his lovely Japanese-American wife, Nikki, a talented poet. As a child, Nikki suffered Manzanar, the World War II concentration camp for Japanese, whether or not they were American-born citizens.

Here, too, I then found David Hilberman and his family. Dave and I had become friends on the picket line outside Walt Disney's Studio in Burbank in the mid-forties when the workers struck the plant. Dave, one of Disney's top animators, a fine artist, had joined the strikers, and when the strike was lost he was among those not rehired. Perhaps it was in meeting old friends, and quickly making new ones, that I found myself back in political activities after years on the sidelines in England. As a result can it be that today I actually feel more energetic and, at the same time, more at peace with myself than ever I can recall?

Soon after arrival, moving in with Kay and the girls and still convalescing, I submitted my plays to the regional theaters. I received a call from Sali Lieberman. He was on the board of directors of the Homestead Players, a community theater across the Golden Gate Bridge in Mill Valley; he told me he and the board had read one of my plays and wanted to do it.

I had revised it somewhat since the Czech production and changed its title from *The Blossom and the Root* to *In an Obscene Temple*, a quote from Thoreau which is spoken in the third act; his characterization of the land of slavery. I was asked to direct. We had just started rehearsals when a photographer from the *Pacific Sun*, a Marin County weekly, came in and took my photograph. With him was a reporter, and we had an interview on my background, previous professional life, Hollywood Ten, contempt citation, year in prison; all of it.

Two weeks before the play opened, my picture occupied the entire front page of the paper. There was a flattering blurb on the play, followed by a summary of my life's work going back to *The Miracle*, through the theater years to Hollywood and the films I had written. To my astonishment, there they cut my life off. Not a word about the Hollywood Ten or the imprisonment. Whether intended to be out of kindness to me or for the theater's reputation, I'll never know, but their final paragraph reads this way: "Cole left Hollywood in 1947 and devoted himself principally to play-writing. The play in its present form, with the author as director, should prove a unique experience for Marin." It proved to be just a "kindly whitewash." I was indignant and wanted the facts printed. My father was no longer there but sage advice from Sali arrived in time; the theater's relationship with the paper might be damaged. I kept my mouth shut.

At about that time Dave Hilberman had an idea. Kay was teaching sociology at U.C. Extension in San Francisco; why shouldn't I teach Film Writing at San Francisco State College (now a university), where a decade before Dave had found a good job teaching animation? I explained about my lack of academic background, but he said it would be my professional qualifications and not my academic credits that would count. It turned out to be just that way: the following semester I started as an instructor. The kid who didn't want to finish high school suddenly found himself teaching in college! My mother was still alive — she died a few years later at the age of eighty-four — living in Los Angeles, and I couldn't resist phoning, "This is Professor Cole." I teased a bit and then told her. A college "professor" yet! She was just as astonished, and no less pleased, than I.

The gratification which came in the first few months was tremendous, as I found a way to communicate not only the techniques of screenplay writing, but the nature of film-making in Hollywood, its economics and politics. The openly expressed admiration of the students gave me a sorely needed lift. To this day, more than a decade since I was fired from there, some of my students still send me their manuscripts for criticism or phone to tell me of a film they have written that is about to be shown.

The pay, of course, was minimal, but I discovered with relief that I had passed the stage where I was bothered by not contributing an equal share financially to the household (not that *she* ever hinted it). I finally realized — incredible for it to be so belated — that not only was Kay's considerable wealth inherited, but that her income-tax reduction with a husband was far greater than my cost of "upkeep." If only I'd thought of that two decades before, what inner torture and anguish I'd have saved myself! I still continued to do most of the marketing and cooking, and all seemed to be going well enough.

Soon after I began teaching at S.F. State, I learned that S.I. Hayakawa, whose book *Language in Thought and Action* I had studied and so admired while in prison, was a professor of English and the humanities there. I wanted very much to meet him, but I didn't get to. We brushed into each other only once, in a hostile manner, a year and a half later. Among all who knew of my past — and present — their manner toward me was more than tolerant; the faculty amiable, the students appreciative. Once again Hollywood seemed forgotten.

But not for long. In ugly or pleasant ways, the past has a hook for haunting. Some time before, after many months, *Born Free* had finished shooting in Africa and had gone through the laborious process of editing and scoring. Now Carl Foreman personally brought it across the sea to Columbia in Hollywood for the first private preview at the studio. He invited me down from San Francisco for the occasion. There were few in Hollywood who knew "Gerald L.C. Copley" and I were one; it is doubtful that many there, after almost twenty years, even knew or recognized me — and those who might have were very discreet.

But Carl brought me down for a purpose. Trumbo, Lardner, Salt were all working under their own names, as he was. Why not me? It was his determined way of subtly attempting to bring me out of the producers' closet.

A few weeks later, after the film was previewed for the press prior to release and received extravagantly good notices, the word leaked out that "Gerald L.C. Copley" and I were one and the same. I began to receive offers, but, to my dismay, after forty-odd films, including those written on the black market (melodramas, comedies, and the few socially aware films) I had suddenly become the most wanted writer in Hollywood — for animal films! That should have cured me, and it almost did. Hollywood and heroin must be equally tough habits to break — though I have never tried the latter; one "habit" is enough.

Then, on September 3, 1967, a feature article appeared in the *Los Angeles Times Sunday Magazine*, called on the front page "The Unfriendly Ten Revisited." Inside, the five-page article by C. Robert Jennings, was titled "The Hollywood Ten Plus Twenty (1947-1967)." It reviewed the men and their times over the twenty years. Sam Ornitz, so ill when he was sent to a prison hospital, never recovered and died in 1957. There were accounts of the rest of us: Trumbo, Lardner, Scott, Maltz, and of course Dmytryk, all working under their own names for some years; Bessie, Lawson, Biberman and myself still blacklisted. The article didn't go into the reasons, nor probe the question of why some were working and others not.

In my case, I was more than blacklisted. Author Jennings phoned the chief executive at Columbia (name withheld by him) and asked him about the Hollywood Ten. Jennings wrote about the conversation this way:

"Some of them have had their names on films since 1960. Why did Mr. Cole have to use a pseudonym in 1965 on *Born Free*?"

"Lester Cole didn't write *Born Free*. Carl Foreman did."

"Carl Foreman is credited as Executive Producer. Gerald L.C. Copley is credited all by himself."

(Voice rising) "I can tell you that Carl Foreman wrote 90 percent of it. I'll be very honest with you. I'm not aware of anybody else on it." He hung up.

Jennings goes on. "The facts: Foreman admits he had tremendous difficulty engaging Cole to begin with; keeping him on became a matter of principle, and his credit did become an issue. In the end, the studio vetoed Foreman's efforts to use Cole's name."

Why were some of us able to write under our own names and others found even the use of pseudonyms resisted? Jennings doesn't answer that one. I'll try to later on.

That year, 1968, my mother died. At eighty-four, alone, ill, and enfeebled, she had found life unbearable. She took an overdose of sleeping pills and ended it, without a note of farewell to either Blanche or myself. I went to Los Angeles to arrange for the cremation and on the plane, returning, attempting to put my scattered, troubled thoughts together, I picked up a magazine and noted my right hand. To my astonishment, the red scar between my thumb and forefinger caused by the burn she inflicted sixty years ago, a daily reminder of her all my life, had vanished! I do believe that all things are knowable by man, but only as he learns more. Some things have not yet been learned; at any rate, no one has ever been able to explain this phenomenon to me.

By now the Vietnam War was chewing up tens of thousands of the young American draftees and slaughtering hundreds of thousands of Vietnamese men, women and children. The draft was making greater demands on our youth, and the resistance and unrest on the college campuses all over the country was intensifying. Across the Bay, at the University of California in Berkeley, the demonstrations were becoming angrier with each passing day. "Hell, no, we won't go!" was their defiant chant at the induction center for draftees in Oakland, where they picketed. At State College we saw not only similar demonstrations and ever more passionate denunciations of the U.S. aggression, but also the protests of the Black Students Union, which charged discrimination against them, against the hiring of Black teachers, and repression of civil rights.

I was in my second year there; enrollment in my classes was growing in a most gratifying way. But the Black Students Union made its demands for equal opportunities for its mem-

Family reunion. (l. to r.) Sheila, Michael, Lester, David, Dee, Jeffry, Jennifer, Amy, Alexander and Marcella.

bers and for an increase in Black instructors for Afro-American studies. Movements like this in years to come successfully lobbied for affirmative action laws. But in the late sixties the Black students' demands were rejected as non-negotiable by the Regents, and the president, a Mr. Smith, warned them that their threatened strike would be disruptive, and if they dared he would bring in the police.

On November 8, 1968 they dared, and although the picketing was peaceful the mounted riot police, the TAC Squad, came in with clubs swinging. The strike now closed the campus; the police violently forced the picket lines onto the street. On those lines with the students were a number of instructors and professors. We moved to the sidewalk just off campus and continued. President Smith either resigned or was fired

— perhaps because he was ready to accede to the BSU demands? — and, of all people, my once-liberal semantic guide, S.I. Hayakawa, was elevated to this post.

The Regents knew well the man to pick. Hayakawa had, like so many liberals in the Cold War period, changed his political style to fit the times. At the curb just off the sidewalk, where we were picketing, the striking students had brought a pickup truck on which a loudspeaker was mounted; through it they called to students and faculty inside the campus to join their cause.

Hayakawa's political career began at that moment. His beret worn at a jaunty angle, protected by police, he bravely swaggered through the nonviolent pickets, mounted the pickup, and with cameras ready from all the press and TV — evidently he had announced the coming event in good time — flashlights popped and TV cameras whirred as he ripped the wires from the loudspeaker and threw them at the pickets. Yesterday a liberal, today a corporation hero; he thus started the political campaign which finds him now in the U.S. Senate. He was not the only recipient of a reward. John Bunzel, a "liberal" social science professor, acted as his good right hand against the students, and the Regents soon elevated him to the presidency of San Jose State College, where, after some stormy years, he was again kicked upstairs as a senior fellow in the Hoover Institute at Stanford University. Of course, at the end of the term, I and all the non-tenured faculty members who had participated in the strike were fired.

The experience strengthened and inspired me. I wrote my first play in ten years. A student demonstration in front of the Army Induction Center across the bay was reported in the newspapers, and an interview with one of the "Hell, no, we won't go!" students sparked the idea. I knew before I started that a play against the draft, in support of nationwide youth resistance, would have no commercial market, but I wanted to say what I felt for those who would listen. I called it *"Say Uncle! (Sam)."* The title was an obvious metaphor for a big bully twisting the arm of a youth of inferior strength, trying to force him to "Say Uncle!" Upon completion, it immediately went into production regionally where groups such as Students Against the Draft were organized.

It had come off the typewriter as a one-act, sixty-minute play, and that was just as well, since it gave an opportunity for speakers, songs and rallying without making an evening too long. The play soon opened in London, at the Unity Theater, where it played for six weeks. There was more press coverage in London than in all the U.S. combined and, as expected, the conservative press pooh-poohed it as agit-prop, the liberals were mixed, and the left wing very favorable. But all admitted it made its point against the Vietnam War.*

In the U.S. most productions were in California. The long-established Manhattan Playhouse in Palo Alto, under the direction of Judith Dresch, gave it a fine production, and my old and good friend, blacklisted actor Lloyd Gough, came up from Hollywood to help make it a better opening by singing a number of appropriate songs, including some he had written, accompanying himself on his accordion. The play and Lloyd were an instant success, no doubt aided by the strong, activist student movement at nearby Stanford University.

A young director, Joel Eis, then getting a master's degree in dramatic arts, put together a good company that toured central and northern California. After expenses, the receipts went to various groups engaged in draft resistance.

In Oakland we did a benefit performance for the Angela Davis Legal Fund. She had been fired from UCLA for being a Communist. She sued, won back her job, but at the end of the term was fired again. This time they needed no reasons, since she didn't have tenure. Then she was indicted for murder

---

*My overseas activities were not left unnoticed. An FBI report informs on the play this way: "*Say Uncle!*, a play by Lester Cole, is being performed in the Unity Theatre in London. The play is set in an induction office and is an excellent study of draft resistance. . . ."

and kidnapping, in a frame-up trial, which, had she been convicted, could have meant life imprisonment. She fought back. Her fine attornies defended her successfully.

The established press, with few exceptions, ignored *Say Uncle!* In Los Angeles Everett Wile staged it in the theater of the First Unitarian Church, where it played to full houses for its week run. Only *Daily Variety*, on May 6, 1970, took notice of it.* It was not only a fair review, but gave some idea of my determination to expose the maladministration of Nixon, Kissinger and their General, Alexander Haig.

The times seemed to be changing. In 1969 Carl Foreman, once blacklisted, won the prestigious Laurel Award at the annual dinner of the Writers Guild. A year or two before it was given to Sidney Buchman, also blacklisted and an exile. And in 1970 it was bestowed upon Trumbo.

Trumbo's acceptance speech astonished everyone there. Speaking of the blacklist period (ended years before for him and some others), he said about those in the industry who lived through that period:

> Caught in a situation beyond the control of mere individuals, each person reacted as his nature . . . compelled him to. There was good faith and bad, courage and cowardice, wisdom and stupidity. . . . it will do no good to search for villains or heroes or saints or devils because there were none; there were only victims.

This outrageously lofty, ecclesiastical benediction from "on high" upon the scum of the industry and the most vicious, Jew-baiting would-be Negro-lynching Ku Kluxers in Congress started what was to develop, over the years, into open hostility

---

*"After charging that recruitment is 'one of this country's all but hidden enterprises,' Cole examines a crop of draftees reporting for induction and how they are treated when screened. . . . Play is heavy on humor (very black, indeed) and very opposed to the draft. Cole has seen no need to exaggerate for the sake of satire. . . . he has been able to sock his message across without getting too soapboxy. . . . Cole's play would never do for commercial production but for the purpose it's intended, it suits just fine."

among members of the Ten. We had perhaps been forced into unity by a common enemy, but as that force began to dissipate, each went his own way as the years passed; sadly, eventually into some open conflicts.

But then it was apparent only to a few. Ring Lardner sided with Dalton; Alvah Bessie opposed him; Maltz was furious; Trumbo's wife was critical, as were many others, including myself. Some years later Bruce Cook, Trumbo's official biographer, asked us for a quote. There wasn't much to say more than in the above paragraph, except to add that while I never thought of myself as a hero, there were indeed villains, to whom with this soothing balm Trumbo had given the greatest aid and comfort. When he had concluded that speech, the guilty right-wingers cheered; most of the others were stunned. The unpredictable Trumbo had done it again; this time himself a victim — of his own rhetoric.

At this juncture in its history, the Guild found itself in as embarrassing a political position as the Motion Picture Academy of Arts and Sciences had more than a decade before. Then, in the 1950s four blacklisted writers, Dalton Trumbo, Michael Wilson, Nedrick Young and Carl Foreman, had either won Oscars under assumed names or had their names eliminated from the credits of Oscar winners. When this finally came to light, the Academy was forced to remove the ban — it had become ridiculous.

After Trumbo became the third previously blacklisted writer to win the Guild's Laurel Award, the Guild's 1954 anti-Communist Amendment had become an equally ludicrous anachronism. Perhaps it had become known that these men were no longer members of the Party. In any event, the constitutional amendment had become obsolete.

So, some months later, on September 25, 1970, *Daily Variety* carried a front-page story headed: WRITERS GUILD REPEALS BAN ON COMMIES BY 2-1 MARGIN. Though it was apparently never discussed at the meeting, *Variety* recalled, "The industry also insisted [then, in 1954] on a clause that producers need not give credit to a known Communist writer." "Also insisted" — and complied with — seems to indicate that the anti-Communist amendment was producer-dictated. The Guild became the producers' association's watchdog, its staff ferreting out "fronts" and black market pseudonyms with great zeal and efficiency. This cost some of us who slipped through the Guild's net lowered pensions and no residuals for that period before we were reinstated.

But for this accommodation, the Guild, under its new name, Writers Guild of America, West, Inc., received its reward in the 1954 contract. A pension plan was set up, residual payments for films shown on TV were to be paid, and there would be a Health and Welfare Fund. Many writers felt it was more than fair exchange for an anti-Communist amendment, particularly in that period of McCarthy's dreaded power. There were all too many willing collaborators. But all of the above mentioned "rewards" could have been gained by a militant, unified and democratic Guild. Fifteen years before we had won recognition by a threat of a strike. It could have been done again.*

A short time later I wrote to the Guild and asked for reinstatement. On November 2, 1970, I received a reply from Jane L. Buckley, the membership secretary, stating that I had "three avenues open" to me: I could be placed on honorary withdrawal status, if I paid my dues (sixteen years!) in full. I could petition the Council (executive board) to waive the basic dues (from then on) since I was a retiree and eligible for the pension plan. Again, to do this, my dues in arrears would have to be paid in full. The only other alternative, the good secretary advised me, was to be suspended from membership by reason of non-payment of dues. The letter ended this way: "Needless to say, we wish we could be of further assistance. If you have any questions, please do not hesitate to contact us. Sincerely, Jane L. Buckley."

---

*And it was. A unified membership of the Guild won a stunning victory following an eleven week strike in the spring of 1981.

"Needless to say," I *had* further questions. Did they really expect me to pay dues for the years they attempted to keep me from writing on the black market and from being a member of the Guild? It was so preposterous on the face of it that it didn't take long for my opponents on the Council to be forced to retreat. I paid no past dues. My membership was restored. I applied for my pension and it was granted. But because of the blacklist years by the Guild, I received no residuals on films written under pseudonyms (with the exception, somehow, of *Chain Lightning*, which is how they retitled the Bogart picture, *These Many Years*). Like my pension from Social Security, into which I started paying the maximum in 1936 or whenever it started, my last five years, from sixty to sixty-five, the most important, were barren of payments because of the blacklist. So the payments of both are minimal.

The Guild has since then regained its balance, and again I am a member, an "active retiree." Each year I receive a renewed membership card; each month I get the Guild Newsletter; all notices of membership meetings arrive along with other announcements. I have been active with a Committee of Retirees which has succeeded in raising the minimum retirement payments.

At the time, however, the throwing out of the anti-Communist amendment from the Guild constitution did not mean that the industry was throwing out the Waldorf Statement. The Blacklist was still in effect for some, certainly for John Howard Lawson and myself. It was a matter of concern not only financially but, even more keenly, professionally. The Un-American Activities Committee was gone, but its ghost was alive and well in Hollywood. For the vast majority, the past was either forcibly forgotten or happily so. But not for those still blacklisted. And the question never ceased to haunt us: Why could some work and not others? What really had happened? What was behind it? Certainly Lawson and I had screen credits which equaled many of those now back at work.

It wasn't until years later that the shroud of fog lifted; the secret ingredient came to murky light. In or around 1960, Roy Brewer shifted from the IATSE and his post as blacklist Fuehrer to an executive position with one of the minor production companies. At the time I was doing a black market job for Sam Bischoff, who had been executive producer over Burt Kelly for *None Shall Escape* at Columbia. My assignment was *Operation Eichmann*, the quickie described in chapter 17. In a very circuitous way Sam dropped a hint that "things were changing" and there was no need any longer to "go public." To use my own name, all I had to do was write a letter swearing I was no longer a Commie; all absolutely confidential. I said, no, I'd use a pseudonym. I thought no more about it — then.

But for how long had something like that been going on? I have been told that one of the best known and most highly paid women writers in Hollywood got off the blacklist precisely that way in 1960; did a dozen others follow that path to "rehabilitation"? Is that why they went to work under their own names while Lawson, Biberman and I could not? And why, as late as 1965, did Carl Foreman have to put his contract on the line with Columbia to force them to give me screen credit even with the pseudonym "Gerald L.C. Copley" on *Born Free*? With the Writers' Guild constitution refusing membership — and thereby employment — unless writers swore they were not members of the Communist Party — how else could those writers work under their own names? I was forced to conclude that the fanfare of some writers breaking the blacklist was a myth — the blacklist broke *them*.

I couldn't do what they presumably did, yet I desperately wanted, needed, to write films in Hollywood. Perhaps now, with the constitutional ban of the Guild lifted, a new spring had begun for some writers. I sought an agent in Hollywood. My name was known, of course, by all of them, but the old adage in Hollywood is that a writer is as good as his last credit, and while my last credit under the pseudonym was well-known, it was by then seven years in the past. Also, I was then sixty-seven; perhaps time has passed me by. Even though I may no longer have been blacklisted, I might have been considered too old, as were others who never had been involved politically.

I tried. I offered myself to agents. None wanted me. Was I still "tainted"? If I couldn't get an assignment, could I sell a story or an original screenplay?

Woody Allen had made a couple of satiric fantasies, political to a degree, and I thought I'd rewrite my much rewritten novel/play/musical to create a leading role for him. Once more I tore the thing apart, created a central character which I hoped he'd find to his liking, and spent a couple of months re-developing the story. With little real hope — more like desperate but pretended detachment — I sent it off to a friendly producer for whom I'd done some blackmarket work years before. He had recently been associated with a Woody Allen production and was on good terms with Allen's manager. He responded promptly and positively, and felt certain he could present it to Allen's manager with my name on it. He did. It was promptly rejected; I never learned whether my name on the story itself scared the manager.

Written for Allen, there was no second choice, and certainly no general market for a story of its kind. That was it. I swore I was through trying for a breakthrough in Hollywood. Having thus solemnly sworn, I didn't take long to discover I was far from as good as my oath. Hollywood had become the mountain I had to climb, the hated adversary. I refused to stoop, but I couldn't stop trying to conquer.

Less than a month later I was at it again. A play of mine had been put on in the community theater in Mill Valley, a Marin County suburb of San Francisco. Why not rewrite the Lysistrata screenplay and, instead of London, place it in this San Francisco suburb? I could eliminate that which was only pertinent in the early sixties in London, but maintain the inherent antiwar, feminist comedy as it was adapted from Aristophanes' play.

I called the new version *The Athenian Connection*. The title came from the connection between the feminist, antiwar stance of the B.C. Athenian women and those women more than two thousand years later in Mill Valley, California, who had the same feelings about themselves as women. I had made an attempt at an old connection, with a writers' agency in Hollywood, Eisenbach and Greene. I sent them a copy. In a short time the manuscript came back with an extremely brief and brusque rejection: my version added nothing to Aristophanes' original. The implication: neither did I take anything away in my adaptation of the masterpiece! Much later I understood.*

A friend in Hollywood then read it, liked it, and suggested I send it to Sylvia Hirsch, story editor for the writers' department of the William Morris Agency, one of Hollywood's largest and most prestigious. I wrote to Ms. Hirsch and promptly received a most cordial response; she would be delighted to read my screenplay. Off it went.

After a few weeks I heard from her. Starting "Dear Lester," she didn't take long to come to the point: "Several of us have now read your original screenplay; and while we enjoyed it very much, I'm sorry to tell you that we're going to pass on representation. I've been told there is too much of a similarity between this and a picture that Dick Van Dyke was in some time ago that Gar Kanin made called *Man With a Fuzz*. . . . Sincerely, . . ."

Who could have so misinformed Ms. Hirsch about a similarity? The Gar Kanin picture was about a corporation head who refused to keep a man on his job because he grew a beard; what was the similarity between that and women who refuse to sleep with their men if they did not stop a war? But more; the agency "passed" not only representing my script, but also representing a writer whose work they professedly

---

*An F.B.I. report states that they had Eisenbach and Greene listed as my agent. Had they visited them? Obviously. Little more would be required in Hollywood to elicit the kind of response I received.

admired. Once again I swore off Hollywood. Once again it would be "final."

I tried to tell myself that with this firm, "irrevocable" decision, some sort of weight had been lifted from my mind. It would be easier to do so much that needed to be done that I really wanted to do. It was time to stop banging my head against the Hollywood wall.

That year, 1972, the Hollywood Ten were invited to be guests of honor at the Annual International Film Festival in Leipzig, in the German Democratic Republic. Lawson was very ill, Biberman and Ornitz were dead, and all the others, except Bessie and myself, declined for various reasons. The declinations were understandable; for some who had returned to the industry it was once again the fear of "guilt by association," for others either disinterest or rationalized hostility.

Welcomed by Andrew and Annalie Thorndike, whom I hadn't seen since 1962, I found Leipzig wondrously exciting. The festival was one that presented documentary films only, films never seen in the U.S., films most of us never knew were even made — from Africa, Asia, Latin America and from the Socialist countries.

Old friends from England were there, exhibiting films, but perhaps the most awesome of all to be seen were those in the out-of-competition retrospective of famed Soviet documentary film-maker, Roman Karmen. Starting with his earliest work, showing the social development of the primitive peoples in Asia in 1926, his films traced the cultural and industrial development of his country; he filmed front-line action of the Spanish Republican Army and the International Brigade, and captured extraordinary footage of the Soviet Army and its guerrilla fighters in World War II which some years later was to become the major footage in the twenty-part series shown on the NBC network in the U.S. under the title, *The Unknown War*, narrated for American audiences by Burt Lancaster.

Shortly after returning, I wrote an article about the festival

for the *People's World.* The editor asked me if I wanted my
own name signed to it. Suddenly, the most unexpected confrontation: would I sign my name to an article in a Marxist
paper? Would I now, at long last, "come out of the (political)
closet"? A sudden sense of outrage flowed like lava through
my arteries; wasn't it sufficiently frustrating that I could not
use my name on films I might write, must I also conceal it
here in the hopes of eventually returning to the good graces
of the Shahs of Hollywood? I decided it would be under my
own name and only my own name, from then on, wherever
and on whatever I wrote.

Some time later Alvah Bessie quit as film critic and the
editor asked if I'd take over. That was in 1974, and I've been
doing that gratifying chore ever since. For too many years I
had worked for film companies, in most instances writing in
their way what they wanted; now I was writing about the
artistic and social value — and lack of it — in their product
as I wanted to. It was a most gratifying turnabout. Many of
my articles and reviews were reprinted in the *Daily World* in
New York. A new, exciting — and ironic — career had begun:
although they wouldn't permit me to write films for them,
the advertising departments had no objection to inviting me
to the press previews to write *about* their films; those I liked
would bring some money to the box office, which is more
than my name on any film ever did. And if I didn't like the
film, if I panned it — well, perhaps they went by the old
Oscar Wilde maxim, "There's only one thing worse than
being talked about, and that's not being talked about."

I liked this work, and liked the chance it gave me to em-
phasize the role of the writer in films, so long obscured; I
could direct readers toward the writer's basic contribution,
and away from the decades of deception of a film being the
creation of the director and actors.

In 1975 an unexpected reward was an invitation to attend
the International Film Festival in Moscow as press represen-
tative for the two U.S. Party papers.

What changes since I was last there thirteen years before! Gone were the scattered remnants of bombed-out ruins from World War II; new apartment houses, new hotels and other buildings everywhere replaced the old. Seemingly so much had changed, been cleared away, wiped out, yet there remained the emotional scars of those who remembered, those who had fought and others who had suffered every conceivable hardship — scars upon their hearts almost visible to the searching eye. Certainly when you talked with them, the determination to achieve peace in the world, to strive and work for it, could seem to outsiders obsessive. The motivation is not only for themselves and their children, but for the peoples of the world. Who should strive harder for peace than those who lost twenty-two million of their own, far more than all the other warring nations combined? Little wonder war and peace are such frequent themes in their literature, drama and films.

Kapler, Yutkevich, Bella Epstein and Alexander (Sasha) Luria — what a wonderful welcome they gave me. Luria, who back in 1962 had announced one evening at dinner that he was making claim to my son as his "half-father" — "adopting" him — told me of the years since then when Mike had returned. He related aspects of Mike's development I had known little about. I knew, of course, that Mike had come to Moscow on international conferences of psychologists, and how in the intervening years he had become a full professor at Rockefeller University in New York. But I knew little about his contributions as an editor in both English and Russian of many scientific books, published by the Harvard University Press. And in Luria's house, on his desk, was a photograph of him with his godson and namesake, Alexander (Sasha) Cole — my grandson.

Through correspondence I knew that George and Alki Sevasticoglu were gone. With the coming of a democratic government in Greece some years before, the old radical partisan guerrillas were invited to come home. They did, but a short few years later the new government was ousted by the

Fascist Colonels' coup. Once again the partisans were forced to flee, this time to Paris, where George was given a post at the Sorbonne as professor of classic Greek drama. Alki wrote and published two delightful children's books. Their children were grown and in universities. They had survived and were at last serene, but never without a longing for Athens. Home.

At the festival all the guests and invited press — about twelve hundred of us — were housed in the new Hotel Rossiya, a short distance from the Kremlin. It is probably the largest hotel in the world which, apart from accommodating about five thousand guests, houses a large theater-opera-concert hall seating twenty-five hundred, where the festival films are shown. It is equipped with simultaneous translation devices which bring the listeners their choice of English, Russian, French, Italian and Spanish. There is also a smaller theater, a floor below, where the competition of children's films and documentaries is held.

The Festival plays host to more than a thousand guests — film-makers and members of the press from all over the world. All expenses are paid once they arrive in the country, not only the hotel and all meals, but recreation as well. There is a welcome break from the two or three films viewed daily in the two-week competition. On one Sunday a six-hour excursion aboard two luxurious boats takes the guests up the Moscow River, a rare and breathtaking day's outing. And on the second weekend, the guests are invited on the midnight train to Leningrad for a day of sightseeing there and to meet the artists of Lenfilm at a reception that evening before they return to Moscow. We've all heard fables of "royal" treatment; after these experiences, we were convinced it couldn't surpass that which Socialism extended.

Between visits with friends, viewing a couple of dozen films, tape recording notes for articles later to be written, the Moscow River excursion and the weekend in Leningrad, the days flew. Before I knew it, I was saying farewell to old friends and new — and I was on the plane for home.

The articles I wrote expressed my impressions as honestly as they could: if some were glowing, it was because I was. I tried to explain to what degree American film-goers had been conditioned into a narrowed outlook, myself included. Films were produced in scores of countries by people we didn't realize even looked at films, much less made them. We knew of Western European and, to a lesser extent, Russian films, but the Russian people could see the many films made in Peru, Venezuela, Cuba, many African nations and from countries in Asia. Occasionally some of these are shown at U.S. film festivals, but rarely, if ever, are they given commercial distribution. The answer frequently heard is that our audiences would not find them entertaining or interesting. That is probably true; they have been mis-educated *not* to respond to "foreign films." Sadism, violence, sex, brutality, alienation, so-called entertainment films are, with few exceptions, our standard diet. How could they find fascinating a film which showed the struggle of the high mountain Indians in Peru against the usurpation of their life-giving land by the ruling gentry? But millions of Russian "peasants" see those films and find reflections of their own past history in them, a reflection of the reality in which their ancestors fought and died. It's part of their world, be it Peru or Senegal, and it broadens their understanding. Enlightenment can be entertainment, too. Perhaps even more so than "escape."

The late Roman Karmen, famous Soviet documentary film maker and an earnest admirer at the 1972 International Film Festival.

19

A Wider Horizon

It was becoming a time of change. The consciousness, particularly of the younger people who were living in and through the inhumanity of the Vietnam slaughter, soon to be followed by the ousting of Nixon and his "gang of four," revealed a different perspective on accepted myths of the immediate past. Along with this, a flurry of books came out about the blacklist and the Hollywood Ten, revealing many facts which were formerly concealed.

In 1972, sixteen years after the Cogley volumes, Robert Vaughn, well-known actor and not so well-known scholar, wrote his Ph.D. dissertation on the blacklist. Someone encouraged him to enlarge upon it, and the result was the book, *Only Victims*. The title was inspired by Dalton Trumbo's benign benediction in 1970 upon those whom Lillian Hellman, a few years later, was to characterize far more accurately in her book, *Scoundrel Time*.

Vaughn's book was anti-Communist, as were almost all, but it exposed much more about the Committee, and the informers, than had been revealed before, and it received national attention. Perhaps it was the success of this book that started the vogue: Eric Bentley's *Thirty Years of Treason* was followed by Stefan Kanfer's *Journal of the Plague Years*. Kanfer was film critic/editor at *Time*, and his style was somewhat elitist, viewing both sides from a lofty perch with a catch-phrase mixture of pity and contempt. But the books had an impact, as two 1977 films did to an even greater degree: Woody Allen's generally excellent *The Front* and the feature-length documentary, *Hollywood on Trial*. From across the nation students in colleges and universities began to seek interviews from us for term papers and theses; aroused by the revelations of a corrupt government, they now began to see us in a new and more perceptive light.

Impetus was given to some degree to this gathering interest back in December 1974 when the American Civil Liberties Union in Los Angeles gave a highly publicized, well-attended dinner honoring the Hollywood Ten and our attorneys, Robert W. Kenny, Charles J. Katz, and Ben Margolis. Kay and I were invited down from San Francisco, and for me it was an evening of mixed feelings: it seemed everyone was there, so while it was heartwarming to meet some old friends, it was also chilling to turn away from, and be turned away by, other former friends.

Perhaps, then seventy-one, I was becoming cantankerous, too easily annoyed. Kay didn't share my feelings, certainly not the intensity, and that could have been one of the reasons why the rift between us was widening. I was never easy to live with, and perhaps was becoming even less so. When not engaged in constant activity, I had the need for more contact with my own kind of people. I became increasingly restless, irritable. It was then Kay made the suggestion which brought about a wonderful change in my life, making it easier for me to bear whatever might come.

Why not go back to teaching? I can't recall whether she had already given up her own job at the University of California, but she thought I should try; who knew whether or not in the changing climate I might be acceptable? She learned that there was an opening for an instructor in screen writing at U.C. Extension, and I applied.

The administrator of that department, an extremely pleasant young woman, Ginger Richardson, accepted my application and credentials, both as film-writer and former instructor at S.F. State College, and promised to let me know in a short time. As a reference, I gave the name of Allen Rivkin, long-time film-writer, and for some years, after retirement, the public relations director of the Writers Guild and editor of its monthly newsletter.

A very short time later, Ms. Richardson phoned me to say she'd received a most satisfactory recommendation from Mr. Rivkin, and she would like me to start in the fall semester. That was at the end of May. I wrote immediately to Rivkin to thank him.

Apparently he enjoyed the opportunity to reply to Richardson and sent me a xerox of her letter to him and his response. He really had laid it on; a gaudy PR job, a professional "hard sell." After giving my history and the many years we knew each other and the "thirty-odd screenplays of top quality," my presidency in the Guild and other offices, he answered questions regarding his opinion of my teaching abilities thus: "He's a devoted student of filmwriting, communicates with an ability that many politicians would envy. He can teach anything that has to do with screenwriting, to anybody, no matter what level. He had taught at S.F. State College, and my reports have him as a fine educator."

Finally, responding to the question: "Other comments, personal qualities . . . etc.," Rivkin answered: "His charm mesmerizes people; thus they listen and remember. What better qualities does a teacher need?"

I laughed, incredulous, wrote back thanking him, with but one criticism; had he told me in advance how good I was, I would have demanded at least twice the salary.

After a year of teaching, during the summer of 1976, what I had dreaded finally happened. One morning at about nine Kay walked into my office, politely asked to be forgiven for disturbing me at work, and calmly announced that she was leaving the house — and me — at three that afternoon.

It was clear she had planned it some time before, since she said she had bought a co-op apartment, from which the former owner had not moved as yet, and until it was vacant she would live in a furnished apartment she had rented.

I was stunned. Now seventy-one, there was no new life to be started for me, nor did I have any reason to believe she had already launched one. Only as time went on did I realize how, from the beginning almost twenty years before, despite our closeness, there were cultural conflicts growing out of our different environments which blocked the kind of harmony needed. Certainly if it was anyone's fault, it was not hers, and I couldn't figure out how it was mine. Irreconcilable differences, as the lawyers put it.

Generously, she suggested that I stay in the house while I prepare for teaching that fall and finish writing my novel — about four or five months from then. Promptly at three she left. What now? Soon to be seventy-two, how to start over?

Being alone in the house had become unbearable. But I stayed on and worked. I guess I was partly saved by frequently visiting Jack Lawson, now seriously ill. He and Sue had moved to San Francisco to be close to Mandy, their daughter, who worked here. Jack was then past eighty, and Sue but a year younger; Mandy lovingly helped them both, driving them, shopping for them, doing everything possible.

Then a further unhappy distraction; Mason Roberson, a writer, a dear friend and husband of Doris Walker, developed cancer. I would visit him for a few hours at least three times a week. Immobilized after a time, he knew he was dying, and while I did everything I could to try to keep his spirits up, it was he, with infinite courage and love, who helped bring mine back. He knew how alone I felt, and one day humorously suggested that since I was at his house almost daily, why not find an apartment nearby on Potrero Hill? He sent me to a real estate fellow he knew. I told him what I needed, what the upper limit of rent had to be, and I needed a view. He took me to a six-flat building atop a hill only a block away from Mason and Doris's; the view was as magnificent as theirs — a high, panoramic vista through large windows of downtown San Francisco, the Bay Bridge to Berkeley and Oakland, and a vast expanse of the San Francisco Bay. I rented it. It's beautiful. I'm still here.

When I resumed teaching, two months after Kay left, my depression receded to a degree under the great stimulation, the sense of reward, the pleasure of student appreciation. It seemed — and still does — greater than anything I ever experienced as a film-writer.

Nationally, the atmosphere continued to improve. On April 30, 1977, the Departments of the Arts, Humanities and Communications, Society and Culture at the University of California at Los Angeles held a one-day symposium which they titled, "Fear in Hollywood: Red Scare and the Blacklist." The topics to be discussed were anti-Communism, red-baiting, the HUAC Hearings, and the blacklist.

Among the featured speakers announced, subject to availability, were Carl Foreman, Will Geer, Lee Grant, Ben Margolis, Martin Ritt, Martha Scott and "others to be announced." Why so many were unavailable, I don't know, but when the program started at 9 A.M., the huge hall filled to capacity, only Lee Grant, Martha Scott, Ben Margolis, and Howard Suber — whom I did not know and still cannot recall — and I were there.

The two actresses, both forthright and charming, told of their experiences and struggles during that period; Margolis spoke of the historical and legal aspects. I was the fourth speaker of the morning session, and I impatiently awaited my turn. A recent development that apparently went unnoticed by all concerned would be my main point: I had something exciting to report.

When at last my turn arrived, I spoke first of the terror of the period in the early fifties, the fear and unwillingness of many of the accused to take a firm stand, and I then sprung what had so excited me. I asked how many had read the recent Supreme Court decision, less than two weeks before, in which two citizens of New Hampshire — Jehovah's Witnesses — refused to display the motto on the state auto license plate: LIVE FREE OR DIE. They declared it was against their religious beliefs. They were fined, arrested, and then sent to jail for continuing to cover up the words offensive to them after the police warned them. They fought on. When they lost in the Appeals Court, they carried their fight to the Supreme Court, and there they won in a seven-to-two decision. The thrilling, pertinent part for me was the content of that decision. Chief Justice Burger said "it was a matter of supreme importance, coming under the scope of the First Amendment, a protection which includes the right to speak freely or *refrain from speaking at all.* . . . A system which includes the right to proselytize religious, *political and ideological causes* (italics mine) must also guarantee the concomitant right to decline to foster such subjects. The right to speak and to refrain from speaking are complementary components of the broader concept of 'individual freedom of the mind'."*

How this connection with our case escaped all connected with it was beyond me. The audience was stunned when I told them that when our attorneys, before the Supreme Court in 1950, used those *precise words* in our defense, they had been rejected. But now, I said, we were vindicated and had to bring this vindication of the Ten to the attention, not only of the film industry, but to the broadest sections of the American people. And I concluded by saying we must sue for a redress of grievances and another hearing in the Supreme Court.

There was applause and cheers. We broke then for lunch, and scores of students, professors and film people crowded around us and turned to Ben Margolis and asked him if he

---

Wooley vs. Maynard, U.S. Supreme Court, April 1977.

would take the case again. Margolis had, unknown to me since I'd seen him last, apparently altered his political stance. He jerked a thumb in my direction and said, "If he can raise the money, sure." I was stunned. I said nothing.

Bob Kenny had died; Charlie Katz was seriously ill after open-heart surgery, and I didn't want even to mention it to him. I wrote letters to a score of newspapers telling of our vindication. To my knowledge, none of the letters appeared.

I was again invited that summer, 1977, to the Moscow Film Festival. On the way, stopping in New York, I went to see Leonard Boudin, noted civil liberties attorney. He had read the decision, said I was absolutely right, and when I eagerly told him I wanted to raise money so we could sue for a redress of grievances, or at least a rehearing in Court, he wryly said there was one slight obstacle: the Supreme Court has a law which states that a rehearing must be applied for within twenty-five days of a decision. We were just twenty-seven years too late.

At last the matter got one limited airing. Carey McWilliams, editor emeritus of *The Nation*, wrote and then had printed a fine article on the relationship of the decision to our case. But it did not advance our cause. Maybe I'd find another way. The Guild?

After visiting in New York with my sister and friends, a few days later I took off for Moscow. And there the idea receded in my mind, for the time being, as I enjoyed meeting old — and now older — dearly loved friends.

Once again there were surprises among the films shown. There was a remarkable feature film from Bengladesh (yes, from that remote, independent nation once the eastern part of Pakistan), a land known to us only for its floods and hungry, illiterate peasants. Who in the U.S. knew before I learned and passed it along in an article that they had made fifteen feature films there in the past dozen years, exhibited all over Asia, Africa and the Socialist countries?

I saw a beautiful, deeply moving film made in North

Korea, showing the personal tragedy of a family torn apart by the division of the country into hostile parts. Would it ever be shown in the U.S.?

How many were aware that in the Soviet Union there are not only film studios in Moscow and Leningrad, but one in every major republic and some not so major ones? Not only in the Ukraine and Georgia, but in Uzbekistan, Mongolia, Kazakstan, including the one in the almost unknown Republic of Kirghiz. From wherever, each film is made both in the language of its republic and in Russian.

The films from Kirghiz are particularly extraordinary. Movies frequently have a tendency in the USSR as elsewhere to reflect in their characters the regional culture in a way which makes their motivations unclear to people from other lands. But from the writings of Chinghiz Aitmotov, Kirghizian novelist, dramatist and screenwriter have come films which have in them people universally understood. Such writings are the works of genius. His characters live everywhere, and everywhere people identify with their problems. In recent years such films as *Jamilia* and *The First Teacher* have had only a few commercial showings in the U.S., but I believe whoever saw them will find them hard to forget.

I had the privilege of meeting Chinghiz Aitmotov at a reception given at one of the embassies. We spoke of comparative conditions for film writers in our respective countries. While writers there enjoy better conditions in many ways, the problem of director domination has not been eliminated, although, unlike here, the writer is consulted and has some voice in the decisions — if not the final word. Aitmotov sees the director's prominence as a historical hangover which goes back to the days of silent films. I was gratified by his emphatic agreement with me regarding the role of writers and their need for control of their material.

The writer, I have long maintained, is to film what the composer is to a symphony. The director is the conductor of the writer's composition. It is all too common to hear and see advertised "Altman's *Nashville*," "Altman's *M*A*S*H*," and perhaps somewhere in small print the names of the writers. But one never sees advertised Leonard Bernstein's *Fifth Symphony* and, far below, in small letters, "Music by Beethoven."

The finished film is not unlike the recorded performance of a symphony. The conductor directs the skills of the musicians — in film they are the actors, cinematographers, designers and all the technicians who create a collaborative work of artistic merit. The writer as composer is the director of the director; read a screenplay — the previously included sequence of *Rosy Ridge* is an example — and it becomes evident. The writer is not a member of the orchestra, not one of the fiddles, cellos, trombones or percussions. This downgrading of the writer is a conscious act employed for one purpose only — to prevent the writer from achieving what should be his: control of his own creative work. If the director doesn't like it, or it doesn't suit the producer, they are free to get another story, or if they own the material, another writer and do it over. They should not be free arbitrarily to mutilate the writer's work — without even seeking his permission.

Also unforgettable were the films from Africa, and particularly one called *Xala*, written and directed by Ousmane Sambene, novelist, dramatist, film writer and director from Senegal. Like almost all the films from the so-called Third World — there is only One World — Sambene's films show the struggle of his people against reactionary neocolonialism. In *Xala*, he portrays how his own people, after gaining independence from France, remain subservient to that country through corrupt leaders. Unemployment, hunger and resistance are revealed with powerful ironies, sharp comedy and ridicule of those "Uncle Tom" Blacks who seek to imitate their former — and still secret — white masters. Sambene, from his writings and former film success, finances 50 percent of the cost of his films; by Senegal law the government is forced to supply the other half. So, although government-supported, his films are banned in Senegal as revolutionary, subversive. He laughs at this irony, but he is frustrated and angry; his films are made for the enlightenment of his own people. The best he can do is show them there in "underground" cinemas. But in the rest of the world he strives to help people understand what is going on in Senegal, and search for parallels in their countries. His films are seen in the U.S. only in film festivals and occasionally in small "art" houses.

Not surprisingly, at this 1977 Festival, the U.S. press was represented by only two papers: *Variety*, by Ron Holloway, head of the West Berlin office, and myself from the *People's* and *Daily World*. David Rintels, president of the Writers' Guild, and John Furia, Jr., also from the Guild, were there to attend an International Film Writers Conference following the Festival. Other American guests were officials from film festivals held annually in New York, Chicago, Los Angeles and San Francisco and a few others. A totally unexpected and enlightening event was an invitation to a cocktail party and reception at the American Embassy. The U.S. press — Holloway and myself — and the officials from the various festivals were invited to meet the *official* U.S. delegation, which was headed by Jack Valenti, president of the Motion Picture Producers' Association (Eric Johnston had long since gone to his reward) and the other two delegates, film stars Kirk Douglas and Ellen Burstyn.

Holloway of *Variety*, an expert on East European and Soviet films, took this opportunity to interview Valenti and I was a fascinated listener. Rather goodnaturedly, Valenti grumbled about the disparity in film grosses in the two countries; with 220 million population in the U.S. the annual internal gross revenues were about $2 billion. The Soviet Union, with about 10 percent greater population, had an internal gross of $4 billion, double ours. Ruefully, he went on to say the U.S. industry would like to get a slice of that $4 billion by selling more of our films there. He was optimistic; hopefully it would be worked out during this visit.

Of course, what he didn't say, or didn't realize, was that

while gross revenues in the USSR were double ours, their admissions are a fourth as much, from 25 to 75 kopeks, which makes attendance there *eight* times greater. And, of course, it is the same in the theater: In the U.S. some years ago, a Ford Foundation survey showed that only 3.5 percent of the American people ever saw a live drama; in the USSR even the smallest district either has a repertory theater or is visited by touring companies regularly throughout the year.

Moreover, the films they show are not only Soviet-made. They are brought from fifty lands. Whereas Ousmane Sambene is hailed throughout the USSR, here he is known to but a handful of people, mostly film students at the universities or those who attend festivals.

It is amazing how calmly and philosophically, if not quite good-naturedly, the Soviets take the distortions and contradictions of the U.S. press and the Voice of America. Shortly after his return to this country, Valenti stated on the air and in interviews that it was impossible to make an equitable film deal with the Soviets because of the differences in producing and distributing films; the opposite of his optimistic remarks when in Moscow.

The director of Sovexport Films, V. Mayatsky, replied that it was hard to learn what made Valenti change his mind so suddenly. And he went on: "The Voice of America distorted the real situation. . . . After a long interval, the USSR and the U.S. signed an agreement on cultural exchange. From 1958 to 1974, Sovexport Film bought ninety-nine U.S. films. Over the same period U.S. companies bought forty-eight Soviet films. In 1974-1975 we bought for distribution eleven U.S. full-length pictures, while U.S. film companies bought only seven Soviet films." And then Mayatsky came to the heart of the problem: "True, when we select films we take into account the tastes of the Soviet audience, and we do not buy, and are not going to buy, films that glorify war, racial discrimination, violence, and pornography. . . . It is a well-known fact that the Soviet Union distributes U.S. and other foreign films on a wide scale, while the distribution of Soviet films in the U.S. is very limited."

That last sentence, if anything, is an over-generous understatement. "Very limited" indeed! The brilliant Japanese-Soviet coproduction, *Durzu Ursula*, screenplay by Kurasawa and a Russian writer, and directed by Kurasawa, won both first prize at the Moscow Film Festival and the Hollywood Academy Oscar for the year's best foreign language film. It was bought here but for more than a year after winning the award it was buried in vaults, and after that could be seen only in brief appearances at small independent houses. Some Soviet films are bought and *never* distributed; perhaps the price the U.S. distributors get from USSR distribution of their films pays for keeping Soviet films frozen in vaults. Certainly the beautiful Aitmotov films, *Jamilia* and *The First Teacher*, reached only the most limited audiences. I have never been able to find any response by Valenti to Mayatsky's rebuttal.

Before leaving San Francisco for the Festival, I had been asked by an actor friend to phone an old uncle and aunt in Moscow and say "hello," and, if I had time, to meet them. Despite the hectic activities, I made time. Meeting Joe Levy was an unforgettable experience. He was eighty-four, perhaps all of five foot three, and weighed about a hundred pounds. But he was lithe and lively. It was a warm sunny afternoon, and we sat in the little park outside the hotel. Soon my questions led to his telling the story of his life: how he and his young wife left Russia in 1916, during the war, and came to New York, where he became a master electrician. They joined the Communist Party in 1926, and when the depression hit the U.S. in 1930 and he was out of a job, he read in the *Daily Worker* that skilled mechanics were desperately needed in the USSR. They returned, went to work and for a year lived with practically no furniture, no beds; they ate and slept on the floor. Then their furniture was shipped from

New York by a relative and their little apartment became home.

At that point he walked me a short block to the Metro station. We went down the stairs. "You see those lights?" he pointed to the various chandeliers that illuminated the beautiful, immaculate station. (Works of art everywhere, graffiti nowhere.) "I put them there, forty-five years ago. Them and hundreds like them, all through Moscow. Me and other workers. This subway is ours. We built it. You know how much it costs to ride on it, anywhere, fifty, sixty miles? Three kopeks. Four cents. We did it." His pride shone: his work, his subway. As we walked back to the bench, he told me that he worked for twenty-eight years in the subway, extending it in every direction, more than a hundred miles. Then he reached retirement age. "You know, doctors, hospitals, from the beginning — all free. And now you know how much my pension is? Eighty percent. Eighty percent of what my wages were. And my wife. She was a translator. Same thing. Eighty percent, each of us." He looked at me challengingly, as if to say, you got something like that, maybe?

I shook my head, looked at this obviously Jewish-looking man, Joe Levy, and asked, "You know, with all these Jews going to Israel, what about anti-Semitism here? In America, that's what most of the Jews talk about. Anti-Semitism."

He shook his head. "Since 1931, once, only once did anything happen to me. A few years ago my wife and I — I wish she could have come today, but her arthritis is terrible — we were out for a walk on a Sunday, and we're passing a church a few blocks from our flat, and people are coming out of church, and we know most of them and say 'hello' and they say 'hello' but there's one woman, she's new. You could tell by looking at her she was fresh from the country. And she could tell, one look at Joe Levy, she could tell by my nose, my face, what I was. So her face screws up in disgust, she spits at my feet and like she's vomiting says, *'Jude!'* So I step in front of her, she's maybe six inches taller than me, and put my face up to hers as far as I can and say, 'Missus-from-the-country, you're speaking to Joe Levy, master electrician and Communist. You understand? In this country human beings don't say things like that.' So she backs away, kinda scared." He laughed. "A coupla days later I'm walking down the street and there she comes. She sees me and, no kiddin', she kinda bows and smiles and says, 'Good morning, Comrade'."

Then he warmed to the subject. "Listen, young man!" Me, at seventy-three, he called a young man! "I got here lots of relatives. A nephew, he's a doctor. He wants to go. Not to Israel. To America. Why? Because here he makes wages like a coal miner and in America he hears on the radio doctors are millionaires so he wants to be a millionaire. But Jews have it good here, if only they don't worry about millions.

"Scientists, doctors, musicians, writers, artists — in proportion to the population they are three, four to one more in all them professions. You know, maybe, that Jews are Party members two to one over other people? That says nothing, maybe?" He looked at his watch; it was time for him to go. He embraced me, said goodbye, and to give his and his wife's love to their nephew.

I watched him stride away, straight and strong, and shook my head in wonderment. I would have quite a tale to tell his nephew.

I came home to find that Jack Lawson had died. Sue, herself close to eighty, frail and ill, moved in with her daughter. Then, to the gratification of hundreds of writers, young and old, and countless friends and admirers, the Writers Guild sponsored a memorial, on September 8, in Los Angeles. The Guild theater was crowded with old friends. In the Guild newsletter, published the following month, all the speeches were printed, preceded by a glowing foreword, which said, in its introduction, that the memorial had been held " . . . for our distinguished colleague and first president of the Screen

Writers Guild. . . . over a two-hour period, many of his friends paid eloquent and deep-feeling tribute to him."

It was a moving affair. I flew down to L.A. with Sue Lawson and Mandy, and her brother Jeff met us there. Carl Foreman, a member of the executive board, was chairman, and spoke first. He praised Jack for his tireless efforts on behalf of the Guild, a man he revered as ". . . the selfless donor of his strength, time and intelligence. . . . I never knew anyone who gave more of himself to the concern of others." He then introduced as first speaker the president of the Guild, David Rintels, who made it clear to any and all who did not know or had forgotten. He spoke of the relentless fight Jack made for ". . . our rights as artists, and our rights as labor. . . " and noted how, as a consequence, ". . . none was more blacklisted than he." That struggle for our rights was indeed the reason for the blacklist.

Rintels was followed by old friends and colleagues: Edward Eliscu, Maltz, Donald Ogden Stewart cabled from London; Alvah Bessie, Abby Mann, John Bright and finally myself. I spoke of the early days of the Guild, when Jack, John Bright, Brian Marlowe and I were among those who organized the first meeting of writers in February 1933. I recalled our struggle to gain recognition; the blacklist and imprisonment, not for Communist "subversion," but, as Rintels had said, for ". . . our rights as artists and our rights as labor." I didn't spare those who were culpable: I reminded them, too, how in 1954 the Guild, terrorized by McCarthyism, passed a constitutional amendment which carried out the producers' wishes and also blacklisted us. And I told how, a few months before Jack died, I brought him the news of the Supreme Court decision which in effect exonerated us, and how he urged me to do something about it — our vindication had to become widely known. Although it was too late to get legal restitution, it was not too late for the Guild to act. I then urged the president and board members present to press through the Guild membership a resolution calling on the producers, in the light of the Supreme Court decision, formally to rescind their 1947 Waldorf Blacklist Statement. In that way, Jack would be truly honored, and the Guild could be proud of having succeeded in restoring the First Amendment in Hollywood.

There was applause, but nothing came of it. The once-fighting Guild, while honoring one of its founders and first president with words, in deeds had become an industry pussy-cat. Even an establishment figure like Allen Rivkin, public relations director, has been quoted as saying, "The Guild has become little more than a collection agency for TV residuals" (payments to writers for reruns of films on TV).

As a consequence, despite some of the enormous salaries and exorbitant prices for screenplays a few were receiving, the majority of the Guild members are in an increasingly critical economic situation.

In his retiring speech as president two months later, David Rintels said to those screen and TV writers who had earned more that year than ever before: "I congratulate all 1486 of you." What he did *not* say when congratulating "all 1486 of you," was that the Guild membership was then 4,252, which meant that 2,766 members either didn't earn more or earned less, or were unemployed. Later the same year, the Guild published in the newsletter the average income of those who had worked. The compilation showed 21.9 percent only up to $2,000 annually; 10.4 percent from $2,000 to $4,000; 17.8 percent from $4,000 to $10,000; and 8 percent from $10,000 to $15,000. Thus, while 41.6 percent of the membership earned from $15,000 to $75,000 and over, 58 percent of *those working* earned less than electricians, mechanics, plumbers, carpenters or painters in the industry.

In the early 1930s, when we were fighting to organize, one of our chief opponents was MGM's Irving Thalberg. From his high chair, he looked down and ridiculed us, asking, "Are you artists or plumbers? Plumbers may need unions, but not artists." Today, almost fifty years later, more than a majority of our "artists" earn less than a majority of plumbers.

Moreover, while nobody tells a qualified plumber how to do his job, qualified writers have *no* control over their work. It's something we've always wanted and cried for, complained and cursed about, but never had the guts to fight for. Not that we didn't have models for how it could be done; playwrights in the Dramatists Guild not only have control of their material, but have the final word on the cast and the director.

And as the labor pool of "artists" grows, salary averages decrease. Today the Writers Guild has over five thousand members. The rate of unemployment is higher than ever. The con game used is clear: once every couple of years a university film school graduate will sell a screenplay for an enormous sum. *The Sting*, starring Robert Redford and Paul Newman, reportedly brought its young authors a jackpot, $350,000. Highly publicized, that news spread over the nation's campuses, and a year later it was reported that there were thirty-one thousand students taking courses in film-making, writing, directing. What a field day — what a labor pool — for the industry! I make a point of warning my students at the start of each semester of the hazards they will encounter. But such is the power of film, creative work, that this Jackpot Syndrome doesn't faze many. I warn them they will have to work as waiters, taxicab and bus drivers, or in factories — and write at the same time. They accept this. I know how they feel. I've never stopped trying either.

That December, at the end of the fall semester, the university administration did a "Survey of Student Opinion": a questionnaire was given each student. Their responses weren't signed, or shown to me. They were slipped into a box in the office of the building.

A week later I received xeroxed copies of the anonymous responses with this note: "Dear Lester, These are a joy to read. Congratulations on a fine job." [signed] Ginger Richardson.

I read them with a sense of wonder, growing joy and, I must confess, bursting pride. Could Allen Rivkin have been accurate in his estimate of me, what seemed, when I read his recommendation, the grossest flattery?

The survey started by asking the students to rate instructors from 1 (poor) to 5 (excellent). Their rating for me was: no 1, 2, or 3, one 4, six 5s; two 5 plus, and one 10. Their answers to the follow-up questions were incredible. I was totally unprepared for their reactions: To the question, What aspects of the course or teaching particularly pleased you, responses were like this: "Class energy very high." "Having Lester Cole here: KNOWLEDGE." "Professional handling of class — seminar form." (Where and how did I learn *that*?) "The instructor's personal experience with the subject matter." "The especially good critiques of our work and his suggestions." "It was an honor and a pleasure to benefit from Mr. Cole's experience." "The course was taught by an extremely intelligent and gifted man who has almost half a century of writing experience for us to learn from." And on and on, music to my eyes.

They know about my approach to life and to film, and if some don't I tell them in the first session. No doubt they suspect I am still a "Red," but it never becomes a subject for discussion. It is a seminar on screen-writing, not politics. I am accepted because of what I have and willingly give. Their responses to the questionnaire left no doubt for me. I felt, when I finished reading them, as if I'd shed ten years — along with some irrepressible tears of gratitude for their generous repayment.

Kay and I have been separated since 1977. I miss her still. Some — far from all — of the pain is gone, and most of the irrational anger. It is far easier now for me to see that she might have been right. I remember the note I found on my desk one morning some years back, which simply stated she'd be gone for a couple of days and for me not to bother either of her daughters since they would not know where she would be. And finally, she emphasized I was to leave them alone and bear in mind that like herself, neither of them was *my mother*!

That seemed to be the clue. Could I really have been leaning on Kay in that manner all those twenty years? Was she oppressed by a feeling that I was using her as a substitute for my own mother? (And all the time I felt as if I were her father!) Did the scar that mysteriously disappeared ten years before between my right thumb and forefinger, after being there sixty years, still remain somewhere else — in my mind, my heart? It must have, and perhaps this frantic note she left that day is a clue to whatever unhappiness I must have caused her over those two decades. The pain may be gone, but not the memory, and the sadness.

Sometimes, among large and gratifying compensations, there are even more gratifying small ones. I was driving home from the market one morning, in 1978, the radio tuned to a talk show. A writer and his actress wife were talking about and promoting their new book, something about the annual migration of swans that stopped to rest and feed in a pond on their estate in Long Island. Suddenly I was startled; I recognized the stuttering voice of an old "friendly witness," Budd Schulberg, who — his father, a millionaire in the twenties and early thirties — had been head man at Paramount. Budd was among the earlier elite Party members to turn informer, who "sang like a canary," as the cons would say at Danbury.

Listeners to the radio program were invited to call in and ask questions. I sped home, got on the phone, waited anxiously, and just three minutes before the show was to end I was put on. A caller only gave his first name, and I was introduced as "Lester, who was interested in your interest in birds." The name Lester apparently rang no bell then, and he asked pleasantly what it was I wanted to know.

I was prepared; I'd thought of nothing else since I raced home to the telephone twenty minutes before. "Why did you write about swans and not canaries?" I asked.

"Canaries?" He was puzzled.

"Canaries, yes. A bird you really know." I was suddenly so angry I was shouting. "You know all about canaries because you *are* a canary! Aren't you the canary who sang before the un-American Committee? Aren't you that canary? Or are you another bird, a pigeon — the stool kind."

There was an audible gasp at the other end. Schulberg was once again stuttering as he had done in his youth. He finally managed to say, "L-l-lester? Lester Cole! L-l-lester, I've been wanting to see you all these years. I want to explain. I really c-can. I —"

"Just sing, canary, sing, you bastard!" I'd lost control in my fury. I could have done much better had I remained calm.

I was cut off at that point. But sometimes little things like that can make your day.

A short time later a letter arrived from Cedric Belfrage which made my day in a far more positive way. He had received a temporary visa to come back into the country for thirty days at the request of the British Broadcasting Company. They were in Hollywood making a TV documentary about Hollywood in the twenties and wanted Cedric to tell of his experiences there in those long-gone days. Cedric reminded me that it was 1977, just fifty years since we first met; could I come down for a weekend while he was there? We would celebrate the fiftieth anniversary of our friendship.

I immediately wrote I could and would. Fifty years! My thoughts went back to those first days in the twenties, and then to twenty-five years later, when Cedric's ordeal had been at least as bad, if not worse, than mine. After the success of his first book, *Away From It All*, an in-depth account of his first trip around the world in the depression-ridden thirties, he soon thereafter, with two associates, James Aronson and John McManus, founded an independent, progressive weekly, the *National Guardian*. All three were outstanding journalists, and their paper was read widely as they exposed the Nixons,

Thomases and McCarthys and supported those who had become their targets — the Ten, Julius and Ethel Rosenberg, Alger Hiss and others. In the early fifties, Senator Joe McCarthy made Cedric a target; here was an Englishman on a permanent visa trying to subvert the activities of such patriots as himself. On the stand Cedric refused to answer McCarthy's demand that he reveal his political beliefs and affiliations, and he was deported. But not before he was kept for more than three months in prison, in a miserable hole on Ellis Island, in New York Bay — and when the sun was positioned right, in the shadow of the Statue of Liberty.

Today Cedric lives with his wife in Mexico. He has written nine books, among them the distinguished *American Inquisition,* and he is an editor of the tri-lingual magazine published in Mexico, *Third World.*

It was a beautiful reunion; the fiftieth anniversary of an unbreakable friendship.

1977 at Russya Hotel, Moscow Film Festival. Professor Albert Johnson (Film History and S.F. Film Festival), Yolanda Stevens, a director of the L.A. Film Festival (Filmex) and the author.

20

Within Sight Of Another Shore

There has been a tendency among many of those who remained in the Party to be bitter and harshly critical of those who left. I'm not innocent of such feelings at times, but at others I know that not only was the pressure on some almost unendurable, but others felt they had just cause for leaving. There have been criticisms of the Party over the years and some of them were indeed justified. To this day, struggles remain over sectarian attitudes, both in the leadership and the rank and file; doubts about policy which do not often get serious consideration by leaders, either on a local or national level; and many other complaints. By no means are all the complaints justified; but when the need to leave is overpowering, the methods become varied.

I remember when one prominent writer in 1960, seeing friends back at work, "went public" even though he was not in need of the money. In the article he wrote in a prominent national magazine, he didn't claim to have been duped, doped or seduced into joining the Party; aside from his own, he gave no names, betrayed no one. He wrote:

I was a member of the Communist Party . . . in whose ranks
I found some of the most thoughtful, witty, and generally
stimulating people in Hollywood. I also encountered a number of bores and unstable characters, which seemed to bear
out Bernard Shaw's observation that "revolutionary movements tend to attract the best and worst elements in any given
society."*

Unstable characters? Of course. He, Trumbo, me; unstable
— we're everywhere. Instability is a built-in part of modern
society. It's just that most of us can only see the instability in
others. It helps us if we understand which is the chicken,
which the egg, and neither came first. But we do know that
trade unions didn't create the twelve-hour day and child
labor in the English cotton mills; it was the other way around.
Marx and Engels' *Communist Manifesto* didn't create capitalism. Capitalism, child labor, the twelve-hour day created
the Communist Manifesto.

Since it came into the world in 1847, the *Manifesto* has
influenced millions of people who have joined Communist
parties in all countries. Many join, many leave. Depending
upon a multitude and complexity of conditions, sometimes
more join than leave; sometimes it is the other way around.
(The trend is toward increase, I believe.) Sometimes leaving
is for sincere reasons, which are believed legitimate and certainly to be respected. I respect such departures. But when,
as among some of the Ten, a few felt the need not only to

---

*It seemed clear enough then to those who know him which of these two elements —
the best and the worst — he believed himself to represent. However, one of his best
friends, the late Dalton Trumbo, once disputed that, or at least his implied claim to
be above whatever "unstable characters" were then around. Trumbo, something
less than a moderate drinker himself, wrote to this individual in 1947, telling him he
was not being influenced by the complaints of others about our friend's drinking, of
his getting "goat drunk," but — and the letter concludes with these words: "And
while I'm at it, I'd rather you didn't drop around the house any more. If you have
anything to take up with me, just drop me a note by hand. I don't mind having you
around, and certainly Cleo doesn't, but I'm not going to have you scaring my kids to
death in one of your goddam fits. Sincerely, your friend, Dalton Trumbo." The
letter was published in 1970.

advertise their dissent, but profit by it with cash rewards, it is not unreasonable to suspect the motive. The reasons the person gives for leaving cannot be accepted as genuine.* Such rewarded defectors know there will be three certain consequences: they will benefit themselves, they will weaken those they left behind — or fell behind — and will cause doubt among whoever might be considering enlisting. With their paid-for advertisement of departure, they become adversaries, not merely resignees.

The Cold War period of the 1950s — and now again in the 1980s — is not an easy time for middle-class intellectuals to be attracted to Marxism. In the 1930s it was not only emotionally magnetic but intellectually and socially fashionable. But when the Un-American Activities Committee and then McCarthy shattered the shelters of some of us and we found ourselves "outside" with "bores and unstable characters," "lesser people," looked down upon by those whose peers we once were, many among us saw themselves isolated, they felt an intolerable loneliness. They had to regain status. It was probably worse than the possibility of economic deprivation, which some of them had no reason to fear.

I think I understand their fears and their pain. It was my good luck to have a background that makes my needs different from theirs. There may be some truth in the dour warning by the oil corporations that U.S. oil wells are running dry, but not my old well; it's still pumping a steady flow of energy.

Hollywood may be behind me (not that I've given up my fight and right to write for films!), but how much better the alternatives seem: my film writing classes at U.C.; my work as film and dramatic critic for the *People's World*; the frequent lectures at universities on the history of film and the U.S. industry. A year ago I was invited to Hofstra University on Long Island as one of the lecturers at Prof. Walter Miller's annual Writers' Conference, and last September French Tele-

---

*As witnessed in Victor Navasky's recent book on the Hollywood informers, *Naming Names* (New York: Viking Press, 1980)

vision invited me to participate in Paris in a panel discussion on McCarthyism, with none other than Roy M. Cohn, the late and unlamented Senator McCarthy's right underhand man as an opponent — what fun! And this summer to Rhode Island University.

While at Hofstra University a young professor, Robert Lowery, sought me out. He was a scholar devoted to the history and literature of his torn and divided land, Eire, and most particularly to the never-to-die writings of the great working-class dramatist and poet, Sean O'Casey. He told me a national committee had been formed to honor O'Casey's hundredth birthday on March 30, 1980. The sponsors were most impressive: Brooks Atkinson, Lillian Gish, Raymond Massey, Paul Robeson, Jr., Cedric Belfrage, Mordecai Bauman, Barrows Dunham, and dozens more. Would I, he wanted to know, join this list of sponsors and organize a West Coast committee? It could plan a series of evenings in which there would be productions of his plays, readings of his poems and autobiographical works, and to coordinate a labor salute on his birthday with one to be held in New York. For that evening Michael Mullen, long-time president of the Irish Transport and General Workers Union, and Eileen O'Casey, Sean's widow, would be coming from Dublin to the U.S. They could, if we set up an evening, travel to San Francisco from New York for the occasion. And would I become a sponsor of the events?

I was honored and accepted with pleasure. Almost instantly I recalled how, not too long after Gorky's writings were inspiring me, O'Casey's early plays were companion pieces; in years to come they both were models I would ever seek to emulate even though I knew I would never succeed in coming close to their achievements. I told Lowery of the excitement I felt when I first met Sean and Eileen at one of the Sunday afternoon get-togethers at the home of Ella Winter and Don Stewart in London. At that time, already in his eighties, Sean's working-class heritage remained as firm as it had been all his life, throughout his plays and the six volumes of his memoirs. Lowery gave me some material, copies of his *Sean O'Casey Review*, a quarterly publication, along with brochures on the plans for coming events, and I took them back with me to San Francisco.

The first person I contacted was Padraigin McGillicuddy, who was in charge of the creative and cultural programs for KPFA, the Berkeley radio station of the Pacifica Network. She immediately, enthusiastically took over the chairmanship of a committee and within days brought together an enthusiastic working committee from the Bay Area Irish community: Leo Downey, actor and director, Renee Gibbons, her longshoreman husband Lew, and many others. Plans began to formulate for production of O'Casey's plays in theaters and on TV — actors, musicians and others all eager to participate.

Our first main task was coordinating the *Labor Salute* with the one in New York. Theirs was to be held on March 25, ours would be a dinner on Sean's birthday, March 30. Feverish plans, the publicity, the selling of tickets — could we pull it off, get fifty, sixty people to attend at fifteen dollars per person, the profits, if any, to go to the Sean O'Casey Scholarship Fund? A week before the dinner it seemed bleak.

But then came the publicity that the president of the International Longshoremen and Warehousemen's Union, Jim Herman, and John Henning, executive secretary of the California Labor Federation, AFL/CIO, would speak. We announced that Michael Mullen and Eileen O'Casey would be guests of honor. We were suddenly deluged with reservations.

Drinks at five, dinner at six. By five-thirty the Delancey Street Restaurant was overcrowded with more than three hundred people. Tables and chairs were rushed from storage. The musicians played with wild enthusiasm. Liquor flowed, dinners were downed, the speeches were received with mighty responses; our own labor leaders, Herman and Henning, along with Mike Mullen and Eileen O'Casey, were cheered for their tributes to the great man's memory. Diane Feinstein,

George T. Kruse, S.F.

Eileen O'Casey at Sean O'Casey's centenary celebration in San Francisco.

mayor of our city, sent a hundred roses and a beautiful plaque to Eileen honoring Sean, and announcing henceforth March 30 officially would be known in San Francisco as Sean O'Casey Day.

Music, dancing, old and new friends celebrating — Irish, Jewish, Black and Asian — a truly international tribute to a truly international genius of the working class.

What a most fitting evening for me to fall in love! Her name is Aisling Gibbons, daughter of Renee, the secretary of our committee. As Irish as her name, blonde, blue eyes, and a smile that is bewitching. She had recited a poem she had composed for the evening, and later we danced a sort of jig to the Irish music, and laughed with pleasure and afterward hugged each other with spontaneous affection. To do that, of course, I had to lift her into my arms because she is not yet three feet tall and then not yet six years old. That was a little more than a year ago, and I doubt that she remembers when we first met, a week before that.

It was at a meeting at her parents' simple flat, in the living room. The old double doors to the bedroom could not slide closed, and at six o'clock Aisling's favorite TV program, *Sesame Street,* was playing. But it interfered with the meeting, and her parents insisted that she turn it off. Finally, after many defiant protests, she resentfully obeyed. Then she came to face the six or eight committee members, her oppressors. She took stage center, she placed her hands on her hips and in a cold, measured manner announced, "I hate Sean O'Casey."

By the time of his birthday celebration she had changed her mind completely. This is the poem Aisling composed; her mother wrote it down:

> Happy birthday, Sean O'Casey.
> My mother loves you
> and I love you too.
>
> My mother is working for you
> and If you were here with us
> I know you would like the show.
>
> Your spirit was there
> But I didn't see it.
> Now you are really dead
> And buried.
>
> Still if you were alive
> I would like you
> And you would like me too.

He would love you, Aisling, as everyone who cares about children and the world in which they will live their lives must love you and want all children to be secure against nuclear madness and those who dream of first strikes.

Ousmane Sambene, novelist and film director (l.), and interpeter, interviewed by the author for TV at S. F. State University in 1979. Sambene's outstanding films are all too infrequently seen by U.S audiences.

Fast approaching seventy-seven I feel more than merely alive; I have the will to remain strong in mind and body to stay in the fight. I did think it would be all over for me a month ago when suddenly without warning my younger son Jeffry, a mere forty-one, was suddenly stricken with a strange disease, pancreatitis, and died within forty-eight hours.

The grief was unbearable. I don't know how I survived. Do I owe it to my son Michael, his children and Jeff's? To the Gorkys, the O'Caseys, the Aislings, to friends everywhere? If so, it is a debt I happily pay.

All of me is not, cannot, be within these pages. I've experienced personally more than it is relevant to tell. Politically I've touched upon some of my share in conflicts. I've seen heroic, selfless sacrifice and calculated cunning for gain of wealth and power. I've had good luck and bad, witnessed loyalty and betrayal, made never-to-be-forgotten friends and never-to-be-forgiven enemies — in and out of the Party.

Looking back, inevitably along with the happy memories are the regrets, some bitter and few without self-criticism. I get solace, I think, from Friedrich Engels' statement: "Until there is world socialism, man remains in a stage of his pre-history." In that context — and in that refuge — I feel unshaken in the belief that I have remained within my pre-historical stage as a part of the working people from whom I came and with whom I shall continue the fight for the genuine needs of all people.

Like the writer I quoted earlier I too can look upon myself in the framework of G.B. Shaw's dubious drollery — that in all revolutionary movements "the best and the worst elements" can be found. But they exist not only in revolutionary movements; as Engels indicates, it is true on all levels of society and social relations. And equally strong is my belief that while I'm far from one of the best, I'm some distance from some of the worst.

I truly feel myself to be somewhere in between, one of the vast sea of struggling humanity, the ever growing number of swimmers determined to reach the other shore, where mankind's true history will begin.

As best I know how to tell it, this has been the story of my swim, with and against the tides.

Appendix

Feature Films for which Lester Cole received screen credit.

1932. *If I Had a Million* (Paramount). Story credit (with 18 others). *p. 112.*

1933. *Charlie Chan's Greatest Case* (Fox). Adaptation, with Marian Orth. *p. 132.*

1934. *Pursued* (Fox) Screenplay, with Stuart Anthony. *p. 132.*

1934. *Sleepers East* (Fox). Screenplay. *p. 132.*

1934. *Wild Gold* (Fox). Adaptation, with Henry Johnson. *p. 132.*

1935. *Under Pressure* (Fox). Screenplay, with Borden Chase and Noel Pierce. *pp. 134-5.*

1935. *Hitch Hike Lady* (Republic). Screenplay, with Gordon Rigby. *p. 145.*

1935. *Too Tough to Kill* (Columbia). Adaptation, with J. Griffin Jay. *p. 135.*

1936. *Follow Your Heart* (Republic). Screenplay, with N. West and Samuel Ornitz. *p. 145.*

1936. *The President's Mystery* (Republic). Screenplay, with Nathaniel West. *pp. 146, 149, 159, 172.*

1937. *The Man in Blue* (Universal). Screenplay.

1937. *The Affairs of Cappy Ricks* (Republic). Original screenplay.

1937. *Some Blonds are Dangerous* (Universal). Screenplay.

1938. *The Crime of Dr. Hallet* (Universal). Screenplay, with Brown Holmes.

1938. *Midnight Intruder* (Universal). Screenplay, with George Waggner.

1938. *The Jury's Secret* (Universal). Screenplay, with Newman Levy.

1938. *Sinners in Paradise* (Universal. Screenplay, with Tom Lennon.

1939. *Winter Carnival* (Wanger-United Artists). Screenplay, with B. Schulberg and M. Rapf. *p. 158.*

1939. *I Stole a Million* (Universal). Original screen story.

1929. *The Big Guy* (Universal). Screenplay.

1940. *The Invisible Man Returns* (Universal). Screenplay, with Kurt Sidomak. *pp. 158, 172.*

Source: John Cogley, *Blacklisting* (Fund for the Republic, 1956).

1940. *The House of Seven Gables* (Universal). Screenplay, dialog director. *pp. 172-3.*

1941. *Footsteps in the Dark* (Warners). Screenplay, with John Wexley. *p. 179.*

1941. *Among the Living* (Paramount). Screenplay, with Garrett Fort. *p. 179.*

1942. *Pacific Blackout* (Paramount). Screenplay, with W.P. Lipscombe.

1943. *Night Plane from Chungking* (Paramount). Screenplay, with E. Felton and and T. Reeves. *p. 186.*

1943. *Hostages* (Paramount). Screenplay, with Frank Butler. *pp. 191-7.*

1944. *None Shall Escape* (Columbia). Screenplay. *pp. 202-6.*

1945. *Objective Burma* (Warners). Screenplay, with Ronald MacDougall. *pp. 206-8.*

1945. *Blood on the Sun* (Cagney-United Artists). *pp. 14, 218-21.*

1945. *Men in Her Diary* (Universal). Adaptation.

1946. *Strange Conquest* (Universal). Story, with Carl Dreher.

1947. *Fiesta* (M-G-M). Original screenplay, with George Bruce. *pp. 229-31.*

1947. *The Romance of Rosy Ridge* (M-G-M). Screenplay. *pp. 226, 229-53.*

1948. *High Wall* (M-G-M). Screenplay, with Sidney Boehm. *pp. 256, 276-7.*

  + six more, including *Born Free*, (*pp. 381-2, 390-1*) under pseudonyms on the black market.

Index

443